Public Speaking

Choices and Responsibility

Public Speaking
Choices and Responsibility

Second Edition

WILLIAM M. KEITH AND CHRISTIAN O. LUNDBERG

CENGAGE
Learning·

Australia • Brazil • Mexico • Singapore • United Kingdom • United States

Public Speaking: Choices and Responsibility, Second Edition
William M. Keith, Christian O. Lundberg

Product Director: Monica Eckman

Product Manager: Kelli Strieby

Content Developer: Kathy Sands-Boehmer

Associate Content Developer: Karolina Kiwak

Product Assistant: Colin Solan

Media Developer: Jessica Badiner

Marketing Manager: Stacey Purviance

Content Project Manager: Dan Saabye

Art Director: Marissa Falco

Manufacturing Planner: Doug Bertke

IP Analyst: Ann Hoffman

IP Project Manager: Farah Fard

Production Service: MPS Limited

Compositor: MPS Limited

Text Designer: Dare Porter, Real Time Design

Cover Designer: Dare Porter, Real Time Design

Cover Image: DrAfter123/Getty Images

For product information and technology assistance, contact us at
Cengage Learning Customer & Sales Support, 1-800-354-9706
For permission to use material from this text or product,
submit all requests online at **www.cengage.com/permissions.**
Further permissions questions can be emailed to
permissionrequest@cengage.com.

Library of Congress Control Number: 2015943723

Student Edition:

ISBN: 978-1-305-26164-8

Loose-leaf Edition:

ISBN: 978-1-305-65517-1

Cengage Learning
20 Channel Center Street
Boston, MA 02210
USA

Cengage Learning is a leading provider of customized learning solutions with employees residing in nearly 40 different countries and sales in more than 125 countries around the world. Find your local representative at **www.cengage.com**

Cengage Learning products are represented in Canada by Nelson Education, Ltd.

To learn more about Cengage Learning Solutions, visit **www.cengage.com**

Purchase any of our products at your local college store or at our preferred online store **www.cengagebrain.com**

Printed in the United States of America
Print Number:01   Print Year: 2015

Contents

Preface   xi

PART 1   FUNDAMENTALS OF GOOD SPEAKING   1

1 PUBLIC SPEAKING   2

Introduction: Why Learn Public Speaking?   3
Speech Is Powerful   4
   The Power of Public Speaking to Change the World   4
   The Power of Speeches to Change Your World   5
   Speaking Connects You to Others: Democracy
     in Everyday Life   6
   The Conversational Framework   7
The Communication Process   9
The *Public* in Public Speaking   10
Speaking Is About Making Choices   12
   Preparation   13
   Informing   14
   Persuading   15
The Speaking Process: Preparing and Performing   16
Thinking Through Your Choices   17
   Your Responsibilities (Chapter 2)   17
   Your Audience (Chapters 3, 4)   17

   Your Goals (Chapter 5)   18
Creating Your First
  Speech   19
   Informing and Arguing
     (Chapters 11,12)   19
   Research (Chapter 6)   20
   Organizing (Chapter 7)   20
   Finding the Words (Chapter 8)   21
Giving Your First Speech   22
   Delivering the Speech (Chapter 9)   22
   Overcoming Anxiety (Chapter 9)   22
   Presentation Aids (Chapter 10)   22
Making Responsible Choices   23
   Good Speeches Are the Result of Choices   24
   Taking Responsibility Means Respecting the Audience   24

American Red Cross

2 ETHICS AND THE RESPONSIBLE SPEAKER   26

david hancock/Alamy

Introduction: Why Ethics Matter in
  Public Speaking   27
Ethical Pitfalls in Public Speaking   29
   Deceptive Speech   29
   Inappropriately Biased Speech   31
   Poorly Reasoned Speech   32
Seven Principles of Ethical Public Speaking   33
   Be Honest   33
   Be Open   34
   Be Generous   34
   Be Balanced   35
   Represent Evidence Responsibly   36
   Take Appropriate Risks   36
   Choose Engagement   36
How to Avoid Plagiarism   38

How to Create an Ethical
  Speech   39
   Respect Your Audience   39
   Respect Your Topic   40
   Present Other Views and
     Treat Them Fairly   42
Avoid Fallacies and
  Prejudicial Appeals   44
   Name Calling   44
   Glittering Generalities   44
   Inappropriate Testimonials   44
   Plain-Folks Appeals   45
   Card-Stacking   45
   Bandwagoning   45

3 UNDERSTANDING AUDIENCES AND PUBLICS 48

Introduction: Those People Sitting in Front of You 49

Audience Analysis 50

The Literal Audience: Demographics 51
Problems With the Demographic Approach 52

The Rhetorical Audience 53
The "As" Test 54
From "Me" to "Us" 55

Types of Rhetorical Audiences 55

Adapting Your Speech to Your Audience 57
Identify Common Interests 57
Make the Most of Shared Experience 57

Work from Common Premises 58
Be Directive 58

Two Views of the Audience: Marketing vs. Engagement 59
Marketing 60
Engagement 60

The Audience and the Public 61
Advancing the Public Conversation 63

Your Ethical Responsibilities to Your Audience 63

4 BECOMING A SKILLED LISTENER 68

Introduction: Public Hearing and Listening 69

Types of Listening 70
Passive Listening 70
Active Listening 70
Critical Listening 71

The Ethics of Listening 72

Obstacles to Good Listening 75
Distractions 75
Your Mental Zone 76

Taking Good Notes 77

Giving Constructive and Useful Feedback 80
Criticize Speeches, Not People 82
Be Specific 82
Focus on What Can Be Changed 82
Be Communication Sensitive 83

PART 2 CREATING A GREAT SPEECH 85

5 TOPIC AND PURPOSE 86

Introduction: Picking a Topic and Defining Your Purpose 87

A Strategy for Picking a Topic 88
What Interests You? 89
What Will Interest Your Audience? 89
What Is the Occasion? 90
What Is Your Purpose? 91
What Is Your Thesis? 91

Finding a Topic Among Your Interests 92
What Do You Already Know or Care About? 92
What Do You Want to Know More About? 93
Brainstorming 94
Choosing One of Your Topic Ideas 95

How to Focus Your Topic for Your Audience 96
Geography or Location 96
Past, Present, or Future 96
Typical Audience Interests 97

Speaking Purposes and Speaking Situations 97
General Purposes of Speeches 98
Types of Speaking Situations 98
Time Constraints 100

The Thesis Statement: Putting Your Topic and Purpose into Words 101

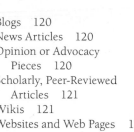

6 RESEARCH 105

Thomas Lohnes/Getty Images

Introduction: Becoming an Expert   106

Researching Responsibly   107

The Research Process   109
Figuring Out What You Already Know   109
Designing a Research Strategy   111
Deciding Where to Go   111
Making a Methodical Search   113

How to Conduct an Online Search   114
Creating Search Terms   114
Focusing Your Search   116

Gathering Your Materials   117

Reading Your Materials and Taking Notes   118

Evaluating Sources   120

Blogs   120
News Articles   120
Opinion or Advocacy
    Pieces   120
Scholarly, Peer-Reviewed
    Articles   121
Wikis   121
Websites and Web Pages   122

Revising Your Claims   122

Organizing Your Research Information   123

Choosing the Sources for Your Speech   124

Citing Your Sources and Avoiding Plagiarism   125

Getting Help From a Research Expert   126

7 ORGANIZATION 128

Ap Images/Rachel La Corte

Introduction: Getting Organized   129

The Basic Three-Part Structure   130

The Introduction   131
Functions of an Effective Introduction   132
Elements of the Introduction   133

The Body   135
Functions of the Body   136

The Conclusion   139
Functions of the Conclusion   139
Elements of the Conclusion   140

Patterns of Organization   140
Chronological   141
Spatial   142
Cause and Effect   143

Problem-Solution   144
Topical   144

Monroe's Motivated
    Sequence   146
Attention   147
Need   147
Satisfaction   147
Visualization   148
Action   148
Combination   148
Choosing the Order of Points: Primacy vs. Recency   150

Arranging Your Supporting Materials   150

Outlining   151
Outline Structure   152
Preparation and Delivery Outlines   152

PART 3   PRESENTING A GREAT SPEECH 155

8 VERBAL STYLE 156

Bob Daemmrich/Alamy

Introduction: What Is Style, and Why
    Does It Matter?   157

Characteristics of Effective Style   158
Concrete and Lively Language   159
Respectful Language   160

Classifying Verbal
    Style: Figures and
    Tropes   161

Figures   161
Figures of Repetition   162

Figures of Contrast 164

Tropes 167
Tropes of Comparison: Metaphor and Simile 168
The Trope of Substitution: Metonymy 170

Tropes of Exaggeration: Overstatement and
  Understatement 171
The Trope of Voice: Personification 171

Matching the Style to the Topic and the Occasion 172

9 DELIVERY 174

Introduction: Stand and Deliver 175
Speaking or Talking? 176
Creating Focus and Energy From Your Anxiety 177
Types of Preparation and Delivery 179
Speaking From Memory 179
Speaking From Manuscript 180
Extemporaneous Speaking 180
Impromptu Speaking 181
Staying on Time 181

Types of Speaking Aids 182
Using Your Voice Effectively 183
Volume 183
Speed 185
Articulation 186
Inflection 187

Using Your Body Effectively 188
Standing 188
Walking 189
Using Gestures 190

Communicating Credibility 190
Making Eye Contact 190
Choosing Your
  Appearance 191

How to Practice Delivering Your Speech 192
Practice, All the Way Through, at Least Four Times 192
Practice in Front of an Audience 192
Practice Making Mistakes 193
Breathe, Breathe, Breathe 193

Answering Questions from the Audience 193
Anticipating Questions 194
Interpreting the Questions 194
Giving Your Answers 195

Group Presentations 196
Cooperation 197
Coordination 198
Delivering the Group Presentation 199
Rehearsing the Group Presentation 199

iStockphoto.com/laflor

10 PRESENTATION AIDS 201

Introduction: Adding Media to Your Message 202
Why Use Presentation Aids? 203
Principles for Integrating Presentation Aids 204
Static Visual Elements 207
Pictures and Photos 207
Charts and Graphs 210
Maps and Diagrams 213
Text 214

Moving Images 215
Audio 215
Non-Electronic Media 216
Handouts 217

Posters and Flip Charts 217
Objects 217

Demonstration Speeches and Presentation Aids 218
Presentation Software 219
Delivering Your Speech With Presentation Aids 222
Preparing to Use Digital Media 223
Developing a Backup Plan for Digital Media 223

Ariel Skelley/Blend Images/Getty Images

PART 4 KINDS OF SPEECHES   225

11 INFORMATIVE SPEAKING   226

Introduction: Telling It Like It Is   227
Goals of Informative Speaking   228
  Present New Information   229
  Provide New Perspectives   230
  Generate Positive or Negative Feelings   231
  How to Choose an Informative Goal   232
Responsibilities of the Informative Speaker   233
Topics for Informative Speeches   235
  Objects   236
  Events   236
  People   236
  Processes   237
  Ideas   237
Techniques of Informative Speaking   238

  Defining   238
  Describing   239
  Explaining   241
Choices That Make
  Information
  Effective   243
  Keep It Simple   243
  Connect Your Topic to Your Audience   243
  Use Supporting Material Wisely   244
  Choose Effective Organizational Patterns   244
  Choose Effective Language   244
Alternative Speech Formats   245
  TED Talks   245
  PechaKucha   247

AP Images/Gillian Jones

12 BEING PERSUASIVE   250

Introduction: Giving the Audience Proofs   251
Ethos: Why Audiences Should Believe You   254
  Classical Dimensions of Ethos   255
  Why Are You Speaking on This Topic?   256
Pathos: The Framework of Feelings   257
  Appeals to Positive Emotions   257
  Fear and Other Negative Appeals   259
  Framing   260
Logos: Who Needs an Argument?   262
Making Connections: The Process of Reasoning   264
Types of Arguments   264
  Arguments from Examples (Inductive Reasoning)   265
  Formal Arguments (Deductive Reasoning)   265
  Causal Arguments   266
  Arguments from Analogy   267

  Arguments from Signs   268
  Arguments from
    Authority   269
When Reasons Go
  Bad   269
  Fallacies of Appeal   270
  Fallacies of Causation   273
  Inductive Fallacies   274
  Begging the Question: The Fallacy of Circular Reasoning   275
What About the Other Side? Dealing
  with Counterarguments   276
  Why Addressing Counterarguments Is Persuasive   276
  Tips for Dealing with Counterarguments   277

MAURICIO LIMA/Getty Images

13 SPECIAL TYPES OF SPEECHES
AND PRESENTATIONS   280

Introduction: Adapting Your
  Skills to New Challenges   281
Speeches at Life Transitions   282
  Toasts   283
  Eulogy   285
  Graduation   287

Speeches at
  Ceremonies   289
  Introducing a Speaker   289
  After-Dinner Speaking   291
  Presenting an Award   292

David T. Foster III/Charlotte Observer/MCT/
Tribune News Service/Getty Images

APPENDIX 1: SAMPLE SPEECHES   295

Informative Speech   295

Why Laughter is the Best Medicine by Michael Fisher   295

Persuasive Speech   296

Statement to the Iowa House Judiciary Committee by Zach Wahls   296

Special Occasion Speech   298

"I am an African." (Statement on Behalf of the African National Congress, on the Occasion of the Adoption by the Constitutional Assembly of the Republic of South Africa Constitution Bill) by Thabo Mbeki   298

APPENDIX 2: SAMPLE OUTLINES   302

Informative Speech Outline   302

Why Laughter is the Best Medicine by Michael Fisher   302

Persuasive Speech Outline   304

Statement to the Iowa House Judiciary Committee by Zach Wahls   304

Special Occasion Speech Outline   306

Statement on Behalf of the African National Congress, on the Occasion of the Adoption by the Constitutional Assembly of the Republic of South Africa Constitution Bill 1996 by Deputy President Thabo Mbeki   306

Endnotes   309

Index   312

Preface

The ability to engage an audience with skill, elegance, and clarity can have a decisive impact in students' lives. The difference between success and failure in a student's academic work, personal relationships, and vocational path often depends on the ability to create ethical and effective speeches. Even though future success is a good reason to cultivate skill in public speaking, it is not the only reason. In an increasingly globalizing and information-saturated world, students who become more engaged, informed, and responsible public speakers may well be one of the last and best hopes for our civic and democratic life together. In an era of hyperpartisan politics and creeping disillusionment with public discourse and the political system, our best resource may be a return to the ancient arts of rhetoric and public speaking. These arts can teach us how to really listen to, respond to, and respectfully engage with our fellow citizens. This book seeks to remake an art with ancient roots for modern times, or, in more contemporary terms, to remix an ancient beat for the information era.

We wrote *Public Speaking: Choices and Responsibility* because we believe firmly that public speaking matters profoundly to our personal and collective futures. This text, we hope, embodies a vision of public speaking that is accessible, easy to engage, and relevant to our students without sacrificing the time-honored traditional lessons of public speaking. In contrast to many approaches to public speaking, which present a catalogue of tips and techniques for giving a speech, we have attempted to create a simple framework for helping students learn to be better public speakers. Our framework is compact, simple, and easy to teach and learn. The essence of teaching public speech is in helping students to make informed choices about how to approach a speaking situation, and in helping them to see and take responsibility for the implications of their choices.

This second edition continues the focus of the first edition on *making choices* and *taking responsibility*. But we have sharpened our approach to this theme based on feedback from our readers and instructors. We have reordered and revised the chapters to reflect a more intuitive approach to skill building in public speaking. We have expanded the opening examples for each chapter by including video and other resources that add to the instructional value of these examples. We created a more comprehensive coverage of types and organizational formats for speeches by adding a section on Monroe's Motivated Sequence, and by expanding our treatments of the diverse speaking situations that students will encounter in the modern world, including some new approaches to informative speaking—TED and PechaKucha.

Also, we have added resources to help students learn and instructors to teach outlining, by expanding our coverage of outlining and by adding sample outlines to the speeches in the Appendix. We have deepened our treatment of argument by including a section of fallacies. Finally, we have integrated the ancient insights of the rhetorical tradition with cutting-edge research in modern rhetorical theory, social, and even hard sciences, highlighting the intersections between the two in a new **Remix** feature interspersed throughout the chapters.

NEW TO THIS EDITION!

- The chapters have a **new order**—to create a more natural progression from basic skills to contexts and genres of speaking.
- Each chapter **begins with a vignette** that builds directly on a video of a student speech available in MindTap, allowing for a quick preview of the chapters topics and skills.
- **Group presentation** has been moved to Chapter 9 to emphasize the continuity of skills between solo and group delivery.
- The **Monroe Motivated Sequence** has been added to Chapter 7 on organization, showing how it adds distinctive organizational forms and purposes.
- **TED talks and PechaKucha** are included in Chapter 12 to show how these vital new forms add to students' choices about how to give compelling and effective informative presentations.
- More emphasis is given to **outlining**, with new examples for students' use in the Appendix.
- Extended treatment of **fallacies** is included in Chapter 12, emphasizing their key features and distinguishing them from good arguments.
- Each chapter has an exciting new feature—the **Remix**. Remixes bring together the best of research in business and social science to bear on the practical questions of how to become an excellent public speaker.

We are excited about each of these additions to the second edition. We believe that these changes will enhance and extend our original focus on making choices and taking responsibility as the core of public-speaking pedagogy. We provide readers with a broader range of tools drawn from ancient insights, classical rhetorical theory, and research in persuasion. An expansion of these tools augments the core insights of the first edition. This expansion is significant because more choices increase the possibilities that a speaker can competently employ to analyze and learn to implement.

For us, "making choices" means seeing every public speech as a collection of decisions that starts with inventing a topic, moves through effective research, organization, and delivery, and ends with successful interaction with an audience. "Taking responsibility" means owning your choices, both by making them intentionally and by accepting the obligation to be responsive to the audience. With these two concepts forming the core of this book, we believe we have provided a set of guiding principles that ties many of the best insights of public-speaking pedagogy together around a central theme and that satisfies the demands of the current generation of students for broader civic and social engagement.

The style of the book also reflects our concern not only to engage students but also to inspire them to use their voices to make a difference in their communities, future workplaces, and the broader public sphere. Many of our examples are directly relevant to students' everyday lives; others are drawn from issues that occupy the front pages of newspapers, websites, and social media sources. In both cases, our goal is to provide students with examples that are relevant and engaging and that demonstrate the importance of public speaking to the broader health of civic life.

To create a text that is intuitive, easy to teach and learn from, and engaging to students, we have placed special emphasis on significant themes. In the introductory chapter we emphasize the world-changing power of public speech, and we introduce students to our central concepts of making choices and taking responsibility for them. Our goal is to "put the public back in public speaking" by introducing students to the idea that every speech targets a specific strategic goal (informing or persuading an audience, for example) and simultaneously forms a part of the larger public conversation around issues important to each of us.

In addition, students need to understand that this is also the best approach to speaking in professional and business contexts. Speeches here have to be well argued and researched and clearly organized, just like those in the civic context. If a "public" is a group of people with a common set of concerns, there are publics both internal and external to any business or organization. The basic skills of good choice-making can be applied to nearly any context.

Chapter 1 is devoted to help get students up and speaking, and more important, to give them a basic understanding of the choices that go into an effective public speech. We provide a brief, early overview of the process of creating and delivering a public speech. Perhaps most significant for many first-time speakers, this chapter tackles the issue of communication apprehension head on, offering effective introductory advice for dealing with public-speaking anxiety.

Because this book is so centrally concerned with responsible speaking in personal, work, and public contexts, Chapter 2, addressing ethics, is the first substantive chapter of the book. We believe our approach to ethics will resonate with contemporary students because, instead of simply producing a list of do's and don'ts, we provide a set of principles for thinking about ethical public-speaking practice as an intrinsic element of every communicative interaction. The chapter treats all the standard topics in an ethics chapter—including properly citing sources, accurately representing evidence, avoiding deception and prejudicial appeals—but it does so in the broader context of encouraging students to think about the health and quality of the relationship they are establishing with their audience.

To be ethically sound and strategically effective, good public speaking should begin and end with thinking about the audience. In Chapter 3 we discuss how thinking about the audience influences speakers' choices and how to take responsibility in composing and delivering speeches. Not only do we talk about skills at the core of good public speaking—for example, analyzing and adapting to the audience—but we emphasize thinking about public speaking as an opportunity for engaging the audience in a conversation around issues of personal and public concern. Our goals in this chapter are to take advantage of the current sentiment among students, promoted in colleges and universities, for greater public and civic engagement and to demonstrate to students that in addressing a specific audience, they also are making their views known in the context of a broader public conversation.

For the model of public speaking as a part of a broader public conversation to be successful, we believe a public speaking text should present more than just the best ways to speak to an audience. Thus, Chapter 4 addresses how we should listen. One of our goals is to help students to be better audience members and more responsive speakers by emphasizing the role of active, critical, and ethically sound listening. We include detailed advice on eliminating impediments to good listening, taking good notes, and giving constructive feedback. But perhaps more notably, we believe that privileging listening in the public speaking classroom is a pivotal first step toward improving the quality of public conversation in that it emphasizes paying attention to the claims of others as a necessary part of participating in a robust and respectful public conversation.

In the next three chapters we move from a basic framework for making choices and taking responsibility in public speech toward a practically oriented treatment of how to make effective choices in selecting a topic and purpose (Chapter 5), doing effective research (Chapter 6), and organizing your ideas and information (Chapter 7). Chapter 5 provides students a practical rubric for making good topic choices that best balance their interests, their goals for interaction with the audience, and the nature of the public-speaking situation. We provide easily implementable solutions for picking a topic area, defining a purpose, generating a thesis statement, and focusing the speech in light of the occasion and character of the audience.

A culture of search engines and social media has fundamentally changed the way by which students relate to information, and any public-speaking pedagogy worth its salt has to take into account this sea change in information culture. Chapter 6 faces head-on the unique challenges of researching in a digital world, providing students with a detailed guide to navigating a research context that is substantially more challenging than it was even a decade ago. Again emphasizing the central role of making choices and taking responsibility, this chapter on research provides a detailed, easy-to-follow, step-by-step protocol for designing a research strategy. Because contemporary students do research primarily online, we start with a discussion of all the research options available to them and provide concrete instructions for searching the Internet and other sources effectively. Given the changes in student research practices, we place heavy emphasis on methodical searching, including designing and keeping track of search terms, and on focusing research efforts amid the near-avalanche of online sources from which students can choose. Because today's student often struggles with what to use and how best to use it, we devote parts of the chapter to evaluating the credibility of sources and to thinking critically about the role of evidence in the composition of a good speech.

Chapter 7 teaches students how best to integrate their claims, arguments, and evidence in a lucid and compelling format that engages an audience effectively. This chapter on organization presents a rubric from thinking about introductions, signposting, the body of a speech, and a good conclusion. Instead of simply offering a catalogue of possible speech formats or deferring to the nature of the topic for inventing an organizational pattern, however, we discuss organization as a choice that, like any other, entails specific advantages and drawbacks. Thus, students should come away with a set of resources for developing a capacity for critical thinking about organizational choices.

Chapters 8 and 9 deal with verbal style and delivery, applying the same basic framework for making choices and taking responsibility that we have woven throughout the text. Chapter 8 addresses the best of the rhetorical tradition's reflections on lively language use, borrowing from a wide range of contemporary and pop culture discourses to discuss effective choices for the use of figures and tropes, including treatments of repetition, contrast, comparison, substitution, exaggeration, and personification. We conclude this chapter by reflecting on the ways the speaker's topic and the occasion might serve as a guide to the style choices good speakers make. Chapter 9 extends this same line of thinking to choices in delivering a speech. To help students negotiate these choices, we discuss various types of delivery—from memory, from a manuscript, extemporaneously, with the help of a presentation aid, and so on. We conclude this chapter with discussions of how best to practice and effectively handle audience interaction.

We follow physical delivery with a detailed and visually rich Chapter 10, which applies the principles of choice and responsibility to the use of presentation aids. Whether the student is using a static visual aid such as a chart, moving images, an audio clip, or presentation software, applying the basic framework of choices and responsibility can provide helpful insights. This chapter includes an integrated section on how to give a demonstration speech, which by its nature has a multimedia element. It concludes with a pragmatic, detailed discussion about integrating presentation software into a speech without leaning on it as a replacement for good public-speaking practices. Here we discuss a number of messy but critically important practicalities that go into the effective use of presentation software, including how to think about delivery with presentation software, how to practice with and use presentation software in the classroom, and how to develop a backup plan.

Chapter 11 focuses on informative speaking, beginning with thinking about how our contemporary context and news media in particular have changed the way we think about information. More than ever, the culture broadly, and our students specifically, have begun to think about the notion of "spin" in presenting information. Our goal in this frame is to help students think about responsible choices for presenting information in a way that is clear, well organized, and useful for the audience. The chapter returns to the theme of topic selection to deal with the unique challenges of picking a good informative topic, and then moves on to discuss techniques for informative speaking and the set of choices a speaker might make to ensure that information is helpful for the audience.

Chapter 12 updates Aristotle's three modes of proof—logos, ethos, and pathos, or rational argument, the speaker's character, and emotional appeals—to give students concrete guidance in composing and delivering an effective speech. Though our inspiration is ancient, we draw from contemporary examples to provide a basic framework for thinking about how best to convince modern audiences through appeals to reason, character, and emotion. This chapter places special emphasis on processes of reasoning, not only to help students give better speeches but also to help them sharpen their critical thinking skills.

Chapter 13 concludes the text by focusing on other types of speeches and speech occasions. Even though a first course will focus appropriately on basic informative and persuasive speeches, with classmates as the main audience, students will encounter many other speaking situations in the world, and these will present new communication challenges. We believe the skills to meet these challenges will be extensions of the skills already learned. Students can easily learn to give effective and compelling speeches at life transitions and ceremonial occasions. So we believe we have produced a public-speaking curriculum that is

- comprehensive, but systematically organized around a coherent system for making good speech choices and taking responsibility for them
- simple to learn and to teach, always returning to the themes of making choices and taking responsibility
- rich in practical advice and concrete detail for composing and delivering speeches
- focused on the biggest struggles and conceptual issues faced by public-speaking students
- an effective reworking of ancient arts for the modern world—faithful to the best insights of the rhetorical tradition but responsive to the contemporary student in its use of examples, composition and delivery practices, and style
- a curriculum that puts the civic and relational character of public speaking in the foreground of choice making.

We have included a number of instructional features to advance these goals. We have tried to compose a visually engaging book, with images that match the diversity and vitality of contemporary public culture. Each chapter begins with a vignette that ties students' actual work to the content of the chapter in story form and ends with review and discussion questions. We also have included two major kinds of interactive features in the text to keep students engaged. **Try It!** presents an exercise students can do while reading the text, providing an immediate opportunity for hands-on practice with the concepts in the book. Instructors can use the Try It! boxes for in-class work, group work, think-pair-share exercises, or homework. The second feature, **FAQ** (Frequently Asked Questions), channels the spirit and style of its online inspiration. FAQ boxes anticipate and answer students' questions about various parts of the text, providing a brief interlude for thinking beyond the immediate curriculum and toward some of the bigger questions implied in learning public speaking.

The following special resources for students and instructors are designed to streamline teaching and facilitate learning complete the learning package for *Public Speaking: Choices and Responsibility, Second Edition.*

MINDTAP RESOURCES

MindTap®

Public Speaking, Second Edition features an outstanding array of online supplements to make this course as meaningful and effective as possible. **Note:** For students to have access to the online resources for *Public Speaking, Second Edition,* these have to be ordered for the course; otherwise, students will not have access to them on the first day of class. These resources can be bundled with every new copy of the text, or ordered separately. Students whose instructors do not order these resources as a package with the text may purchase them or access them at **cengagebrain.com**

Contact your local Cengage Learning sales representative for more details.

Cengage Learning's *MindTap* for *Public Speaking: Choices and Responsibility* brings course concepts to life with interactive learning, study, and exam preparation tools that support the printed textbook. Student comprehension is enhanced with the integrated eBook, interactive teaching and learning tools including quizzes, flashcards, and interactive video activities. Unique to this program are the Making Choices simulations, which help students identify the moments of choice in preparing a speech, and guide them in making ethical decisions based on their audience and speaking goals. These simulations are built around key topics and concepts in the book, from choosing a focus and theme to selecting sources and visual aids and more.

YouSeeU

With *YouSeeU*, students can upload video files of practice speeches or final performances, comment on their peers' speeches, and review their grades and instructor feedback. Instructors create courses and assignments, comment on and grade student speeches, and allow peer review. Grades flow into a gradebook that allows instructors to easily manage their course from within MindTap. Grades also can be exported for use in learning-management systems. YouSeeU's flexibility lends itself to use in traditional, hybrid, and online courses.

Outline Builder

Outline Builder breaks down the speech preparation process into manageable steps and can help alleviate speech-related anxiety. The wizard-format provides relevant prompts and resources to guide students through the outlining process. Students are guided through topic definition, research and source citation, organizational structure outlining, and drafting notecards for speech day. The outline is assignable and gradable through MindTap.

Speech Video Library

Speech Video Library gives students a chance to watch videos of real speeches that correspond to the topics in *Invitation to Human Communication*. Each speech activity provides a video of the speech; a full transcript so viewers can read along; the speech outline—many in notecard and full sentence form and evaluation questions so students are guided through their assessment. While viewing each clip, students evaluate the speech or scenario by completing short answer questions and submitting their results directly to their instructor.

Additional MindTap Study Tools

 Flashcards is a classic learning tool. Digitally reimagined, flashcards detect the chapter a student last opened, then shows cards for that chapter.

 Flashnotes.com is an online marketplace full of study guides, notes, flashcards, and video help created by students, for students.

 Merriam-Webster Dictionary enriches the learning experience and improves users' understanding of the English language.

 Notebook Integrating Evernote technology is an app that aggregates student annotations and notes into a single consolidated view.

 ReadSpeaker Text-to-speech technology offers varied reading styles and the option to select highlighted text to reinforce understanding.

 NetTutor® staffed with U.S.-based tutors and facilitated by a proprietary whiteboard created for online collaboration in education.

Sharing and Collaboration

 Google Docs Instructors and students share dynamically updated text documents, spreadsheets, presentations, and PDFs.

 Kaltura Simple video, audio, and image uploading tools open a wealth of instructional, testing, and engagement opportunities.

 Inline RSS Feed Send timely, valid feeds to students—within the Learning Path or as a separate reading —with the option to add remarks.

 Web Video Easily incorporate YouTube videos as a separate viewing activity within the Learning Path or directly within a reading assignment.

ConnectYard This MindApp social media platform fosters communication among students and teachers without the need to "friend" or "follow" or join a social network.

RESOURCES FOR INSTRUCTORS

Public Speaking, Second Edition features a full suite of resources for instructors. These resources are available to qualified adopters, and ordering options for student supplements are flexible. Please consult your local Cengage Learning sales representative for more information, to evaluate examination copies of any of these instructor or student resources, or to request product demonstrations.

Instructor's Resource Manual. The Instructor's Resource Manual provides a comprehensive teaching system. Included in the manual are suggested assignments and criteria for evaluation, chapter outlines, and in-class activities. PowerPoint slides also are included.

Cengage Learning Testing, powered by Cognero. Accessible through cengage.com/login with your faculty account, this test bank contains multiple choice, true/false, and essay questions for each chapter. Cognero is a flexible, online system that allows you to author, edit, and manage test bank content. Create multiple test versions instantly and deliver through your LMS platform from wherever you may be. Cognero is compatible with Blackboard, Angel, Moodle, and Canvas LMS platforms.

Acknowledgments

I would like to thank all the students I've taught over the last 30 years. I have learned so much about teaching public speaking from them. I also owe heartfelt appreciation to the teaching assistants I've worked with at Oregon State University and the University of Wisconsin–Milwaukee. Their creativity, freshness, and passion have kept me inspired more than they know, and they have improved my teaching immensely. Chris Lundberg is the best coauthor imaginable, and I owe him more than I can say. And finally, enormous thanks to my wife Kari—you make everything possible.

—Bill Keith

I would like to thank Bill Keith for being a fantastic coauthor and colleague, and Beth Lundberg for putting up with us in the process of writing this book.

—Chris Lundberg

We would like to thank the amazing team at Cengage: including Monica Eckman, Editorial Director; Nicole Morinon and Kelli Strieby, Product Managers: Kathy Sands-Boehmer, Content Developer; Karolina Kiwak, Associate Content Developer; Colin Solan, Product Assistant; Lisa Boragine, Digital Content Designer; Marissa Falco, Art Director, Daniel Saabye, Project Manager, Permissions staff: Ann Hoffman, Farah Fard, and Julia Geagan-Chavez; and Stacey Purviance, Marketing Manager.

—*Bill Keith and Chris Lundberg*

Reviewers

We are grateful to all the reviewers whose suggestions and constructive criticisms have helped us shape *Public Speaking: Choices and Responsibility:*

Debra Bourdeau, Embry-Riddle Aeronautical University; Charla Crump, Clarendon College; Katherine Dawson, University of Louisiana at Monroe; Staci Dinerstein, William Paterson University; Catherine Donnelly, Kings College; Catherine Donnelly, Lone Star College; Marvin Elliott, Kentucky Christian University; Jeremy Estrella, Portland Community College; Karen Foss, University of New Mexico; Annemarie Fleishman, Milwaukee School of Engineering; Amy Fountain, Mississippi State University; Rebecca Franko, California State Polytechnic University; Katharine Fulton, Iowa State University; Joseph Ganakos, Lee College; Lisa Hebert, Louisiana State University; Heather Heritage, Cedarville University; Ronald Hochstatter, McLennan Community College; Jenny Hodges, St. John's University; Teresa Horton, Baker College; Kristyn Hunt, Lamar University; Cathy James, Mesa College; John W. Jordan, University of Wisconsin-Milwaukee; Marilyn S. Kritzman, Western Michigan University; Philip Lane, Miami-Dade College; Kimberly A. Laux, University of Michigan-Flint; Melody Lehn, University of South Carolina; Melanie Lea, Bossier Parish Community College; Danielle Leek, Grand Valley State University; Tami Martinez, Indiana University South Bend; Maryann Matheny, Campbellsville University; John Nash, Moraine Valley Community College; Jean Perry, Glendale Community College; Narissa Punyanunt-Carter, Texas Tech; Ken Robol, Beaufort Community College; Douglas Rosentrater, Bucks County Community College; Caroline E. Sawyer, University of Memphis; Amy Schumacher, The George Washington University; Kim Smith, Bishop State Community College; Roberta Steinberg, Mount Ida College; Burton St. John, Old Dominion University; Joseph Steinitz, University of Iowa; Juan Taylor, Schoolcraft College; Mary Triece, University of Akron; Karol Walchak, Alpena Community College; Wade Walker, Louisiana State University; Edward Wallace, Campbell University; Christopher Westgate, Johnson and Wales University; Joshua Young, University of North Dakota; David Zanolla, Western Illinois University and Naomi Young, Grossmont College.

PART 1 FUNDAMENTALS OF GOOD SPEAKING

CHAPTER **1** Public Speaking

CHAPTER **2** Ethics and the Responsible Speaker

CHAPTER **3** Understanding Audiences and Publics

CHAPTER **4** Becoming a Skilled Listener

DrAfter123/Getty Images

PUBLIC SPEAKING

LEARNING OBJECTIVES

- Explain why public speaking is powerful and worth mastering
- Contrast the public and civic dimensions of public speaking with other types of communication
- Define the special responsibilities of a public speaker
- Identify the stages and choices necessary to compose and deliver a speech
- Describe communication choices at each stage of the speech creation process

CHAPTER OUTLINE

- Introduction: Why Learn Public Speaking?
- Speech Is Powerful
- The Communication Process
- The *Public* in Public Speaking
- Speaking Is About Making Choices
- The Speaking Process: Preparing and Performing
- Thinking Through Your Choices
- Creating Your First Speech
- Giving Your First Speech
- Making Responsible Choices

Colt has to give a speech for his class, and he wants it to be about a problem that has been bugging him for a while: Do speeches even matter anymore? Given all the technology that people carry around with them, what's the deal with communication these days? His problem is that he doesn't know what to do next. How can he develop and research the topic? How should he think about his classmates as audience? How should he organize the speech and choose the right words? It all seems so confusing, and he's not even sure where to start. He needs some basic principles and overview of the process.

Overview

To become an effective speaker, first you'll want to understand a few basic principles about public speaking as a communication activity. This chapter will give you an overview of the communication process, highlighting the difference that public speaking can make in your life and in the lives of the people listening to you. You will learn about the process of composing and delivering a public speech, focusing on the variety of choices you have to make when you give a speech. Finally, to get you started on the process of composing and delivering a speech, we will walk you through the basic elements of speech preparation, which are the topics of the subsequent chapters.

MindTap®
Start with a warm-up activity about Colt's speech, and review the chapter Learning Objectives.

INTRODUCTION: WHY LEARN PUBLIC SPEAKING?

Caution: The contents of this book can be dangerous. Dangerous—but also powerful. Whether used for good or for ill, speech is one of the most powerful forces in human history. Sometimes it has been used to unite people around a common democratic goal—for example, to advance the cause of civil rights. Other times dictators have used speech as a powerful weapon. But however it is used, speech can change the world. More important, *your* speech can change *your* world in big and small ways.

The principles we'll introduce will help you give better speeches in almost any context, even when your goal is modest. They will help you learn to be a better public speaker—clearer and more persuasive, but also more engaged, responsible, and well reasoned.

We often hear that public speaking is just about clear communication. It is in part, and people sometimes assume that anyone can do it without much effort or thought. But

MindTap®

Read, highlight and take notes online.

performance counts too—actually getting up and talking in front of other people. You may be surprised to find out by the end of this course, however, that getting up and speaking in front of other people can be the easy part. In this book we would like to introduce you to the range of skills that go into preparing, producing, and delivering a speech, skills that will make you a more effective advocate for yourself and for the people and ideas you care about.

You may not be in this course to change the world: Many students take a public speaking course because it is required. But taking this course, working through this book, and adopting your instructor's advice on how to be a better public speaker will make you more successful not only in class but in your everyday life and beyond the classroom.

You are about to become part of a tradition that stretches back thousands of years. So stick with us. We hope to convince you of the power of words, of the world-changing capability that each of us has if we learn how to develop and use it responsibly.

Whatever brought you to this class, public speaking is necessary not only for your education and career but also for your life and for the health of our democracy. We will argue that *speech is powerful* and that *speech matters*.

What's a Remix?

Public speaking is not only an ancient art. It is also a topic of study for people in a number of modern fields. Studying it well requires that you read and think through a "mashup" of sorts, incorporating timeless insights about speaking with fresh new angles on the art of speech. So what are we remixing here? In these boxes we will remix the tradition of public speaking by including recent work on public speaking topics from social sciences, the humanities, and even from the sciences. We'll also include some sources for further reading if any of these ideas grab your attention.

SPEECH IS POWERFUL

rhetoric Term for the study of how language, argument, and narrative can persuade an audience.

The study of public speaking began in ancient Greece. For the Greeks, public speaking was part of the broader field of **rhetoric**, the study of how words could persuade an audience. In the modern world, many people associate public speaking with manipulation, and the term *rhetoric* with "empty talk." They may say, "Let's have less rhetoric and more action." Although it is true that talk is sometimes empty, good speech also can be a form of action, motivating people to make important changes in the world. To see why, the first thing to understand is that because speech is powerful, *your* speech can be powerful.

The Power of Public Speaking to Change the World

One of the first people to write about the power of public speech, the Greek philosopher Gorgias of Leontini, claimed that "speech is a powerful lord." Twenty-five hundred years later, abundant evidence supports Gorgias's insight. Speech and speeches have been used to both good and bad ends. They have introduced and converted many to the world's great religions. They have helped to elect presidents and overthrow dictators. They have begun wars and ended them. Winston Churchill's and Franklin Roosevelt's speeches rallied the British and U.S. populations during World War II. In the 19th century, Elizabeth Cady Stanton spoke out to make people aware of the rights of women. In the middle of the 20th century, the speeches of Martin Luther King showed people in the United States how to think differently about civil rights and issues of race and racism.

"We need the power of words *to speak a better world into existence.*" Speech, used effectively, should motivate us to make changes on our campuses, in our communities, and as a nation. It also should help us make better decisions about the kinds of changes we make. We need the ability to speak with clarity and conviction, but we also need to be able to listen with attention and respect to other people's viewpoints. Thus, one of the biggest challenges of our time is to learn how to speak in a way that generates cooperation and insight, and that avoids division and narrow-mindedness.

But what can learning how to speak well do for you? After all, you probably will not be in the position of addressing the nation in a time of war or convincing Congress to change a law. The point of this course is not to change you into an Elizabeth Cady Stanton, a Winston Churchill, or a Martin Luther King.

The Power of Speeches to Change Your World

Even though speeches can change the world, common sense tells us that they also can make a big difference in your individual history. Every day, people speak in courtrooms, boardrooms, and classrooms to persuade others of their points of view or to inform others about things they need to know. A good speech can make all the difference in winning a lawsuit, pitching a business idea, or teaching people about something that might change their lives significantly. And, ultimately, that is the point of this book: Because speech is such a powerful tool, we should learn to use it as effectively and as responsibly as we can.

The skills you will learn here also will make you a more effective speaker in your career. If you want to come across as the candidate to hire when applying for a dream job, being well spoken is a crucial part of your success. If you prepare well for the interview, thinking about how to present yourself as a fitting and capable candidate, if you perform well by speaking clearly and articulately, if you make a persuasive case, and if you invite the participation of the interviewers by fostering a good dialogue, you can be a shoo-in for the position. By the same token, if you pitch a business proposal to a supervisor, a client, or a lender, you will have to project an attitude of competency and meticulous preparation, as well as to speak articulately and build a relationship with your listeners.

The basic principles are similar for any speech, whether it is delivered on the Senate floor, in a State of the Union address, in a business meeting, or before a local community group. In each instance, you will have to plan carefully what you will say and how you will say it, and to build a relationship with the audience.

FAQ Why start by talking about the Greeks?

We have inherited many ideas about communication and its relationship to public life from ancient Greek and Roman (also called "classical") practice. The founders of the United States used them as models; many classical principles and terms they developed are still useful and relevant. For example, in Chapter 12 we'll examine persuasive appeals in speaking through the lens of the classical distinction among *ethos*, *logos*, and *pathos*.

FAQ Can speeches really change the world?

Here are some speeches that helped to change the course of history. If you would like to learn more about any of them, access them online.

"Against Imperialism," William Jennings Bryan
"Acres of Diamonds," Russell H. Conwell
"Mercy For Leopold and Loeb," Clarence Darrow
"Statement to the Court," Eugene V. Debs
"Farewell Address," Dwight D. Eisenhower
"1976 DNC Keynote Address," Barbara Jordan
"Inaugural Address," John F. Kennedy
"I Have a Dream," Martin Luther King
"Every Man a King," Huey Long
"The Ballot or the Bullet," Malcolm X
"Farewell Address to Congress," General Douglas MacArthur
"Pearl Harbor Address to the Nation," Franklin D. Roosevelt
"The Fundamental Principle of a Republic," Anna Howard Shaw
"Declaration of Conscience," Margaret Chase Smith

FAQ *Can speeches really make a difference in my life?*

Here are some examples of the kinds of speeches that can change the course of your life if you deliver them effectively:

- The speech you give as an answer to the job interview question, "Tell us a little bit about yourself"
- The speech you give when you pitch an important business idea
- The speech you give when you are trying to persuade people in your community (for example, a town council or a neighborhood association) to change something in your community that should be changed.
- The speech you give when convincing a loved one to do something—to enter a long-term relationship, for example, or to support you in an important project
- The speeches you give to convince others to vote for a candidate or a law that affects your everyday life

democracy A system of government in which people govern themselves, either through direct votes on policy issues (*direct democracy*) or by electing officials who deliberate and make decisions on their behalf (*representative democracy*).

unity Harmony among related parts.

pluralism The coexistence of numerous ethnic, cultural, political or religious groups in one nation.

stakeholders The people who have something to lose or gain as the result of a decision or policy. They have an *interest* in that decision.

Speaking Connects You to Others: Democracy in Everyday Life

A good public speech, no matter what the context, ultimately strives to reach the best ideals of **democracy**. If you have a dollar bill in your pocket, take it out. The Great Seal of the United States is reproduced on the back of the bill. On the left side is a pyramid inside a circle, and on the right side is a circle with an eagle in it. The eagle has a small scroll in its mouth. If you look closely, you will see the Latin phrase *E pluribus unum*, meaning "From many, one." The many people who make up the United States are all united—we are all in this together.

Democracy works, or at least we will be able to make it work, only if we recognize the fact that we are many people with substantial differences in opinion, race, class, sexuality, gender, religion, and belief. But we also strive to make from these differences a common identity, or at least a common commitment to democracy and the well-being of our fellow citizens.

Public speaking, at its best, is about respecting that common commitment: Public speaking is about the **unity** of democracy. But it is also about respecting the **pluralism** of democracy—namely, that we have to speak and listen in a way that preserves the important differences that make each of us who we are.

Now you may be saying to yourself, "Wait a minute. I was hoping to get some communication skills out of this class that I could use in business, for my job." Actually, you will get that, and more. Successful and effective persuasion and informative speaking in politics, business, and even personal life can invoke the highest democratic values. Why? Because speakers who make good decisions consider the effects of their words on all **stakeholders**,

"From many, one" on the U.S. dollar bill expresses an important part of democratic life.

Aaron Amat/Shutterstock.com

or all the people who have something at stake in the decisions. Skilled speakers not only know how to adapt to their audience of stakeholders, but they also understand their audience's diversity.

The Conversational Framework

In this book we'll distinguish different approaches to communication, especially public communication. Speakers are never *just* informing and persuading; there is always a larger context that creates mutual responsibilities between speakers and their audiences. To sharpen the picture, let's compare advertising and democracy as contexts for communication. They represent fundamentally different approaches to public discourse and different ways of understanding this mutual responsibility.

In advertising, a company is trying to sell something, to get someone to buy something. Ads target specific groups of people called market segments—men between 30 and 40, for instance, or working women who live in urban areas, or Twitter users. Advertisers are successful when sales increase; their responsibility to their audience is fairly limited, and communication is usually in just one direction.

In contrast, in the context of democracy, communication is among people or citizens "thinking together." Decisions should emerge as a result of the mutual exchange of arguments, information, and points of view. Democracy is big and messy; imagine it as an enormous system in which

different ideas and arguments circulate, being expressed (and maybe changed) at many different points. Sometimes it's you and a friend talking about what the government should do about student loans; sometimes it's you reading a debate about student loan finances in the newspaper or on a website. Sometimes it's your roommate watching an argument being mocked on a satirical news show, and sometimes it's your parents attending a community meeting to hear what people say.

If you're paying attention, you are part of the larger public dialogue, and you might even be putting in your two cents. Even if you don't see yourself as particularly political, you might be surprised if you keep track for a few days of how often you think and talk about public issues; you can't help it—they matter.

Clearly, this is very different from advertising. Democratic conversation, or dialogue, aims to solve problems, not to sell products. It involves everybody, not just a target consumer audience. To be successful, arguments have to be adaptable to men and women alike, older and younger, and of different races, religions, regions of the country, income, education levels, and so on. Advertising bypasses differences such as these by selectively targeting a smaller audience of people who have something in common.

Suppose a student is going to give an informative speech on a surprising or controversial topic, such as the campus need for transgender bathrooms. An advertising approach probably would start by defining the target market as the types of people most likely to be sympathetic to sexualities that are different from their own and would ignore everyone else. It's difficult to imagine, however, how the student would give a speech to a class and ignore many or most of the people in it.

In contrast, in a democratic conversation or dialogue, the speaker would begin by identifying the larger public issues that connect to the availability of transgender bathrooms: equality, civil rights, and the increasing acceptance of gay and transgender people. The speaker would be placing the issue of transgender bathrooms within larger discussions that have been going on for 10, 50, or maybe 150 years, portraying the issue as part of a larger conversation about civil rights or equality.

Public Speaking and Democracy

At one time, teachers taught public speaking courses by having their students memorize and deliver great speeches, learn ornate hand gestures, and focus in excruciating detail on pauses, tone, and vocal flourishes. If you were taking this class in the 1800s, you might have had to master hand movements to go along with a text that you were memorizing, and to do this, you might study something like this:

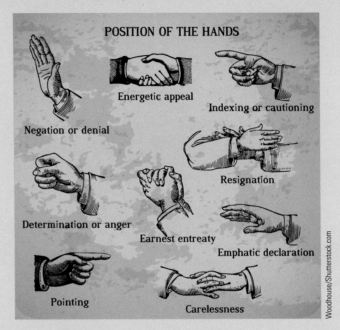

POSITION OF THE HANDS

Negation or denial

Energetic appeal

Indexing or cautioning

Resignation

Determination or anger

Earnest entreaty

Emphatic declaration

Pointing

Carelessness

Woodhouse/Shutterstock.com

But starting around the 1900s, and continuing until today, public speaking has focused more on helping people to compose and deliver materials that they wrote, in a clear conversational manner. Why the change? Well, when education was the privilege of a small segment of society, knowing how to deliver a riveting version of a speech from ancient Greece might have been a useful skill. But now, public speaking instruction, including this book, focuses on the idea that the goal of public speaking is to help students find their voice so they can advocate for themselves and for the things that matter to them. This is part of a larger historical trend to see higher education as a good for a greater number of people and, by extension, to prepare more people for productive lives in the workplace and in the broader democratic sphere.

An accompanying turn in public speaking, then, was to see the point of a good speech as more than just helping students really nail vocal flourishes or hand gestures, or to show how well they could recite ancient poetry. The new point of public speaking was to see it as the ability to communicate in one's own voice to an audience of peers—to other people who were also in public listening and speaking and talking about matters of common interest.

For more information, check out:

J. M. Sproule, Inventing Public Speaking: Rhetoric and the Speech Book, 1730–1930. *Rhetoric and Public Affairs.* 15:4. 2012

Zeam Porter speaks at a public hearing about a proposed transgender policy for high school sports. Porter identifies as transgender. Can just speaking up, and speaking out, make a difference to public discourse?

As another example, consider a speech about yoga. In a public speaking class, is it the speaker's job to "sell" yoga to her classmates? Probably not. But she could present the information she gained from her research on yoga in the context of public conversations about health, athletic performance, or even spirituality.

Our point here is that while you are learning many new techniques in public speaking class, such as outlining, research, and delivery, you also will learn new ways of understanding the kind of communication that makes up truly *public* speaking. It isn't quite like talking to friends about movies and music, and it isn't like a sales pitch. Public speaking is the adventure of taking your turn in one of the amazing ongoing public conversations that are happening right now.

In short, speech is powerful, and it matters in ways that you may not have thought about too much, but after taking this course, you'll never hear a speech the same way again. Now let's look at an overview of the actual process.

THE COMMUNICATION PROCESS

In this book, we'll often refer to communicating in the context of public speaking as *rhetoric*, but with a different meaning than you're used to. As we noted, today the term *rhetoric* is often negative and refers to discourse that is empty, insincere, and pompous. In its classical sense, however, rhetoric is about the art of speaking, and it requires at least three components:

- a speaker,
- a listener, and
- some means of sharing facts, ideas, reasoning and information between them.

There might be a conversation between two people or among several people, as in a group discussion. Or, as in public speaking situations, there might be one speaker and a large audience. Or the medium might change: One person writes a letter or email to another, or a letter is published in the newspaper and is read by thousands of people. Even though the "speakers" and "listeners" are not physically present, we can still use the terms *speaker* (writer) and *listener* (reader) because the communication situations are parallel: In all of them, the speaker is trying to accomplish something with the listener, using language. Of course, there are also differences: Speakers in person generate nonverbal cues to meaning, and for writers, layout, design, and color can communicate more than the words say, or sometimes something different from what the words say.

Tai Lihua of the Chinese People's Political Consultative Conference (left) joins a panel discussion in Beijing with the help of a sign language interpreter. Are the Deaf who use sign language truly speaking?

For most of us, "speaking" involves opening our mouths and having audible words come out. But if you are Deaf, speaking means using your hands to create American Sign Language (ASL) or American Signed English. And what about the many of the public speeches that are written in advance, some existing only as texts? Many "speeches" inserted into the *Congressional Record*, for example, have never been spoken aloud. We mention ASL and written speeches to emphasize that "speaking" is a complex phenomenon and to encourage you to think about what speech is and how it is generated.

TRY IT!

YOUR RHETORICAL SITUATIONS

Make a list of the most common rhetorical situations you engage in.

- Who are the most common listeners? Why?
- Are these situations usually face-to-face or electronic? Why?
- Which ones are easiest? Most difficult? Why?

THE *PUBLIC* IN PUBLIC SPEAKING

An audience is not the same as the people listening or reading by chance; people who happen to overhear a conversation are not the audience for the conversation. Audiences are made up of a variety of people, with different beliefs, values, and life experiences. And the speaker wants something from all of them—their attention, their patience, their comprehension, their openness, a change of mind, a change of action.

Much of the time, speaking (and writing) is not only an expression of the speaker's thoughts but is also, in an important sense, tailored *for* the audience. Speakers need to know something about their audience so they can adapt to the audience. Just as in ordinary conversation you say different things (or the same thing in different ways) depending on whom you are talking to, speakers adjust their topic and presentation to their audience. **Adaptation** is one of the central concepts of rhetorical communication.[1]

adaptation Adjusting a topic, arguments, and presentation to fit a particular audience.

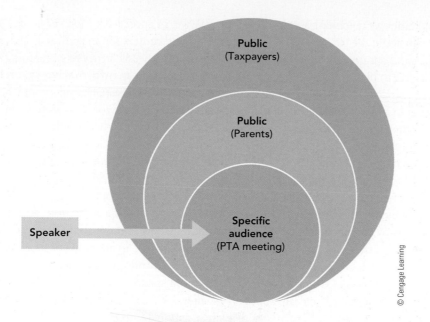

FIGURE 1.1
Audience members belong
to more than one public.

Is the audience ever more than just the people in the room with the speaker? To explain why it is called *public* speaking, we have to consider the concept of a **public**, a group of people who share a common set of concerns.

In Figure 1.1, the speaker is attempting to influence or inform an audience whose members belong to more than one public. For example, the audience at a PTA meeting will be part of the public that cares about the fate of children as well as the public that pays taxes. If the speaker is making an informative presentation about the current state of student achievement in the district, she will have to think about a specific public in deciding what information is relevant and how to frame it.

Yet, the diagram in Figure 1.1 is incomplete. Why? Because it pictures the speaker as separate from or outside of the public. However, when you are speaking *to* an audience in public, you are speaking *with* an audience composed of fellow members of your public. The speaker portrays herself and the audience not as opposed to each other ("I care about one thing, and you care about something else") but, instead, as part of the same public ("Here is what *we* care about"), as shown in Figure 1.2.

public A group of people who share a common set of concerns.

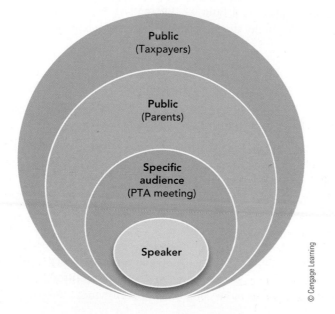

FIGURE 1.2
The speaker and the
audience both belong to the
same publics.

Whether we're looking at informative, persuasive, or special-occasion speaking, we'll generally talk about the *public* as a way of talking about the context for an audience. This is necessary because speakers need to understand who the audience is if they're going to adapt their information to the audience. For example, if you were giving an **informative speech** on the idea of a taxpayer bill of rights, the public most likely would consist of "people concerned about tax policy." Or if you were giving a **persuasive speech** arguing for changes to make student loan programs more widely accessible, the relevant publics would be "people concerned about access to education" and "people who believe education is essential to the economic success of the United States." Even a **special-occasion speech**, such as a eulogy at a funeral, can be addressed to a public; if the deceased volunteered at the Humane Society, her friends will talk about how her accomplishments mattered to people who care about animals.

The concept of the public allows us to differentiate public speaking from advertising and other forms of private and personal communication (there is more about this in Chapter 3). The concept of the public provides a way for you to connect to an audience in an ethical and effective way by focusing on interests that concern them not just as students in a classroom but also as members of a broader citizenry. When you speak in class, you will be addressing a public only if the things you talk about are of interest to your audience members, not just as fellow classmates but also as members of a larger national public.

informative speech A speech in which the primary purpose is to educate the audience about a topic.

persuasive speech A speech in which the primary purpose is to change the audience's opinion about a topic or to encourage them to take a particular action.

special-occasion speech A speech made on the occasion of a life transition (such as a wedding) or at a professional event (such as introducing a speaker).

SPEAKING IS ABOUT MAKING CHOICES

It may seem a little strange to think about speaking as making choices. Isn't speaking just saying what you're thinking? If you reflect for a moment, though, you may realize that you often are sure of what your thoughts are only as you are saying them, and you may say them differently depending on the person you're talking to.

In creating a speech, you make **choices** about what to say. Two thousand years ago, when public figures in classical Greece and Rome wanted to give a speech, they might turn to a rhetorician (called a *logographer*, or "speechwriter") to figure out how to compose and deliver the speech. Now, most of us do this for ourselves. Ancient rhetorical practice was organized around the canons (sets of rules or principles) of rhetoric, which broke the process of speaking into five parts: (1) Come up with content, (2) organize it, (3) choose words for it, (4) memorize it, and then (5) deliver it.

We teach public speaking a little bit differently now, and in this book we propose a simplified and updated model that focuses on the choices you will need to make to give a successful speech.

choices In public speaking, the choices are about topic, information and arguments, organization, visual aids and other supporting materials, and type of delivery.

First, *preparation*: How will you prepare your speech? What do you want to say? What information and arguments will you use to support your claims? How will you organize the speech and move from point to point? What words, images, or technology will be needed in creating a compelling experience for the audience?

Second, *performance*: How will you deliver or "perform" your speech? What tone, pace, and gestures will you use? You will have to make sure that you speak clearly, loud enough for the audience to hear, and you will have to eliminate distracting speech and body tics. Few speeches are memorized nowadays, but you will have to decide how to master the information in your speech and create materials such as notecards or slides that allow you to deliver it.

When you think of public speaking, performance, or **delivery**, probably comes to mind first. Images of shaking knees, sweaty palms, and a nervous stomach are common, but effective preparation can result in more comfortable performances. Preparation means planning

delivery The act of making a speech to an audience.

the best way to present your message so the audience will respond favorably. You will have to think about the audience's interests in this topic and in listening to you talk about it. You also will have to think about the audience expectations and predispositions. Finally, you will have to give the audience a stake in what you are saying by providing an opportunity for the members to participate. They may respond by asking questions, and you should have a strategy for dealing with their questions, but you also should give them an opportunity to participate by changing their beliefs and/or actions as a result of your speech.

Preparation

The moment when you stand up and give your speech may not be the most important, or even the most difficult, part of the process. Although the performance components may trigger the nerves that make your stomach shaky as you think about giving a speech, the *preparation* that goes into deciding what to say is more difficult and probably more important than the performance. Great delivery with nothing much to say isn't effective communication. We all admire and enjoy a great performer, and sometimes we assume that a musician's or an actor's talent is responsible for the impressive concert or play. Actually, no matter how talented, the artist has invested a huge amount of careful preparation into creating that compelling event for the audience.

PREPARATION CHOICES CHECKLIST TRY IT!

Run through the following checklist when you are preparing a speech:

- How do I want to structure the speech?
- What arguments do I want to use?
- What kinds of research will be most helpful to do and to present to the audience?
- What sources and ideas will the audience find most credible?
- Am I taking into account possible objections or rebuttals to my arguments?
- What is the product of my preparation? A memorized speech, notes, images? And how should I use them?

The most crucial part of speaking may well be the thought that goes into it. Why? First of all, good delivery depends on good preparation; the preparation that you put into your speech beforehand may be one of your best defenses against feeling nervous about, or even overwhelmed by, public speaking.

Speaking should be *communication*. You should say what you think, or better yet, you should present the best information and your most thoughtful opinions about our subject matter. In contrast to acting, which involves saying someone else's words, public speaking is speaking your *own* mind. In the case of an actor, it's unclear exactly who is communicating to the audience. The writer? The actor? A combination? In public speaking, it's all about you. You are both writer and "actor." So, although the way you give a speech may be a kind of performance, you should think of speaking as a process that allows you to say what you think to someone in particular.

Deciding what to say implies making some important choices based on your opinions and on the materials and tools that are available to you: ideas, arguments, images, words, and metaphors. This means that you have to put work into preparing your speech, a process we call invention. As an illustration, let's look in more detail at the kinds of choices speakers make when they prepare speeches that inform and persuade an audience.

MindTap

Watch a video, and do an interactive activity.

Public speaking is above all communication.

istockphoto.com/Luvo

Informing

Many times as a speaker, you are trying to convey information to an audience. Sometimes you are in the role of an expert, sometimes a sort of teacher; in other cases you are more like the messenger delivering the news, like a reporter. In each case, you are trying to get information across to the audience clearly and effectively.

Some people mistakenly assume that if you know what you're talking about, you'll automatically be clear, but that's not necessarily true. Think back to some of your least favorite teachers. They may have been experts, but they may not have been very good at communicating their knowledge.

Why is that? How can expertise and good communication be two different things? It happens because communication is not only about the knowledge in the speaker's head but about the audience as well. Audiences can't understand things they don't understand. That seems obvious, but many speakers disregard it. To explain or clarify something, you have to assume that the audience doesn't understand it already, and then choose to explain it in terms of the actual current knowledge of this group.

Making Choices: Example 1   Suppose you are faced with explaining a new university regulation to a group of students on your campus. The university has decided that "any drug or alcohol-related tickets or arrests involving students will have academic repercussions." Right now, you, the reader, (like the hypothetical audience) are probably wondering what that means—"repercussions?" As a speaker, you have some choices:

- First, you have to decide what your role will be. Are you speaking on behalf of the university or as just a student?
- Even though you'll cover the same information in either case, if you're speaking as a student, you'll highlight benefits or consequences for students, including yourself. If you speak on behalf of the school, you may feature the reasons for the decision and what it means for the school.
- Depending on which way you go, you'll change the order of points (probably putting the ones most important to the audience last), and you'll change any charts or illustrations you use, because these highlight the things that will be most memorable for the audience about the information.

Persuading

Sometimes we want more than just to have the audience understand us; we want them to believe or do something. By *persuasion*, we mean all of the ways that speakers can attempt to influence audiences, from informing them about a topic to arguing that they should change their beliefs or inspiring them to action. All of these are "persuasive" in the sense of attempting to influence the audience. Even in an informative speech, speakers adapt it to the audience, trying to make sure that the audience not only understand but also care about the information.

Making Choices: Example 2   You probably are so used to making choices about what to say that you don't realize that you are always choosing what to say and how to say it. As a simple interpersonal example, suppose you'd like to get your friend Brian to go to a movie with you on a Friday night. You start with "movie" and "Brian," but from there you have a lot of choices. You have to decide whether you think he automatically will want to go to a movie or if you'll have to convince him. If you're going to convince him, you'll consider what would motivate him. Is he looking for a relaxing time after a hard week? Is he bored with his job and looking for excitement? Does he enjoy dinner before a movie, or does he like a big bucket of popcorn with his flick? You might research what movies are playing, and you may choose one based on what kind of movie Brian likes. Or you may try to convince Brian to see the movie *you're* interested in. If Brian were someone you didn't know well, you might have to approach the request more formally; with a fairly close friend, you can be more informal.

Without realizing it, all of these choices may flash through your head before you decide to say to your friend, "Hey, bud, want go and check out the midnight showing of *Donny Darko*? You know you love that flick, and we can grab some food afterward." Your process for public speaking will be similar: You need to interpret the audience and purpose (whom you're talking to and what you want from that audience) and, as the next example shows, there are always choices about that interpretation.

Making Choices: Example 3   Let's say you have been asked to give a presentation to the city council asking for a change in the zoning laws for a skateboard park. Your audience consists of the city council members, who will vote on your proposal. So, what are your choices? You probably don't need to know much about the city council members personally, because they probably don't make zoning decisions based exclusively on their being a man or a woman or white, Asian, or Hispanic. Their decisions are more likely based on their functions as city council members: interpreting the law and serving the public interest. What you want to say about your topic is determined to a large extent by what you want to convince them to do, but your approach to these council members and how you want to persuade them requires some strategic choices.

Why should the city council change the zoning laws? Because it will benefit you and your friends? Naturally, you think that it will, but will that move city council members? Probably not. Can you argue that it benefits them? Yes, but be careful: You're not talking about benefiting the council members personally but, rather, you're arguing about their *role* as council members: They should care about benefits to the city. How would the new park benefit the city? Presumably it will generate some tax revenue and perhaps some part-time employment.

However, because council members have to think about the good of the city, they'll have to consider two problems: What if noise from the park bothers the neighbors or skaters get rowdy? You'll have to address those issues clearly, or you can't expect the council to take you very seriously. As you decide what to argue, you also should think about language choices. You might think about how you want to address the members ("Sir" and "Ma'am" versus "You guys"), and about how you want to describe the skate park. Will it be in terms that get them visualizing it ("Imagine all these kids exercising and staying out of trouble") or in terms that support your argument ("Data on skateparks show they're good civic investments")? You might use analogies to national or state parks. You may even think about how you'll dress for the occasion—will it be in skater clothes or something more formal? You'll have to consider which would be better, and why. Skater clothes might show that you're in touch with the future users, but something more formal might show that you should be taken seriously.

THE SPEAKING PROCESS: PREPARING AND PERFORMING

Now that you have an idea about a public speaker's choices, let's look at the actual process. What do you have to do to give a speech? It's useful to see preparation as having two parts: the analysis and the "writing" of the speech. First, you will have to *think*—analyze—what you want to say in the particular situation for your particular audience. Then you will have to *create* a speech that is well organized, is crafted for maximum effect, and has good supporting arguments. After that, you're ready to *speak*; you will have to deliver the speech in such a way that it not only will be listened to but also will be heard and acted upon by the audience. Here's is a brief outline of the process:

Prepare:

- *Choose a topic:* What things are important to you that you would like to say to your audience?
- *Audience:* Who will be listening, and what is their interest in the topic?
- *Goals:* What do you want the audience to do, either by learning, acting, or changing beliefs?
- *Arguments:* What claims, propositions, or ideas would you like the audience to believe?
- *Research:* How will you support your arguments with evidence, statistics, quotes from experts, and other materials that lend credibility to your case?
- *Organization:* How will you put your points together to have a clear pattern that is easy for the audience to follow?
- *Words:* How will you phrase your ideas to be both clear and compelling to the audience?

Responsible public speakers approach different audiences in different ways. A town council meeting is different from a classroom and from half of Congress.

Perform:

- *Delivery:* What choices will you make about performance of the speech? How will you act (for example, will you make an effort at eye contact?), and what choices will you make in verbal style (tone, pitch, rate, emphasis, clarity) to make sure that your speech has maximum persuasive effect?
- *Anxiety:* What strategies and techniques will you use for managing your nerves?
- *Speaking Aids:* Do you need any visual aids? What purpose will they serve? What technology is available? How can you integrate these into your speech?

THINKING THROUGH YOUR CHOICES

To preview how the chapters of this book will walk you through these steps of the speaking process, we'll use the example of Danielle, who is trying to figure out how to give a speech persuading other students to donate blood. Each part of speech preparation involves a set of choices, and Danielle needs to recognize both *what* her choices are and *how* to make them responsibly. First, the analytic part of preparation: Think about who your audience is, and your goals regarding this audience.

Your Responsibilities (Chapter 2)

First, Danielle has to orient herself to what we'll call the *ethical* dimensions of this speaking situation. She needs to ask herself what her relationship is to her audience. Does she want to get donations and doesn't care how she gets them? Even if Danielle isn't willing to lie to get people to donate, she still might employ half-truths or misleading statements. This stance toward the audience shows a lack of rhetorical or communicative responsibility, because it divides Danielle from the audience ("I'm persuading *you*"). A more responsible approach would create a context in which Danielle and the audience together are coming to understand the mutual benefits of blood donation ("*We* need to do something about the local blood shortage"). Before Danielle can start thinking about what to say, she needs to clarify what she intends to do with, or to, the audience in this situation.

[handwritten margin note: what to do w/ info]

Your Audience (Chapters 3, 4)

Now Danielle must think about the nature of her audience. She can think about her audience in general terms, especially the obstacles that might prevent members from being blood donors already. Some students are busy with schoolwork plus jobs or family or all three. Other students may be uninterested. Either way, Danielle knows that her speech has to be entertaining and informative, and that it must give the audience a reason to show up at the blood donation station and be poked with a needle for little or no compensation.

After she takes these general issues into account, she might think more specifically about the actual group she will address: Is it a random sampling of students in a course, a volunteer group, or a campus social group? At this point, Danielle will need to think about why people are in the audience in the first place and then to think about how she can use the picture of the audience that she is developing to motivate them to give blood. Finally, she'll probably realize that a couple of specific fears about blood donation might come into play with any audience: Some people are afraid of blood, and some people are horrified by needles. She'll have to take those fears into account at some point in her speech. In addition, some people fear (wrongly) that they can get a disease just from giving blood.

Her issue—the blood supply—is one that concerns us all, so it is *a public* issue. What kind of public is her audience of college students relative to the issue of blood donation? Despite all

[handwritten margin note: what kind of audience, obstacles they might face "public issue"]

iStockphoto.com/Grmarc

Is there a difference between a student asking other students to donate blood and the Red Cross asking for donations?

clear call to action

the differences in students (older, younger, urban, rural, male, female), can she find a common characteristic that gives them a reason to say yes to blood donation?

Here is where Danielle's rhetorical creativity comes in. She can *describe* the audience to themselves. They are busy college students, yes—but they also are people who might get sick or injured and need some blood at the hospital. "Potential blood-bank users" may not be how the students think about themselves, but it's a true description, and it's relevant to Danielle's purpose: It transforms the audience into a public, with a mutual interest in blood donations. Another possible public would be "people who value public service." Many college students either fall into this group or wish they did, and Danielle can give them the opportunity to perform a public service.

Danielle will have to speak in a way that helps the audience listen and to *want* to listen. This includes the use of tone, pacing, and transitions to keep the audience involved. Danielle also will have to present arguments in a balanced way that takes into account the needs, expectations, and predispositions of the audience. She also will have to present herself as a person who is open to and respectful toward the opinions of the audience members. She will have to give all the evidence needed for them to make an informed decision, and to provide concrete steps for them to take if they choose to donate blood. Finally, Danielle should allow the audience time to ask questions, if this is appropriate, and to answer the questions in a clear, engaging, and nonconfrontational way.

Your Goals (Chapter 5)

Danielle has to assess the situation. In this case, she already has a topic (sometimes that's not the case). What are her goals? She should clearly distinguish between her personal goals (what she wants to accomplish) and her goals with the audience (what she wants her speech to accomplish). She can't just say, "Hey, donate blood, because if I get in good with the blood bank people, I'm set for an internship, and that would be a big résumé booster." That's her personal goal; she will benefit if she can get more blood in the blood bank by recruiting more donors. Her goal *with the audience* would be to persuade the students to donate blood voluntarily through the campus program. But this goal has some inherent challenges: Why donate blood on campus for a few cookies when you might be able to get money somewhere else for selling your blood *plasma*. Danielle would like to get students to want to show up at one of the campus sites. She doesn't have to control or manipulate them or make them into better people; she just has to get them to see why it would be right to donate. Danielle wants to choose a goal that is appropriate not only to the situation but also is defensible.

CREATING YOUR FIRST SPEECH

Once Danielle has made some tentative decisions about her audience, her goals, and the audience's relationship to her topic, she will start creating her speech, the second part of preparation.

Informing and Arguing (Chapters 11, 12)

For Danielle to persuade her audience, she'll have to provide information about blood donation and, for this specific situation, reasons why students should donate, and then she'll have to choose the best reasons. (Her choices here will both determine and depend on her research, as discussed in the next section.) These reasons will be the **argument**, in which the conclusion is, "I should donate blood." Arguments give reasons and evidence, and Danielle has several choices. She can choose examples as evidence:

argument A claim backed by reasons—logic and evidence—in support of a specific conclusion.

Here is a person who was saved by donated blood.

She can make public arguments:

Donating blood is an important public service.
You or someone you love might be in an accident some day, and you want make sure the local hospital has a ready supply of your blood type.

She also can present arguments based on emotion:

When one of your family members is hurt, there's nothing more comforting than knowing that there's an army of volunteers there to support you, even though they don't know you, because they were willing to give the gift of their blood.

Danielle should brainstorm many arguments from which to choose the ones that the students in her audience are most likely to understand and that connect to them the best. She may have to confront the realization that her reasons for donating blood may not be the same as the audience's reasons. She can choose to use any, all, or none of the following brainstormed reasons to make her case:

- It's fun!
- You can help others.
- You have an obligation to help.
- The blood bank needs you.
- Other people will need your help.
- Sick people need your help.
- It's easy.
- You'll feel great about yourself after you do it.
- There's no risk in giving blood.
- What if you needed blood?

What will help her choose among these reasons? She'll need to select the arguments that are most effective with the specific audience/public she has chosen to address. Even if there are many good reasons to do something, they aren't equally good to everyone. If she has chosen to address her audience as college students, which of these arguments will mean the most to them *as college students?* The ones about idealism? Community? Ease of giving? We'll return to these questions in the chapter on persuasion (Chapter 12) and discuss how reasoning will help make this choice.

Research (Chapter 6)

Once Danielle has chosen lines of argument, she'll have to do some research to find the facts and information that will fill out her reasoning. She could, of course, just get up and freestyle her speech, but this would be a failure of her responsibility to her audience. To become thoroughly informed, Danielle needs a research strategy: She needs to figure out where the best sources are and then read enough of the literature on blood donation to make some reasoned conclusions. To do this, she must have an organized approach to research that evaluates multiple perspectives instead of just cutting and pasting from a discussion board or a wiki.

Danielle has an enormous variety of sources to choose from: interviews, news stories, pamphlets, journal articles, web pages, Wikipedia, books, and so on. But she needs to choose her sources carefully and allow the audience to evaluate their credibility. She also needs to use the research responsibly, offering as full a picture of the facts as possible. Her speech will be more effective if all the statistics are from credible sources, such as the American Red Cross or the American Medical Association, rather than from something like www .saveavampiregiveblood

Good research makes Danielle more credible, and it can give her more choices about how to present her reasoning. But most important, research fulfills the trust she wants the audience to place in her. If she says that donation is safe, she must have the research to back that up.

Organizing (Chapter 7)

Once Danielle has chosen her arguments and assembled research to support them, she is ready to choose how to organize her speech. This happens at two levels. First, she has to decide the best order for her two or three main arguments. Perhaps civic duty is her strongest argument, but if people fear disease or needles, she may have to focus on that argument first, to clear away misunderstandings. Otherwise, audience members may not be able to hear her powerful arguments about civic duty because they're thinking, "Wait! Isn't this dangerous?"

Persuasive speakers know that they must rely only on credible sources to back up their words. The American Red Cross website, for instance, is a reliable source for information about blood donation.

Second, she has to decide how to structure the body of the speech. What is the best order for her points? If the most important point goes last, which one *is* most important? How are the points related to each other? Their relationships (for example, just another reason or cause and effect) will help her choose clear transitions between the points, which will help the audience understand her argument more precisely.

She also has to decide how to **frame** the speech in the introduction and the conclusion. The introduction, in a sense, will introduce the audience members to themselves and also set the tone for the speech while previewing the arguments. The conclusion will bring the arguments together in an appeal for action.

frame The context of relevance to the audience, for the information or arguments of a speech; often articulated in the introduction and conclusion.

The first few sentences basically lay out the relationship between speaker, audience, and topic. Look at some possibilities and what they are likely to mean to the audience:

1. If you give blood, I could win a prize in a competition that my sorority is having.

   Meaning for audience: The blood donation is a means for the speaker to benefit.

2. If you give blood, the survivors of the recent disaster will do much better.

   Meaning for audience: The donation will help others.

3. If you give blood, you'll feel great about yourself, proud of your engagement.

   Meaning for audience: The donation will help the audience members.

Danielle must choose a frame that will effectively *introduce* her arguments to the audience, so it has to be consistent. Introduction 1 wouldn't work with a speech that was mainly about altruistic reasons for audience members to give blood. In a speech focusing on how blood donations help others, the conclusion would have to support the frame by providing a vivid example of someone whose life was saved or improved thanks to donated blood.

Finding the Words (Chapter 8)

An important set of choices involves the words that Danielle will use when she speaks. Not every single word, but the key terms that connect her and the topic to the audience. For example, what is the subject of the speech? It's about blood (which is intrinsically gross to a lot of people), and she's asking her audience to do something with the blood. But what? Is it

> a donation?
> a gift?
> a contribution?

Of course, these words have similar meanings, but they have slightly different implications. *Contribution* suggests a group effort, whereas *donation* makes the blood sound equivalent to money (and the common metaphor for the place where the blood is stored a blood "bank"). *Gift* is an emotionally and culturally charged term that seems more personal than the others; people who have never made a donation or contribution in their life know all about gifts. The best word depends on the frame of the speech and the choices Danielle has made about her arguments.

As another example, what words could Danielle use to say that blood donation is a "good" thing?

worthy	excellent
valuable	honorable
necessary	helpful
commendable	admirable
splendid	cool
marvelous	really fine
precious	awesome

This may seem like too many choices, but spending some time choosing the three or four key terms in the speech will help you get the parts of your speech to hold together. In addition, it can help set the tone of the speech. Notice, for example, that the choices at the end of the list are much more informal and slangy than the earlier ones. In some situations, this might be appropriate; in others, it might not be—depending on the choice of audience and frame.

Language choices can go well beyond vocabulary, as we'll see in Chapter 8. These include uses of language such as metaphor and other tropes. An exciting or appropriate metaphor, such as Martin Luther King's "I've Been to the Mountaintop," can easily pull together an entire speech and help the audience not only understand it but remember it as well.

Suppose that Danielle has decided that the best frame and audience for this speech is that students should see themselves as members of a larger community and take some responsibility for what happens in that community. One choice that would help her to express this idea vividly to the audience would be a figure of speech that makes the plastic bag of donated blood a symbol for community itself—"This is community in a pint-sized bag." The complexities of public health problems and the volunteer blood donation system can be reduced to the image of the bag itself, allowing students to imagine their connection to the larger community when they imagine the bag. Rather than being scary or icky, the bag of blood becomes a symbol of hope and commitment.

GIVING YOUR FIRST SPEECH

Danielle, like most people, imagines that the hardest part of the process is delivering the speech. As we'll discuss later, that's probably not true—though it's true that people worry about it the most!

Delivering the Speech (Chapter 9)

Many of Danielle's choices about delivery involve how she will prepare and practice the speech. She'll have to decide if it will be extemporaneous (spoken from notes) or written out and either read or memorized (the more difficult options). Once she decides on a type of preparation, she'll have to practice it, either by herself or in front of a small, friendly audience, thinking especially about staying within her allotted time.

Of course, delivery matters. Danielle will want to deliver her speech clearly, not too fast or slow, and with appropriate feeling and emphasis. In Chapter 11, we'll talk about how to practice your speeches and refine all these elements.

Overcoming Anxiety (Chapter 9)

Anxiety probably will be a problem for Danielle, as it is for everyone, including some of the most seasoned speakers. Though we will address this topic in greater detail in Chapter 9, for your first speech in public speaking class, you can remind yourself that your classmates are in the same boat as you, and you can focus on all the preparation you have done and just let the speech give itself.

Presentation Aids (Chapter 10)

Danielle knows that her audience will appreciate visual images or media accompanying her speech. She may decide to bring some pictures or to use a program such as PowerPoint to highlight important points, display graphics, and show images. First, she will have to consider

Visual aids are often helpful in emphasizing your important points when used effectively.

a number of logistical issues, especially whether the setting is media-friendly. Danielle will have to decide just how image-rich she wants her presentation to be. If she uses too many images, props, or slides, the audience may feel either overwhelmed or distracted from what she is trying to say. If she relies too much on the images or media, she is at risk of letting the media use her instead of using the media to enhance her speech. She will have to decide which images and text enhance her message and which ones drown it out. We will discuss these issues at length in Chapter 10, with the goal of giving you some ways to manage visuals in your speech.

If all this seems like a lot to think about in preparing a speech, keep in mind that we'll give you techniques for breaking the process into easy, manageable steps. Moreover, if Danielle does all these things, she will not only have the confidence in her speech that she needs to counteract her anxiety, but she is also likely to give a powerful and effective speech. Even better, Danielle's speaking abilities will improve with every speech that she composes using this process—as will *your* speaking abilities. The skills that Danielle is honing in making a speech about giving blood will help her in the future, preparing her to make the kind of speeches that will change her personal history for the better, and perhaps make a difference in the lives of those around her.

MAKING RESPONSIBLE CHOICES

Let's bring together the concepts and processes of this chapter. What you learn in a public speaking course is how to make good communication choices and how to take responsibility for them. Our aim in this book is to expand your choices in speaking and give you more and better ways of making those choices, enabling you to take responsibility for them.

Good Speeches Are the Result of Choices

What's a *good* speech? When the speaker is free from nervousness? When it gets big applause at the end? Most people imagine that a good speech has something to do with getting what you want or transmitting information properly or getting the audience to think as you do. Although these outcomes may happen, they don't by themselves define good communication.

"Good communication" is a bit ambiguous, because it is pulled between choices that are *practically* good (effective in persuading your audience, getting what you want in the short run) and choices that are good because they are *responsible* (what you would want if you were in the audience). The best communicators make choices about how to write and deliver a speech that are both practically effective and ethically responsible. *Responsible and ethical*, for this context, are intertwined—taking responsibility for your choices is an ethical stance. Thus, your communicative ethics are revealed in the choices that you make in crafting a persuasive speech as well as the choices that you make in terms of your orientation to your audience (the kind of relationship are you creating with them as you step up to speak).

There are many possible good relationships with an audience. They always depend on the specific case, and a good persuader can tell the difference between an appropriate and an inappropriate approach. So, good rhetoric, or good communication, actually is fairly straightforward (though not simple in practice). It's about making choices and being willing to take responsibility for them. The responsible and ethical speaker chooses the appropriate goals for the audience and situation and the appropriate means to achieve those goals. In this sense, the story of Danielle serves as an example of what a speaker has to do to give a good speech: making the best choices for the audience and the situation.

Taking Responsibility Means Respecting the Audience

Rhetoric and persuasion get a bad name when they are used irresponsibly—when the means or the goals disrespect audiences, ignore their interests, or treat them as less than fully rational participants in the process. There's a simple way to prevent these abuses: Be ready to take responsibility for your choices. Imagine, at any point in a speech, someone in the audience asking, "Why did you say that? Argue that? Use that metaphor? Organize your speech that way?" If you can give an answer, you're taking responsibility. If you can't, you're not living up to the requirements of public persuasion.

Many people find ways to reject responsibility for their own talk. Here are a few:

- Well, I don't know why I said that—it seemed OK to me.
- Oh, I hoped you weren't going to notice that.
- One of my sources argued that, so why not?
- It seemed like the only way to do it.
- The material just seemed to require this presentation style.
- Everybody does it this way.
- It's just conventional to say that—who cares?
- It's the truth.
- There isn't any other way to say it.

If you're not taking responsibility, either you don't respect your audience or you don't care about being effective. Respecting the intelligence of the audience and treating potential points of disagreement respectfully is an important part of persuasion and will make your speech more successful. As we pointed out earlier, the "public" part of public speech is connected with the best ideas of democracy, and democracy requires respect for disagreement.

Summary

Let's put it all together: *public* and *speaking*. Public speaking is powerful because it means communicating with other people in a way that respects their interests and also holds open the possibility of change. Speech changes society and can change your life as well. Public speaking addresses other people not only as individuals but also as members of a public, as fellow citizens in a democracy, as people motivated by common interests. Public speaking is deliberative, which means that the goal of a public speech is to create knowledge, to make better and more well-informed decisions about issues of common concern. Finally, public speakers make choices and take responsibilities for their choices; they make choices about content, organization, words, delivery, and visual aids to create a compelling speech.

MindTap®

Reflect, personalize, and apply what you've learned.

Questions for Review

1. Why will it benefit you to become a better public speaker?
2. Why does public speaking matter?
3. What's the relationship between preparation and performance?
4. What are the elements in a good public speech? What does a speaker have to think about in preparing a speech?
5. What does the idea of "public" mean in public speaking?
6. What is communication? What distinguishes public speaking from other types of communication?
7. How is public speaking related to democracy and to civic life?
8. How can speakers take responsibility for their choices?

Questions for Discussion

1. How do you think public speaking will make a difference in your life, both as a speaker and an audience?
2. Can the connection of public speaking to democracy extend to everyday speeches, especially in business and personal settings?
3. What are examples of irresponsible speech? What are the negative effects of irresponsible speech?
4. In your opinion, what makes a speech succeed or fail? What makes one speech persuasive and another speech fall flat?
5. Do you think the idea of a public is relevant in our current political and social situation?

Key Concepts   MindTap®

Practice defining the chapter's terms by using online flashcards

adaptation	frame	rhetoric
argument	informative speech	special-occasion speech
choices	persuasive speech	stakeholder
delivery	pluralism	unity
democracy	public	

2 ETHICS AND THE RESPONSIBLE SPEAKER

david hancock/Alamy

LEARNING OBJECTIVES

- Explain what it means to communicate ethically
- Summarize the main reasons why ethics matter to public speaking
- Identify various ethical pitfalls for speakers
- Apply the seven principles of ethical public speaking to your own speeches
- Define plagiarism and explain how to avoid it

CHAPTER OUTLINE

- Introduction: Why Ethics Matter in Public Speaking
- Ethical Pitfalls in Public Speaking
- Seven Principles of Ethical Public Speaking
- How to Avoid Plagiarism
- How to Create an Ethical Speech
- Avoid Fallacies and Prejudicial Appeals

Cara has a topic in mind, and it means a lot to her. It's important, it's very much in the public eye, and she knows a lot about it. So that's all she needs? Maybe. The hard part is that the topic is highly controversial, and people on both sides are passionate about it. So Cara is really worried about being fair. She wants to present her side strongly, and even advocate for it. But she has to think through how to do that without being unfair to the other side, or being unfair to the audience in the way she makes her case.

Overview

In this chapter you will learn why ethics matter in public speaking, and how to make better ethical choices. This chapter will help you become more aware of the practices that contribute to or detract from ethically sound relationship-building with your audience. It will help you make choices based on mutual responsibility and good reasons rather than on manipulation and deceptive arguments. We will address the implications of deceptive, biased, and poorly reasoned speech as well as provide positive principles to help guide your public speaking choices. We also will address the issue of plagiarism— using other people's work without giving them proper credit. Finally, we will discuss how to create and deliver speeches that contribute to an ongoing conversation with your audience. You may want to revisit this chapter as you work through the book.

© 2017 Cengage Learning

MindTap®

Start with a warm-up activity about Cara's speech and review the chapter Learning Objectives.

INTRODUCTION: WHY ETHICS MATTER IN PUBLIC SPEAKING

The Greek term *ethos*, which is the root word for our word *ethics*, means both "character" and "habit." **Ethics** can be defined as the principles that govern people's actions, or as habitual moral behavior. Some of the ethics of public speaking are probably obvious to you: You should not fabricate quotations or facts; you should not misrepresent the sources that you quote; you should not intentionally mislead your audience; and you should not knowingly use weak logic or faulty arguments. Most people agree that these practices are ethically shaky, whether in day-to-day conversation, in speeches delivered in or outside the classroom, or in another means of communication (such as writing, texting, or instant messaging).

MindTap®

Read, highlight, and take notes online.

ethics Rules, standards, or principles that govern people's conduct, or habitual moral behavior.

In a public speaking class, unethical speech can affect your grade, because your instructor will hold you responsible. But in any setting, unethical communication practices also can harm your reputation, limit your effectiveness as a communicator, and damage your relationship with the people with the with whom you are communicating. What if you were to persuade members of your audience to make a significant change in lifestyle based on shoddy evidence? What if this change harmed their health or well-being in some way?

When ethics in public speaking is based on the relationship between speaker and audience, the goal of public speaking becomes more than simply influencing or informing them. "Effectiveness" in the narrow sense of getting your own way is not a good test for ethical acceptability. Throughout history, speakers have used deception and manipulation to persuade audiences to do things that were wrong. Even if a speech is effective in moving an audience, this doesn't mean that the speech is ethically good.

Ethics and Effectiveness

In this chapter we would like to make the case that you should engage in ethical speaking practices because it's the right thing to do, and because the choices you make collectively define your character as a person. But if you aren't convinced by those claims, you might consider being ethical because the perceptions of your ethics make a big difference in how people respond to things that you ask them to do (for example, in asking them to change a belief, an attitude, or an action in a speech).

A good bit of research bears out this claim, but some of the most interesting work on ethical communication and personal effectiveness comes from studies of interactions between bosses and workers in the workplace. This will come as no surprise to readers who have worked for very good or very bad bosses: A study (Walumba et al., 2011) of employee satisfaction and productivity found that employees were more willing to do what their bosses asked of them if they perceived their bosses to be ethical, that they had more confidence in their ability to achieve tasks, and that they were willing to work harder for the good or the organization.

Other studies have borne out this same relationship between being perceived as ethical and being effective in achieving goals in contexts as diverse as television news and science communication. The bottom line is this: Aristotle said that an audience will be more favorably disposed towards you if they think that they can trust you, and that you have their best interests at heart. As we study this dynamic in more and more areas, it appears that Aristotle's insight has been borne out.

For more information, see:
F. Walumbwa, D. Mayer, P. Wang, H. Wang, K. Workman, & A. Christensen, "Linking ethical leadership to employee performance: The roles of leader–member exchange, self-efficacy, and organizational identification," in *Organizational Behavior and Human Decision Processes*, 115 (2011), 204–213.

Because your words can affect your audience, you need to steer your listeners in a direction that is both effective in changing their minds *and* good for them. To do this, your speech has to be based on sound evidence and arguments. If your goal in public speaking is to connect with your audience on a topic of importance to you, you should do everything you can to build a good relationship. This relationship is the most important

The goal of ethical speaking is to create a trusting relationship with the audience, a skill at which the Dalai Lama, for instance, excels. Do religious systems of belief, such as Buddhism or Christianity, encourage or discourage ethical communication?

AP Images/Ashwini Bhatia

important component of public speaking, and it is the core from which all the choices you make should flow.

Your choices entail more than just avoiding ethical pitfalls such as lying, misrepresenting sources, and knowingly making weak arguments. Ethical public speaking also requires responsibly using and citing evidence in your speech, employing sound reasoning, and delivering your speech in a clear and accessible manner. Good speakers take these steps to nurture their relationship with their audiences.

FAQ Why do I need to worry about ethical choices? Aren't I just conveying information from my research?

In a sense, yes—often you're relaying things you've learned to the audience. But you don't relay *everything*—you can't—which means that you're making choices. And if your audience questions your choices ("Why didn't you mention . . . ?"), you have to be able to take responsibility and explain the reasons for your choices. So every communicator, no matter the context, by definition is forming some kind of ethical relationship with the audience.

ETHICAL PITFALLS IN PUBLIC SPEAKING

Deceptive speech, inappropriately biased speech, and poorly reasoned speech represent potential pitfalls in building an ethically sound relationship with your audience. In this section we highlight what you should try to avoid in speaking. Let's start with lying, or the pitfall of deceptive speech.

Deceptive Speech

Consider the following thesis for a speech:

> Lowering the drinking age to 18 will help young people, and college students in particular, to drink less.

Wait—is that true? Will lowering the drinking age help young people to drink less? Would there be anything wrong with defending that thesis if it weren't true? Is it morally wrong to say something untrue? Your reflex response may be, "Of course it's wrong," but this is a more complex question than it may appear at first. In everyday speech, we often say things that are untrue, but our intention is not always to deceive. Sometimes we just have the facts wrong. For example, if you argue in a speech that 80% of college students binge-drink, you simply may be mistaken, but not necessarily lying.

However, if you decide it's OK to say, "Everybody on campus drinks," because some exaggeration is good for making your point, your choice will be hard to justify. That little bit of hyperbole for the sake of making an argument can have serious negative effects, because students' drinking habits are influenced heavily by their perceptions of what "everyone" is doing.[1]

Part of what makes an intentional lie wrong is that the misrepresentation or omission is *done for the speaker's advantage.* Liars know the truth but either hide it or make the audience believe something different, and usually they do so for their own benefit. For example, if you're trying to convince an audience that a certain political candidate is terrible when she is not, you probably are doing so in the hope that people will vote for your favorite candidate. An intentional lie deceives for the purpose of accruing some benefit for the liar.

Sometimes, however, an intentionally deceptive statement does not have a destructive or self-serving purpose. For example, if a friend asks whether you like the new shirt he bought, you might say yes even if the answer is no. The motive behind socially acceptable white lies like this one is to avoid hurting someone's feelings, whereas the goal of intentional deception, such as lying about an opposition candidate, is to benefit the liar. The difference is motive.

TRY IT!

WHEN LYING MIGHT BE ETHICALLY DEFENSIBLE

Of course, if you were protecting an innocent person from a murderous mob by hiding him in your house, you might be justified in telling the mob that he isn't there. Even though honesty is a good ethical goal, protecting the life of an innocent victim might justify a bit of deception to avoid a more significant ethical evil.[2] Brainstorm more instances of ethically defensible lies.

Despite the distinctions between different kinds of lies, most of us agree that lying is an ethically undesirable choice, and the ethical goals for our speeches ought to be to avoid harm, promote good, and maintain the quality of our relationships. Thus, though lies may be acceptable in some narrow instances, they are not justifiable in public speaking, because the goal of a good relationship in public speaking is to give audiences as accurate a version of the facts as possible so they can make good decisions on the basis of the evidence presented.

TRY IT!

REASONS TO BE HONEST—AND NOT TO BE

From your personal experience, make a list of all the advantages and disadvantages of honesty in communication. Then compare it to the lists of other people in the class. How similar or different are they? What do you think accounts for the differences?

Deceptive speech has three distinct drawbacks for your audience and your relationship. First, deceptive speech practices can induce your audience to act on or believe in things that are untrue. Second, deception can damage your credibility. If your audience begins to wonder whether you're being deceptive, either because something doesn't sound quite right or is known to be untruthful, you will lose credibility. Third, the technical choices you make in speaking—deciding what to say, how to say it, what details to include, what to leave out—are ethical choices. If you're willing to lie for a public speaking grade, you're cultivating a habit that may be harmful to your character.

Inappropriately Biased Speech

All speeches come from a viewpoint unique to the speaker. The question, however, is whether you let your personal perspective, or **bias**, shape *all* the evidence or information that you present in your speech. Because an ethical public speaker respects the intelligence of the audience, your goal is to make your case while letting the audience members make up their own minds based on their own reasoning skills. As a result, when you're speaking, you ought to make choices that do not rely on bias and that allow listeners to see multiple legitimate positions on your topic.

bias Your own personal perspective.

Distinguishing between advocacy and bias is important. **Advocacy** means presenting a strong case for your perspective or leading your audience toward a change in a belief or an action. Being an advocate means that you are willing to give other perspectives a fair hearing. You may be advocating lowering the drinking age, but as an advocate, you're aware of, and address, the reasons why people might disagree. Showing bias, on the other hand, means that you intentionally misrepresent, leave out, or unfairly downplay alternative perspectives. Bias Biased presentations ignore the reality that reasonable people can and do disagree.

advocacy Making a case for a perspective, a change in belief, or a particular action.

Bias, or, on Being Fair and Balanced

Research on bias is interesting. On one hand, research shows that when audience members perceive significant bias in a speaker, they tend to respond in one of two ways: If audience members share the speaker's bias, they may respond with approval (if they notice the bias at all), and if they do not share the speaker's bias, the perception of the speaker's bias will cause the audience to resist the speaker's conclusions. So far so good. On the other hand, though, some evidence indicates that when a speakers go *too* far in avoiding the perception of bias, acting as if they have no preexisting opinion when the audience expects one, an attempt to eliminate bias can create audience resistance to the speaker and the speaker's claims—perhaps because the audience thinks that speakers are not being fully honest about their motives.

The theory here suggests that the best thing to do is to be honest about your dispositions on a topic, and then to try your best to be charitable toward the other opinions in presenting them.

For more information, see:

E. Knowles & J. Linn, *Resistance and Persuasion* (Mahwah, NJ: Lawrence Earlbaum and Associates, 2004).

Think about it this way: As a speaker who is providing information, you will be at your best when you treat your topic the way you expect your teachers to treat topics: You give the most complete picture, without leaving out facts or ignoring areas of dispute. For example, if you were giving an informative speech about the effects of lowering the drinking age, you would present the evidence on both sides. By the same token, if you were giving a persuasive speech, you certainly would advocate your position, but not by leaving out or discrediting alternative viewpoints. For example, in a persuasive speech advocating lowering the drinking age you might legitimately say the following:

> **Some scientific evidence justifies the claim that legal drinkers are, on average, more responsible drinkers.**

Is strong advocacy of your position consistent with being open to other points of view?

MindTap®

Watch a video, and do an interactive activity.

argument An assertion (a claim) supported by evidence, expert opinion, data, or a logical chain (grounds).

claim A statement to be proven or agreed to.

grounds Evidence, expert opinion, data, or a logical chain in support of an argument.

reasoning Making good arguments that are supported by good grounds.

In contrast, this would be an inappropriately biased statement on the topic:

Just think about the negative effects of Prohibition. Obviously, setting the drinking age at 21 makes things worse in the same way.

The difference between advocacy and bias is a matter of the choices you make. Notice that in citing "some scientific evidence" in the first example above, the advocate does not back off her claim that lowering the drinking age is good. Instead, she qualifies it with the word "some" to acknowledge disagreement.

In the second example, the speaker chooses to ignore criticism altogether, which can be a surprisingly ineffective persuasive strategy. Listeners who disagree with the speaker will be put off by the suggestion that they are being unreasonable. In contrast, the first statement is on solid ethical ground because it respects the intelligence of the audience, acknowledges an alternative viewpoint, and suggests that there are sources to consult in coming to a reasoned decision.

Poorly Reasoned Speech

Deception and bias are two common ethical pitfalls in public speaking, and the third is poorly reasoned speech. We will show you how to create a well-reasoned speech more extensively in the chapters on research and persuasion (Chapters 6 and 12). For now, we will discuss the ethical implications of knowingly making poor arguments.

What is an argument? It is not a shouting match or a heated back-and-forth between two or more parties. An **argument** is a **claim**, or something you would like to prove or get another person to agree with, that is supported by some **grounds**, that is, evidence, expert opinion, data, or logical chain. **Reasoning** is the process of making good arguments that are well supported by solid grounds.

The process of reasoning can go wrong in a number of ways. (We'll have more to say on this in Chapter 12, discussing reasoning and persuasion.) Here are some examples:

- *Claims without any support.* If you say, "Eating a strict diet of rutabagas is the path to a healthy life," but you don't provide any data, expert opinion, or studies to back up the claim, your argument is incomplete and, therefore, poorly reasoned.

- *Claims with weak support.* If you say, "You should invest heavily in pork bellies, because I read a really great advertisement from the Pork Council that said investments in pigs will really pay off," you have provided some grounds for your claim, but because your support is a small and arguably biased sample, it doesn't justify your claim.
- *Claims with inappropriate support.* If you say, "You should go to Disneyland for spring break, because the Food and Drug Administration (FDA) recently found that aspirin is still safe," you have provided support that does not justify your claim. Though most examples are not this obviously defective, speakers commonly cite evidence that has little to do with the conclusions they want the audience to make.

One of your most important choices in preparing a public speech is how you will back up what you are saying with data, studies, logic, and expert opinion. If you intentionally make claims without support or with weak or inappropriate support, you can mislead your audience all too easily. If audience members recognize poor reasoning, this will damage your relationship with them and your ability to inform or persuade them. If they do not realize that you are making claims based on shoddy support, they may end up acting against their best interests.

SEVEN PRINCIPLES OF ETHICAL PUBLIC SPEAKING

Now that you know what to avoid, what steps can you *take* to ensure that your public speaking choices are ethical? Here are seven principles that will help you to be an ethical and credible speaker:

1. Be honest.
2. Be open.
3. Be generous.
4. Be balanced.
5. Represent evidence responsibly.
6. Take appropriate risks.
7. Choose engagement.

Let's see how each of these principles works in practice.

Be Honest

Honesty really is the best policy. However, it's easy to forget that sometimes. Given what you know about your audience and what you want to achieve in your speech, you may be tempted to say things that aren't lies but that you know will mislead. For example, it would be misleading to claim that real estate is a foolproof investment because "in 2006, investors were routinely seeing 20% growth!" The real estate market worsened significantly in 2008, so your implication that it has remained the same since 2006 is just not true.

The more complete the information you give your audience, the more honest you are about the topic. Sometimes being honest means letting the audience see the limitations of your argument or your supporting data. You might think about being honest in these terms: It is always better to back your facts and claims with reasoning that *you* would find clear, well supported, and logically sound.

THE CONSEQUENCES OF DISHONESTY **TRY IT!**

Think back on a couple of fibs you've told, whether small or big. Think about why you told them. For each one, do you think the other person, if he or she knew the truth, would still consider you to be an honest person? Why or why not?

Feverpitch, 2010/Used under license from Shutterstock.com

It would be dishonest to pretend in a speech about investments that the real estate market has not suffered in the last few years.

Be Open

Do you have a specific motivation for making an argument? Perhaps you have direct personal experience with the issue, or perhaps you want to talk about the benefits of a product that you sell in your spare time. Open communicators ensure that their audience understands that their motivations for talking about an issue are clear. Less ethical communicators sometimes are selective about what they reveal about their motives and predispositions toward the topic.

If you have a personal motive, such as specific experience with or a vested interest in your topic, you should say so. Not only is your openness likely to increase your persuasive appeal, but it also tells your audience why you are interested in the topic.

Openness applies not only to your topics but also to the kinds of reasoning you use. For example, your political position influences the kinds of arguments you make. Explaining where you stand gives the audience a chance to think critically about your speech and points of agreement or disagreement. In addition, being open means being open to having your opinion changed. We discuss this idea in Principle 6: "Take appropriate risks."

Be Generous

Ethical public speaking requires that you place the audience's interests above your own. You should use your speaking time for the good of the whole as opposed to pushing an agenda that benefits only you. A public is a community, and your speech should put the community first.

You won't always have just one goal in speaking. Your primary concern should be to help the audience members by informing them about your topic, but realistically, you may be pursuing other goals at the same time, such as getting a good grade or impressing that special someone in the second row. Those are legitimate goals. But you should convey to audiences the sense that you are speaking primarily for *their* benefit. Try to make sure that your audiences will recognize that you want to expose them to some sound reasoning or to become aware of a beneficial change in their thinking or actions.

As an audience member, you don't like to think you are being manipulated for the speaker's gain. Choosing to speak for the benefit of your listeners is the ethical option because you have your *and* their best interests at heart. Your common interests help you form a genuine connection with your audience.

Be Balanced

Balance, or presenting both sides fairly, is the other side of the bias coin. Some speakers always try to balance their presentations, acknowledging views they don't agree with, but others focus exclusively on their own side, hoping the audience will forget the other side. The extent to which you include objections to, evidence against, and counterarguments to your position determines the level of balance in your speech.

More important, you should treat these arguments with the respect they deserve. You appreciate it when a speaker interprets your position fairly before critiquing it. Philosophers call this the Principle of Charity ("Always interpret others in a way that maximizes the truth and rationality of what they say"), and it's associated most closely with the work of Donald Davidson.[3]

Here's an easy test of your speech's balance: Ask yourself whether a person who holds an opinion opposite of yours will think you're being fair in your presentation of the opposite argument. Are you are giving the best possible version of the opposing argument? Have you captured the nugget of truth in it? People on the other side of a dispute are rarely stupid or crazy, even if you vehemently disagree with them.

When we address hotly contested issues, we should treat opposing viewpoints with the same respect we would like our arguments to receive. Choosing to give a balanced presentation of the facts in your speech is ethical because it allows the audience to come to an informed conclusion. In addition, your speech may be persuasive because you have chosen to address the counterarguments against your position fairly and disarm them.

balance Presenting alternative perspectives fairly.

Radius Images/Alamy

As a listener, you don't like to feel manipulated. What strategy does that suggest to you as an ethical speaker?

Represent Evidence Responsibly

When you cite a piece of evidence (such as survey results, statistical data, or a quotation), the audience should know the name of your source, what your source said, and where to find the source for fact-checking or exploring the topic further. Why? First, it is unfair not to give credit to someone else's work. This is plagiarism, the academic equivalent of stealing (look up your school's policy against plagiarism on the school website). Second, if you pass off someone else's work as your own, you deny your audience the ability to truly assess the credibility of the claim you are making.

Responsible use of sources requires the following:

- A citation that is complete enough to allow audience members to find it easily if they want to check on it themselves.
- A fair presentation of what a quotation says or what information means, if audience members don't or can't look up your source. When you modify quotations or data to suit your needs, it undermines your audience's ability to think about your claims. Let the opinions and work of others speak for themselves.

The irresponsible use of sources has become easier to spot, thanks to Internet search engines. Your instructor or classmates can do a quick search and easily catch you modifying or creatively "borrowing" ideas from others. The consequences for your grade, your credibility as a speaker, and even your academic standing could be severe. More important, it is a good ethical habit to properly present and attribute the work of others that informs your speech. You would expect the same from someone using your speech or writing.

Take Appropriate Risks

Risks in public speaking include building relationships, taking stands on issues, and giving your audience information that helps them think differently about a topic.[4] You're not only putting yourself on the line by giving a speech, but you're also putting your ideas up for public scrutiny. Though taking such risks can seem uncomfortable, the alternative is to give speeches about topics that everyone already knows about or that they already agree with.

The choices you make in regard to risks entail two ethical challenges. The first challenge is taking a large enough risk. You might not step out of your comfort zone to speak to audience members who disagree with you; you might just "preach to the converted." In doing so, you invite the following question: Why didn't you take the opportunity to do something meaningful, to make a change in your audience's opinions, actions, or understandings of the world for the good?

The second challenge is taking risks that are too large, straying into territory that you don't have good support for or that your audience will be unable to hear. For example, a speech insisting that everyone should join a doomsday cult because aliens are about to take over the world would be taking too large a risk in terms of what could be proved and in terms of what most audiences would find plausible and be able to evaluate and act on.

Thus, one of the principles for composing an ethically good and persuasive public speech is to take on an appropriate degree of risk for the situation. Test your choices using the self-risk test: Are you willing to put your beliefs and commitments at risk in an ongoing public dialogue? Do you approach the potential interaction with the audience as if it might change your mind at some point? In other words, do you go into the speech thinking, "Well, I hope this works, but I'm open to modifying my views based what I hear?"

Choose Engagement

Done well, a good public speech is an invitation for vigorous public conversation—for an exchange of ideas and opinions that benefits the speaker and the audience.[5] When we talk about civic engagement in this book, we don't mean just speaking in a given space (a city council meeting, public hearing, or community organization's gathering) but making speaking choices that open you to a potential dialogue with your audience.

A lecture is one-sided, but a conversation requires back-and-forth. Speakers can actively discourage audience participation—they can go well over time limits, they can speak in an inaccessible or an intimidating manner, or they can ignore obvious cues that the audience has lost interest, can't follow what is going on, or would like to ask questions. To make your speech the opening to a conversation, you should choose to invite your audience to participate in your speech. This doesn't mean letting them have their say in the middle of your presentation. It means you are speaking in a way that allows them to understand, digest, and engage with your ideas.

What might get in the way of your audience's engagement in your speech in this way? You might speak too quickly; you might use obscure or jargon-laden language; you might bombard the audience with too many facts; you might speak in a boring monotone or otherwise fail to hold members' attention. Speaking in a way that stifles audience participation and response is unethical not only because it harms your relationship with the audience, but also because it prevents ideas from undergoing public scrutiny.

For the audience to engage your speech, you must present your ideas simply, with structure, and at a pace that is digestible for the majority of the people listening to you. These are skills you'll develop as you practice your speech, and we'll discuss some specific ways to improve them in the chapters that follow.

As you might guess, engagement also means that you are open to audience feedback in the form of questions or commentary on your speech. You should engage audience questions (if the program or speaking format allows) as thoughtfully and deliberately as possible, and you should see feedback as an opportunity to sharpen your speaking skills. (Check out Chapter 13 for more on dealing with audience questions.)

Inviting your audience members to express their viewpoints is ethical because they contribute to an ongoing conversation about important issues. Whether your audience provides

Engaging with an audience is a skill you can learn. You don't have to have Ellen Degeneres' charisma to make engagement work for you in a public speaking situation. Is being direct, and maybe a little funny, effective in forming a relationship with the audience?

Kevin Winter/Getty Images

feedback in class or in conversations after class, the best goals of public speaking are served when your speech is an invitation to a larger conversation about an issue.

HOW TO AVOID PLAGIARISM

If you compose and deliver your speech following these seven principles, you will be well on the way to giving an ethically sound speech. However, one breach of these principles is so important that it must be discussed in depth—plagiarism. **Plagiarism** is the act of using the language, ideas, or arguments of another person without giving the person proper credit. Several of the seven principles we just discussed offer strong ethical reasons for avoiding plagiarism:

- Plagiarism is not *honest* (Principle 1). If you do not give proper credit to your sources, you are implicitly claiming that the language, ideas, and arguments in your speech are entirely yours.
- Plagiarism does not respect the spirit of *openness* (Principle 2) because it conceals your sources, which prevents your audience from evaluating their credibility.
- Plagiarism is not *generous* (Principle 3) because it does not give other people credit for the work that they have done in writing, thinking, and making their ideas public.
- Finally, plagiarism does not *represent your evidence responsibly* (Principle 5), because your audience needs to know who created a quote, an argument, or an idea in order to understand its context and to track down and fact-check what you say.

We live in a culture awash with sampled songs and pirated movies, in which your laptop's cut-and-paste function has made it easier than ever to use other people's creations, ideas, and creative work—with or without attribution. It is unavoidable that you will be influenced by the ideas and styles of arguments from the sources you read while researching your speech, but "borrowing" without crediting the source is clearly unethical. To illustrate, let's consider some examples, from the most blatant acts of plagiarism to a few practices that are on the borderline of ethical behavior.

- *Blatant and egregious plagiarism:* If you find a speech online and read it word for word, passing it off as your own, you clearly are plagiarizing. What your instructor expects from you, and what audiences expect from you outside the classroom context, is not simply to stand in the front of the room and say something. You must do the work to research the speech, compose and organize your arguments, and really think through your topic. Delivering someone else's speech as your own is a clear-cut case of intellectual theft, and you should not do it.
- *Uncredited "borrowing" of quotes, facts, and figures:* Sprinkling into your speech large portions of text copied from other places without giving credit is plagiarizing, even if you composed the material that surrounds the copied parts. If you use a quotation in a speech, you must say where it came from, and you have to include that information in your speech's bibliography (see Chapter 6).
- *Paraphrasing or minor modifications:* **Paraphrasing** is rewriting or modifying text so its original idea and flow of argument are essentially unchanged. Speakers do this because it is easier to paraphrase an idea than it is to create original ideas and arguments. So if one of your sources says,

> **Global warming will create significant environmental effects, including inducing a rise in sea levels that will threaten coastal areas,**

and you simply replace a few words, saying,

> **Global climate change will produce a number of significant environmental effects, including a rise in ocean levels that will threaten our coasts,**

plagiarism The use of the language, ideas, or arguments of another person without giving proper credit.

paraphrasing Making minor modification of the wording of someone's idea or argument; requires citing the source.

you're plagiarizing. The rewritten version of this sentence contains only a few minor changes in phrasing; the original idea is unaltered. When you use a paraphrase like this in your speech, you must cite the original source.

- *Appropriating ideas:* All public speeches will borrow ideas from other people's work to some extent, and this is actually one of the great benefits of public speaking—it takes work that authors and researchers have done into the broader public sphere in front of a new audience. There is a risk here, however. If you introduce into your speech an idea that you wouldn't have come to on your own, you must give credit to the source where you found the idea.

When it comes to plagiarism, you have a choice: giving credit or inappropriately taking someone else's words, ideas, or arguments. When in doubt, give credit! Chapter 6 describes how to take good notes as you research your topic, so you won't forget or misplace critical source information.

How do you avoid plagiarism in your speech? You can take two easy steps to stay on the safe side:

1. *Give credit for every quotation, statistic, and argument you use in your speech.* This step is as simple as preceding the quotation or fact by saying where you got it: "The World-watch Institute claims that global warming will induce a rise in sea level," or "The Heartland Institute produced a study that claims global warming is not a result of human emissions." Or you could start your speech with a quote, and then follow it immediately with, "This quote, which was drawn from the Intergovernmental Panel on Climate Change, underscores the importance of addressing climate change."
2. *Provide complete citation information in your bibliography.* Include the author's name, title of the work, date of the publication, page numbers, and other information that will enable audience members track down the source; Chapter 6 will cover the details of citing a source and compiling a bibliography.

The bottom line is that you will use a variety of different materials, which all will influence your speech in some way. If you give proper credit to these sources,

- you will advance your case with rigor and strength,
- you will act generously, and
- you will give the audience the chance to engage with your materials.

If you don't give proper credit, you're engaging in an intellectual version of stealing, and your speech, your ethos, and your character will suffer accordingly.

HOW TO CREATE AN ETHICAL SPEECH

What other kinds of ethical concerns should you be thinking about in preparing your speech? From the moment you decide to speak about a topic that interests you and is important to you, you have a number of choices regarding how you will present and organize your material for your audience. These include choices about respecting your audience and your topic, presenting more than one side and dealing with disagreement, and avoiding prejudicial language.

Respect Your Audience

The seven principles of ethical public speaking ultimately imply that public speaking should be about *relationship* and *conversation.* Because a public speaking situation is about building a relationship with the audience, it's fundamentally a *cooperative* setting. The speaker and the audience are working together to come to points of agreement and to mark off points of disagreement. When the audience and the speaker disagree, their disagreement should be understood in the broader context of the cooperative relationship. Although it is easy to get into a heated exchange with a stranger whom we will never see again, we are more careful about how we disagree with our friends, or with anybody with whom we have an ongoing friendly relationship.[6]

The choices that you make in public speaking dictate the ethical character of your relationship with the audience. Is that relationship premised on honesty or on deception? Are you open about how you came to your conclusions and to having your opinion changed, or are your processes of reasoning closed off to the audience? Are you speaking in a generous and balanced manner, or are you unfair toward people who might disagree with you? Are you representing the work of others fairly and in a way that helps the audience to evaluate your case, or are you misappropriating or hiding your sources? Are you open to risking yourself and your ideas for the sake of your audience, or are you unwilling to put your ideas on the line? Are you choosing engagement, or are you attempting to manipulate or otherwise exclude your audience's participation? Obviously, if you want to build a relationship that is both effective and ethically sound, you want to make choices that emphasize the seven principles of honesty, openness, generosity, balance, fair representation of evidence, appropriate risk taking, and engagement.

At the core of all these principles is reciprocity, the Golden Rule. As a speaker, you should think, speak, and argue like you would like to be spoken to. Put another way, you should employ the same perspective toward the speech that you are asking your audience to take. Obviously, you want your audience to pay attention, listen thoughtfully, and be open to change on the basis of your speech. Consequently, you should choose speaking practices that allow your audience members to pay attention, that create the opportunity for them to listen thoughtfully, and that give them the opportunity to make an informed change in opinion based on clearly cited, well-documented, and solid evidence.

To apply the Golden Rule, ask yourself these questions at each point in the composition and delivery of your speech:

Have I made any choices I'd want to conceal? Why?
Do my choices respect the audience's freedom to choose based on solid arguments?
Would knowing my purposes and techniques change anything for them?

Finally, you may have a responsibility to an extended audience, a *community* of relevant people. If you're talking about AIDS prevention and your audience members don't know much about this topic, it might be easy to mislead them, intentionally or not. But you can check your ethical intuitions by making yourself responsible to a community of people who *do* understand AIDS prevention. If you'd be willing to take responsibility for your speaking choices with an expert in the audience, or if you'd be comfortable having your remarks on the front page of tomorrow's paper, you're respecting your extended audience. If you wouldn't be comfortable, ask yourself why. What about your speech *wouldn't* you like to take responsibility for?

Respect Your Topic

The next important choice is how you will respond to the research you have done on your topic. We call this "respecting your topic" because whatever your preconceived notions, research and expert opinion should guide how you think about your topic. Respecting your topic means that you should compose a speech based on your research rather than cherry-picking research to support your preexisting views.

Realistically, when most people prepare a public speech, they often already know what they would like to say. What this means in practical terms is that people often research their topic to find evidence that supports their preexisting opinions. Letting your agenda drive your research as opposed to letting your research drive what you eventually will say may result in

The Golden Rule

The idea of reciprocity is at the heart of many of the great religious, ethical, and philosophical systems. Here is a list of a few of the various versions of this significant ethical insight from thinkers and religious texts in a broad diversity of traditions:

- Ancient Greek philosophy: "Do not do to others that which would anger you if others did it to you."
- Baha'i: "And if thine eyes be turned towards justice, choose thou for thy neighbor that which thou choosest for thyself." Epistle to the Son of the Wolf 30
- Buddhism: "Hurt not others in ways you yourself would find hurtful" Udana-Varga, 5:18
- Christianity: "In everything do to others as you would have them do to you; for this is the law and the prophets." Matthew 7:12
- Confucianism: "Do not unto others what you do not want them to do to you." Analects 15:13
- Enlightenment philosophy: "Act as if the maxim of thy action were to become by thy will a universal law of nature." Kant, *Groundwork for the Metaphysics of Morals*
- Hinduism: "This is the sum of duty: do naught unto others which would cause you pain if done to you." The Mahabharata, 5:1517
- Humanism: "Humanists affirm that individual and social problems can only be resolved by means of human reason, intelligent effort, critical thinking joined with compassion and a spirit of empathy for all living beings." The Humanist Manifesto II
- Islam: "Not one of you is a believer until he loves for his brother what he loves for himself." Fortieth Hadith of an-Nawawi,13
- Judaism: "What is hateful to you, do not do to your neighbor: that is the whole of the Torah; all the rest of it is commentary." Talmud, Shabbat, 31a

List drawn in part from https://tanenbaum.org/wp-content/uploads/2014/02/The-Golden-Rule.pdf

ethically suspect choices. It violates the rule of reciprocity regarding opinion change and the principle of risk. You can't expect your audience to be open to your opinion if you're unwilling to be changed by your research or to follow where it is leading you. Of course, you may find after extensive research that your opinion still seems right. If so, good for you, but remember that it's important to go through the process of not only checking but also shaping your opinion as your research dictates.

A number of concrete practices can help you be responsible to the existing body of research on your topic.

1. *Pull research from a broad set of sources.* If, for example, you are politically liberal, you naturally will be tempted to go to primarily liberal sources, and if you are a conservative, to go to primarily conservative sources. Picking your sources on the basis of their ability to confirm your biases closes you off from the variety of differing perspectives on your topic, and is ultimately irresponsible to the broader lines of thought that make up the literature on your topic. So, for example, if you want to make the case that the war in Iraq was bad, or was good, for national security, you need to do research in both conservative and liberal publications. Similarly, if you are giving an

informative speech about health food, you should balance your research with sources on conventional as well as alternative medicine.

2. *After researching a number of perspectives, make some choices about which arguments are the most credible.* This requires hard work and thinking. Which sides of the argument are most appealing to you? Why? Which claims are most well supported? Who offers the best evidence and arguments? On the basis of these choices, you should start to form an opinion about what you want to say about your topic, primarily based on the most defensible conclusions.

3. *Once you have started making preliminary conclusions, ask yourself who would disagree and on what grounds.* This question will help you check your natural tendency to let sources that appeal to you do all the work for your speech without considering alternative arguments.

4. *Be willing to revise your conclusions based on new evidence.* If you have formed a provisional opinion about your topic based on your reading but you stumble across some really compelling new evidence, you have to be willing to change your mind.

5. *Include the main disagreements between differing perspectives that led you to decide on the case you want to make,* or the angle on your informative topic that you want to take. For example, if you are giving a speech about health care policy and you would like to argue that reform is worth the costs, you should cite the opposing arguments and explain why you came to your position despite the good objections of some critics.

In the end, respecting your topic is about letting evidence and arguments influence what you will say, as opposed to simply confirming what you already thought. This practice is ethical because it both forces you to be honest about your views in your speech and ensures that your audience can make a well-informed decision about your topic.

Present Other Views and Treat Them Fairly

Informing your audience about divergent viewpoints is a necessary component of your speech. A few techniques for treating disagreement fairly follow.

First, recognize that people with opposing viewpoints don't disagree on absolutely everything. Usually the big disagreements in public life are about priorities or a few critical assumptions. Think about our public debates on the role of the government in promoting social

Suppose you want to give an informative speech about the health benefits of practicing yoga, which promotes muscle and bone health. What is the other side of the picture that balances these benefits, and where would you find out about it?

iStockphoto.com/Evgenyatamanenko

goods (such as health, education, welfare, or any number of social policy issues). Though the tenor of public debate may not respect this fact, most well-intentioned advocates on both sides of any crucial issue agree about more than they disagree about.

Some people, for example, think that the government should stay out of health care, while others think that the government ought to take a more active role in ensuring health care coverage for all U.S. citizens. The advocates on either side of this issue agree on a surprising number of things. Both sides would like to expand access to health care and to lower the cost of coverage. Both sides would like to promote efficient and effective health care delivery. Where the two sides disagree is usually whether the government's intervention hinders or helps to achieve these goals. To treat such disagreements fairly, employ the following techniques:

- *Foreground shared commitments.* What goals and values unite the majority of opinions, even ones that differ, around your topic?
- *Be clear about the central points of dispute.* Your job as a speaker is not only to say what you think but also to specify your position on grounds that those who disagree with you would recognize. If you do this carefully, you not only will help your audience make an informed decision, but also will put yourself in a good position to discuss the merits of opposing viewpoints.
- *Make the best possible case for alternative viewpoints.* Audiences know when you are intentionally presenting alternative opinions in a bad light. If you want your audience to engage with your topic and, more important, to grant you credibility in talking about it, present opposing viewpoints in a charitable light.
- *Make your grounds for disagreement explicit.* Once you have framed alternative viewpoints, be explicit about why you don't agree with them, and present a well-reasoned case for your position in the light of potential objections.

When should you identify opposing arguments? Probably throughout your speech, whenever they become relevant. For example, if your speech about raising the gas tax has three major points (raising the tax will create incentives for conservation, lead to the development of more efficient technologies, and produce significant new revenue), you might use an opposing argument as the introduction to a major point in the speech:

> **Raising the gas tax will create greater incentives for efficiency. Because an increased tax makes operating a car more expensive, drivers will have an economic incentive to cut out unnecessary travel. Some have argued that raising the tax will not have this effect, however. For example, a study by Gas Inc. argued that demand for driving is inelastic—that is, raising the cost of driving does not reduce gas use, because people will simply pay more to go where they want to go.**

At this point, evidence to the contrary usually would be introduced, often preceded by the conjunction *but*:

> **But recent studies of states that raised their gas tax show that the cost of driving is a significant factor in the choices drivers make about where to go.**

To complete the argument in an ethical and balanced way, at this point you would say why you believe one study and not the other:

> **Historical data from state gas taxes shows that the conclusions that Gas Inc. came to are not quite right. At a certain point, increases in the cost of gas do affect driving behavior, inducing more people to carpool, use mass transit, or avoid unnecessary trips.**

Being balanced doesn't mean that you can't advocate for one side. Rather, being balanced means presenting multiple perspectives on an issue and then providing your audience with the grounds that brought you to your conclusions.

AVOID FALLACIES AND PREJUDICIAL APPEALS

In public life, speakers make choices about not only *what* they are arguing or asking for but also *how* they argue or ask for it. You don't have to be on a college campus long before you are solicited by people gathering signatures for petitions. They often begin by asking, "Do you have a minute for [the issue]?"—for example, "Do you have a minute for the environment?" This is, by definition, a loaded appeal. It is set up to make you feel like a loser if you say no.

appeal An attempt to influence an audience.

An **appeal** is an attempt to influence the audience (see also Chapter 12). Some appeals rely on the strength of the evidence or logic that undergirds them, and other appeals rely on prejudicial language. Language is prejudicial when it attempts to distract the listeners from thinking critically and making a decision based on the merits of the evidence.

In this section, we'll describe name-calling, glittering generalities, inappropriate testimonials, the plain folks appeal, card-stacking, and bandwagoning—a few of the logical fallacies and unethical appeals that rely on drawing your attention away from the merits of a claim.

Name Calling

Name calling is sticking a label on people or ideas that prejudges them as good or as bad.

We can't afford civil liberties for *terrorists*.

When you call somebody a "terrorist," you have already made a number of judgments about what they did and why. However, you've provided no evidence or arguments, just assertions hidden under a negative label.

We must reject marijuana—it's a *drug*.

The implication "therefore it's bad" isn't supported by any arguments, so this name calling is just a way of short-circuiting real dialogue. After all, ibuprofen is a drug, and it's widely regarded as beneficial.

Glittering Generalities

Glittering generalities connect a person, an idea, or a thing to an abstract concept, whether positive or negative. The speaker expects the goodness or badness of the abstract concept to transfer to the topic, just by being mentioned in the same sentence.

It's the *patriotic* choice.

Everybody on every side of every issue thinks their position is the patriotic one, and they may be right! In a democracy, equally patriotic people can disagree, so it's unfair to attempt to bypass discussion through an appeal to patriotism.

Inappropriate Testimonials

Inappropriate testimonials rely on good will toward a celebrity rather than expertise.

Hey, it's the *president* recommending this.

No matter who is president, just being president does not offer adequate support for an argument. Of course, not all testimonials are unethical, because we should be influenced by people we trust in the areas where they have expertise or experience. But "Trust me" (or "Trust him") isn't a substitute for real reasons and dialogue.

Plain-Folks Appeals

Pretending to identify with the audience's (assumed) tendency to avoid complexity or unfamiliar ideas is a plain-folks appeal.

> **I don't know much about economics, but I know I can't run a deficit in my bank account.**

Perhaps the economy would be easier to manage if the federal budget were like our personal bank accounts, but it isn't. There are good deficits and bad deficits in a national economy, and you have to make the case for your view, not just throw up your hands.

Card-Stacking

Card-stacking (as in stacking the deck in a card game) uses evidence selectively to prove a point, especially by allowing one or two extreme examples to stand in for a whole range of evidence.

> **Cheating is rampant on this campus! Did you hear about those crazy cheaters in Biology 101?**

A card-stacking argument that student cheating is a widespread problem might focus on a few shocking episodes and never bring up the majority of students who are honest in their course work.

Bandwagoning

Arguing that "everyone" believes or is doing something is an attempt to get the audience on the bandwagon.

> **Everybody knows that big banks can't be trusted.**

This kind of claim isn't a logical argument. It's more like bullying, implying there's something wrong with *you* if you don't believe what "everyone" believes.

In conclusion, composing an ethically sound public speech requires making choices that treat your audience as you would like to be treated. You would like to hear solid information and arguments presented in a clear, compelling, and honest manner. You would like to be able to have a basic grasp of the various perspectives on the issue, and you probably would like some guidance on how to sort through the different claims regarding a change in opinion or action.

Ethics and the Audience

One way of thinking about ethics that we have suggested here is to think about how speaking ethically changes or influences you. So, for example, you are the culmination of individual choices that you make, so you should be ethical if you want to be a good person, or you should speak ethically because it helps you to achieve your goals. Another strand that we've been discussing is the idea that you should speak ethically because your speech plays a role in shaping the audience, and you might want to consider exactly what kind of world you are helping to bring into existence.

This is one of the great insights of the rhetorician Ed Black. In a classic essay in rhetorical studies, Black argues that instead of just focusing on whether or not a speech is successful in achieving its goals, we also can make an evaluation of a speech based on the kind of audience that it calls into existence. To make this argument, Black points out that there is a difference between an author (the actual person who sits and writes a story, for example) and the way that we might think of the persona that author is constructing in how he or she tells a story. Black says that just as there is a difference between authors and the personae that they portray, there is a difference between the actual audience that hears a speech and the kind of people that the speaker intends the audience to become by hearing the speech. So, for example, if your speech is chock full of fear-mongering and nastiness, not only do you intend the audience to be moved by fear and nastiness, but in some small way you are training your audience to be the kind of people who are moved by fear and nastiness. And that is the point in everything we have been saying in thinking about ethics—your speech, both what and how you deliver it, has effects, and you are responsible for those effects. Because you are responsible for the outcomes, large or small, you should think about exactly what kind of world you are trying to speak into existence. Hopefully, for ethical speakers, the answer is that they are trying to make the world a little better than it was before they spoke.

For more information, see:
E. Black, "The second persona," *Quarterly Journal of Speech*, 1970, 56:2.

Summary

Public speaking can be ethically wrong in a number of ways: lying, misrepresentation of facts, poor reasoning, plagiarism, poor citation of sources, and intentional use of manipulative or deceptive appeals. All of these ethical lapses can damage the relationship between you and your audience. You should feel great after having delivered a well-researched, well-thought-out speech, and you should feel even better if you do it in a way that you can be proud of from an ethical perspective.

Cultivating ethical public speaking as a skill can make a significant difference in your life, and perhaps even in the world. Maybe someday you will convince business colleagues to undertake a profitable change, or you will help your community overcome a pressing challenge. The key to making a difference, whether large or small, is to see each public speaking opportunity as a chance to build a relationship with an audience and to point the audience toward some greater good. Each chance you have to speak lets you take part in a larger ongoing conversation and to make positive changes.

MindTap®

Reflect, personalize, and apply what you've learned.

Questions for Review

1. How do relationships and conversations relate to communication ethics?
2. What are the seven principles for ethical communication?
3. How is bias an ethical problem for speakers?
4. Choose three of the prejudicial appeals described in the chapter and give an example of each.

Questions for Discussion

1. Is it always wrong to lie? Explain why or why not, and give examples to support your answer.
2. Choose three of this chapter's principles for ethical speaking, and give an example of how a speaker might fail to uphold each of them. How could each of these ethical lapses be corrected?
3. How do you usually evaluate whether communication is ethical? List your personal criteria and be prepared to defend them.
4. Do you disagree with any of the principles in this chapter? Why or why not? Use examples to prove your point.
5. We have identified a number of ethical faults in this chapter. In your opinion, which are the worst? Which are nearly acceptable, and when? Give examples to back up your claims.

Key Concepts   MindTap®

Practice defining the chapter's terms by using online flashcards

advocacy	bias	paraphrasing
appeal	claim	plagiarism
argument	ethics	reasoning
balance	grounds	

LEARNING OBJECTIVES

- Differentiate types of audiences
- Analyze how the identity of the audience influences your choices, and explain how your choices influence the identity of the audience
- Distinguish between the literal audience and the rhetorical audience
- Explain the distinction between marketing and engagement as approaches to the audience
- Explain how your interaction with an audience fits in the broader context of the public and democratic conversation

CHAPTER OUTLINE

- **Introduction: Those People Sitting in Front of You**
- **Audience Analysis**
- **The Literal Audience: Demographics**
- **The Rhetorical Audience**
- **Types of Rhetorical Audiences**
- **Adapting Your Speech to Your Audience**
- **Two Views of the Audience: Marketing vs. Engagement**
- **The Audience and the Public**
- **Your Ethical Responsibilities to Your Audience**

I n looking out over the class, Tiffany wonders how she is going to make her speech work. She's fairly sure it's about a stance that's unpopular with most students: becoming a vegetarian. Tiffany finds it easy to talk to her vegetarian friends about it, but she hasn't had much success with her cheeseburger-loving friends. How *do* you talk to people when you have trouble seeing the common ground? She has to find a way to think through her choices about how to construct an audience-friendly speech.

MindTap®

Start with a warm-up activity about Tiffany's speech, and review the chapter's Learning Objectives.

Overview

To give a successful speech, understanding and connecting with your audience is crucial. This chapter begins by providing you with a way of thinking about audiences and gradually moves outward to the ways your interaction with a specific audience is part of a broader public conversation. To start, we offer a set of tools for analyzing your audience. Second, we provide you with resources for adapting your speech to your audience members, with the goal of helping you to make effective choices about the best ways to engage them as you persuade or inform them. Next we discuss the idea that audiences are also part of a larger public dialogue. We conclude this chapter with an argument for understanding your audience as part of a broader public conversation, and we talk about your responsibilities to the audience.

INTRODUCTION: THOSE PEOPLE SITTING IN FRONT OF YOU

Effective public speaking requires you to connect with your audience. If you deliver a carefully researched, well-argued, stylistically powerful speech but fail to engage your audience, your speech will not be effective. Connecting with the audience requires you to develop skills in analyzing your audience and, on the basis of analysis, adapting your speech to it and engaging its members.

MindTap®

Read, highlight and take notes online.

- Analyzing your audience means thinking about the makeup and motivations of your audience so you will have a sense of the best way to make your case to them.
- As we discussed in Chapter 1, adapting to your audience means writing, framing, and delivering your speech in a manner that will maximize the chances that the members will not only hear you but also may change their opinions, beliefs, or actions in response to your speech.

Analyzing and adapting to your audience are fundamental skills for responsive communication. Communication is always directed to one or more persons in some way. Letting them know what is on your mind is the goal of *expressive communication.* In contrast, the goal of *responsive communication* is to engage the other persons and elicit a response, so it must take into account their opinions, motivations, beliefs, and character. Inexperienced speakers often focus on themselves: "What do I think?" "What do I feel like saying?" Although, of course, the speech starts with the speaker—you have to have something you want to say—to be effective, you have to include the audience in the choices you make in both planning and speaking.

In public speaking, you want not only to make your opinion known but also to influence how your audience thinks about your topic—whether your goal is to inform audience members, to persuade them to take action, or to honor someone on a special occasion. In each of these cases, achieving your goal requires making choices to tailor your speech carefully to the audience.

Though you have specific goals in mind for each audience to which you deliver a speech, a public speech is also a turn in a larger conversation. As a communicator, you should think about your audience as a partner in an ongoing public conversation. Your goals in speaking and your choices in composing and delivering your speech should move a public conversation forward. Thus, for any public speaking situation, you will have to develop an understanding of the audience so you can foster a relationship and strengthen the quality of public conversation in your community and beyond.

We begin by giving you tools for analyzing and engaging specific audiences: asking "who, what, where, when, and why" questions about each audience and viewing the audience as a rhetorical, as well as a literal, audience.

AUDIENCE ANALYSIS

audience analysis Surveying your audience's beliefs, values, experiences, and motivations.

Audience analysis means thinking about the beliefs, values, experiences, and motivations that characterize your audience. Of course, an audience usually is made up of people with different, beliefs, values, experiences, and motivations. Still, you can try to answer some questions about the general tendencies of your audience. You might think about these questions as the "who, what, where, when, and whys" of audience interaction:

- *Who* is in the audience?
- *What* opinions does your audience already have about the topic you are presenting?
- *Where* are you addressing the audience? What things about the context or occasion might influence your audience members' interest and dispositions?
- *When* are you addressing the audience? This is not just a matter of the time of day, but also why your topic is timely for the audience.
- *Why* would your audience be interested in your topic? Why should these people make a particular judgment, change their minds, or take a specific action? In other words, how does your goal intersect with their interests, concerns, and aspirations?

literal audience The group of people sitting in front of you, as you begin to speak; they can be described in demographic categories.

This analysis will help you figure out how to make effective choices in your speech.

Skillful public speaking requires you to identify the common factors that unite an audience's opinions and the possible points of persuasion. A good speaker also can convince the audience to find new areas of commonality. But this task requires more than simply identifying who is in the audience and what they think.

rhetorical audience What the literal audience can become when you convince the members to think or act differently.

The important distinction here is between the **literal audience**, or who the audience members are as you get up to address them, and the **rhetorical audience**, or who the audience members can become when you convince them to think about themselves—and your topic—differently. The literal audience is the group of people sitting in front of you, who have opinions and ideas that are all their own; they are the audience of marketing and advertising. The rhetorical, or possible, audience consists of those whom your speech can transform by convincing them to think differently about their worlds. The rhetorical audience is the audience you choose to address. Let's look at each audience in detail.

THE LITERAL AUDIENCE: DEMOGRAPHICS

Analyzing the literal audience requires you to make a series of educated guesses about the commonalities among the people in the room. These guesses are based on knowledge (or assumptions) about the demographics of the audience. **Demographics** are the standard categories we use to understand who people are. They are classifications that can give a rough picture of essential characteristics of the audience, such as the following:

> **demographics** Population characteristics, such as age, gender, or income.

age	political commitments
gender	sexual orientation
race	educational level
socio-economic status (class)	occupation
religious beliefs	income
nationality	

For example, you know that all the people in your public speaking class are likely to be enrolled at the school. Because they are students, you can make some educated guesses about how they think about the world and what issues concern them (20-something college students think about the world differently than older or younger people do). You also can make educated guesses, based on their age, about other things that might influence your speech, such as media consumption habits, political leanings, and a number of lifestyle issues. For example, most people under 40 have never used a typewriter or a rotary phone.

Jim West/Alamy

Demographics help us understand some superficial characteristics of a group of people, such as age, gender, and race. For a public speaker, however, a deeper understanding of the audience is necessary—and possible.

TRY IT! **EXPERIMENTING WITH DEMOGRAPHICS**

Pick any topic that is interesting to you, whether from popular culture, sports, the arts—anything. Write it down. What could you do to adapt this topic to an audience of traditional age (18–22) college students? List two ways in which the topic is relevant to them. Now imagine giving the same speech to a business or professional audience from diverse backgrounds. Would the topic be relevant in the same ways? Add two new ways to your list. Finally, imagine that you are giving a speech on the same topic at a senior citizen center. What difference would this change in audience make for your speech? Add two more differences. Now look at your list of ways in which your topic is relevant. How similar or different are the things on the list? Why do you think that is?

You also might make guesses about your audience based on educational level or professional experience, which will dictate the kinds and complexity of topics that you can treat. You might even make some guesses about your audience based on the racial or gender composition—though you have to be careful to avoid stereotyping. Different life experiences because of race and gender influence how people think about the world, but it is dangerous to presume that people can be defined by their race or gender. You also have to remember that you can't tell someone's race, age, or maybe even gender just by looking across the room at them. Someone with light skin may self-identify as African American, and our guesses about age often are wrong.

Although demographics can be useful, you shouldn't assume that you automatically know what someone thinks or values because that person is female or male, Chinese or Jewish, age 15 or 50, or a college professor or a plumber. Instead, you should take the diversity of your audience as a clue to the diversity your speech must address.

Problems With the Demographic Approach

Relying on demographic data alone won't allow you to make good choices about how to engage with your audience. Why? Your information may be incomplete or inaccurate. Even if you get the demographics right, you can't assume that you know people's positions or values based on their demographic characteristics. Generalizations are really just stereotypes, and these tend to be an undependable way to assess people's actual beliefs or commitments.

Another problem is that if audience members don't fit the demographic implied by the topic, they have no reason to listen. If the speech argues, "Women should get yearly pelvic exams," the men in the audience have no reason to listen—unless you expand the audience to all people who care about the health of women. As another example, suppose the speaker starts a speech about a new diabetes-testing device with the question, "Do you have diabetes?" That makes sense for the topic, but if the answer is no, those audience members will tune out. They have no reason to care about the device—unless you expand your definition of the audience to include everybody who cares about someone who has, or could have, diabetes.

A focus on demographics also can lead you away from finding a common ground for the audience. Demographics focus on differences and toward treating the audience as a fragmented set of groups rather than as a single group that you are trying to persuade or inform. The fragmentation makes it hard to make choices: Do you choose arguments for the men or the women? For the rich or the poor? White or Asian?

Your challenge, then, is to make choices in your speech that cut through the inherent diversity of your audience members to find commonalities and address your speech to all of them. Use demographic information about the audience as a starting point, but then move beyond these differences to find points of commonality. For example, if you are giving a speech about the negative effects of Title IX (the federal law that requires funding equity for men's and women's sports teams), and your audience has both men and women in it, you should, of course, find a way to address male and female students' concerns simultaneously. But suppose you have an all-guy audience. Does that mean you can assume that no one is in favor of Title IX? Of course not. Not only may some audience members have a sister or a girlfriend who benefits from Title IX, but some men may favor it in principle even if it decreases funding for their favorite sport.

THE RHETORICAL AUDIENCE

Speakers can make better speech choices by focusing on the audience they want to create rather than just the demographic characteristics of the bodies sitting in the room. It's not the audience you are given that should guide your choices; it's what you *make* of the audience. What makes your speech effective is your skill in designing the persuasion that provides you with an audience suitable for persuasion, or a rhetorical audience.[1] The answer to questions such as, "Which arguments should I use? Which evidence should I offer?" is always, "What makes my point best to my rhetorical audience?"

How do you create a rhetorical audience? By *addressing* them it in a certain way, you can create a particular relationship, a particular "us."[2] You already are familiar with the idea of "addressing" an audience, because you do it interpersonally. When you greet someone, you use some form of address. To a friend, it might be "Hiya, Rudy." To the clerk at the convenience store, it's likely to be "Hi," with no name. To a teacher, it might be "Hello, Dr. Jones." But if you were to go up to Dr. Jones one day and say, "Hi, Bob," it would cause some confusion. When you address someone as a friend or as a teacher or as a sales clerk, you are defining your relationship.

The same process operates in many communication contexts. Suppose you ask out a fellow student for coffee. Are you asking the person "as a student, let's talk about the homework" or "as a potential friend, let's get to know each other," or "as an expert, please will you tutor me." "Student," "friend," and "expert" are different roles that the same person can inhabit, so they are different rhetorical audiences.

You should make clear, in your approach, which audience (which role) you are addressing. You might even address—and so bring into existence—a role that the other person didn't even think of: "Hey, are you worried about the tuition situation here? I am. I think we need to talk about what can be done." Now the audience is not "fellow classmate" but, rather, "fellow tuition-payer at our school." The other students may not have ever thought about themselves that way before, but your mode of address invites them to take the role of tuition-payer in listening to you.

The point about rhetorical audiences is that you are not simply bound to what a demographic analysis can tell you about an audience. You also can invite the audience to relate to your topic through a different lens—a lens that you create. The ways that you may invite an audience to engage a topic are bounded only by your rhetorical imagination and creativity.[3]

THE RHETORICAL AUDIENCE **TRY IT!**

What's the difference between literal and rhetorical audiences in the same situation? Directions: Describe both a literal and a rhetorical audience for each of the following speech goals. For example, if the speech goal is to persuade people to recycle, a literal audience would be "the 18- to 30-year-old students in front of you who are mostly from the city you live in and work part-time jobs," and a rhetorical audience would be "people who care about saving the earth."

- Inform an audience about a proposed piece of legislation.
- Persuade someone to take a public speaking class.
- Give a wedding toast.
- Persuade someone to avoid texting and walking at the same time.

How do the answers differ? What does this tell us about audience?

The "As" Test

How do you figure out what audience to create? You can start, if you like, with demographics, and ask yourself about likely roles that cut across categories and include the whole group. From among those roles, ask yourself which ones would make your audience members most open to changing their perspective on your topic. Or you can start with your topic (which you intuitively thought was appropriate to this group), and try to imagine the different possible audience roles for which you could design arguments.

A useful tool for choosing a rhetorical audience is the **"as" test**. For example, instead of addressing your audience members in their roles as 20-somethings and college students, you could address your audience *as*

"as" test A tool for choosing a rhetorical audience as people in a specific role in order to change their perspective on your topic.

Americans	curious people
citizens	voters
consumers	taxpayers
music lovers	drivers
achievers	people who care about their health
compassionate people	

Many more roles are possible. In principle, a rhetorical conception of your audience allows you to pick a role or perspective that not only helps them relate to your topic but also invites them to forge commonalities despite demographic differences.

TRY IT!

THE "AS" TEST

Imagine that you knew nothing about the demographics of your audience for a topic that interests you. Pick three categories from the "as" list and say how you would modify your approach to the speech for each category.

The rhetorical role of the audience can influence a number of choices that you make in your speech. You might address the audience directly in their rhetorical role. For example, in a speech about online piracy, you might say, "As consumers of media, all of us are concerned with the quality of music that contemporary artists are producing." Inviting an audience to take up a specific role also can influence your choices about words and verbal style. For example, if you want to invoke the idea of people who have to make difficult choices about what they can and can't afford during a financial downturn but you want to avoid inviting them to think of themselves as cash-strapped consumers, you might say, "Budgets are tight, resources are not infinite, and we have to make some difficult choices about health care."

A limitation to the idea of the rhetorical audience is that you can't magically make the audience into anything that you want it to be. You will have to use judgment about what roles you think your audience might be willing to assume. If you want to give a speech on the benefits of recycling, you can't assume that the rhetorical audience consists of "people who care about recycling." That sounds good—it's convenient!—but it misses a crucial point: You're speaking about recycling because you think some people don't know a lot about recycling or don't care about it very much. If you assume that the audience already knows a lot, why are you speaking? Instead, you might choose as your rhetorical audience "people who care about the environment" (because recycling helps reduce pollution and garbage) or "people who care about prices" (because recycling can make certain products cheaper). In general, a rhetorical audience of "people who wanted to hear this speech and agree with it" doesn't help you make choices that will reach people in your audience who don't fall into that category.

How would you describe the audience for 2014 Nobel Peace Prize winner Malala Yousafzai of Pakistan?

From "Me" to "Us"

As you think about the audience you will choose to address, you are directing your attention, to an extent, away from yourself. Most of the choices you make in planning your speech take your audience into account. But your orientation toward your audience is also a component of your speech. Sometimes speakers can appear to be lecturing or talking down to their audiences, because they create a distance between themselves and the audience. Listen to the difference in these two pairs of theses:

> **You should all do more recycling.**
> **We all need to do more recycling.**

> **You need to know more about energy conservation.**
> **We all could be better informed about energy conservation.**

In the first sentence of each pair, the speaker seems to be saying that she is different from the audience: smarter, more knowledgeable, and more moral. Audience members may find that off-putting, as if they were children being lectured. In the second sentence of each pair, the speaker includes herself in the speech. This makes a lot of sense. If you are calling a community into being, asking the audience members to see themselves as all affected by a problem, you will be more effective if you are speaking as a member of that community.

Similarly, whenever you listen to a speech and evaluate it, you should ask yourself, "Who does the speaker think I am? What does he or she want from me? Is that appropriate?" You should expect the speaker to address you in terms that you can relate to. For example, if the topic of the speech is obesity, and you think you are pretty fit, you may think, "What has obesity got to do with me?" You should expect the speaker to address people like you in the speech: "Obesity is everyone's problem, because…."

TYPES OF RHETORICAL AUDIENCES

Now that we have the idea of the rhetorical audience in hand, we can generalize a little bit into *types* of audiences. To divide them up this way, we need the idea of *interests*. Interests are something we have relative to a given rhetorical role, such as student, consumer, taxpayer, or citizen. So, for example, as a taxpayer, I have an interest in taxes being low. As a student at a public university, I have an interest in my tuition being low, so I have an interest in taxes being a little higher. As a citizen, I have an interest in the tax system being fair and doing its intended job. Not all interests are financial. You can be interested in fairness, justice, artistic merit, and all sorts of other things, depending on the situation.

Audiences may (generally—not every person) have, or not have, an understandings of their own interests, because of knowledge about a topic. That's where communicators come into the picture, to clarify the relationship between facts and interests. If you didn't know that your taxes supported a certain government program, you didn't realize that you had an interest (one way or another) in that program. If you didn't realize that downloading from Torrent sites is stealing, you didn't realize that your general interest in fairness/lawfulness is relevant to your downloading habits.

Whether you are thinking about informative speaking or persuasive speaking, interests are always relevant. If you want to convey information, you also have to show why the information is relevant or interesting to the audience. If you want to persuade people to take an action, you have to have show that the action is consistent with their interests, or follows directly from them. Take a look at the speech (available on MindTap) on "College Student Volunteering and Civic Engagement." Alyssa addresses her audience as students, and as students she sees that they have an interest in personal education—self-improvement and skill development that will advance their career and personal plans. For another audience, for example accomplished and experienced professionals, the relevance of those interests is low, and others may be more relevant. They may be interested more in giving back to the community *using* their experience than in gaining experience. So Alyssa addressed a relevant rhetorical audience and targeted its salient interests.

Let's look at some general kinds of audiences. These categories can be useful to you in thinking through your choices about how to develop a topic. For informative speeches interests help you think about framing the information ("Why should you care about this information? Why does it matter to you?"), and for persuasive speeches, interests help you think about the challenges you will face in constructing arguments for them.

- *Sympathetic audiences:* Here, rhetorical audiences already see their interests aligned with yours. You can just add to and amplify the agreement, adding information and substance. On most college campuses, a speech about "We need more and cheaper parking" will find a friendly response.
- *Apathetic audiences:* Apathetic audiences don't care about a topic, because they don't know they *should* care about it. This a great opportunity for a speaker to show the audience members that their interests are aligned with knowing about this information. The speaker identifies a rhetorical audience, its interests, and then shows how the information is relevant. For example, most people don't know a lot about the concept of "net neutrality," and they surf the web and use Netflix in happy ignorance of the term. But if they did know what was at stake, they'd want to know a lot more.
- *Hostile audiences:* Sometimes rhetorical audiences are fairly sure that they *do* know what their interests are, and they are the opposite of what you want to propose. The challenge here, while respecting their understanding of their own interests, is to convince the audience that either another interest should take precedence or that there is another interpretation of the interest. For example, because the cost is much lower, most students find themselves automatically in favor of textbook rental. Yet, as students, they have an interest not only in price, but also in quality, and there is an argument that although the current textbook system could be improved, moving to rentals forces professors to use books that they don't like, or that aren't very good, and these texts thus diminish students' educational experiences.
- *Occasional audiences:* These are audiences that have gathered for a specific purpose. Sometimes it is a special occasion, and their expectations are dictated by it. If you speak at a funeral, attendees are interested in hearing you remember and praise the deceased. If you

Is a hostile audience a problem—or an opportunity?

speak at a graduation, the audience is interested in hearing you speak about the meaning of this life transition. On such occasions, you are free to talk about lots of different things, and to be creative, as long as you can tie your talk back to the basic interests of the occasion.

ADAPTING YOUR SPEECH TO YOUR AUDIENCE

Adapting to the audience doesn't mean just telling people what they already know or want to believe. It means creating a bridge between a version of audience members' identity and beliefs and what you want them to believe. The following are several resources for building this bridge.

Identify Common Interests

What are the interests or goals that your audience members, as _____ (fill in the audience you've chosen to address), could reasonably be expected to have? Tying your arguments to a goal that people would have in the role you're addressing enables you to adapt to your audience members while advocating a policy or proposition that they might initially have rejected or found implausible, or even presenting information that they don't really care about. For example, if you're giving an informative speech on the registration process at your school, you can be sure that everyone who registers has similar interests, such as getting the classes they want and getting through the process quickly.

Make the Most of Shared Experience

In many cases, the audience you create will have a set of common experiences. You can use these for your argument: "Everybody knows how annoying it can be to stand in line and deal with the registrar." You can organize your speech in terms of these experiences: "Everybody knows the registration process: First you get the class schedule, then you attempt to register, and then you try to find another set of classes. At each stage, you're paying for things you don't need." You also can emphasize the topic through verbal style: "Registering for classes is like playing the lottery."

Work from Common Premises

Your audience may share common assumptions. Bringing these to the surface can provide points to support your argument: "Getting the right courses is important, or we wouldn't put so much work into the registration process."

Be Directive

Your creation of the audience can be normative. You can tell your audience who they should be.

> As students, we *should care* about the negative influence of big sports at our school because...
>
> As U.S. citizens, we *need to be interested* in other countries' opinion of us because...

Dr. Martin Luther King and the Address to the March on Washington

Dr. King's speech in 1963 is the most famous speech of the second half of the 20th century, and one reason is the way it constructs its audience. What kind of audience did King have? Partly it was an occasional audience: In the midst of a growing public discussion about civil rights for African Americans, the attendees were there for the occasion of this second March on Washington (the first one was in 1942).

This audience was likely to be sympathetic. But King also realized that he was being broadcast on radio and a text of the speech was likely to be circulated widely, so he had to expect that anyone in the United States might be in his audience. Some of this secondary audience might be apathetic, and parts might be actively hostile to his message, and to him. In the context of the Cold War, calls for civil rights might even be seen as "communist" and un-American.

So this is his problem in designing the speech—how to construct a rhetorical audience to include the 250,000 people standing in front of him and also invite everyone else in the country. His solution is to make the audience of the speech not just advocates of civil rights but *Americans* in general, in a specific sense of American that he defines in the speech. What the speech does brilliantly—so much so that we can still find ourselves to be the audience for it—is to define "American" in terms of principles that ensure no contradiction between being a real American and being in favor of civil rights for all. How does he do this?

King constructs his audience in a number of ways. One way is to track the repetitions (technically, *anaphora*, see Chapter 8) in the speech; repetitions usually highlight what the speaker thinks is most important. First, he calls on history. In the opening passage, he repeats the phrase "one hundred years later" (after beginning with, "Five score years ago," a nod to Lincoln's Gettysburg Address). The year 1963 is a hundred years after the Emancipation Proclamation freed slaves in the secessionist states. King thus begins by alluding to the outcomes of the Civil War, in which at least three things were at stake: the legality of slavery, the question of federalism (i.e., Does federal law trump state law?) and the citizenship status of former slaves. Two of these questions were settled definitively by the war: Slavery became illegal, and federal law, on constitutional issues in particular, trumped state law. Yet, in the hundred years since the war, as King points out, African Americans had not achieved legal or political equality.

But "Now is the time." King leaves history and begins talking about the present, which is the concern of those in his audience on the Washington Mall, and also the flashpoint for those who will be hostile his message. He disassociates himself from the legal strategies of the NAACP ("the tranquilizing drug of gradualism"), as well as from more radical approaches to gaining civil rights. He insists, however, that the issue can't be put off, and that "we will never be satisfied" until equality is achieved.

Then he goes into the most famous portion of the speech, urging listeners to "go back" to their home cities and states and continue to fight. Why? Because "I have a dream." King's account of the dream, in which the United States thoroughly acts on the implication of its founding principles, is electric, and he paints a vivid picture of that world. It's certainly a compelling vision, and hard for anyone raised as an American to reject. He has faith in that vision of America, and "with this faith," the future can be transformed.

King then taps into the emotional side of patriotism, invoking a childhood song, "My County Tis of Thee," and integrates the entire nation into the speech by declaring that we (notice the "we" here) should "let freedom ring" from every part of the country, including those in turmoil over civil rights at that time.

By invoking the words of the core documents of U.S. history, its ideals and symbols, King creates a rhetorical audience, positioned to understand the civil rights movement as integral to their idea of themselves as Americans.

TWO VIEWS OF THE AUDIENCE: MARKETING VS. ENGAGEMENT

The conceptions of the literal audience and the rhetorical audiences imply different approaches to interacting with an audience. To see how, let's look at the differences between a familiar type of communication, marketing, and engagement, one of the principles of ethical speakers that we discussed in Chapter 2.

We all live in a sea of advertising and marketing, and we're totally familiar with it. Marketing is about convincing audiences to change their behavior, based on their existing

Francis Miller/Time & Life Pictures/Getty Images

Did King give a policy speech (the Civil Rights Act was facing Congress at that time) or a celebratory speech?

Table 3.1 Two Approaches to Audiences

Marketing	Engagement
One-way process	Two-way process
Demographic segments	Commonalities
Stereotypes	Self-risk
Means to an end	Deserving respect

beliefs and motivations; and engagement is about changing the beliefs and motivations of the audience (see Table 3.1). Our purpose in drawing this contrast is to show that even though marketing is an entirely legitimate activity, it operates from assumptions that are different from public speaking, and those assumptions become clearer in the contrast. Marketers are trying to create awareness that will foster sales, and to do that, they don't target messages to a general public but, instead, to highly specific demographic slices, reduced to a specific age range, gender, income, ethnicity, and so forth. Given enough research, marketers can make good guesses about the interests of many of the people in a given demographic slice, and what appeals to them. Marketers can, in a practical sense, stereotype audiences, but the limitations of the stereotypes don't affect their usefulness; being right 50% of the time is enough to get good results. In a public situation, though, ignoring half the audience isn't helpful.

Marketing

When you are selling something, your relationship to your audience has four characteristics:

- *One-way process.* When you're selling a product or a service, your goal is not a dialogue with your potential customers. You don't expect new ideas or mutual interests to crop up; you're doing something *to* them, not *with* them.
- *Demographic segments.* Marketers divide their audiences into demographic segments: old, young; rich, poor; college education, only high school; urban, rural; and so on. Marketers are interested in difference, in finding the specific groups of people most likely to buy their product or service.
- *Stereotypes.* Through research, marketers know who is most likely to want their soda sweet, their pants loose, and their cars big. Stereotypes such as these, if based on solid research, can be highly reliable, but they are still just generalizations: Some young people like Cole Porter, and some older people like Jay-Z. Stereotypes need to have only enough truth to generate some sales.
- *Means to your ends.* In marketing, the audience members are means, not ends in themselves, deserving of respect. Marketing is premised on using people rather than engaging them. Although a salesperson may try to convince people that she's helping them, which sometimes might be true, in the end she just wants to sell her product because it's her job.

Engagement

Communication in any democratic framework requires genuine engagement, recognizable by everybody involved. A democratic framework is, of course, an integral part of the institutions that form our government. But it also can be the framework for lots of organizational and small-group settings. Whenever a group of any size decides to listen to everybody and give equal weight to everyone's insights and arguments, this group has adopted a democratic framework. To what does genuine engagement commit you?

- **Two-way process.** Real engagement includes both talking and listening. As a speaker, you have a responsibility to treat the audience in the way you'd like to be treated, which boils down to the Golden Rule, discussed in Chapter 2. Although public speaking is part of a public dialogue, it isn't actually conversation, and your audience may not always be able to respond. But you still have responsibility to address the audience *as if* the members were going to respond and have their turn.

- **Commonalities.** Public speaking that's engaged doesn't segment the audience and deal with every demographic difference piecemeal. Instead, the democratic imperative is to talk to the whole audience, because everybody is part of this conversation. The skilled public speaker finds a way to speak across differences of identity, beliefs, and values.

- **Self-risk.** If you see your speech as part of a larger dialogue, you approach it as if someone in the audience might change *your* mind. You can test your speech choices using the "self-risk" test described in Chapter 2: Are you putting your own beliefs and commitments at risk?[4]

- **Deserving respect.** In the public dialogue, if you're speaking to an audience members who have little knowledge about your topic, it might be easy to mislead them. As we pointed out in Chapter 2, you can assess the integrity of what you are asking your audience to believe or do by imagining that this is an audience of experts.

MARKETING VS. ENGAGEMENT `TRY IT!`

Pick an issue that is important to you. If you were marketing the issue, how would you approach your audience? How would your approach change if you were to opt for an engagement approach?

THE AUDIENCE AND THE PUBLIC

The hallmark of successfully engaging your audience is your recognition of a common interest in your topic. In other words, to be an effective public speaker, you should see your speech and your audience as part of a larger public conversation. So this section will help you understand the broader public context of your audience.

As defined in Chapter 1, publics arise out of the common experience of a shared problem. For example, the people whose drinking water is polluted by an industrial polluter form a public, as do the people angered by the lack of choice among news outlets because of reduced competition in the news business. Whether your topic is large or small, local or global, your job as a speaker is to create and address a concerned public.

FAQ *What makes an issue a public issue?*

Private Issue	Public Issue
Tuition bills are putting a drain on my social budget.	It would be better for the university to reduce tuition for all the residents of the state.
I hate cigarette smoke.	The university should ban public smoking for the sake of health of the students, faculty, and staff.
I need to go on a diet.	The state and local governments should work to provide resources and education about healthier eating in schools and universities.

© Cengage Learning

You participate in public conversations in two ways in public speaking class: (1) as a speaker addressing public problems, and (2) as an audience member participating in issues of public concern. Both of these ways of participating in public matters are broader than your specific community. A community is made up of the people who share a common location (they live in the same town) or institution (they work at the same company or go to the same school or church).

In contrast, a public, as American philosopher John Dewey explained, is a set of individuals with a common set of interests because they perceive a common problem.[5] These individuals probably don't know each other personally, and they may never meet, but *if* they were to meet, they would be able to relate to each other on the basis of cost of gasoline, pollution of local lakes and streams, lack of good candidates for state office, or some other topic. For example, people all over the United States are concerned about the future of our safe drinking water supply. Though each of them have their own private needs and perspectives, live in different parts of the country, and have different individual circumstances, they are all united by a shared concern.

TRY IT!

JOINING THE PUBLIC DIALOGUE

One of the goals of public speaking is to give each of us a voice in local and national public dialogues.

- List three factors that limit the access of average citizens to local and national dialogue.
- Which barriers affect you most directly?

Ideas that you present in a speech may influence a member of your audience to blog about them, speak about them to another community, write an editorial, or engage in broader dialogue beyond the classroom in some other way. The point is that your participation in the great conversation around public ideas extends beyond your specific community, because your ideas, if persuasive, may carry beyond your speaking situation.

Diverse groups of citizens can be united by their common concerns.

Make brief lists for each of the following:

- What problems most affect your daily life?
- What problems do you think present the biggest challenge for your future?
- What problems most affect the daily lives of your friends and family?
- What problems present the biggest challenges for your friends' and family's future?
- What problems most affect the daily lives or futures of all people in the United States?

In what ways were your answers to each of these questions similar? In what ways were they different? What does this tell you about the big "public" problems? Which ones should we be most concerned about? What can we do about them?

Advancing the Public Conversation

Speaking to a public means speaking in a dialogue to a group of people whom you treat as reasonable, interested, and engaged partners. In speaking to a public, you are speaking to your audience about an issue of common concern, using a common vocabulary. This means speaking in a way in which all the players in the dialogue can have meaningful input regardless of their age, gender, sexual orientation, religion, race, or class.

In a successful public speech, the speaker and audience are on the same side. You are both the "us" discussed earlier in this chapter. The "public" in public speaking means that you establish commonalities with people you may not know personally. When you look at an audience of strangers, you don't have to panic because you don't what their personal beliefs and values are. That doesn't matter to a *public* speaker. Instead, a public speaker will ask these questions:

- What public, exactly, should listen?
- Why should this public listen?
- What common goals might we share in speaking and listening to each other?

YOUR ETHICAL RESPONSIBILITIES TO YOUR AUDIENCE

Because your speaking choices define the character of your audience and the way it engages with your topic, you have a responsibility for the connections you are inviting the audience to make. Does your speech invite the audience to understand issues in a deeper, more nuanced way? Does it lead the audience to value and fairly evaluate the positions of all the relevant participants in the public debate?

Public or Publics?

At one time, you could be pretty sure that the audience for a speech was limited to the people who were sitting in a room and listening to a speaker. But in an ever-expanding media environment, any speech potentially can be heard by more people than are in a room for a speech. Of course, this has been the case for a while. When certain people (political leaders, celebrities, and so on) speak, the speech might be distributed to a broader audience by radio, newspapers, or news media. But now, with the advent of cameras in cell phones, and with easy distribution through social media and YouTube, any speech potentially can have a life that extends beyond its initial delivery.

This has implications for you, because you have to think that what you say or do in any given instance potentially can be seen by anyone from this time forward. This is a fact of modern life, and it has interesting implications for how we think about the idea of the "public" in public speaking.

Borrowing from scholar Michael Warner, we'll call this phenomenon, which allows speeches (or really anything in public life) to have a media-driven life beyond their initial presentation *circulation*. Circulation means that speeches and ideas can go much farther than they did before, at a significantly quicker rate than in the past, and can be seen and heard by audiences that speakers might not have expected.

Because there's so much digital stuff circulating out in the world, we also live in an environment with many more things for people to look at, listen to, and engage with. And in this world, it's harder to predict what people will be looking at, or even to know if these days we share in common many texts, experiences, or ideas. Maybe it doesn't even make sense to talk about one "capital P" Public that has a shared experience. Warner suggests that in this environment it may be more appropriate to talk about lots of little publics all paying attention to their own things rather than to talk about one uniform Public that shares similar tastes and experiences in media.

These little publics come together by paying attention to the issues that interest and engage them. So it makes sense for the modern public speaker to speak as if the "Public" is not just a group of people out there waiting to consume speeches. Instead, individual publics form because people pay attention to a text or an idea, and that text or idea unites them in some small away. For example, a public of fans of your favorite sports teams might read the same blogs and have a shared experience around that practice. Or fans of a gossip blog might form their own public around mutual interest in celebrities. So the question for you is this: What specific public do you think will pay attention to and engage with your ideas?

For more information, check out:

M. Warner, Publics and Counterpublics, *Quarterly Journal of Speech*, 88(4), 2002.

One way to think about why your speaking choices matter to audiences is to presume that *the world we speak comes into existence*. What does that mean? It means that the world can be seen as a collection of smaller individual worlds created by people communicating. The words that people speak in one place can change the way that people think and act in other places. It means that the habits we use in speaking help to create our social context and also affect the way other people respond to us.

TRY IT! **WORDS CREATE WORLDS**

The words we use to describe things make a real difference in how we think about them. Discuss with a small group what difference the following descriptions make in how we think about each of these topics:

- Downsizing vs. firing
- The war on terror vs. the global struggle against violent extremism
- Slacking vs. relaxing
- High fructose corn syrup vs. corn sugar

In the largest sense, *speakers are responsible for the world their choices create*. If you speak in a way that demonstrates a lack of concern for your audiences, deceives them, or aims only for your benefit, they are likely to respond in kind. For instance, in addressing the students and administrators at a university board meeting, you should try to make the best, clearest, and most compelling argument possible. But you also hope that your audience will listen to what you have to say and consider its merits. Indeed, your argument will have the best chance if you also listen carefully and consider other peoples' viewpoints, opinions, and objections. If audience members perceive you as deceptive, manipulative, or self-serving, they will likely respond with resistance, deception, or manipulation. In public speaking, the habits of speaking we develop also imply habits of listening, responding, and being part of a community.

So taking your audience into account is about more than just guessing their predispositions toward a specific topic and saying something interesting. Public speakers are making a difference, no matter how small or large, when they speak in public, to a public. Doctors make a difference to our health and so are bound by the Hippocratic Oath, an ancient ethical code of physicians that includes this promise: "I will prescribe regimens for the good of my patients according to my ability and my judgment, and never do harm to anyone." Likewise, public speakers should "prescribe regimens" for the good of their audiences according to their ability and judgment, trying to avoid harm to anyone.

Some speeches can help audiences by giving them information that they might not have already; some speeches can change people's opinions and possibly their actions; and some have changed the course of history. Because speech is such a powerful tool, you have a responsibility for how you speak. For example, framing a speech about lowering the drinking age in terms of students who die in car crashes creates a different world than a speech framed around the idea that a beer or two isn't going to hurt anyone. Either frame might be effective, but which one is the responsible choice?

Kristoffer Tripplaar/Alamy

In a speech at Columbia University, United Nations Secretary-General Ban Ki Moon galvanized his audience with appeals to universal human values.

Here are two basic tests for whether your choices are responsible in relation to your specific audience and the broader public.

- *First, does your speech create a benefit for everyone,* including you, or is your speech responsible only to your own needs and values? A speech with political implications should benefit you and your fellow citizens.
- *Second, is your speech responsible to your audience and its context?* Answering this question means understanding what arguments will motivate your audience members and allow them to achieve the change you intend. Your speech should give the audience the tools needed to take action on your topic. A speech that argues for getting rid of gravity or figuring out how to go back in time is a detour into fantasy unless the speaker can provide action steps that the audience can take to accomplish these goals.

In the end, these two responsibilities of public speech mean that you'll have to adapt what you say to different contexts and different audiences, as discussed earlier in the chapter. The ways you speak at home with your family, at lunch with a friend, and in front of an audience that you don't know should differ depending on what you are trying to achieve, how you can help the audience achieve this change, and why your audience is listening.

To decide what choices are responsible for a specific speech, ask yourself these questions about your audience:

- What is the best way I can cultivate a relationship with this audience in this context?
- What expectations does this audience have of me?
- What can I expect the members to do with the points I am making in the speech?
- What common goals and ideals can I reference in making my case?
- And, finally, what changes in opinion, belief, or action am I calling for?

The habits you use in addressing audiences will make a difference not only in how they respond to you but also in whether your speech can help shape the public conversation for the better. If you cultivate an ethic of responsible, engaged, well-reasoned speech in your public speaking classroom, you will be developing habits that reach beyond your time in school and encourage others in your class to do the same.

Summary

In a public speaking setting, the audience consists of the people to whom you are communicating and for whom you make the choices that compose your speech. These choices set the tone for your relationship with your audience. This relationship affects how you and your audience will act in the future. Because public speaking is tied so closely to democracy, public speaking provides an opportunity to practice decision making with others. An effective speech not only can teach people about the specific contents that you would like to impart but also can bring the audience and speaker together in thinking about difficult public problems.

As a speaker, you'll consider not only *who* is in your audience and *what* these people will want to hear, but you'll have to decide *how* you want to address them. In other words, you need to know who your literal audience is and who you want your rhetorical audience to become. The "as" test will help you figure out the possible ways you might appeal to your audience—for example, as fellow students, as concerned citizens, or as members of the human race. The choices you make in defining how you want to address your audience determine what you will say to your audience and what ideas you will select and highlight in your speech. To make the most of a public speech, you will have to make careful choices and you must take responsibility for the effects of these choices.

Questions for Review

1. What is an audience, and how is it related to a public?
2. How does engagement influence how you understand an audience?
3. What are the different ways to analyze an audience? What are the strengths and weaknesses of the demographic approach to audience analysis?

Questions for Discussion

1. It's important to think carefully about how to address your audience. What problems do you think require better speaking to solve? How would you address an audience regarding any of the problems you think should have better critical deliberation?
2. Try to think of the last time you were an audience member and you felt manipulated by a speaker (or even an advertisement or an infomercial). What did the speaker do or say that made you feel manipulated? How did it make you feel?
3. How will choices about how to address an audience influence your decisions in putting a speech together—choices about the order of points, possible arguments, and types of evidence?

Key Concepts   MindTap®

Practice defining the chapter's terms by using online flashcards.

"as" test	demographics	rhetorical audience
audience analysis	literal audience	

LEARNING OBJECTIVES

- Distinguish between hearing and listening
- Contrast passive, active, and critical listening and their uses
- Define and explain some of the ethical issues that confront listeners
- Identify obstacles to listening and how to avoid them
- Evaluate which note-taking techniques work best for you
- Develop strategies for giving effective, constructive feedback

CHAPTER OUTLINE

- Introduction: Public Hearing and Listening
- Types of Listening
- The Ethics of Listening
- Obstacles to Good Listening
- Taking Good Notes
- Giving Constructive and Useful Feedback

n class, Tanya is bored. She has trouble paying attention to the many speeches. While other students are speaking, she thinks about her homework for other courses, her work schedule, and her plans for Friday night. She knows that she should be paying more attention because the teacher keeps asking questions after each speech, but Tanya just can't seem to focus. She has noticed that this happens when she's listening to teachers in her other classes, too. She wishes she knew how to listen better.

MindTap®

Start with a warm-up activity about listening and review the chapter Learning Objectives.

Overview

If public speaking is a conversation between a speaker and an audience, "public listening" is every bit as important as "public speaking." In this chapter you will find out how you can be a more active, engaged, and critical listener. We'll start by distinguishing between simply *hearing* a speech and *listening* to a speech—which entails not only hearing but also actively engaging and attempting to understand the content of the speech. To further define good listening practices, we discuss the differences between passive, active, and critical listening. Because listening is one-half of the process of a public conversation, we also address the ethics of listening, which entails a set of practices and prescriptions about how you should think about listening. Finally, we will discuss the some of the most important impediments to good listening and a number of practices that can enhance your listening experience, including taking notes and giving feedback.

INTRODUCTION: PUBLIC HEARING AND LISTENING

You can't control whether the speeches you have to listen to in the public speaking classroom or beyond are intrinsically interesting to you, but you can control how you choose to engage with them. So what can you do to be a better and more engaged listener?

The answer begins with the difference between listening and hearing. Sometimes as an audience member you may hear a speech, but you are not truly listening to it. You may register individual words and sentences, but you are not thinking about what you are hearing, and you

MindTap®

Read, highlight, and take notes online.

retain little of the speech the moment that it is finished. And then there are times when you hear a speech and truly listen to it—that is, you engage the ideas in the speech; you actively think about the concepts; and you have paid enough attention to have good recall.

We can *hear* a speech in another language, but we can't *listen* to it because we don't know the language. Hearing is just the act of receiving the sounds; listening is actively processing what you're hearing. If you can't *hear* a speaker, you can move closer or ask him or her to speak up. If you are having trouble *listening*, the techniques in this chapter will help you.

As an audience member, you need to know how to listen actively and critically, engaging with the speaker's message. As a speaker, you also need to know about listening, because you are trying to get people to listen to you or help them listen to you in the most productive way. The more you know about what makes messages easy or difficult to listen to, the better you will be prepared to engage with your audiences.

TYPES OF LISTENING

There's no one best way of listening. What's "good" in listening depends on what you're trying to accomplish, what you want to learn from the speaker, and what you think the speaker wants from you. We'll talk more about these factors and their part in good listening, but first, what are your choices of listening styles?

Passive Listening

passive listening Listening that does not actively engage the ideas and arguments of the speaker.

Passive listening is listening that doesn't actively engage the speaker's ideas and arguments. It makes you a bit like a sponge: You're merely attending to what's coming from the speaker and not thinking much about it; it runs across your mind like rainwater across the roof. You're not analyzing it, questioning it, applying it to yourself, or making an effort to remember it.

Passive listening is what most of us do when we're watching television or a movie. We just let the experience happen, with the words and ideas washing over us and leaving whatever traces they may while our brain goes into neutral. Entertainment media don't ask for your engagement, but a speaker does, because, at its best, public speaking is a dialogue between speaker and audience. Passive listening is like zoning out in a conversation.

Passive listening be a bit rude to a speaker, and it probably won't produce a great experience for you either. If you expect a speaker to grab your attention and hold your interest no matter how little effort *you* make, you'll probably be disappointed and bored. You probably won't be able to produce meaningful questions and take up your end of the larger conversation.

> **TRY IT!** **YOUR PASSIVE LISTENING PROFILE**
>
> List the top three situations in which you are a passive listener. What are the consequences of passive listening in these situations? How do you feel about these outcomes? How hard would it be to change this habit?

Active Listening

active listening Listening attentively for the meaning and relevance of the speech.

Active listeners aren't waiting for the speaker to make sense—they actively seek to make sense out of what they hear. **Active listening** seeks the meaning and the relevance of what's being said. Suppose a speech is about concealed carry laws, which regulate carrying a gun in your pocket in public places. An active listener will be thinking, "Why does this person care about guns? Gun laws? Why do I care?"

Meaning includes not only the topic but also the speaker's frame or position. *Relevance* is the connection between your interests and the speaker's interests, and you can listen to see how much those converge.

YOUR PERSONAL ACTIVE LISTENING CHALLENGES   TRY IT!

List three situations in which you have the most trouble being an active listener. For each one, say *why* active listening is hard for you. What could you to do to improve your listening in these situations?

We listen to a speech in real time: We can't stop it, slow it down, or rewind. That means that the speaker and audience will have to work together for the speech to make sense. Speakers have the responsibility to provide enough organizational structure that the audience has a chance of following their ideas and line of reasoning. The audience's responsibility is to pay enough attention to put the pieces together, to make something meaningful out of what the speaker is saying.

Making sense out of a speech takes some work. Most of us benefit from either taking notes (which forces you to create a structure for what's being said) or making mental summaries of what you hear ("OK, the first point was about the history of gun laws, and so now the second point is about current law"). Active listeners typically find speeches more interesting than passive listeners do, because a speech that makes sense—that *you* help make sense of—is always more engaging than a speech that just washes over you. Table 4.1 summarizes the differences between active and passive listening.

Critical Listening

Critical listening goes a step beyond active listening. **Critical listening** means listening with the goal of evaluating what is said in addition to listening actively for meaning and relevance. An evaluation is different from a preference. If you like your hamburgers with ketchup but not mustard, or movies with action over ones with romance, that's a *preference*. But if you're *critically evaluating* a burger or a movie, you're applying the standards that are appropriate in the context regardless of your personal preferences. "This kind of movie is not to my taste, but it's very well done on its own terms" is an example of critical evaluation.

The same strategy applies to a speech. Critical listeners listen for what's good and bad about the speech and don't let their evaluation be affected by their personal opinion of the speaker or the subject. Critical listeners ask themselves whether the speech is effective or ineffective, whether its arguments are strong or weak, whether its supporting evidence is relevant or irrelevant, and whether its conclusions are logical or illogical. A critical listener always asks why the information in a speech is true and how we could confirm that it is true.

critical listening Listening to evaluate what is well done and poorly done in a speech.

Table 4.1   Active vs. Passive Listening

Active Listeners	Passive Listeners
Engage what the speaker is saying, thinking about the meaning and relevance of the claims	Just take things in, not really paying attention to specifics
Pay attention to where the speaker is going, and put the pieces together by taking notes or making mental summaries	Don't reflect on the content of the speech
Think of lots of questions	Don't think of questions

British author and former nun Karen Armstrong asks audiences to think critically and listen respectfully about religious differences in speeches about her Charter for Compassion project. Why is religion an especially difficult topic about which to listen?

Jeff Morgan 02/Alamy

In sum, these are the qualities of critical listeners:

1. They *think* about whether the speaker has produced appropriate evidence to justify the claims in the speech.
2. They *ask* themselves about what the speaker is *not* saying and what topics or information the speaker is avoiding.
3. They *appreciate* a well-organized, logical argument.
4. They *sort* through relevant and irrelevant parts of a speech and focus closely on the relevant parts.
5. They *assess* the strong points of a speech, and say so, but they also offer constructive criticism about the weak points.

Passive, active, and critical listeners differ in the kind of feedback they give:

- Passive listeners usually say only something about themselves, such as "I felt like it was interesting" or "It held my attention."
- Active listeners are able to say something descriptive about the speech, such as "Here's what I heard you say in your speech" or "These seemed to be your main arguments."
- Critical listeners are able to say something evaluative about the speech, such as "Here's the point that worked best," "This is where your arguments were least persuasive" or "A metaphor could have made your point clearer."

THE ETHICS OF LISTENING

The choice to be a good listener has a necessary ethical component. As an audience member, you have an ethical and a civic obligation to listen carefully and critically. First, you have an obligation based on creating a reciprocal relationship—that is, as we discussed in Chapter 2,

Fred "Mr." Rogers, spoke often at college graduations, and his speeches embodied, for his audiences, an ethic of gentleness and dialogue. Do you think that people can be taught, from an early age, to listen ethically?

a relationship that goes both ways. Ethically, you have responsibility to match the speaker's effort with equal effort in listening; your willingness to listen shows respect for the speaker.

You also have an obligation to listen as you would expect to be listened to. If public conversation is a grand dialogue in which everyone gets a turn, it's important to make each speaker's turn count by paying attention to a speech as you would like to be paid attention to. Just as everyone should get a chance to speak, so, too, should everybody be a good listener.[1]

In previous chapters we discussed the dialogic aspects of public speaking; rather than being a one-time event, a speech is a special type of ongoing conversation in which only one person speaks at a time. Your speech responds to things others have said (you may even refer to them in your speech), and you expect others to respond to you by asking questions and giving you solid feedback. As a turn in an ongoing conversation or dialogue, a speech will be effective only if the audience is listening critically enough to be able to respond.

The ethical components of listening not only include being an active and engaged listener, but also include a set of concrete considerations. The following behaviors allow you to both listen and improve the environment for the whole audience to pay attention:

- *Be ready to listen.* You need to be fully mentally present to the moment of speaking, so you should avoid thinking about other things or performing other tasks (such as reading, doing homework, or texting) while the speaker is preparing to speak.
- *Visibly pay attention.* Your actions create a positive cue for the speaker when you are paying attention, and they create a negative cue when you are visibly distracted. Paying visible attention (eyes on the speaker, pleasant facial expression, taking notes, not fidgeting too much or playing with technology) can affect a speaker's ability to

Public forums, such as this board of education meeting, can be challenging communication situations. They require participants to think hard about how to balance their need to speak with their responsibilities to other speakers.

RosalreneBetancourt 2/Alamy

give the best speech he or she can. In addition, if you look bored or disengaged, other members of the audience might decide to tune out, too. But if you look interested, that signals to your fellow audience members that the speech is worth listening to.

Eliminate potential distractions for yourself and others. This means doing some obvious things, such as not talking during the speech, turning off your cell phone, not using your computer for non-speech-related activities (such as watching videos, poking your friends on social media sites, instant messaging). This also includes more subtle distractions such as preparing for your own speech or loudly shuffling notes.

- *Respect the forum.* Because public speaking can turn a classroom into a participatory, democratic forum for the exchange of ideas, your behavior should show respect for the nature of the forum. You should show up on time or wait to enter the room if you are late and someone is already speaking. If you have to leave early, you should excuse yourself between speeches. Making faces or noises to indicate your disagreement while the speaker is talking reduces the atmosphere of mutual respect that's needed for a forum to function as a dialogue.

- *Practice good turn-taking.* Do whatever you can to respect the time in the public speaking classroom. If you're next up to speak, move to the front of the room as efficiently as possible. If there's feedback time, raise your hand and wait to be recognized. Then make your point and move on, allowing the speaker to respond and leaving time for others to give comments. Just as speakers should stay within their allotted time, audience members should make their questions or feedback concise.

Ethical listening strategies are crucial not only to the public speaking classroom but also to an ethically robust civic and community life. One common gripe about modern life is that people don't really listen to each other anymore. On many notable public issues, we find passionate advocates for all sides of a cause who can make their case effectively but who do not do a particularly good job of paying attention to the arguments of people on the other side. We may hear others, but we often do so only for the sake of lining up our counterarguments before we have truly listened to the logic of another person's claims. Ethical listening means listening with an open mind, attempting to give the most charitable reading possible of what others are saying, and giving them the benefit of the doubt before arguing with them.

Enhancing your skill in listening has two significant benefits for you as a member of the public. First, it will allow you to listen carefully to the arguments of people whom you do not agree with, which either may change your mind or at least make you a better advocate for your causes. Second, it will make you better at listening for the quality of arguments, the soundness of evidence, and the strengths and shortcomings of various positions on difficult public issues. Thus, the listening skills that you hone in the public speaking classroom will make you a more competent citizen and member of the general public.

OBSTACLES TO GOOD LISTENING

Listening is hard work. Not only do you need to listen actively, critically, and with an open mind and to be courteous, but you also have to deal with external and internal obstacles.

Distractions

You're ready. Paper out, pen in hand. Mind clear and focused on the speech that's about to start, on which you know you'll have to give comments. And then a huge truck rolls by outside the classroom. Next, you hear a little clicking sound and see that the person next to you has a phone out, under the desk, and is texting. Wait, do you smell something? What is it? It must be the worst cologne ever. And then . . . you realize that you've missed the introduction to the speech.

Distractions make it hard to listen because we're paying attention them instead of the speaker's words. Some distractions are built into the setting. You may be too far back to see or hear the speaker clearly. Perhaps the room is too hot or too cold.

Outside distractions of all kinds are often referred to as "noise," and sometimes they are literal noise—nothing is as annoying as a jackhammer in the background. Or someone near you is snapping gum. Or the visuals may have too much information or too-small text, and in the effort to see them, you may forget to listen.

In these situations, it takes an effort of will to pull yourself back into the moment and begin to listen actively. What will help you focus? Certainly note-taking is one way. (We'll discuss note-taking strategies shortly.) Sometimes it also helps to acknowledge silently to yourself, "That jackhammer is really annoying," and then redirect your attention to the speaker.

distractions Obstacles to paying full attention to a speech.

DISTRACTION AWARENESS TRY IT!

Make a list of what's distracting you right now, as you're reading, whether it's in the environment or in your head—or in your headphones. How long is that list? What could you do to shorten it?

Another kind of distraction consists of stereotypes, which are like a kind of noise in our head that makes hard to listen carefully to someone. As we pointed out in Chapter 3, stereotypes are generalizations based on a single dimension of the person, such as age, gender, race, religion, or job.

> He's talking about legalizing marijuana—he's just a pothead.
> She's speaking about sexual harassment. Because she's a woman, she must have been a victim of it.
> He's too old to "get" video games.

MindTap®
Watch a video, and do an interactive activity.

Such stereotypes imply that people "like that" are all alike. If you assume, for example, that all Asian students are math nerds, you may have difficulty actively and critically listening to an Asian student's speech about the current art scene at your school.

Of course, most of us have been taught the limits and unfairness of stereotypes, but we tend to stereotype people anyway. So, as listeners, we have to be alert to whether we are stereotyping. This means being aware of the assumptions you're making as you listen. In a sense, this means you have to listen critically to your own listening, questioning whether you are being fair to the speaker and the material.

A third kind of distraction is more subtle but perhaps easier to control. Your focus may drift a bit from listening to the content of a speech, and you may find yourself focusing on some aspect of the speaker. This is natural. The speaker might be attractive or not, charismatic or not, dressed conventionally or oddly—"Look at that tattoo!"—and we can't help but notice. We all focus at times on qualities of speakers that we do or don't like.

Although outstanding delivery or a pleasing appearance is certainly an asset, for the active or critical listener, it plays only a supporting role and shouldn't become a distraction. Sometimes when the delivery is notably dramatic and engaging, audience members will be so caught up in it that they have trouble listening to what actually is being said. This is why some people are suspicious of elaborate, theatrical delivery: They fear that it will lead them away from critical listening.

Sometimes audience members will be distracted by what they see as mistakes or errors in delivery: poor posture, mispronunciations, a slight speech impediment, or small stumbles over words. As active and critical listeners, we have the responsibility to do our best to listen past these things for the content of the speech. If we're actively engaged as listeners, we realize that the point of the person's speaking is not to present a perfect appearance or delivery but to share ideas and arguments. The kinds of flaws that matter include those we discussed in Chapter 2, such as bias in the presentation of evidence and unethical appeals.

Your Mental Zone

A final set of obstacles comes from inside you and is not related to the speaker. The first happens when you aren't "in the moment." You might be thinking about problems at home or at work, worrying about an exam or a paper that's due, or anticipating an upcoming party. And then there's the habit of always wondering if you have any new text messages or an update on a social media site. But if you're thinking about these things, you're not really in a position to listen actively and critically. To redirect your thoughts, try admitting to yourself that you have something on your mind and acknowledge that you should make time to think about it later. Then turn your attention back to the speaker so you will miss as little as possible.

A second internal obstacle to good listening can be your preconceptions about the topic—for instance, "yoga is boring" or "gun laws are stupid." To listen critically, you have to set aside your existing ideas about the speaker or the topic. After all, a person who's been boring or illogical in the past might be really interesting and logical today. Whether you like someone won't help you critically evaluate what he or she is saying in a speech.

You have to try to be open to what's being said in this specific speech. Being open means being willing to try on ideas, like a piece of clothing, to see if they might "fit" with your beliefs and values. You can ask yourself, "OK, what would I be giving up if I were to accept what the speaker is saying as valid?" Maybe you've always identified yourself as someone who dislikes conservatives. But this speech advocates a "conservative" idea. Can you listen in a way that allows you to evaluate its merits independently of whether it's conservative or not? Being open requires an active effort to put aside, or bracket, your preconceptions for the time you're listening. In the end, of course, as a critical listener, you'll make a critical evaluation what was said, and you may end up rejecting it or deciding to think about it more, and in either case you gave it a fair chance.

Why is it hard to talk frankly about yourself to a group of people?

Wavebreak Media LTD/Alloy/Corbis

A third challenge to your focus is internal objections, or the "yabbut" problem. Sometimes, when we really disagree with a topic or argument, we mentally object to every point the speaker makes, thinking "Yeah, but…" and generating a counterargument. In a sense, this is good, because it indicates our critical engagement with the speaker. But if we spend too much time doing mental refutations, we may miss some of what the speaker is saying. The mental noise we generate is simply too loud to allow us to focus on the speaker, and we risk misunderstanding the arguments and refuting the wrong things. The solution in this case is to refocus on the speaker and on note-taking. You also could use an asterisk or other special symbol in your notes to mark points where you think the speaker went wrong. The symbol will help you locate the points you want to ask questions about after the speech.

TAKING GOOD NOTES

Note-taking is a key tool of active and critical listening. The best listeners are often good note-takers, whether their notes are on paper (or screen) or in their heads. Why? Taking notes is a way of translating the words being said into ideas. To translate, you have to pay careful attention not just to words but also to their meaning and context. For example, the word *fair* can mean dividing things equally (everyone gets the same amount) or proportionately (each person gets a different amount according to a rule or principle such as seniority or need). If a speaker says the word *fair*, as a note-taker you have to decide, based on what you're hearing, which meaning is appropriate, because that will determine what you write in your notes.

Taking good notes is a crucial skill for students, and for everybody else. When words go in your ears and out your hands, you understand and remember them better. Yet, note-taking can be a little mysterious—What are you going to write down? Everything? Just an outline? Key words? How will you decide what to write or skip?

Most note-takers use one or a combination of the following techniques to record the speaker's main points and show their relationship and the structure of the speech:

FAQ *If have a good memory, do I need to take notes?*

Yes. Although notes do help you remember, they do more than that. They are your on-the-spot interpretation of what the speaker means, so they help you to be a critical listener.

FIGURE 4.1
Outline Style Notes

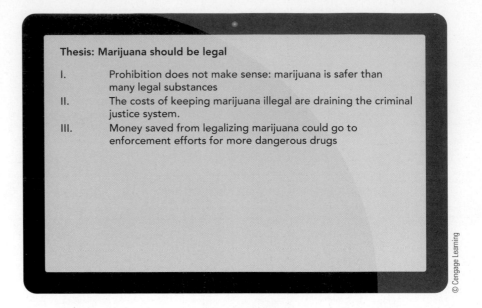

Thesis: Marijuana should be legal

I.   Prohibition does not make sense: marijuana is safer than many legal substances

II.   The costs of keeping marijuana illegal are draining the criminal justice system.

III.   Money saved from legalizing marijuana could go to enforcement efforts for more dangerous drugs

© Cengage Learning

- *Make an outline* (Figure 4.1). As you'll see in Chapter 6, speakers should provide verbal signals—such as *first, next,* and *finally*—and transitions—such as *in addition* and *in contrast*—indicating the structure of their speeches. Speakers also usually identify their thesis, or main point, and use previews and reviews of their arguments. These will help you make an outline with your notes.
- *Indicate the relationship between ideas with arrows and lines.* For instance, when the speaker says, "Here's my second reason for advocating gun control," you'll know that

Dr. Hans Rosling, a Swedish doctor and public health advocate, uses slides to make his information clear. Concise, high-contrast visuals such as the ones accompanying his speech at a recent TED conference make it easy for listeners to take notes.

AP Images/Sipa

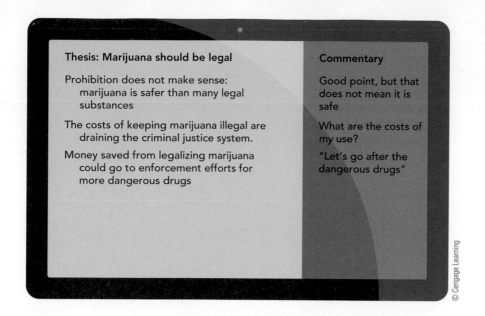

FIGURE 4.2
Cornell Style Notes

this is the second main argument the speaker is making, and the first one is finished. So you can mark your notes accordingly, perhaps by drawing a line across and starting a new section. Phrases such as "in other words" and "for example" signal descriptive material that illustrates a point the speaker has just made. You could use an arrow to indicate the relationship.

- *Comment on the concepts and arguments in the speech with the two-column Cornell System* (Figure 4.2). On the left side of the page, record the flow, or structure, of the speech, and on the right you can put key words, questions, and comments.
- Use a concept map or an idea cloud to diagram connections among concepts or arguments (Figure 4.3). Because speeches are linear, this may not be the best way to capture a speech, but it works well for some people. To make a concept map, start by writing down the speaker's main ideas or concepts (from the thesis and the preview in the speech's introduction). Put those roughly in the center of a piece of paper, with circles around them. Then, in the course of the speech, you can create additional nodes for their subpoints. You can draw lines between the different circles to indicate relationships between the speaker's points.

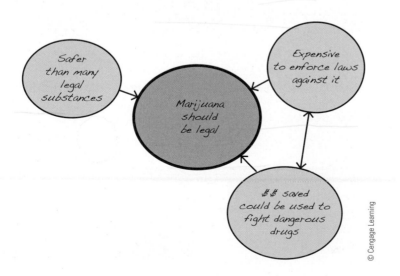

FIGURE 4.3
Concept Map

Taking Notes

Every note-taker develops a personal system, which takes into account some practical concerns:

- If you write too much, you'll fall behind the speaker; if you write too little, it won't be useful to you later.
- Most people find that abbreviating common words works well, in the way you would do when texting, such as *bc* for *because* and *btwn* for *between*. The abbreviations used in texting are familiar and useful to many people.
- If an unfamiliar and difficult word comes up, write an abbreviation and the definition next to it the first time you write it down, such as "chthonic = © = underground." Then every time you see © in that set of notes, you know it refers to that word. But if you can't figure out your abbreviations later, then you'll have cryptic notes that you can't use.
- Should you take notes on paper or on your laptop? Research by Pam Mueller and Daniel Oppenheimer (*Psychological Science*, June 2014, *25*: 1159–1168) suggests that taking notes on a keyboard results in "shallower processing," meaning less intellectual engagement with the materials, translating into reduced understanding and memory. Laptop or tablet notes are still worthwhile, but good old pen and paper may be the gold standard.

GIVING CONSTRUCTIVE AND USEFUL FEEDBACK

critical feedback A substantiated opinion about what worked and what didn't work in a speech.

constructive criticism Specific feedback about strengths and weaknesses, with specific suggestions for improvement.

In public speaking class, you'll be giving feedback to other speakers as a listener and an audience member, and you'll be getting feedback from your audience as a speaker. This is known as **critical feedback**, your argued opinion about what worked and didn't in a speech. Everyone needs this kind of feedback to improve as a speaker; if no one tells you what's working and what isn't, you can't grow in sophistication and effectiveness. But even **constructive criticism**—criticism that is well thought-out and useful—is still hard to hear.

How would you complete the following sentences?

When I am criticized, I feel…
When I am criticized, I often think …
When I am criticized, I tend to react by …

Are your reactions less than positive? You're not alone. Even criticism that we know is legitimate can provoke negative feelings. Keeping in mind that other people feel the same way as you do about criticism can help you deliver constructive criticism to *others* in a way that it will be heard, and it can help you hear criticism of *yourself* and take away something useful from it.

Unrealistic assumptions sometimes can act as a filter and transform criticism—valid or not—into negative feelings that prevent us from responding positively and learning how to improve. These assumptions include the following:

- Everyone should like me.
- People who criticize me don't like me.

FAQ *I dislike critical people. Why do I have to be one?*

The word *critical* often means being negative to someone personally. We are using it in a more positive sense here, referring to feedback that contains enough analysis so recipients can understand what they did well and where they could improve. The speaker's best friend is someone who takes the time to separate strengths from weaknesses—and talk about both.

Many of us don't like to see hands go up for questions. Do we have a responsibility to answer questions?

- I don't make mistakes.
- Criticizing my work demeans me as person.

If your instructor says, "Please rewrite this paper and edit more carefully," but you hear "You're a horrible writer," you probably won't be motivated to write an improved paper even if the teacher's criticism is reasonable.

Be aware of your reactions to criticism of your speeches. Try to keep your feelings and spontaneous reactions under control until you've reflected impartially on the feedback and consciously *decided* which elements are appropriate and useful. This isn't easy, but it's a skill that does get better with practice.

Because you're in a position to evaluate speeches critically, as a good listener you can help other speakers improve—just as they can help you. To play this role, you have to be able to give feedback, positive and negative, that speakers can really use.

Four tips for giving feedback the speaker can use are:

1. Criticize speeches, not people.
2. Be specific.

People at Occupy Wall Street rallies used hand signals to give feedback to speakers.

3. Focus on what can be changed.
4. Be communication-sensitive.

We'll discuss each of these tips in turn.

Criticize Speeches, Not People

Just as a good teacher does, you should be criticizing or praising only *this* specific speech or *this* performance, not the person giving it. Many students want to say after a speech, "She was good." There's no question that it's great to get personal encouragement from audience members, and you shouldn't hesitate to give it ("I really enjoyed your speech, Kim"). But that isn't critical feedback.

To be useful to the speaker, you should say *why* the speech was good:

Your introduction was really effective because it made the information concrete.

The same goes for weak or ineffective speeches:

I found the transition to point 2 unclear and confusing.

Make sure that you don't say things about the speech as if they were about the person. Saying "That speech was lame" doesn't help the speaker at all, and it might seem insulting and distract the speaker from other feedback that would improve future speeches.

Be Specific

"That was boring" isn't specific enough to allow for improvement. It's better to think about *why* it was boring and give those reasons without using the insulting label "boring."

Try to identify the specific part of the speech you want to give feedback about:

I thought your evidence in point 2 was especially strong because the sources were clear and familiar. But point 3 really wasn't convincing because I couldn't follow the connections between the evidence and your claims.

The extent to which you can be specific usually reflects the amount of thought you've put into the feedback, and speakers will take the most thoughtful and detailed criticism the most seriously. Even praise isn't useful if it's too general.

Focus on What Can Be Changed

Make sure that what you're criticizing is something the person can actually change. It's pointless, for example, to critique someone for speaking English with an accent. Similarly, if the topic was assigned, the speaker didn't choose it, so no use criticizing it.

But the speaker did choose how to develop and organize the speech. If you want your criticism to be useful, try to provide specific ideas about how the speech could have been developed or written differently. It's helpful to encourage speakers to revisit their choices.

If you're listening and taking notes carefully, you often can identify one or two central choices that, if changed, would improve the speech. For example, the speaker might have been assigned the topic "crime on campus." The biggest choice in a speech with this assigned topic is probably going to be between talking about crime in abstract, statistical terms and talking about crime in personal, specific terms. This is a core choice about how to frame the speech and how it's going to relate to the audience. So as an audience member, it's less helpful to say, "Wow, crime is really boring," than to say,

It seemed like your choice to approach the topic abstractly made it hard for the audience to connect to it and get interested in it.

Be Communication Sensitive

Sometimes the way a critique is phrased can make a difference in whether the speaker takes it seriously. Wording and tone can suggest you're stating a fact rather than your opinion. For example, "This speech was under-researched" can come across as harsh. You can correct for this by remembering that your critical reaction to the speech is *your* reaction; it is not a fact, and therefore it is debatable.

Incorporating **I statements**, such as "I feel" or "It seemed to me," can soften your critique for the speaker, and they also show you acknowledge that other listeners, including the speaker, may legitimately disagree with you. So you can make the point that the speech was under-researched with I statements such as these:

> I wondered whether adding more research would have strengthened your argument overall, especially in point 2.
> It seemed as if the second point was much shorter than the others, and I wondered how much stronger the speech would be if it were better developed.

Finally, remember that it's usually more effective to balance positive and negative feedback so your critique doesn't seems like an endless list of "wrong…wrong…wrong." Constructive criticism not only should describe how improvements can be made but also point out what worked well.

> I thought the introduction did an excellent job of catching our attention by focusing on a famous case of government waste.

I statements Judgments (criticism and praise) phrased in terms of "I" rather than "you."

Summary

Learning to listen is just as important to developing your skill as a public speaker as learning to put together good arguments and eloquent phrases. Developing your skill in listening is important because it helps you to be a better audience member. By conquering distractions and learning to listen actively and critically, you can learn a lot about good speaking from paying attention to and dissecting the choices of other speakers. Effective note-taking makes listening more effective. If you listen closely, you'll have a better grasp of the choices that speakers make, and you can give a better assessment of the strengths and weaknesses of their choices than if you weren't paying attention. In addition, your constructive feedback and criticism can help others improve. Every speech, whether you're somewhat bored or totally engaged, is a new opportunity to learn something about right and wrong ways to give a public speech.

MindTap®

Reflect, personalize and apply what you've learned with a Speech Simulation.

Questions for Review

1. What is the difference between hearing and listening?
2. What are the different kinds of listening—passive, active, and critical? What kinds of things does a listener do when listening passively, when listening actively, and when listening critically?
3. What distractions or challenges get in the way of good listening practices?
4. What are some ways of taking effective notes?
5. What techniques make feedback effective? What makes feedback ineffective?

Questions for Discussion

1. Why is good listening an important skill for being a better public speaker? How might skill in listening translate to your effectiveness as a citizen or as a member of your community?
2. What kinds of feedback are most important to you? What makes you likely to take feedback seriously? What makes you ignore feedback?
3. Is it ever good to be a passive listener? Why or why not? Use examples to prove your point.
4. Find the video of a speech online. It might be a commencement address by Fred Rogers ("Mr. Rogers"), a presidential speech, or one of the examples on the site that goes with this book. Listen to it once, straight through; then listen to it again while taking notes. How different was your experience? Did you "hear" the same speech the second time, or a different one?

Key Concepts   MindTap®

Practice defining the chapter's terms by using online flashcards.

active listening	critical listening	I statements
constructive criticism	distractions	passive listening
critical feedback		

PART 2 CREATING A GREAT SPEECH

CHAPTER **5** Topic and Purpose

CHAPTER **6** Research

CHAPTER **7** Organization

DrAfter123/Getty Images

5 TOPIC AND PURPOSE

Roberto Westbrook/Getty Images

LEARNING OBJECTIVES

- Differentiate topic, purpose, and thesis statement
- Analyze topic selection from the perspective of the audience, the speaker, and the occasion
- Construct specific speech topics from general topic areas
- Compose general and specific purposes for your speeches
- Draft thesis statements

CHAPTER OUTLINE

- **Introduction: Picking a Topic and Defining Your Purpose**
- **A Strategy for Picking a Topic**
- **Finding a Topic Among Your Interests**
- **How to Focus Your Topic for Your Audience**
- **Speaking Purposes and Speaking Situations**
- **The Thesis Statement: Putting Your Topic and Purpose into Words**

Adam has been thinking a lot about a concept he learned in another course—*cyberbullying*. It seems important to him, and relevant to his friends' experiences. But would it make a good speech topic? What makes a good speech topic anyway? Is a topic good because everyone already knows about it—or because they don't? Should it be interesting to the speaker—or to the audience? Adam has to figure out if the topic of cyberbullying is going to work for his speech class.

Overview

One of the most important choices in composing and delivering any speech is the topic you would like to talk about. But choosing a subject is not all there is to it. An effective public speech requires that you decide what you would like to achieve by presenting your topic in front of a specific audience, the purpose for your speech. These two elements, your topic and your purpose, are the starting point for your relationship with the audience and for the choices you'll have to make to best achieve your goals in the speech. In this chapter we'll cover strategies for finding a topic and coordinating it with the purpose of the speech, whether to inform, to persuade, or to mark a special occasion. If you understand your speech as a part of an ongoing public conversation, picking a topic and a purpose can be both straightforward and rewarding as long as you consider your interests, the interests of the audience, and the demands of the specific speaking situation. Finally, we will discuss how to craft a thesis statement that captures the essence of your speech.

© 2017 Cengage Learning

MindTap®

Start with a warm-up activity about Adam's speech, and review the chapter's Learning Objectives.

INTRODUCTION: PICKING A TOPIC AND DEFINING YOUR PURPOSE

A public speech is built out of specific choices. Some choices are small—the merits of one word versus another. Other choices are bigger, including how you will organize your speech and decide the best way to make your overarching argument. But the first choice you have to

MindTap®

Read, highlight, and take notes online.

topic The subject of a speech focused to fit the audience, the purpose, and the situation.

make is what to talk about, your **topic** All of your other choices in composing and delivering a speech flow from this primary choice.

The strategy for picking a topic that we lay out in this chapter consists of two basic choices. The first choice is selecting a topic that works for you, your audience, and the specific occasion. The second choice is deciding how to narrow that topic to a specific purpose and create a thesis statement reflecting that topic and purpose.

A STRATEGY FOR PICKING A TOPIC

Picking a topic may be easy if you're intensely interested in one or more issues. In that case, your challenge may be to decide which topic to pick. Other times, you may not know exactly what you would like to talk about. In both cases, the advice is the same: You need a strategy for topic selection. An effective topic choice requires a bit more work than just deciding on a whim that you would like to talk about a topic currently of interest to you, or surrender to the idea that you find the least boring.

Picking a topic requires that you coordinate three important considerations, drawing on some of the concepts about audience that we introduced in Chapter 3—in particular, the ideas of audience, public, and adaptation. A good speaker understands the audience in relation to a public, which defines a set of interests, and then adapts the speech to those interests. The three considerations for selecting a topic are your interests, the interests and needs of the audience, and the nature of the occasion or speaking situation.

1. *Your interests:* Decide what is important to you. What do you spend your time thinking about? What are you passionate about, or at least interested in talking about and researching?

2. *Your audience's needs and interests:* What do you imagine would interest your audience about a given topic? What does your audience need to hear about the topic, and what information or persuasive claims would be useful?

When James Franco is speaking at his own roast, how much freedom does he have in choosing a topic?

FIGURE 5.1
The Three Considerations in
Topic Choice

Your interests

The occasion or speaking situation

The interests and needs of the audience

© 2014 Cengage Learning

3. ***The specific occasion or speaking situation:*** What is the occasion for the speech? Why is the audience gathered to listen to you, and what kinds of content and style do you think is expected of you?

These three considerations can provide a rubric for choosing a topic, and they will remain helpful as you move to defining the purpose of your speech.

The best topics are found where your interests, the interests and needs of the audience, and the demands of the occasion overlap (see Figure 5.1). If you ignore any of these three considerations, the quality of your speech may suffer. For example, if you're talking about something that your audience is interested in and is appropriate for the occasion but you're uninterested in the topic, you're unlikely to speak with energy and conviction, and you're unlikely to be motivated to do the work of researching and composing an effective speech. If you're talking about something that interests you (suppose you like to talk about term versus permanent life insurance) and is appropriate for the occasion (an informative speech) but is uninteresting to your audience, you are unlikely to keep your audience for very long. Finally, if you're talking about something that is of interest to you and your audience ("Is dubstep annoying or awesome?") but that is not appropriate to the occasion, you are unlikely to give a successful speech.

MindTap®

Watch a video, and do an interactive activity.

© 2017 Cengage Learning

What Interests You?

The first consideration is what topics interest you. If a list doesn't immediately jump to mind, you might think about markers of your interest. What kinds of TV programs and movies tend to draw your attention? Can you recognize any consistent themes? When you read or browse the Web, what are the usual subjects? Do you have hobbies or activities at work or outside of the classroom that you would like to share with an audience? Even seemingly small interests can make an interesting speech topic.

Say, for example, that you are one of the millions who really like cooking and cooking shows. You don't have to give an informative speech on how to cook a perfect egg to make use of this interest. You could take up issues of good nutrition or trends in food and eating. You could talk about the implications of agricultural subsidies, or you could make the case for eating locally. If you are careful and creative in thinking about your interests, you're likely to discover a range of potential topics that interest you. A little later in the chapter, we'll offer a number of ways to find a speech topic among your interests.

What Will Interest Your Audience?

You also should think about the interests and needs of your audience. Instead of asking yourself, "What am *I* going to do with this speech?" it's better to ask, "What are *we* going to do with this speech?" In earlier chapters, we've discussed public speaking as conversation, and here's just one way where that approach begins to pays off. When you've identified some topic areas of interest to you, ask yourself these questions about your audience:

- What would the audience be interested in, or could be convinced to be interested in, on the basis of the topic's impact on the audience as a group?
- What does your audience need to hear? What aspect of the general topic area should the audience be informed or persuaded about?

In other words, the more fully you are able to put yourself in your audience's shoes, the more effective your choice of topic and purpose will be.

In Chapter 3, we discussed audiences and speakers as participants in a larger public conversation. If you think about your audience as people who care about health, a whole set of topics comes to mind. If you think about your audience as people who care about jobs and careers, another set of topics comes to mind, and so on. The point is that you don't have to start with just yourself or some random topic; you can begin thinking about topic choice by thinking about the audience. In a few pages, we'll discuss in detail how to focus your topic to fit your audience's interests.

What Is the Occasion?

Second, as you choose your topic, consider the occasion. Whether you are giving a sales presentation, endorsing a political candidate, requesting an exemption from a university

Will Allen of Milwaukee, Wisconsin, received a MacArthur Foundation Genius grant. Does that automatically make him an interesting topic?

regulation, or speaking to your public speaking class, the speaking situation may impose some constraints that can affect your topic selection. You need to talk about an issue that you can effectively fit within your time limit, and you need to talk about subject matter that is both accessible to and acceptable for an audience of your peers. Later in the chapter, we will discuss types of speaking situations.

Fitting with the occasion, when you consider the occasion, this also includes thinking about the moment. Two videos in the MindTap Speech Video library illustrate that point. In *Why Laughter is the Best Medicine,* Michael's enthusiasm about the topic is contagious. But he's also chosen a topic that will interest the audience, because everyone likes to laugh, and he's chosen an approach ("Hey, it's *good* for you"), which gives him a good reason to talk about it with the audience, so it fits his interests, his audience and the occasion. In *Together We Can Stop Cyberbullying,* the speaker has chosen a topic that he thinks is important and shows that by bringing his personal experience as a "tutor and mentor." He also makes a great case to the audience members about why they should care about it, both intrinsically (he gives some disturbing examples) and because it might happen to any of us. It works well in the classroom context because he can discuss the problems and solutions in a 10-minute speech.

What Is Your Purpose?

Your purpose is another critical choice point. Your task is to figure out what topics can suit you and your audience simultaneously. Of course, at the most general level, your purpose is to give a good speech. Good speeches make a connection with the audience, advance the quality of collective conversation, and inform, persuade, or engage.

But these general goals are not specific enough to guide the choices that you need to make in composing a speech. So, to determine the **specific purpose** of your speech, take a look at where your interests and your audience's interests intersect. This intersection is in part your personal preference and in part the audience's need, which we discussed earlier. Your specific purpose is to fulfill a specific need for your audience as it relates to your topic.

specific purpose   The need that your topic can fill for your audience.

For example, imagine that you want to take up the general topic of food, and you are convinced that locally produced food is better for you, your audience, and the environment. Your general topic (food) drives toward a specific purpose. In this case, you would like to inform your audience about the benefits of eating locally or to persuade them to change their eating habits to emphasize local foods. Of course, your specific purpose could go the other way too: You could try to convince your audience members that local foods are costly, more energy- and labor-intensive, and not that much better than foods coming from a distance. Either way, your specific purpose flows from your interests and your assessment of what your audience should do or think about your topic.

What Is Your Thesis?

Finally, you have to translate your topic and purpose into a thesis statement. A **thesis statement** is a one-sentence summary of the argument that you would like to make or the information you would like to present. This statement identifies your topic, embodies your goal, and sets the stage for all the elements in the speech that follow it. Actually, a good thesis statement will help you compose an effective speech. As you are drafting it, you can ask, "Does this fact, piece of information, point, or argument support the thesis statement and help me to advance my case?"

thesis statement   A one-sentence summary of your topic and your goal.

We will discuss thesis statements in more length toward the end of the chapter, but for now, think about thesis statements as being like short movie trailers, which give a succinct

FIGURE 5.2
The Process of Choosing
a Topic

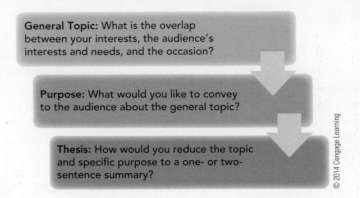

idea of what the movie is about. So for our local food example, in which the specific purpose is to convince the audience to eat locally, the thesis statement might be something like this:

> **We should all emphasize local foods in our diets, because locally grown food tastes great and is better for the environment.**

Notice that this statement identifies the general topic area (food) and the purpose (to get more people to eat more local food) and condenses this purpose into an argument by emphasizing the benefits of local eating for the audience. Overall, your goal in this process of choosing, focusing, and defining your topic is the best fit possible for your audience and the situation (see Figure 5.2).

So far, we've discussed how to pick a topic, define a purpose, and move toward a thesis. Next, we'll look in detail at ways to find and focus on your topic.

FINDING A TOPIC AMONG YOUR INTERESTS

As we've said, one place to start looking for a topic is your own knowledge and interests. Even if you want to begin with a certain public—people who are concerned about health or the environment or success or some other topic—you have to identify what publics *you* belong to or are important to you. You can start by asking yourself what you already know and what you want to know.

What Do You Already Know or Care About?

On what subjects are you expert? Does the answer tell you something about the publics of which you are a part? Everybody has many kinds of expertise, whether they realize it or not. You've done many things in your life so far, and these things have given you knowledge that others may not have. Maybe you play one or more sports or a musical instrument, or maybe you're an expert gamer. Perhaps you've had jobs or internships that gave you interesting insights or knowledge. Your major classes obviously define a kind of expertise, as does any course where you mastered the material because it moved you. Reflecting on any of these experiences might help you choose a topic area that's meaningful and relevant to you and that you can make interesting for your audience.

As mentioned earlier, be sure to consider your audience as well as yourself when you are reflecting on possible topics. For instance, referring to our example of a speech about the drinking age in Chapter 2, people who are old enough to drink have an interest in this topic that is very different from those who are still under age. Similarly, some college students feel

How did Angelina Jolie end up choosing refugees as her "cause," and the subject of frequent speeches?

Paul Morigi/WireImage/Getty Images

that alcohol is an important part of their life, and it's something they care about; however, others have little interest in alcohol or other people's alcohol consumption.

What Do You Want to Know More About?

Another great way to explore possible topics is to think about what you wish you knew more about. A specific topic, say, cloud computing or cancer vaccines, may have caught your imagination. Or you may have noticed a problem, such as a local source of pollution, or a campus group that you don't think has sufficient funding.

Often, we see items in the news or while surfing online that pique our interest. Not everything you find this way will work for a speech, but once you're in a public speaking class, it's worth keeping a little list you can go back to for ideas. Perhaps, for example, you'd like to know more about tuition, how it's set, why it goes up, or where your tuition dollars go.

FAQ What if I don't want to know more about anything?

Everybody has some curiosity. You couldn't get through school if you didn't. But often people self-censor: When they think about the things that interest them, they immediately decide, "Oh, no, that wouldn't work." So when you're brainstorming, be gentle with yourself. Write down everything that comes to mind, and evaluate it later.

REMIX

Brainstorming

How does brainstorming work? William Duggan, a researcher at the Columbia Business School who studies entrepreneurship and strategic intuition, has an interesting approach to this topic. He argues that the ideas about brainstorming that many of us have are based on a picture of the brain that modern neuroscience has abandoned. Duggan argues that we should not see brainstorming as turning off our more rational or critical "right brains" to let our creative "left brains" run free. Instead, the human brain is always using both our rational and our creative faculties to weave together things from our history with old and new concepts in the context of new experiences. And the really innovative stuff in brainstorming happens in that magic movement between our experiences, our concepts, and the creative connections that we make between ideas and the world.

So, Duggan argues, the most effective kind of brainstorming is the kind we have suggested here: Start with some general concepts that inform a choice (in the case of picking a topic, we have suggested that you start with your interests and experience) and then break each of these general concepts into smaller components: Why is it that you are interested in the things that you are? If, say, you are interested in college sports, why are you interested in them? Why college sports and not pro sports? What is it about watching or following sports that keeps you interested? Or, in the case of your experiences, what is it about your experiences that you think might be relevant to another audience? Why? Are your experiences relevant because they create opportunities for others to learn and grow? To avoid mistakes? Do you have a unique perspective as a result of your experiences? Why is it unique?

In other words, you do not have to put pressure on yourself to think of wildly innovative or creative topic ideas that strike you like a bolt out of the blue. Instead, creativity comes from working through a process. The key to brainstorming (and to innovation generally, argues Duggan) is to begin with a rough or general instinct about a problem, and then to break down your initial instinct into smaller elements. In the process of breaking down larger ideas down into smaller parts, these smaller ideas can come together in new and unexpected ways. That is where creative ideas come from.

This view of the creative process fits exactly with the ancient rhetorical idea of *invention*, which is the word that ancient Roman rhetoricians used for the process of generating the content of a speech. Their word for invention did not mean "to create something from scratch": it meant a kind of discovery, a guided search for ideas, which was primarily about figuring out what already existing concepts you could find and put together in new ways to craft a persuasive case.

For more information, see:
William Duggan, *Creative Strategy: A Guide for Innovation* (New York: Columbia University, 2012).

Brainstorming

Suppose you've thought about what you already know and what you'd like to know, and you're still drawing a blank. Don't give up. Brainstorm instead.

First, list everything you're interested in. Try to imagine all the things you would like to learn about if your time and money were unlimited. You could list anything from the moon and the stars, to how buildings are constructed, to the science of concrete, to how officials decide to site and time traffic lights, to what makes people smarter or stronger, or why college is important, or how Jon Stewart became so popular. Whatever it is, write it all down. Save this list.

Now, write down the major experiences of your life: home, family, school, travel, work, hobbies, places you've been (whether the hospital or Washington, DC), and things you've done (competed in sports, won an award, worked at a camp).

Next, go through both these lists and look for *keywords* or key phrases. These are words and phrases that come up more than once or that seem especially vivid to you.

Finally, go to a search engine (such as Google, Yahoo, or Bing), and enter some of your keywords or phrases. Comb through the hits and see what comes up. Is there something here that looks like a speech topic? You'll want to be patient doing this, because for any given search term, you'll get a huge number of hits.

You also can see how your term relates to other people by combining it with the words *news* or *current* events. Type in the words *news blood donation* and see what you get; the hits near the top are likely to be reports about research on blood, policies about donation, problems with shortages, and so on.

Cut and paste to a file the links that catch your eye. Do this for five or six of the terms on your brainstorm list, and you'll certainly have some excellent speech topics, ones that come from your own life and experiences.

Another option is to talk to a librarian at your school. If you talk to someone who deals with topics of all kinds on daily, you might get some very good additions to your brainstorming.

FINDING TOPICS CONNECTED TO YOUR PUBLICS TRY IT!

Brainstorm some topics that matter to you. If this seems a little too broad, you might begin by thinking about specific areas, using the "as" technique from Chapter 3. So what matters to you in a given role:

- As a student at the university—is there a service that the campus needs or a policy you'd like to see changed?
- As a member or future member of a professional community—what should your classmates know about your career, occupation, or business interests?
- As a consumer—what should or shouldn't people be buying? Do you know something about a product or a brand that would help your listeners make better choices?
- As a citizen of your city or state—what local policies or practices bother you? What are the actions that make you say, "If I were running things, this would be done differently!"?
- As an American—what federal policies or practices are working well and should be expanded? What issues should we be paying attention to that we are not?
- As a human being—there has to be something that you are passionate about that you would like to share with your audience. What is it?

Your answers to these questions indicate publics to which you belong, and to which your audience will belong as well.

Choosing One of Your Topic Ideas

Once you've generated some topic ideas, you'll have to think about how to choose one. Researching and presenting will be easier, and you'll be more effective, if you care about the topic. But if you're *incredibly* passionate about the subject, beware: It might not be the best choice because you may not be objective enough to take the audience's perspective, and you may give a speech aimed only at yourself.

You probably shouldn't play it too safe by picking something that's so well known or universally understood that it's boring. Instead, go for something that seems novel or represents a new angle about something familiar.

If you have only 5 to 10 minutes to speak, a topic that's too broad or too obscure won't work. If it would take 15 minutes to give the audience the background information to understand your point, you won't achieve your goals in a 10-minute speech.

Table 5.1 summarizes the advice on choosing a topic.

Table 5.1   Topic Choice Dos and Don'ts

Do	Don't
Brainstorm by listing all the things about which you already have an opinion.	Pick a topic you don't care about because it seems easy or feels safe, or you have already done all the research.
Pick a topic that interests you, preferably one that you care about.	Pick a topic on which you are so passionate you don't have any perspective.
Pick a topic that contains some element of controversy or that has an angle your audience may not expect.	Pick a topic that everyone already knows about.
Pick a topic about which you can explain to audience members why they should care.	Pick a topic so obscure or difficult that you won't be able to connect it to the audience in the time allotted.

HOW TO FOCUS YOUR TOPIC FOR YOUR AUDIENCE

Often, the topic area you've chosen will be too broad. It would be easy to talk about a topic area such as obesity or decriminalizing marijuana for an hour without scratching the surface, but you probably have only 5 to 10 minutes for your speech. You can't squeeze it all in, so you'll have to narrow your topic. Yet you also don't want to narrow your topic so much that you have nothing to talk about. Finding the happy middle is the key here. Your goal is to give a complete and self-contained speech in 5 or 10 minutes, not a small part of a larger speech.

How do you narrow your topic? You have to find a subtopic, a piece of the larger topic. You've already established your interest in and connection to the topic area, so you should focus it according to the audience's likely interests. You can play around with possibilities, considering different rhetorical audiences and different subtopics, trying to find the best fit.

As examples, let's return to the topics of obesity and decriminalizing marijuana and consider the potential rhetorical audiences that would allow us to narrow these topics.

Geography or Location

Sometimes you can narrow a topic by looking at it in terms of "our city," "our state," or "our campus." Each location defines a particular rhetorical audience and public. For example, the epidemic of obesity strikes differently in different parts of the country, and the statistics differ significantly for urban and rural folks.

The criminality of marijuana also depends on state and local laws and their enforcement. Some are more tolerant than others, and in some, possession is already legal, so you might focus only on the local obstacles to and consequences of decriminalizing marijuana.

Audience members naturally will perceive a greater relevance for something that is happening, or could happen, nearby. If you are giving a persuasive speech, local actions are more likely to be meaningful to your listeners than those on a larger scale.

Past, Present, or Future

Some timeframes may be meaningful than others to a specific audience, so timeframes also can narrow the focus of your speech. Probably a student audience doesn't care much about the history of obesity, but they may care about the future. If current data project that 1 in 3 people will be obese by age 32, then in a class of 25, about 8 people are likely to become obese—and they might be anyone!

Table 5.2 Finding Your Topic Focus

Too Broad	Just Right	Too Narrow
Persuasive speech: We need better health care.	The federal government should adopt a single-payer insurance system.	Someone should give *me* better health insurance.
Informative speech: Recreational drugs are bad.	Methamphetamine use is dangerous.	That guy in the back row is always high.
Persuasive speech: People should care about stuff more.	College students should take a more active role in local elections.	You should come to the environmental interest group meeting tonight.

The history of drug laws, and how the use and possession of marijuana became a federal crime in the 1930s, is important in setting a context for current debates. The history also is fascinating on its own, because it's a common assumption that drugs always have been illegal when attitudes about drugs actually have changed radically in the past—so they could change again in the future.

Typical Audience Interests

You also might think about what interests are characteristic of your specific rhetorical audience. With regard to the topic of obesity, college-age students might worry about the "freshman 15" (a documented 15-pound weight gain that many college students experience) or about increasing numbers of their peers who are either obese or have conditions to which obesity contributes, such as diabetes. From another perspective, everybody at some point becomes a consumer of health care, and because the prevalence of obesity lowers the general health of the population, it tends to make everyone's care more expensive. Some students will be covered by their parents' health insurance, but one day everyone will be funding his or her own insurance or health care, so obesity matters even for people of average weight.

Some students may be interested in being able to use marijuana freely, but that won't be your whole audience, so framing your speech as if your whole audience were recreational drug users wouldn't be appropriate. However, if reducing costly drug prosecutions would free-up government money that could improve public schools and universities, it would serve the interest of every student.

Table 5.2 gives examples of extremely broad and narrow versions of topics (the left and right columns) and ones that would be just right for a classroom speech.

FAQ What can I do to learn more about my audience in public speaking class?

If your classmates seem like strangers to you, it's much harder to know what topics will interest them. Taking advantage of class activities, such as group work or study groups, will allow you to get to know students in your class.

SPEAKING PURPOSES AND SPEAKING SITUATIONS

In ordinary conversations, you rarely have to think about your goals for some situation. If you're at a party, your goal might be to learn more about the person you're talking with and letting him or her learn about you. If you're interviewing for a job, you're sharing information in a way that highlights your skills and experience and demonstrates why you're right for the job. If you're shopping for a new TV, you'll probably go in with some questions and preferences, and you want the salesperson to tell you what you need to know to make a buying decision.

A public speaking situation requires consciously thinking about the situation and your purpose. Sometimes the situation determines the purpose. At a funeral, for instance, you should praise the person who has passed away. In other cases, you have more freedom to set your goal. If you're talking to a community group about the problems of tagging and graffiti, you might choose between being mainly informative or mostly persuasive.

General Purposes of Speeches

general purpose Type of communication act: information, persuasion, or engagement.

The **general purpose** of your speech is the kind of communication act you would like to accomplish with the audience. The way we think about speaking purposes today is based on a set of categories from the Roman rhetorician Cicero. Cicero identified three general purposes for speeches: *docere*, Latin for "to teach or inform"; *movere*, "to move or persuade"; and *conciliare*, "to engage with the audience." (Sometimes the term *delectare*, "to delight, please, or entertain," was used in Roman rhetoric to describe this purpose.)

With some changes, these categories still work well for us today. When you speak, your purpose can be to provide some new information to the audience, to move the members to some change in their thinking or behavior, or to comfort or inspire them. Here, in more familiar terms, are the three general purposes of speaking, which were introduced in Chapter 1:

1. *Informing* is your purpose when you are giving the audience members information that you think might be useful in their making decisions or understanding events in their lives. As we'll discuss in the next chapter, speaking to inform doesn't mean that you are just a passive conduit of information; as a speaker, you are choosing and shaping information in ways that will be most effective for your audience.

2. *Persuading* is your purpose when you are trying to change minds or actions of the audience. Persuasion requires you to appeal to the audience's trust, emotions, and reasoning.

3. *Engagement* is your purpose when the main point is the audience's engagement with the speech itself. The speech may be funny, sad, or inspiring, but even though it may convey information to audience members incidentally or help to change their minds, its primary purpose is to draw the audience into the experience.

Your *specific purpose*, discussed earlier, is the general purpose that has been tied to your topic and your audience. If the topic were "parking problems on campus," the specific purpose could be "*informing* the audience about parking problems on campus," "*persuading* the audience why parking is a problem on campus and how to solve that problem," or "*having some fun* with the frustrations of the parking situation on campus." Your purpose also is related to the occasion for your speech, your *speaking situation*.

Types of Speaking Situations

Outside of the public speaking classroom, the occasions that call for you to speak will often dictate what you are speaking about. You may be asked to give a pitch at a business meeting, to give a speech honoring someone, or to motivate your organization to adopt a specific policy or proposal. But in the classroom setting, you'll often have the chance to choose your topic. This is an important choice, one that demonstrates your understanding of your audience and your purpose.

The Classroom Situation In the classroom, first make sure you are clear about the assignment. Your syllabus will identify, for each graded speech you give, your goal or general purpose: Informing, persuading, and entertaining or commemorating are typical goals of classroom speeches.

But presenting a good speech doesn't mean just meeting the minimum requirements for the assignment. Speaking is communicating, and classroom communication is real, in many ways. Your speech will have real effects on your classmates. It may bore them, annoy them, inspire them, enlighten them, or confuse them. Which of these you want to do depends on your purpose. If you're just going through the motions, with no real goal, your speech probably won't be that good, and you won't be training yourself well for situations in which you do want to have a real impact.

Invited Speaking Situations   An advantage of an invited speech is that you often have information about the situation and its constraints before you go in, which helpfully reduces some of your choices. A group often has a purpose and will make clear why it's invited you to talk. For example, if the international student association at your school asks you to talk about your experiences studying abroad, you have a pretty good idea of both the topic (studying in another country) and the purpose (sharing information and insights). If someone asks you to speak to a class or a group about a blood drive, you know you'll be talking about blood, the need for donations, and you'll be trying to persuade people to donate.

Being invited to speak can reduce the uncertainty about the purpose and expectations for the situation. But even though you've been invited, you still will have to work to win over audience members, who may not know exactly who you are or why you're there.

Public Situations   In a public situation, it's likely that you'll be one of several speakers, and that a meeting has been convened for a specific purpose. In some cases, that purpose is

Staff Sergeant Salvatore Giunta, the first living soldier after the Vietnam War to be awarded the U.S. Medal of Honor, was invited to award a scholarship in his name at his own high school.

Everett Collection/Newscom

to make a decision. At a school board meeting, for instance, members of the public will be allowed to each speak for a few minutes about a certain policy before the board votes. At a zoning hearing, citizens may get to speak about whether or not a specific business should be located in their neighborhood.

Before you speak in situations like these, you'll want to think carefully about how your contribution can make a difference in the final decision. Many times, speakers have only a short time at the microphone, and they produce a rapid-fire list of complaints and concerns. It often is more effective to state one solid argument that the governing body can use in making its decision.

Sometimes, public settings are forums or town halls. In these situations, speakers are encouraged to make short speeches in which they share their feelings or experiences. These settings often are more about getting all the available points of view and aren't well adapted to argument and dialogue. In such situations, your goal is to be vivid, memorable, and relevant. You want to say something that people will remember because it's relevant to the question at hand and because it reflects something personal about you.

Business Settings Often, business speeches are either a presentation or a pitch. The *presentation* is a kind of informative speech that shares information, either to make sure that everyone is fully informed or to help managers with decision making. Presentation goals include clarity and relevance above all. You want to be sure that you are telling your coworkers exactly what they need to know, and they need to understand it clearly. In general, less is more in an informative presentation; presenting only the most relevant information will help you to avoid wasting everyone's time.

The *pitch* is something like a sales presentation, although what you are "selling" can be an idea, such as an advertising theme, or a service, such as your consulting or accounting expertise, or a product, such as your office collaboration software suite. The basic structure of a pitch is problem/solution (organizational patterns for such a speech are discussed in Chapter 7). The presenter describes a problem, then provides the idea, product, or service that solves the problem (you may have noticed that advertisements often take this form as well). To pitch your case effectively, you have to convince people not only that you understand their problem but also that your solution is the right one. An effective pitch requires a lot of background research to ensure that you fully understand your client's or coworkers' needs and interests.

Time Constraints

Time constraints are a given in almost all speaking situations. There is a simple rule here: The more time you have, the broader your topic, the more challenging your purpose, and the more ambitious your thesis statement can be. Alternatively, the shorter your time, the more disciplined you will have to be in choosing your topic and purpose. Of course, expanding the amount of time that you have does not necessarily mean that you should choose a larger topic, nor does it mean that you have to choose a more ambitious purpose or thesis statement. Nor does a short time mean you can't achieve important goals.

This rule is essential for speeches intended for the public speaking classroom. Sometimes, students can get hung up by not having enough to say to fill the allotted time. To guard against this problem, pick topics that are sufficiently fertile and purposes that are challenging enough to require the full speech time.

The more common problem with time constraints is topics and purposes that require more content than time allows. The following considerations can help you balance your topic selection with the allotted time:

- Does setting up the topic or the major issues surrounding it require a lot of explanation? For example, convincing people to eat more local food is a simpler topic than a detailed description of American agricultural and food policies.
- Is your intended topic so far out of the range of your audience's expertise or experience that you will have to spend significant time defining terms or explaining arguments?
- Does the topic translate easily into a compact thesis statement? If you are having a difficult time framing a thesis statement in one or two sentences, it may be a sign that the topic you have chosen requires too many different arguments and kinds of evidence to make your case elegantly.
- Are you overloading your topic and purpose with unnecessary arguments? The easiest test of this point is to sketch out the points that you would like to cover, and then to ask if each of them directly supports your thesis statement.

Choosing a topic will thus require you to balance several different factors: time limits, the size of the topic, and your goals.

THE THESIS STATEMENT: PUTTING YOUR TOPIC AND PURPOSE INTO WORDS

Once you have chosen a topic and a purpose appropriate for your time limit and audience, the next step is to combine the topic and purpose in a form that your audience will grasp easily: the *thesis statement*, a one-sentence summary of the topic and purpose together. The thesis statement ties together your narrowed topic and your purpose.

The thesis statement should come right after the first part of the introduction (which you'll see in Chapter 7 is called the "narration") to let your audience know exactly what your speech is about.

If you have trouble formulating a thesis statement, go back and reconsider some of your choices:

- Did you do enough research?
- Have you included the audience?
- Does the thesis statement fit your general purpose?

Table 5.3 and Table 5.4 show thesis statements for informative and persuasive speeches about the two topic examples we've been using—obesity and the decriminalization of marijuana.

If you were giving an informative speech about obesity, you might present your thesis statement to your audience like this:

Table 5.3 Informative Thesis Statements

	Marijuana Speech (Informative)	Obesity Speech (Informative)
Topic:	Marijuana	The extent of obesity
Purpose:	To inform the audience about the history of marijuana	To show that obesity is widespread and to detail some causes
Thesis Statement:	In the next few minutes, we'll examine the history of marijuana as an illegal drug, from 100 years ago to the present.	In this speech, I would like to help you understand the extent of the obesity epidemic and some of its causes.

In this speech I would like to help you understand the extent of the obesity epidemic, and some of its causes.

Or this:

Today, I'm going to analyze the phrase "obesity epidemic," explaining what obesity is and why it's an epidemic.

You don't have to say, "I'm going to inform you about obesity," to make your purpose clear to the audience, though sometimes that is a useful way to construct your purpose and thesis statement.

If you were giving an informative speech about marijuana, you might present your thesis statement this way:

In the next few minutes, we'll examine the history of marijuana as an illegal drug, from a hundred years ago to the present.

This formulation also tells the audience that the organizational structure will be chronological (organized by time periods).

Another thesis statement for a speech about marijuana could be:

Today, I want to describe the positive and negative health effects of marijuana, for teens, adults, and for college students in particular.

This statement of purpose and thesis has the advantage of including a preview of the three points of the speech (teens, adults, and college students).

Table 5.4 Persuasive Thesis Statements

	Marijuana Speech (Persuasive)	Obesity Speech (Persuasive)
Topic:	Marijuana enforcement	The extent and harms of obesity
Purpose:	To persuade the audience that marijuana is not harmless	To convince people that obesity is a significant problem
Thesis Statement:	Today I'll present a significant amount of evidence why you shouldn't believe marijuana is a harmless drug.	I'd like to argue that obesity is directly, or indirectly, a problem for all Americans, including everyone in this room.

Muriel Bowser, Mayor of Washington DC, will preside over the District of Columbia joining four states in legalizing recreational marijuana use. How could you incorporate her into a speech about the legalization of pot?

A persuasive thesis statement on obesity might look like this:

I'd like to argue that obesity is directly or indirectly a problem for all Americans, including everyone in this room.

"I'm going to persuade you that obesity is a problem" is unlikely to be an effective thesis statement. Because it announces an outcome rather than an intention, the audience can take it as a challenge and mentally respond, "No, you're not!" and stop listening. It's better to state what you want to do, as in the following example, rather than your expected outcome.

Today I'll present a significant amount of evidence that proves you shouldn't believe marijuana is a harmless drug.

PRACTICING THESIS STATEMENTS   **TRY IT!**

Pick two topics from your brainstorming list and turn each into a thesis statement (either persuasive or informative) that reflects your position on the topic. Check that the thesis is neither too broad nor too narrow, that it aims at an issue of common concern, and that there is a way of thinking or acting that would help or interest your audience. Would *you* like to hear a speech organized around this thesis? Do you expect that most of your audience members would?

Summary

Picking a topic can be a challenge, but only because it sometimes seems like you have to pull it out of thin air. The process of picking and refining a topic is easier if you follow a few simple steps and ask a few questions of yourself at each step in the process:

1. *Think* about what topics matter to you or that you would like to know more about, and compare your list of interests to a list of topics that might matter to the audience. *Brainstorming* might help you generate these lists.

MindTap®

Reflect, personalize, and apply what you've learned.

2. *Define* the situation: Where and to whom are you speaking? What is this audience interested in, or what should be important to the members that they might not know already? Focus your topic so it is appropriate to the time you have been given to prepare and speak.

3. *Choose* the general and specific purposes for your speech. Given the situation and your goals, what are you trying to accomplish with your audience?

4. Once you have a topic and general and specific purposes appropriate to your situation, *create* a thesis statement. Make sure the thesis is focused enough for you to do a credible job of supporting it but broad enough to be of sustained interest for you and your audience.

Picking a topic can seem daunting at first, but if you start with what interests you and think about what might interest your audience, you will likely find some good areas of overlap. If you work through each of these steps with some thought and intention, you will be well on the way to picking a topic that works for you and for your audience.

Questions for Review

1. What factors should you consider in choosing a topic? How do speaking situations, as described in the text, make a difference in your choice?
2. What are the best ways to narrow a topic? Give examples of overly broad and overly narrow topics.
3. What are the steps in the process of brainstorming?
4. What are the general purposes for speaking?
5. What are the speaking situations, and how do they differ from each other?
6. What is a thesis statement? What makes a thesis statement effective?

Questions for Discussion

1. What kinds of topics do you think are too difficult to talk about in public? Why?
2. What topics interest you? Do the topics have a common thread you would like to hear about? Do you think your potential audience shares any of these interests?
3. Can you make a topic interesting if the audience is not concerned about it already? How?
4. Pick a topic you've heard about in the news that really bores you. What would it take for *you* to become interested? Do a little online research and see whether you can come up with three interesting angles on this topic.

Key Concepts   MindTap®

Practice defining the chapter's terms by using online flashcards.

general purpose	thesis statement
specific purpose	topic

CHAPTER 6 RESEARCH

LEARNING OBJECTIVES

- Describe the importance of responsible research choices
- Outline an effective, efficient research strategy
- Create search terms for focused online searches
- Gather relevant research materials
- Discover the note-taking approach that works best for you
- Evaluate the credibility and usefulness of different sources
- Effectively organize research materials and choose the most useful ones
- Correctly cite your sources

CHAPTER OUTLINE

- Introduction: Becoming an Expert
- Researching Responsibly
- The Research Process
- How to Conduct an Online Search
- Gathering Your Materials
- Reading Your Materials and Taking Notes
- Evaluating Sources
- Revising Your Claims
- Organizing Your Research Information
- Choosing the Sources for Your Speech
- Citing Your Sources and Avoiding Plagiarism
- Getting Help from a Research Expert

Robert and Dixie have been assigned to speak on either side of an issue, a kind of "pros and cons" format. They chose home schooling as their issue. Each has a general position on it (Dixie is in favor, and Robert against) but they admit they just don't know that much about it. So what now? How do they become well enough informed to give a speech on the topic? Where should they even start? How can you keep track of your research? Do you have cite it?

Overview

Research is necessary for an effective public speech. This chapter will help you make responsible, well-crafted, and carefully executed research choices. First, we will help you figure out what you already know and translate that knowledge into a research strategy. Next, we will provide some concrete tips on where to go for research (including other people as well as the Internet and the library), how to design a good search query for search engines and databases, and how to narrow your search. After that, we will address what you need to do once you have collected your research material, including how to read through it, take notes, and evaluate which sources are worthwhile. Finally, we will deal with how to use your research process to refine your arguments, choose and organize your quotations, and give proper credit for the sources you use in your speech.

MindTap®

Start with a warm-up activity about Stephanie's speech, and review the chapter's Learning Objectives.

INTRODUCTION: BECOMING AN EXPERT

MindTap®

Read, highlight and take notes online.

Researching, composing, and delivering an effective public speech requires you to acquire some expertise on your topic. You don't have to be the kind of expert who can produce original facts, figures, and data and publish groundbreaking work regarding your topic. But you do need to become enough of an expert on your topic to translate the research that you have done to an audience that may not have the same background or comfort with concepts and terminology that you have developed in your research. On your topic, you are the expert for your audience's purposes. You should cultivate enough expertise on your topic to bring new insights to your audience and to speak with confidence and credibility.

The audience members may know nothing about your topic. If this is the case, what you say could help shape their opinions, so your words should be backed up with some reliable information. Or you may be speaking in front of an audience that already has a good base of knowledge about your topic—and some strong opinions. In this case, your credibility depends on having a good grasp of the literature about your topic.

Expertise matters. For example, consider how a few medical experts changed the way we think about vaccination. In 1998, the prestigious British medical journal *The Lancet* published a study claiming a strong link between the autism and early childhood vaccination for measles, mumps, and rubella (MMR). The findings were widely publicized, and a movement against vaccination emerged. Parents worried that if they vaccinated their children, they would put their children at risk for developing a serious developmental disorder. Immunization rates declined significantly. According to an investigation by London's *Sunday Times*,[1] in Britain before the study, 92% of children were vaccinated against measles, mumps, and rubella. After the study, vaccination rates declined by 12%, and similar declines were reported in the United States. In Great Britain, the number of cases of measles rose from 58 in 1998 to 1,348 in 2008, and similar increases occurred in the United States.

Yet, it turns out that the study reported in *The Lancet* was based on flawed evidence, with a number of good reasons to question its claims. For example, although there has been a significant increase in diagnosed autism in the last few decades, there has been only a slight increase in MMR vaccinations. Children who aren't vaccinated have a similar risk for acquiring autism as children who are vaccinated. Moreover, the increase in autism didn't start at the same time as the introduction of the MMR vaccination.[2]

What does a story about bad laboratory research have to do with the kind of research you will conduct for public speaking? Plenty. Even though you probably won't be presenting laboratory research to the public, the way you put together your research about your topic—including the quality of your arguments and the sources you choose—will make a difference in the way your audience thinks about your topic.

The sources, ideas, and arguments that speakers use to justify a position in public have public implications, guiding the way that people think about significant problems. The question to keep asking yourself is whether the research you present in your speech will help your audience members to make better choices, perhaps changing their habits, their votes, or the way they think about the world. Citing bad research can perpetuate dangerous myths, and it might cause your audience to jump to unsafe conclusions. You have the choice and the responsibility to make sure the conclusions you come to in your speech are well founded and well supported by high-quality research.

RESEARCHING RESPONSIBLY

In a good presentation, the points are delivered in an articulate, well-organized manner using high-quality research from reliable sources, which are cited properly. Whether you undertake your research conscientiously can make the difference between misinforming your audience members and providing them with a truly helpful answer to a significant problem. In other words, you have choices about how you find and use research in your speech. Because these choices have implications, you have to engage in the process of researching, citing, and using information in your speech as if it matters to your audience.

Sometimes research seems like an annoyance—necessary for an assignment, but not all that important if your topic isn't obscure or controversial. But you shouldn't think about research as a process you can complete by just going through the motions. No matter how well you think you know a topic, responsible research will reveal new possibilities for argument and invention, giving you more choices. You might find incredibly persuasive support for your opinion, or you might change your mind as you unearth the best counterarguments against your position. The fact that you don't know the outcome is the best reason to research—in fact, it is *the* reason to research.

Theo Wargo/Getty Images

Geoffrey Canada speaks often on behalf of the Harlem Children's Zone, a pioneering school he founded. Do you think he should do and present research about his own work?

Do you need more reasons to conduct responsible research? You probably can't be clear and persuasive about your topic if you have only a hazy understanding of it. Actually, haziness in their speech is one of the ways to spot people who are trying to manipulate or deceive others into agreeing with them. We are naturally suspicious of a speaker who doesn't offer good evidence for his or her claims. When speakers demonstrate mastery of the details in their speech, we tend to trust them more. Having a well-researched speech helps the audience see your claims as plausible and avoids creating the impression that you're talking about something you don't know much about.

TRY IT! **FINDING OUT WHEN RESEARCH IS NEEDED**

Is it possible for unsupported claims to be persuasive? Try this experiment:

- Choose a topic and write an outline for a speech about it in about a minute, without researching or checking any facts.
- Then share it with a classmate or friend and see how persuasive he or she thinks the speech would be.
- What does your classmate's reaction tell you about research?

If your credibility is one more reason for responsible research, another reason is that your evidence is the audience's evidence; your listeners use the evidence you give them to persuade themselves. The impression made by a charismatic speaker fades quickly, but compelling bits of evidence, useful information, and well-chosen examples may stick in audience members' minds for a long time.

THE RESEARCH PROCESS

[handwritten: ① First: Research topic]

Research can seem like a formidable task if you throw yourself into it without a plan. But if you break the process into a series of manageable steps, you will be well on your way to an effectively researched speech. The keys are knowing where to start and being able to manage the process. The basic elements in the research process are:

1. Figuring out what you already know about your topic
2. Designing a research strategy
3. Organizing a search strategy for the various databases and resources that you will use
4. Gathering your materials, with complete source information
5. Reading and evaluating your materials and taking notes
6. Revising your claims and selecting the information you will use
7. Organizing and selecting research information and integrating it into your speech
8. Generating citations for your materials

In this chapter, we will walk through each of the steps in this process, focusing on practical advice for sharpening your research skills. Although there are many valid ways to engage the research process, having a well-thought-out plan and an organized approach to finding and using your materials is the key.

Figuring Out What You Already Know

Once you have chosen a topic that matters to you (or one has been assigned), start your research process by detailing what you know about your topic already. Make your existing knowledge work for you by forecasting what you would say given just what you know about the topic.

Draft a brief outline of what you might say if you had to give the speech right now, without doing any research. In preparing this outline, ask yourself a few questions:

- What is your opinion on the topic as it currently stands?
- What are the reasons you hold this opinion?
- What arguments and ideas do you think your audience will expect to hear in support of the topic?
- What are the best counterarguments to your position?

Don't worry about making the outline perfect; just get down on paper what you already know. For example, if you were to argue that marijuana should be legalized in your state, you might write down this thesis and three-point outline.

Thesis: Marijuana should be legalized because the costs of keeping it illegal are too high.

1. Enforcing marijuana laws costs too much and takes up valuable law-enforcement resources.
2. The dangers of marijuana use are overstated, and we should be focusing on more dangerous drugs.
3. Making marijuana legal would allow for better regulation of it and would create a significant new stream of tax revenue.

Now ask yourself the questions suggested earlier. Here they are again, with your possible answers.

- What is your opinion on the topic as it currently stands?

I believe marijuana should be legalized because enforcing marijuana laws has large social and economic costs.

- What are the reasons you hold this opinion?

   Because it seems like a lot of law enforcement costs are associated with marijuana laws, and I think these resources could be used elsewhere.

- What arguments and ideas do you think your audience will expect in support of the topic?

   They might expect me to say I'm a marijuana user, but I'm not, so I probably want to present the case in terms of the public policy costs. They might expect a defense that marijuana is harmless, and they might expect me to argue that enforcement is not effective in reducing marijuana use.

- What are the best counterarguments to your position?

   Keeping marijuana illegal lessens marijuana use, and marijuana use creates significant social problems because of addiction and its associated criminal behaviors.

You might notice that a few themes have popped up in your outline. Circle or list these and think about the ways they connect to your thesis. The following points connect to the thesis that marijuana should be legalized because the costs of enforcing marijuana laws are too high:

- Marijuana enforcement
- Rates of marijuana use

Squarelogo/Shutterstock.com

A necessary part of the research process is to figure out what you may know already. For instance, for a speech advocating the legalization of marijuana, you may already know that the use of marijuana for medical purposes is legal in some states but is contrary to federal laws.

- Harms of marijuana use
- Economic and social costs of marijuana laws
- Sources and uses of tax revenue

With this list, you're ready to begin researching. Your goal is to be sure you know something about these themes and that you have facts to back up what you say. With any luck, you will find that your opinion has been confirmed by others, or you may find that you need to change your opinion.

Designing a Research Strategy

Once you have sketched what you already know about the topic, the next step is to design your research strategy, which consists of answers to three basic questions:

1. *Where are you going to look?* A good answer to this question requires more than just saying you will go to an Internet search engine. Skilled researchers rely on a number of different resources to find the best facts, data, evidence, and support for their claims. The next section, "Deciding Where to Go," describes the variety of sources you could try.

2. *How will you look for your sources?* What search terms will you employ, and how will you modify them to get the best results? The section "How to Conduct an Online Search" will offer helpful hints.

3. *What do you expect to find?* It is a good idea to have at least some sense of the kinds of facts, data, and evidence you will be looking for. Your initial outline can serve as a useful resource for this, but you should be constantly doing a mental update of arguments that may turn out to be crucial to your speech.

Your answers to these three questions, which you can write down for reference if you find it useful, will help you orient your research strategy. First, they will give you a focus and a goal to return to if you feel you are getting lost in research or wandering too far afield. Second, they will help you compare your research practice to your research goals. At every point in the research process, remind yourself of your answers to these questions. It's easy to get sucked down a research rabbit hole, pursuing leads that take you farther and farther from where you wanted to go. This is normal, and you may even revise your approach midstream (more on that later, in "Revising Your Claims"), but you also want to make sure you're staying disciplined and connected to your original plan.

Deciding Where to Go

Where should you go, virtually or physically, to look for materials? Three kinds of resources are available to you:

1. electronic media (web-based articles, blogs, and multimedia resources),
2. print media (newspapers, journals and books), and
3. people (informational interviews and other kinds of conversations).

Which is best to start with? The answer depends on the topic you have chosen.

Web-Based Search Engines The big search engines—Google, Yahoo!, and so on—give you a useful place to start, and they will provide you with a wide range of sources. Google has functions for doing not only general web searches but also searches of blogs, news sources, scholarly articles, and books. For each of these search engines, do a general search, a blog search, a book search, and a search for scholarly articles. There are two good reasons to do all these searches: One, you want your sources to be as diverse as possible; and two, for certain topics, you might find relevant evidence in only one area. For example, if you have chosen a

The expansion of search engines such as Google has made research easier than ever, but the challenge is to get the best results from a sea of information.

Annette Shaff/Shutterstock.com

current-events topic, news sources probably are your best bet because books and scholarly articles may be outdated, except for general and theoretical backup. But, if you're talking about a relatively specialized topic—for example, something scientific or something about legal or public policy—a news search may not be your best bet.

Google (www.google.com) is one of the easiest and best places to start a research project. As you've probably discovered, however, the main challenge is not the lack of sources but, rather, the need to narrow your search appropriately. A generic search will give you a broader range of different kinds of sources, linking to home pages for various organizations, news stories, blogs, and other online content. Two more specific functions, Google News (news. google.com) and Google Scholar (scholar.google.com), can help target your search for materials a bit more narrowly. Google News (as well as Yahoo! News at news.yahoo.com) integrates news stories from many newspapers, TV stations, magazines, and wire services. It's a good place to search for topics that are either relatively recent (such as an ongoing political debate) or specific to an individual locality or event (for example, the rising crime rate in your city).

Academic Databases for Journals and Other Periodicals Searching in Google Scholar retrieves academic journals and reports in a single convenient feed, and it also will link you to a number of the major scholarly **databases** (such as JSTOR and Project Muse, whose articles are accessible through your campus library). These large collections of journals will give you a variety of sources in most academic fields. The coverage may not be as specific as you would like for some topics, but academic publications can be helpful in giving you a broader perspective.

databases Searchable collections of information that are stored electronically.

The journal articles and reports accessible through academic databases are peer-reviewed—the gold standard for expert commentary on a topic. So, for example, if your topic is "climate change is induced by human carbon consumption" or "free downloads have hurt the music industry," or any other topic in which some technical expertise would be useful in sorting out a question, such databases can be extremely useful. **Peer review** is important because it means that the accuracy and fairness of the source do not rely solely on the expertise of the person who wrote it, but it also has been reviewed by other experts in the field. If you need help in finding relevant scholarly articles, check the FAQ box on databases, refer to your school library's web page, or talk to a librarian.

peer review Prepublication evaluation of scholarly articles by other scholars or researchers in the field.

Books Searching your library's online book catalog can point you to resources available in extended print format. Searching for books can be a bit more tricky than searching for online resources because books are organized around broader themes than the topic you're researching. This doesn't mean that you shouldn't use books but, rather, that you may have to look at a higher level of generality than you would otherwise. For example, although you may find a number of good books on the topic of marijuana legalization, you also might want to look at more general books about drug policy that contain chapters or sections about marijuana.

Books can be a great resource for your speeches because they often are written for nonspecialist audiences, and their authors have more space to explain their arguments. For each book you think you might want to look at, take a note of the title, the authors or editors, and the call number. You may be able to find the full text of some older books online, but you also may have to track down books at the library, and you'll need all this information.

Interviews and Conversations You may find that you want information that isn't available online or in a library. If you know of someone who could have that information, arrange for an interview or conversation. You might be able to interview an author of an article you found, an official who has experience with your topic, or someone directly affected by your topic. Authors and other experts are superb sources of information, and they usually can direct you to other research resources. Officials with day-to-day experience with your topic can both tell you the significant arguments and issues from their perspective and give you a sense of what directions you might take. Finally, people directly affected by the issues you address can add a personal perspective on what might otherwise be fairly abstract evidence.

To interview someone, you can make initial contact via email or phone. Published scholarly articles often are accompanied by email contact information; if not, they usually will say where the author works, and you typically can find an email contact link on a department home page. Various officials typically list their email contact information on their organization's web page; if not, you usually can find a phone number for someone in the organization who can direct you. If you're interested in talking to someone who is personally affected by an issue, the challenge is to find a person who meets your criteria—usually by asking, emailing, or calling around.

When you contact the person you want to interview, clearly identify yourself, say you are calling for a class assignment, and have a list of questions prepared. You should record the interview, if possible, for transcription after the conversation. If this is not possible, take as extensive notes as possible while keeping sufficient attention on the conversation. You should also assure the person that you will send them your notes after the interview if they would like. If you would like to quote sources you've interviewed or corresponded with, let them know you are going to quote them and where, and give them a draft of the quote so they can review it for accuracy. And be sure to cite them by name and title in your speech.

Making a Methodical Search

To ensure a solid grasp on your topic, and to convince your audience you've done the work necessary to be a minor expert on your topic, you'll want to read and cite evidence from

<aside>
FAQ *What are the best databases for scholarly articles?*

Your campus library will have a database for just about any field that you might find helpful: America, History and Life (history and American studies, via EBSCO), AnthroSource (anthropology, from the American Anthropological Association), Business Source Premier (business journals and articles, via EBSCO), Communication and Mass Media Complete™ (communication studies, via EBSCO), and EconLit (economics, via EBSCO)—and that's just a sampling from the first few letters of the alphabet!

The major general article databases include the Gale Reference Library (for general inquiries) Academic Search Premier, Academic OneFile (great for finding scholarly articles), the CQ Researcher and InfoTrac (good for current events), LexisNexis Academic and LegalTrac (law and public policy journals), JSTOR and Project Muse (humanities), Infotrac, and Science Direct and SpringerLink (sciences). Most college and university library home pages have a list of the databases to which you have access as a student, and a basic description of each.
</aside>

Personal interviews often yield information about local issues that you won't find anywhere else.

as many different kinds of sources as you can. You'll notice in class that the best speeches seem totally complete: The speaker has tracked down information that silences each doubt you had in mind as you listened. You must do the same. If you don't already feel skilled at library research, whether online or in person, take this opportunity to participate in one of tutorials that your college library offers and get know a reference librarian or two; they can be extremely helpful.

You also should be organized and methodical. Keep a running list of the places you have turned to for research. Note the search engines you have gone to, the specific versions you have used (for example, a general Google search, a Google Scholar search, a Yahoo! news search), and any other databases you have consulted (compilations of academic journals, web-sites that have been particularly helpful, library collections that you have used), so you can make sure you've researched all the resources you would like to use, and so you can return to a resource in case you want to double-check a fact or get more details.

HOW TO CONDUCT AN ONLINE SEARCH

Once you've decided where you would like to look, think about how to execute your searches. Online searching offers ease and efficiency, provided you remember a couple caveats: You shouldn't make your searches too general, because there are far more sources on most topics than any one person could read, and search engines are not yet very good at giving you the exact results that will be useful to you unless you invest some thought and effort in creating search terms and focusing your search.

Creating Search Terms

To start your search efficiently, create a list of search terms to use on the Internet and in your library's electronic catalog. Add to, modify, or eliminate terms as you go, based on how productive they are. The common themes that popped up in your initial outline about your topic can be converted into your initial search terms. Your list can have as many subcategories as you have themes for your topic, and if your research moves you in a new direction, you can add new themes and search terms.

Designing a good search requires trial and error. If your search terms are too broad, you will waste time picking through useless sources to find a few gems. If your terms are too narrow, you will miss many useful sources.

Start with one of the common themes as a search term and read the first few articles that turn up from that search. You also could try an "and" search, such as on *marijuana and law enforcement*, or *marijuana and its health effects*. Do "terms of art" (that is, terms that people in the field use frequently) or other concepts occur with any regularity? In working through a first search about our topic example of marijuana legalization, you would find some search terms to add to your list because you would get a sense of what phrases people are using to talk about the issue. For example, after scrolling through the first few search results, you might add the following terms:

"Marijuana reform"
"Marijuana prohibition"
"Marijuana decriminalization"

You also can experiment with synonyms and subtopics. For example, if you started with the theme of "social and economic costs of marijuana laws," you might try "marijuana enforcement" and "marijuana and war on drugs" instead of "marijuana laws." For "social and economic costs," you might try "prison overcrowding," "law enforcement resources," "drug use," and "drug rehabilitation."

Try this process with a few of your themes, substituting search terms that appear in articles you find in your early searches. What new terms do you find? Don't hesitate to modify your list and return to it to brainstorm new approaches if you get stuck.

Google Like a Pro

If you were to take this course 20 years ago, a huge portion of your time would have been spent tracking down research. There were a few searchable electronic collections of articles, but the use of Internet sources was in its infancy—and a lot of the research work would have been done looking up sources, walking around the library to locate actual hard copies, and then maybe even using a copier or a microfilm to reproduce them. Before then, you might have even had to consult a card catalog or an actual paper index.

Thank heavens for the Internet, and specifically for search engines such as Google that allow you to search, retrieve, and look at digital resources without leaving the comfort of your chair. Whereas in the past the problem for student researchers was finding materials, these days the primary problem is having too many resources. You can easily become overwhelmed with the number of hits you get when composing many searches. Sorting through pages of results is not only tiring, but if you aren't careful, it's easy to get a bit lazy and just grab the first couple of hits that seem relevant to your topic. One way to deal with this problem is to be smart about how you tailor a search. Here's a list of advanced search techniques on Google (and some of these techniques are applicable on other search engines as well) that will help you create better, more narrowly targeted searches:

- If you want to search for a specific phrase, put it in quotation marks: Google will often look for terms that appear together without quotation marks, but including the quotation marks directs Google to look for an exact phrase. Exact phrases can be useful in limiting the number of results that you get, and in making sure that the results are germane to your topic.
- Learn how to exclude results: one great technique is to include a minus sign (−) before some words. Typing a minus sign before a term tells Google to leave out results that include the word you choose.
- If you want to search for variants of a word, including an asterisk is a helpful tool. So, if you're searching for variants of the term "night," such as "nightly," "nighttime," and so on, just add the asterisk to the truncated version of the word: night*,
- Try using the search tools button just below the box where you type in your search on a Results page. It will pull up drop-down menus that help you limit your search in useful ways, including limits by date and location. Of course, if you want to produce a really narrow search, the Google advanced search function can be incredibly helpful. To find it, google: "advanced search," or search at https://www.google.ca/advanced_search

For more information see:
https://support.google.com/websearch/answer/2466433?hl=en

FAQ What are some go-to think tanks and advocacy organizations?

There are so many think tanks and advocacy organizations that it isn't feasible to list them all. Here are a few examples, organized by area of expertise and political persuasion, that will give you an idea of where to start.

	Generally Conservative	Generally Progressive
Foreign Policy	The Heritage Foundation	Brookings Institution
Domestic Policy	The Cato Institute	Pew Research Center
Economic Issues	American Enterprise Institute	Center for American Progress
Higher Education	Foundation for Individual Rights in Higher Education	American Association of University Professors

Focusing Your Search

To provide yourself with a good introduction to the material but not get lost in a multitude of sources, you will have to narrow the focus of your search terms continually, moving from more general to more specific searches. If you simply type "marijuana legalization" into a search engine, you will get many sources—indeed, far too many to manage (there were more than 9,910,000 hits on Google for that search term at the time of this writing). You may want to skim a page or two of the results of this search, but the search term is way too broad for your purposes.

In your first general searches, look for any political advocacy organizations, think tanks (advocacy organizations for specific topics that produce materials for the public to use), or other groups that have a specific interest in your topic. Make a note of these websites and organizations and return to them later; they are often a treasure trove of good, though partisan, information. (See the FAQ box for more about think tanks and advocacy organizations.)

As you continue to narrow your searches, you will find interesting new angles and arguments on your topic, and you can begin to revise and refine your outline accordingly. Your goal is to have a good quotation or statistic to back up each of the major claims in your speech. (Chapter 7 will discuss more details about creating an outline of your speech.)

Ai-jen Poo is the director of the National Domestic Workers Alliance. When she speaks, should she be impartial about the issues?

GATHERING YOUR MATERIALS

If you have followed a research strategy patiently, you should be compiling a number of interesting leads for research. At this point in the process, however, you should not be reading your sources closely, nor should you be taking detailed notes on their contents. At this stage, you should simply be gathering materials in an organized way and getting ready to engage them more fully.

You can gather materials electronically or in printed form. If you gather them electronically, you can download the materials (articles, news stories, blogs, and so on) to a folder and then open them individually when you decide to read them. Or you can cut and paste all the materials into a Word document. Compiling one big document of research materials has a couple of advantages: You can easily search your entire research results for key terms using the *Find* command. You also can move quickly between individual documents once you have combined them into a single document.

If you prefer to collect materials in printed form, you will need a system for physically organizing the materials (a set of folders or an accordion file works well), and you probably will have to pay for copying or printing the files. Although collecting in hard copy may be a necessity for various reasons, it also increases the amount of work you will have to do later, because you will have to transcribe quotations and statistics you would like to use into the body of your speech.

Regardless of your method, make sure that you have the complete citation data available for later use. This includes

- the title of the piece,
- the author,
- the journal or book title,
- the publication date,
- the Web address,
- and page range of the piece, if available.

If you download your research materials, this information usually is part of the package. If you are cutting and pasting into a single document, be sure to include this source

[handwritten note in margin: ② next, have all gathered evidence/ materials in seperate folder for easy access/ finding later on]

information or enter it manually. If you are working with hard copies, write the citation data directly on the hard copy or keep a running document that is easy to cross-reference with the hard copy.

READING YOUR MATERIALS AND TAKING NOTES

③ next
Read / take
notes

abstract Summary at the beginning of a scholarly article.

Now that you have a good-sized pile of materials, dozens of files, or a long research document, you can turn to reading and taking notes. Here your challenge will be to read efficiently and to make your reading count by ending up with good notes that you can use for your speech. You will want to be able to locate the quotes, facts, and figures you pulled from the individual documents without having to spend time rereading everything.

To begin, let's talk about reading strategies. Of course you have to read carefully, but you also have to read efficiently. Here are some tips:

- *For journal articles,* first read the **abstract**, the first few paragraphs, the section titles, and the concluding paragraphs. Use the same approach for long news articles, except they won't have an abstract. Reading in this way will give you a sense of the overall argument, and it will clue you in to which sections are most relevant for your purposes. You may even choose to skim or skip a few sections on the basis of this preview.
- *For news articles,* read the first four or five paragraphs carefully. Because news articles typically begin with the most important information, these paragraphs usually will give you the basics of the story. You can skim the later paragraphs to see whether they might have any useful information.
- *For a book,* reading the introduction or preface and the table of contents usually will save you work. Introductions typically walk you through the organization of the book, and you can choose to ignore the portions of the book that are not relevant for your purposes. If the book has an index, use it to look for specific pieces of information.
- *Blog entries* do not have a standard format—so there are not as many reliable techniques for reading them efficiently.

Newspaper articles usually answer the questions "who, what, when, where, why, and how" in their opening paragraphs, so when researching newspaper articles, pay special attention to the beginning.

Design Pics/Jupiter Images

As you read, take notes that will remind you how the research will be relevant for your speech and make it easy for you to fit it into your speech. What kinds of information will be relevant?

- *Arguments* that directly support points in your original outline are obviously helpful, perhaps to quote directly.
- *Background information* can provide context for your speech. In an informative speech, you might note general information about the object, process, or event you are talking about. In a persuasive speech, you might note information that describes current thinking about the problem you are addressing.
- *Facts, statistics, and data* can show the significance of your issue or be memorable because they are unexpected or make a particularly apt comparison. In an informative speech, you might note data that describe how widespread or significant an object, event, or process is. In a persuasive speech, you might note facts and data that speak to the scope and implications of a specific problem.
- *Quotations* from notable people with whom the audience might connect or regard as important can give you or your argument credibility. Other quotations are worth noting because they provide a rhetorically powerful justification for a major point or add explanatory value by using just the right words.

You can manage this part of the process several ways. One efficient method is to compile a *working document*, or a running list of important facts, quotes, stories, and other arguments that might fit into your speech. There is no need to organize these entries yet.

Another method is to identify each note with a *tagline*. The tagline is a short phrase describing the role the fact, figure, or quote might play in your speech. It precedes the actual fact, quote, or paraphrase of an argument, followed by a page number and other relevant source information so you can find it in the original document. It's useful to separate the tagline from the material you're borrowing by putting one of them in boldface if you're keeping a Word document, or using two columns if you're compiling your list by hand. To reiterate, at this point the entries only have to be distinct from one another; they don't have to be organized yet; that part comes later. Figure 6.1 shows what a typical tagline note might look like.

In this smaller, more usable research document, keep a running list of arguments, facts, and quotes distilled from your collection of research materials. As long as your taglines are clear, succinct, and worded consistently, you'll be able to retrieve the information you need by using the *Find* function if you are working in Word.

Your goal should be to produce 5 to 10 pages of arguments for the average speech, with each entry containing a small fraction of the total words in the original research documents.

	Tagline
Marijuana laws increase prison overcrowding	
	Material
"By taking away criminal penalties for low-level marijuana possession, we would be able to keep people out of the prison and the criminal justice system, where they are frequently harmed in various ways."	
	Source note
American Civil Liberties Union, "Marijuana Law Reform" page, last modified 2012, date accessed 5/16/12, p. online. http://www.aclu.org/criminal-law-reform/marijuana-law-reform	

FIGURE 6.1
The tagline method of taking notes

If you make good choices, once you work all the way through your collection of research materials, you should be able to write your speech from the smaller, more distilled research document.

Of course, there are other ways to take notes. Some people use note-taking software such as Evernote. Others use an index card system or more elaborate written notes. However you choose to distill your reading into a more usable form, the same requirements apply: You have to be able to access arguments quickly, find individual items so you can quote or paraphrase them in your speech, and have all the necessary information to cite each piece of material properly.

EVALUATING SOURCES

© 2017 Cengage Learning

MindTap®

Watch a video, and do an interactive activity.

blog A web log, or personal journal, by an individual or a group of authors.

As you distill your research into more usable form, you will be making a number of choices, including the arguments you would like to use in your speech and the evidence you would like to muster to prove them. But you should not choose quotes, facts, or arguments just because they confirm the case you would like to make. You must consider the credibility of the source. You may have found some powerfully worded, on-topic, quotations, but if they aren't from a credible source, you'll use them at your peril.

Let's take a look at how to evaluate the credibility of different kinds of sources.

Blogs

Blogs can be helpful sources of information, but only if the contributors are knowledgeable and trustworthy. You will want to find out what the blogger's qualifications are before you decide to quote from a posting. If evidence of the blogger's expertise is not included in the About section of the blog, you can try a web search for the author's name. A world of difference exists between a blog conversation among qualified academic or public policy sources and one among random members of the public. Because blogs are not edited or peer-reviewed, you should treat the information and arguments you find there with some skepticism; blogs often represent a specific point of view.

FAQ *What is bias?*

Bias usually is contrasted with objectivity: The source is either "interested" or "disinterested." *Interested* means that the source has a stake in the outcome and would like to see things turn out a certain way. *Disinterested* means that the source is neutral and will accept whatever conclusions to which the evidence points.

Even if neither bias nor objectivity exists in a pure form, we can examine whether a source, an expert, or an institution has a bias, relatively speaking, toward one side or another of a controversy. For example, a source may be biased if it has a significant financial, personal, or other incentive to make a particular argument.

Bias does not mean that the position of the source must be dismissed as wrong, but it does mean that you should pay extra close attention to the evidence that supports its arguments, because an interest in one side or conclusion can (often unintentionally) cause people to misrepresent arguments and evidence.

News Articles

News sources can range from highly credible to extremely biased. Nationally recognized, award-winning newspapers and magazines usually have experienced reporters, excellent research staff, dependable fact checkers, and skilled editors. Some examples are *The New York Times*, *The Chicago Tribune*, *The Wall Street Journal*, and *The Economist*. But journalists are not necessarily experts in every area they cover. Staff writers for local newspapers and wire services may not have expertise in every topic they have to write about. Once again, you can go online to research the journalist's background. If he or she is not a specialist, let the article guide you to research done by more qualified writers.

Opinion or Advocacy Pieces

Editorials, position papers, and other opinion or advocacy pieces can give you someone's take on a topic, but you have to be careful about two issues here: bias and

Majora Carter claims to be an expert in environmental justice issues. Can you determine from looking at her website or an online biography whether that claim is justified?

WireImage/Getty Images

qualification. If you cite a really powerful article about legalizing marijuana from www.blazed.com or www.Iheartpot.org, you are not only potentially citing a poorly qualified author, but you also might undermine the perception that you are presenting balanced research on your topic.

Scholarly, Peer-Reviewed Articles

Peer-reviewed articles by scholars and researchers are available on general Internet search engines and in databases such as Gale, InfoTrac, and Academic Search™ Elite, available at your local library or on your college or university library's web page. As mentioned earlier, Google has a specific search portal for academic publications (Google Scholar).

Peer-reviewed articles can be great sources because they have been subjected to a rigorous editorial process and are likely written by people with strong qualifications. Even though they are highly credible, however, they may be too abstract or specialized to be useful for a general audience. You'll need to consider your audience when you consider presenting information for a scholarly publication.

Research studies usually are presented in peer-reviewed articles and generally are good sources of information. Empirical data on your position can help answer questions and provide solid real-world evidence for your claims. Be careful to cite the conclusions of the study appropriately; if you are either mischaracterizing or exaggerating a study's conclusion, you can run into problems.

Wikis

Wikis, such as Wikipedia, are websites whose content is written and edited by the general public. These can be helpful for an introduction to a topic and sometimes can point you to other, more credible sources. Because wikis can be written and modified by anyone, however, they can't be relied upon, by themselves, to present accurate information.

wiki A website whose content can be created and edited by its users.

In general, Wikipedia is not a reliable source except as a possible starting point for your research. Citing it in your speech can damage your credibility by making it seem that you

FAQ *Researching online is just like going to the library, isn't it?*

No. The first rule of Internet research is always this:

Consider the source. Anybody can post anything.

Unlike book and journal publishing, in which a professional system of editing and fact checking ensures the quality of what's published, Internet publishing is cheap and private. What people post is limited only by their time and imagination. Although many print publications have an editorial stance (*The New York Review of Books* is somewhat liberal, *The Economist* somewhat conservative), they still have to adhere to standards of evidence and argument to maintain their readers' trust. Internet materials don't have to meet these standards, and their authors don't have to respond to criticism.

This is not to say that all corporate or personal pages are dubious or irresponsible, just that it's up to you to figure out which ones are. Let the researcher beware! Be suspicious of what you find online, especially if it seems too good to be true. For example, if you go to www.townhall.com, you might think, "Oh, town halls, OK, this should be a good, neutral source of information on public debate and discussion of political issues." You'd be wrong, however; this site is a portal to many ultraconservative websites. Nothing is wrong with one-sided sites—unless you think you're getting a balanced view from them.

have taken the easy way out and that you didn't bother to find more authoritative information to support your claims.

Websites and Web Pages

Websites and web pages can provide a useful source of information and evidence, depending on the objectivity and expertise of their author or sponsor.

- Web pages maintained by faculty, research groups located at universities, and think tanks (such as the Cato Institute and the Brookings Institution) are generally reliable.
- Websites of nonprofit organizations such as the American Cancer Society and government research organizations such as the National Institutes of Health also are generally reliable.
- Corporate web pages often are full of promotional material. Don't use them as your only source about a product or a corporation.
- Personal or private web pages can have links to an immense amount of information on a topic, or they can be one person's ranting. Cite these as a source only after you have checked the author's credentials.

See the FAQ box for some additional insights about researching online.

REVISING YOUR CLAIMS

Now that you've begun to read the research you collected, you may want to refine your argument. If you've researched effectively, you may want to modify your claims, or maybe even change your opinion on the basis of the work you've done. You may need to go back and forth between your arguments and your research several times. Your research may suggest new or better arguments, or you may find that some of your arguments require a little more research.

FAQ *What If I Change My Mind Mid-Topic?*

The big-picture answer (though not the comforting one if you have a deadline) is that changing your mind based on your research is a good thing. It means that you learned something, and writing a speech should be easy now because you have a good understanding of both sides of the argument. You still can use many of your first ideas by introducing them and then explaining why the research or force of a better argument means that you, and therefore the audience, should think about the topic in another, better way.

Sometimes when you've collected and read all the sources you planned to, you can declare victory and say that you've found enough good support for your original proposition to write a speech. At other times, the evidence doesn't cooperate—either because you don't find as much information as you'd like, or because the majority of your research points in a different direction from what you originally intended. These bumps in the road don't represent a failure; they represent the success of your research: You looked and couldn't find good, credible support for the case that you wanted to make.

If this happens, ask yourself what speech you could write on the basis of the research that you've already collected. You may be able to write a solid outline for a slightly different speech than you originally intended. If you have to go back to the beginning with a revised research plan, though, write a new projected outline with the arguments you *are* finding, and look in some new places, using new search terms. By being persistent, methodical, and flexible enough to change your plans a bit, you should be able to create a nice base of research in quick order and arrive at a robust, well-argued case for your speech.

ORGANIZING YOUR RESEARCH INFORMATION

Once you have a selection of quotes, facts, and data that you are comfortable with, you can decide how to integrate them into your speech. The easiest way to do this is to look at all your taglines and group them into like categories. Take note of the most frequent themes and group them into sets of similar arguments. If you've been consistent with your taglines, you should even be able to write a new outline with your taglines serving as the specific points. So, for the hypothetical marijuana legalization topic, the organization outline might look something like this:

I.   Basic facts about existing marijuana laws

    a. Tagline/Quote

    b. Tagline/Fact

II. Social costs of criminalized marijuana

    A.   Overloads the criminal justice system

        1. Prison overcrowding

           a. Tagline/Quote

           b. Tagline/Fact

        2. Takes up law enforcement resources

           a. Tagline/Fact

    B.   Increases criminality

        Tagline/Quote

III. Economic costs of criminalized marijuana

Obviously, such an outline will put you ahead of the curve in terms of writing an outline for your speech (see Chapter 7). But don't be concerned if organizing your research doesn't automatically produce a speech outline or if your speech outline doesn't end up exactly matching the organization you chose for your notes. Your goal here is to organize all your research materials so you can access them quickly when you start writing your speech.

You should have a number of facts, quotes, and other pieces of supporting materials for any given point you plan to make. Order the supporting materials from most useful to least useful, so you can easily pick and choose between them. What makes supporting evidence good? The quality of the source, the extent to which it supports your claim, and other considerations including, for example, how good the quote sounds, or how robust the study data are. To choose the supporting material for your speech, ask whether the individual fact, quote, or piece of data advances your goals, given the specific audience and situation. Let's look at this question in a bit more detail.

CHOOSING THE SOURCES FOR YOUR SPEECH

You don't want to cram *all* your research into your speech. You have to decide which pieces of information will make the cut and appear in your speech. When you write a rough draft for a paper, for example, you do so realizing that you aren't going to keep all of it. Some material will be fine as is, some will be OK but in need of improvement, and some will be destined for the recycle bin. In the same way, you have to gather a large enough body of research so you can make some good choices about what to include in your speech and what served only as background information helping you to understand the topic. (Your instructor might want this material to appear in the bibliography you turn in, however.)

How do you choose? For each piece of evidence you're considering for your speech, ask yourself three questions.

1. What purpose does the information serve for your overall goal? What will your audience understand about the topic if you include this quotation, fact, or statistic? Would the audience miss the information if you did *not* include it? If the material advances an argument crucial to your speech, use it. But if it's on a side issue, even if it's a great quotation, it will distract listeners from your argument.
2. What kind of evidence is it? You probably will serve your purpose best if you have an appropriate balance of facts, quotes, and statistics, because audiences tend to get bored if you include too many of one kind. A speech that is all quotes or all statistics can be difficult to listen to.
3. How good is the evidence? This is not only a question of whether the information helps you prove a point or convince your audience. Evidence is only as good as its source, and, as you've seen, not all sources are strong ones.

When you have polished your research skills, you will find that you will easily discover more sources than you can possibly cite in your speech, so it's important to choose carefully, and cite the sources that best help you make your case to your audience.

only cite sources using

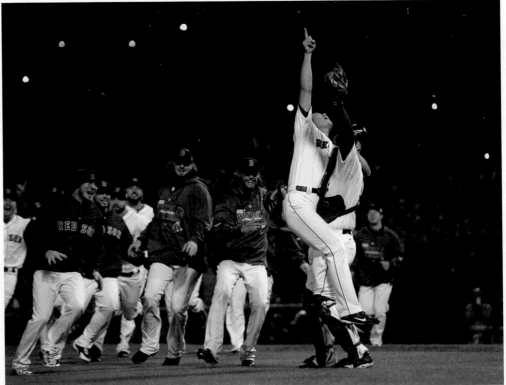

Championships by local teams are exciting for the audience, but are they relevant to every sports-related topic?

Michael Ivins/Boston Red Sox/Getty Images

CITING YOUR SOURCES AND AVOIDING PLAGIARISM

One of the essential choices in research is to give credit where credit is due. There are two reasons. First, showing that qualified people support your claims helps to prove the credibility of your case. Second, giving the audience the necessary information to track down your sources shows that you're confident in your claims and allows the audience to continue the conversation you've started. Perhaps most important, academic life is based on the principle that everyone should get credit for the ideas that they introduce, giving us strong practical and ethical reasons to avoid plagiarism.

In Chapter 2, we made the case for not plagiarizing other people's work. That rule affects you most directly when you're turning your research into a speech. Because the audience usually won't receive a written copy of your speech, it can be easy to plagiarize.

To avoid this potential problem, give credit in two different places. First, you should say, in the body of the speech, where you got the fact, quote, statistic, or argument. This is as simple as naming the person, publication, or organization that produced the information. For example, you might say in your speech: "The National Organization for the Reform of Marijuana Laws said in a 2004 report that...." The main thing is to give your audience a cue that you're relying on someone else's hard work.

Second, you should list the sources that you cite in your speech in a bibliography. A **bibliography** is record of all the sources where you found your information. Think of it as a way for somebody to look up and verify your information, making sure that you represented it accurately. Your bibliography has to be complete enough to allow someone to go to a computer or the library and look up whatever he or she doubts.

A common style for organizing the information in a speech's bibliography is the American Psychological Association (APA) format, which is standard in the social sciences. (See the FAQ box for some examples.) You can think of a bibliography citation as answering four of the journalist's "W questions":

bibliography A record of all the research sources for a speech.

FAQ What does APA citation style look like?

Here are some examples of APA citations for different types of materials you may find in your research.

Book (one author): Larson, Erik. (2014). *Dead Wake: the last crossing of the Lusitania.* New York: Crown.

Book (two authors): Keith, W. M., & Lundberg, C. O. (2008). *Essential guide to rhetoric.* New York, NY: Bedford/ St. Martin's.

Book (edited volume; entire book): Sullivan, J. J. (Ed.). (2014). *The best American essays.* Boston: Houghton Mifflin.

Book (chapter in edited volume): Chao, P. S. (2006). Tattoo and piercing: Reflections on mortification. In L. J. Prelli (Ed.), *Rhetorics of display* (pp. 327–343). Columbia: University of South Carolina Press.

Journal Article (one author): Zigarovich, J. (2015). Illustrating Pip and the terrible stranger. *Dickens Quarterly, 32*(1), 21–43.

Journal Article (two authors): Arendt, F., & Northrup, T. (2015). Effects of long-term exposure to news stereotypes on implicit and explicit attitudes. *International Journal of Communication, 9,* 61–81.

Journal Article (three to five authors): Foulger, T. S., Ewbank, A. D., Kay, A., Popp, S. O., & Carter, H. L. (2009). Moral spaces in MySpace: Preservice teachers' perspectives about ethical issues in social networking. *Journal of Research on Technology in Education, 42,* 1–28.

Magazine Article (no author, accessed online): Laughter is an effective catalyst for new relationships. (20015, March 25). *Science Daily.* Retrieved from http://www.sciencedaily .com/releases/2015/03/150316160747.htm

Newspaper Article (one author, accessed online): Morgenson, G. (2009, November 11). From an idea by students, a million-dollar charity. *The New York Times.* Retrieved from http://www.nytimes.com/2009/11/12 /giving/12STREET.html

Blog Post: Robert Hariman. (2015, March 4). When war is a memory that won't go away [Blog post]. Retrieved from http://www.nocaptionneeded.com/2015/03/war-memory -wont-go-away/

Video Blog Post: UW Madison LGBTCC. (2010, November 22). Stop the silence [Video file]. Retrieved from http://www.youtube.com/watch?v=YFW63cjN6xk

Author = who?
Year = when?
Title = what?
Publication = where?

Your instructor may prefer a different style for your bibliography, but whatever style you use, be consistent, so all the entries are formatted in the same way. Make sure your citations are complete, so your audience won't have trouble tracking them down if they choose to do so. If you have more questions about how to compile a bibliography, talk to your instructor or a research librarian, or take advantage of the online research and citation resources at Purdue University's Online Writing Lab (OWL) at http://owl.english.purdue.edu/

GETTING HELP FROM A RESEARCH EXPERT

Sometimes when you're conducting your research, impressive materials seem to be falling off the page or computer screen. Other times, some additional searching and revision may be necessary to come up with a well-researched speech. No matter what, keep trying! If you don't give up the first time you hit a snag, and if you're flexible enough to revise your speech based on the research you find, you'll be in solid position to give a well-supported speech. Obviously, you can go to your classmates or instructor to compare notes, strategize, and look for more solutions.

But going to the library and talking to a research librarian is one of the easiest ways to get over a research hump. Most college and university libraries have a dedicated staff of people who are eager to help you compile research. Don't be afraid to take advantage of this easy and free way to hone your research strategy. You may save a substantial amount of time and effort by consulting a research expert early in the process, and the skills you gain by doing research alongside a qualified instructor will have benefits for the remainder of your academic career.

The librarian is one of your best resources for helping you efficiently find the information you need.

iStockphoto.com/Alina Solovyova-Vincent

Summary

Research requires you to make a number of choices about how to support the claims in your speech and to make the speech persuasive and useful for your audience. Saying what you think in a clear, organized, and persuasive manner is crucial, but you also have a responsibility to make sound arguments that are well supported by facts, figures, statistics, and expert opinion. If you're organized and persistent, you'll eventually find what you need or make a reasonable revision of your initial hypothesis.

Engage in research with a strategy in mind, combining the knowledge you already have about the topic and techniques for learning new information, balanced against the time you have and the research demands of the project. Decide where you will go for information and how you will execute and refine your search. Next, make choices about how you will gather, evaluate, and organize materials and how you will translate them into notes, or usable chunks of information that you can transform into a speech. After reading the research you've collected, consider whether you need to revise the arguments you intended to make. Finally, choose the quotes, facts, and data to include in your speech, and make sure you properly credit the work of others that you have used.

One last reminder: Take advantage of the many resources on campus for helping you learn to research more effectively. Seeking them out early in the research process will pay off.

MindTap®

Reflect, personalize, and apply what you've learned.

Questions for Review

1. What are your research responsibilities?
2. Describe the process for researching a speech topic. Why is it essential to have a strategy?
3. How will you generate search terms for your research?
4. How should you keep track of your research?
5. How do you properly cite a source, both in a speech and in a bibliography?

Questions for Discussion

1. What are the various ways you might use research in your speech? What, for example, determines whether you need to directly quote someone? When do quotations distract, and when do they help?
2. What makes a good source? What makes a poor source? What are some ways you can tell the difference?
3. What are the biggest roadblocks to research in your experience? What strategies have you used to overcome them?

Key Concepts   MindTap®

Practice defining the chapter's terms by using online flashcards.

abstract	blog	peer review
bibliography	database	wiki

Ap Images/Rachel La Corte

LEARNING OBJECTIVES

- Identify the three main parts of a speech and their functions
- Master the use of previews, internal previews, and transitions
- Describe the patterns of organization and their advantages and disadvantages
- Choose main points and their order
- Justify choices of supporting material and their placement in your speech
- Construct clear and useful outlines

CHAPTER OUTLINE

- **Introduction: Getting Organized**
- **The Basic Three-Part Structure**
- **The Introduction**
- **The Body**
- **The Conclusion**
- **Patterns of Organization**
- **Monroe's Motivated Sequence**
- **Arranging Your Supporting Materials**
- **Outlining**

Trevor decided that he wanted to talk about a sort of weird topic—the etiquette of business meetings. This topic had been discussed briefly in a business course he took, and he became fascinated. He'd done the research and found an impressive amount of information about the topic and thought he understood it very well. Now it seemed like just a matter of repeating it to the audience. But as he sat down to organize the speech, things looked quite different: It was really tough to introduce and organize this information, not nearly simple as "This is what I'm going to talk about. . . ." Trevor realized that he had to think about organization and make some better choices.

Overview

You've picked your topic, thought about audience, and done your research. Now you can start figuring out how to actually put your speech together. Where do you begin? That's the task of *organization*, in which the structure of the talk you'll give actually takes shape. A strong grasp of structure will allow you to take control of the material, to make your information interesting and understandable, and to remember and deliver your speech more easily.

MindTap®

Start with a warm-up activity about Trevor's speech, and review the chapter's Learning Objectives.

INTRODUCTION: GETTING ORGANIZED

Public speaking lies in the middle of a continuum. It's less flexible and improvised than conversation, but it's more conversational and less permanent than a book or newspaper article. Your task in organizing your speech is to choose a structure for your ideas that makes them almost as coherent as a formal written document while allowing you to deliver them in a conversational way. Listening is different from reading, because the words are gone once they're spoken. Your audience members can't scroll back to see what they missed, so you have to find a way to be coherent and memorable without being written down.

Organization allows your audience to follow the logical progression of your speech and helps both you and your audience to remember your ideas. It demonstrates that you are in control of your material, and it also can add persuasive force to your words. You can organize your speech to begin with the overwhelming evidence in favor of your position, to build your argument progressively to a crescendo around your conclusion, or simply to report the facts. Organization is a crucial tool in creating a compelling communication experience for an

MindTap®

Read, highlight, and take notes online.

organization The structure and progression of a speech.

audience; it combines the immediacy and power of a person speaking with the structure and clarity of a written text.

Organization, then, involves much more than telling a joke to introduce the speech and throwing in a few transitions. Organization is a powerful set of tools for connecting your arguments and information to the audience. And we emphasize—as we have before in this book—that for speech to be truly public, that is, for you to speak as a member of a community and for the good of the community, you must make appropriate choices and take responsibility for them. This rule applies to organization as much as the other parts of the public speaking process. You make choices about how to organize your speech, and those choices have implications for how you present a case, and for how your audience responds to your speech.

To choose responsibly, you should be aware of the different effects that you produce by organizing your speech in the different ways we'll discuss below. Your choices can add to the clarity of what you're saying, improve your ethos as a speaker, and make the information more useful and easily digestible for your audience. In this chapter, we'll talk about structure in two stages. First we'll cover the overall structure of the speech—beginning, middle, and end—and in the second half of the chapter, we'll go over the structure of the body of the speech.

THE BASIC THREE-PART STRUCTURE

Not every public speech has an easily identifiable introduction, body, and conclusion. Sometimes people just tell stories (which is its own kind of structure, of course), and in some speeches, such as the President's annual State of the Union address, the speaker works through a number of issues, more like a list. The audience has expectations for how the State of the Union or a personal narrative speech will go and often has more information about the speakers and their purposes than your audience for a classroom assignment or for speeches that aim at public advocacy.[1] As in all public speaking, the audience members and their expectations should influence the choices you make. After all, the President would look a bit silly introducing the State of the Union speech by saying, "Hello, I'm the President of the United States, and today I'd like to talk to you about the state of the Union."

Structure and Persuasion

Edward Tufte has something interesting to say about PowerPoint. He cites a study in which researchers took a section of text in normal paragraph form—the kind of thing you might read in a book—and asked audiences to rate how logically compelling the text was. Then he took the exact same text and presented it to an audience, but this time in bulleted form—the kind of form that you would see in a PowerPoint or Keynote presentation.

Guess what these researchers found? Even though the ideas contained in the two formats were exactly the same, the audiences routinely rated the bulleted contents as more logically compelling. Why? Well, the theory goes that human beings like structure in arguments, and the presence of structure makes a big difference in how we perceive the logical and persuasive value of contents. What is true of visual processing of arguments is potentially true of speeches, and we see clear evidence of this in the frequently repeated tendency of speakers to present arguments in threes. How so?

Our penchant for structure extends to how we like to listen to data: Human beings not only like structure, but particularly like structures that occur in threes. The Romans had a saying that attests to the truth of this principle: omne trium perfectum, or everything that comes in threes is perfect or complete. Kurt Carlson and Suzanne Shu have argued that humans tend to see a "streak" or pattern when there is a third occurrence of a similar type of event. The bottom line is this: Humans like structure, and integrating some structure into your speech, particularly by introducing ideas with three discrete points or even justifications, tends to lend a pleasing sense of wholeness to a claim.

That's why organization is such a crucial part of a speech. Whether you use three points or not, having some structure or pattern to fit into the content of your speech fulfills audiences' expectations that you're presenting your arguments in a deliberate and intentional manner. The presence of some structure to your speech will add to your ethos, too, and to the sense that you have command over your materials because you're presenting them in a carefully planned and deliberate manner.

For more information see:

Edward Tufte, The Cognitive Style of Powerpoint (Cheshire, CT: Graphics Press, 2006); K. Carlson & S. Shu, The rule of three: How the third event signals the emergence of a streak, *Organizational Behavior and Human Decision Processes*, 104(1), 2007, 113–121.

For your class assignments and other public speaking, we recommend adhering to the three-part structure. This isn't just a convention of speech and writing teachers but, rather, a fact about how communication works: You can't start in the middle or abruptly stop and walk away. You have to do some work to get the speech going (the introduction), convey the substance of your point (the body) and do some work to finish up properly (the conclusion). It's always safest to at least provide your audience with a sense of who you are, what your goals are, what you will be talking about, and to end with a conclusion that tells listeners what you want them to do with the information you've provided. Thinking in terms of introduction, body, and conclusion will help you *manage* the process of beginning to speak, speaking, and finishing speaking.

AUDIENCE EXPECTATIONS AND YOUR SPEECH `TRY IT!`

Think about your audience's expectations with these questions:

- What are the primary expectations you think your audience will have of your classroom speeches?
- What are your expectations of other speakers?
- What do speakers do (or not do) to live up to these expectations?
- How does answering this question change the way you think about what is important in delivering your speech?

THE INTRODUCTION

Your **introduction** allows the audience to listen knowledgeably for the important points you will make. Audience members need a bit of structure to help them understand where you are going with a speech and what you would like them to do with it.

introduction The first section of a speech, consisting of the statement of the topic, thesis, and preview.

Without answers to the following questions, the audience won't be sure how to process or respond to the rest of the speech. The introduction has to meet some significant communication needs:

- Who is the speaker?
- Why does he or she want to speak?
- What is he or she speaking about?
- Why should we listen?

TRY IT! | **CHOOSING GOALS**

List three goals that you would like to achieve in your introduction. How would the introduction differ if you were to pick any of the three as the goal of the entire speech?

Even though the introduction is the part of your speech you deliver first, it well may be the last part you will draft. Why? Well, an introduction can come only after you have done your research and decided what you want to say in the body of your speech. You may find it more efficient to save writing your introduction until you have fully laid out what you want to say with the rest of the speech.

Functions of an Effective Introduction

Here's what an effective introduction should do for your speech. Remember—the introduction isn't just a throwaway chunk of talk at the beginning of your speech. It has some specific tasks.

- *Get the attention of the audience:* Give people a reason to listen. Cheesy ways of catching attention (rude jokes, shocking images, strange delivery) aren't needed and aren't helpful. The idea is to catch the audience's imagination (especially visual imagination, the mind's eye) with a snappy and appropriate presentation of your topic.
- *Define the audience and the speaker:* Tell audience members the role you want them to take in listening to this speech (their rhetorical role); define the role you are taking as the speaker.
- *Show why the audience should listen:* Tell the audience members what's in it for them and why this topic is relevant to them. You have to make the case that it's worth their effort to listen to you through the rest of the speech.
- *Develop common ground:* Offer a context that makes sense of your topic for the audience. What's going to be the basis for your argument or persuasion? It might be a belief, a value, or an institution, something audience members all share or belong to. For example, if you're speaking in favor of relaxed environmental laws, you might want to base your speech in arguments about the value of capitalism, free enterprise, and the ability to pull oneself up by the bootstraps. So the introduction should introduce these themes.

FAQ *Shouldn't I start my speech with a quotation from a famous person?*

Actually, it's not always best to start with a quotation. Because *you* are standing there, the audience expects *your* words to come out of your mouth. Beginning with someone else's words can confuse the audience. If you can set up the quotation in a sentence or two, that can work well.

These functions don't always correspond to separate sections of the introduction. You probably won't have an attention point, a common-ground point, and so on—but they all should be accomplished in the course of the introduction. The best way to think of this is that you'll be weaving these purposes together.

President Bill Clinton has had many roles in public life. How should he introduce himself in a speech?

Elements of the Introduction

The entire introduction should not be too long. Usually, it's about 25% of the speech. It consists of the narration, the thesis, and the preview.

Narration   The **narration** is the part of the introduction where you begin to set up what will follow in the rest of the speech. Its purpose is to pique the audience's interest. It doesn't have to be a story (though it can be); it also can be a question, an analogy, or a verbal image that acquaints listeners with your take on the topic and elicits their attention.

Narrations can take two general forms. You can introduce your topic by moving from a general claim to a specific topic in an **inverted pyramid**, or you can use a specific example to illustrate a general theme, which can be called the **Sunday feature** method. Here are examples for a speech about dangerous playground equipment.

Inverted Pyramid

> It's a terrible thing when a child is killed. Children may die from illness, deliberate violence, or accidents. Some accidents are just that and can't be avoided. But others are preventable, and their occurrence is even more tragic when they involve playground toys intended to give pleasure to kids. Statistically, slides more than four feet high are as dangerous to children as guns, and we need to do something about them.

This narration does several things well: It establishes the topic and the speaker's orientation to it. It places the topic in a category—"avoidable deaths of children"—which marks it for action by the audience (as opposed to "horrible stuff we just have to deal with," a category that doesn't require action). It introduces a comparison—guns—which helps the audience see that the slide isn't just playground equipment but, instead, something extremely dangerous.

FAQ *Why not start with a joke?*

Speakers commonly are advised to start with a joke. Jokes and funny stories make a good beginning, but only if you meet three conditions:

1. You must actually be funny (you might seek feedback from others on this).
2. You must have a good joke or story.
3. It must add an insight relevant to understanding the topic.

It is difficult to meet all three conditions in every speech, so beware!

Narration   A story, in a general sense; from the Latin *narratio*, "something told or related".

inverted pyramid   A strategy of moving from a general claim to a specific topic.

Sunday feature   Use of a specific example to illustrate a general topic.

For a group that is familiar with kids, such as parents, this is a good introduction because the category itself certainly will compel their interest. But if the audience is a group of 19- to 20-year-olds without an immediate interest in kids, it may leave these members a bit cold. Remember, the audience is thinking, "What has this got to do with me?" In that case, the Sunday feature approach to narration might work better.

Sunday Feature Example

Remember how much fun the playground was as a kid? Bobby Brady was an average kid. He liked video games, ice cream, and going to the water park. He loved going to the neighborhood playground and trying out all the equipment. He'd swing on the swing, going as high as he could. He and his friend Jorge would rock on the teeter-totter for hours. But Bobby especially enjoyed the slide, climbing up, up, up to the top and sliding down as fast as possible. He doesn't enjoy it anymore. Bobby Brady died last year, after falling from a slide. I wish I could say he was the only one—but I can't. Thousands of children are killed or injured each year at playgrounds, and we need to do something about that. . . .

This narration makes the problem concrete and helps the audience get beyond the abstraction of "thousands of deaths and injuries" by using a single case, Bobby, to stand for all the deaths and injuries. It makes the speaker's position clear, but it doesn't bring in a clear policy frame at the start, asking only for sympathy until the end. That may be acceptable, but it will mean more work on policy implications later in the speech. This introduction grabs and holds our attention by creating a bit of mystery: What's interesting about Bobby? Nothing yet. So the audience, whether parents or not, will keep listening to find out the rest of the story.

Sunday Feature Example 2

You wouldn't think so, but swing sets or slides can be deadly. Sure, kids need to be careful, but they shouldn't get hurt on playthings. We need to do something about the problem of unsafe playground equipment.

This narration is weak. It doesn't develop the problem in any sort of vivid detail, and it doesn't establish the speaker's perspective. If "kids need to be careful," playground equipment isn't the only or primary problem, so the audience isn't clear about what the actual topic of the speech will be or the speaker's position. The attention-getting power is limited by abstraction and ambiguity.

Thesis A clear statement of your subject and/or your argument.

Thesis   The **thesis** should clearly state your subject and/or your argument. You should assume that you are asking for the audience's time and attention—and you will have to work to deserve it. A primary frustration for an audience is not knowing the *point* of a speech—what is it about? Your audience members can't tell how the parts of a speech relate to each other until they know the central point. So, early in the speech, you should make a clear, one-sentence statement of your main point.

The thesis is the hinge point on which everything else in the speech turns. Aristotle claimed that organization was simple: "State your point and prove it." But you've got to have a clear point to do this.

Compare the following thesis statements for the playground speech introduced earlier:

1. Playground equipment must be improved to make it less dangerous.
2. Playgrounds have to be made safe for kids.
3. Playground equipment manufacturers must be held accountable for the safety of their products.

Each of these would be a fine thesis statement—for very different speeches. The arguments for each thesis would be different because the diagnosis of the problem is different. The second thesis just states the problem, whereas the first and third thesis statements suggest a solution.

The Preview The **preview** is a thumbnail outline of the speech, a road map that will help both you and your listeners stay on track. Giving a preview for a speech is sometimes called *signposting*, because it signals the road ahead. Classically, the preview was called the "division of points," because it alerted the audience to the major divisions or sections of the speech.

The best way to think about the preview is this: The body of the speech is divided into two or three main arguments (or groups of arguments), and you'll have to tell the audience what these arguments are so the listeners can recognize them—and how they fit together—when they come along in the speech. The preview, therefore, should be a quick, memorable sentence or two that exactly describes the organizational structure of the speech. Here are two previews, each for a different speech about playground equipment.

preview A brief outline of a speech in the introduction.

> **We'll see that playground equipment poses two main dangers to kids:** *falling* **and** *crushing*.
>
> **To solve the problem of playground equipment, we'll have to look at the** *dangers* **it poses, the** *reasons* **safety hasn't been a priority, and the** *actions* **we can take to ensure that playground safety improves.**

The narration, the thesis, and the preview are ways to introduce your topic and speech to the audience, introduce yourself to the audience, and introduce the audience members to themselves. These elements of the introduction also are preparation for the substance of the speech, the body.

THE BODY

The middle section of the speech, the **body**, is likely to be the longest part of the speech, because it's where you present the bulk of your arguments and evidence to the audience; it's the core of the speech. If you don't have the content for the body, there's not much to introduce or conclude. Whereas the introduction and the conclusion build a framework, the body fills in that framework.

body The core of a speech, where the arguments and evidence are presented.

The body has to make information and arguments clear and, in particular, the *relationships* between information and arguments. As your speeches get longer and more complex, the responsibility to help the audience understand and see connections becomes greater.

Two goals should guide your choices when developing the organizational structure for the body of the speech: attention and understandability.

1. *Attention:* The order of your points and the organizational structure that frames them can help or hurt your how compelling your speech is. For example, if there is a common objection to or misunderstanding about your thesis, you might want to structure your speech to address this in the first point, because the audience may be discounting your (very good) points until the objection has been met. Or suppose you know that the audience is extremely uncomfortable with the solution proposed in your problem-solution topic. You might want to structure your speech to spend more time on the problem that will better prepare the audience to hear your suggestion for dealing with it.

2. *Understandability:* Understandability arises not only from a thoughtfully organized body but also from everything that helps your audience see how the parts fit together: introduction, preview, transitions, internal previews, review, and conclusion. Creating

Phototek/Andia/Alamy

What functions does organization serve for your audience?

a compelling speaking experience requires you to make sure that audience members always know where they are in the speech and understand the relationship of the current point or argument to the whole.

You always have choices about how to organize a body of material, and no matter how natural or easy an option looks, you should ask, "Why this way? Why not another way? How does this organization fit my purposes and audience?" Audience members shouldn't walk away scratching their heads or thinking that their main questions went unanswered because they were bewildered by your choice of organization. That's where responsibility comes in.

Functions of the Body

What purposes does the body of your speech fulfill?

- *Development:* The body develops the two or three main points identified in the preview: the same points, in the same order. This makes listening easier for the audience and also forces you to organize your material carefully instead of just listing it randomly.
- *Arguments:* The body presents arguments for, and addresses arguments against, your thesis. You can organize counterarguments within each point or incorporate them into the structure of the body. (Chapter 12 discusses the details about handling counterarguments.)
- *Supporting Materials:* The body develops your arguments and make cases by presenting supporting materials. Your evidence and examples appear mainly in the body.

The three main elements of the body of your speech are its points, transitions between them, and internal previews.

Points   Your speech should have no more than four or five points, and ideally just two or three points. Why? If you would like the audience to understand and remember the basic structure of your information or argument, it's much easier with fewer points.

Also, you have to be able to *organize* the information you've researched. If you have 14 points in your speech, you're probably just listing them. (In a few pages, we'll discuss organizational patterns.)

Points should be relatively balanced in terms of length and development, including arguments and supporting materials. An outline, discussed at the end of chapter, is a useful way to check for structural balance.

Transitions   **Transitions** are words, phrases, or sentences that link your speech's arguments, points, or sections. They not only signal the movement from one element to another but also alert listeners to where you are in the speech. Effective transitions between points of a speech can help the audience understand the flow of your argument more clearly.

You're probably already familiar with the transitions used between clauses in a sentence: *and, but, because, while, moreover, in spite of*, and *yet*. Notice that grammatical conjunctions such as these link clauses or sentences in different ways:

- *and* establishes a parallel relationship between clauses ("We need to stay informed, *and* we need to vote").
- *but* establishes a contrast between clauses ("We need to be partisan *but* reasonable").
- *because* makes one clause a reason for another ("We all should vote, *because* democracy depends on participation").

Speech transitions work in a similar way. Choose from the groups in Table 7.1, depending on what relationship you want to indicate between arguments or points in the speech. This may require some real thought. It's easy—but boring and not clear—to throw in "and" or "also" between all your points, when what you really want to do is to help the audience by showing the underlying logic of your speech's structure.

That logic appears in your speech in several ways. Transitions are necessary because they provide the redundancy needed in oral communication. They give the audience another

Table 7.1   Transition Words and Phrases by Relationship

Similarity	Part–Whole	Consequence
In addition	A case in point	Because
Also	A specific X is . . .	Consequently
And . . . as well	Another example	Hence
Another	For example	If . . . then
Equally important	For instance	Since
Moreover	Specifically	So
Not only . . . but also		Therefore
Similarly		Thus
Contrast	**Whole-Part**	**Series**
Although	Altogether	After . . . second . . . third
But . . . yet	In all	Following
Conversely	In short	Next
However	More generally	Then
Despite		
Nevertheless		
On the one hand . . . on the other hand		
To the contrary		
While		

Good transitions should be like the passing of a baton between runners in a relay race. When the baton is passed correctly, both runners have their hands on it for just a moment. In the same way, a good transition briefly connects the before-and-after points for the audience.

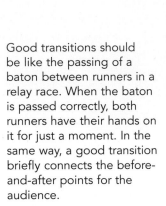

chance to understand you. Although you indicated the structure in the preview, listeners need to be reminded all the way through. Even if the audience members were looking at a list of the points in your talk, they still might need transitions, because it might not be obvious when you had moved from one point to another.

Internal Previews   As your speeches get longer and more complex, you may find that to help the audience, you should give previews *within and between your points* just as you do for the whole speech. An eight-minute speech with two major points certainly will be complex enough to require internal previews within the main points to guide listeners.

For an example of a speech that is complex enough to require transitions and internal previews, see the speech outline in Figure 7.1.

FIGURE 7.1
Basic speech outline

I. Introduction

    A. **Narration:** A day at the polls

    B. **Thesis:** Low voter participation is a serious problem

    (Preview)

II. Body

    A. **(Major point)** Low turnout makes democracy ineffective.

        1. Elected officials don't have a mandate.

        2. Special interests might prevail.

    B. **(Major point)** Low turnout makes democracy unfair.

        1. Law and officials lack legitimacy.

        2. People don't have an investment in outcomes.

III. Conclusion

    (Review)

    Conclusion: We should not tolerate low participation.

    Peroration: *Your* day at the polls.

FIGURE 7.2
Speech body with transitions and internal previews

I. (Body) The problem of low participation

    A. Low turnout makes democracy ineffective.

        (Internal preview) *Low-turnout elections harm* **both** *those elected* **and** *those who vote.*

        1. (Substance of point) *Elected officials* don't have a mandate.

        (Transition) *If the elected officials don't have the mandate, who does? It might be special interests.*

        2. (Substance of point) Special interests might prevail *in policies that affect voters.*

        (Transition) **Not only** *are low-turnout elections ineffective for democracy,* **but** *they can* **also** *create an unjust democracy.*

    B. Low turnout makes democracy unfair.

        (Internal preview) *The unfairness of these elections derives from questions about legitimacy and outcomes.*

        1. Law and officials lack *legitimacy.*

        (Transition) *An illegitimate election may not command the obedience of voters, and for good reason.*

        2. People don't have an investment in *outcomes.*

© Cengage Learning

With transitions and internal previews added in italics, the body of the speech would look like Figure 7. 2.

Transitions and internal previews make a complicated speech easy to listen to. When even the outline looks complicated, these elements will make it clear to the audience.

THE CONCLUSION

The **conclusion** is where you pull your arguments and ideas together for the audience, come to a satisfying conclusion, and leave a good final impression. You *don't* want to conclude your speech by suddenly stopping speaking, then mumble "Any questions?" and awkwardly sit down. The audience has to understand that the speech is over, and what it meant for them. Your conclusion, therefore, is just as important as your introduction and the body of your speech, and you'll want to think it through in advance.

conclusion The last section of a speech, consisting of the review, the restatement of the thesis, and the peroration.

Functions of the Conclusion

You'll want to draw the speech to a close by restating your major points, like your preview did in the introduction. This is the *review*. Similarly, take this last opportunity to make yourself clear by *restating* your thesis. Finally, leave the audience with an appropriate image or emotion as a final impression, in the *peroration*.

The conclusion also allows you to finish speaking. Sometimes, if speakers haven't written a conclusion, they have trouble stopping. Without a conclusion, the speech doesn't sound finished, even to the speakers' ear, and they may just keep going, trying to avoid the awkwardness of suddenly stopping and saying, "Thank you." Use the following elements to put together a solid conclusion.

Elements of the Conclusion

Three elements can help you structure your conclusion into a satisfying wrap-up: review, restatement of the thesis, and peroration.

review A restatement of a speech's major points in the conclusion.

Review   The **review** is a restatement of the major points; it parallels the preview without exactly repeating it. For example:

> **We've now looked the dangers of playground equipment from both falling and crushing.**

restatement of the thesis The second element in the speech's conclusion, which elaborates on the thesis statement in the introduction.

Restatement of the Thesis   The **restatement of the thesis** allows you to reiterate the point of the entire speech. Here, you can show how the main points fit together and tell the audience members once more how you want them to think about this material and what you want them to do with it. The conclusion parallels the thesis but states it more fully, because the audience members now know more than they did in the introduction. Here's an example built on thesis statement 2 in "The Introduction" section of this chapter:

> **The available evidence shows that playgrounds are dangerous for kids.**

peroration The final summary of a speaker's position in the conclusion.

Peroration   **Peroration** comes from the Latin term for the final summary of your position. It draws together the gist of the speech and gives a sense of finality and completion. Here, you might make an emotional appeal, one last push for your argument, as a final invitation to the audience to engage with your speech and your topic. This word also is used to describe the final summations by attorneys in a jury trial.

Writing a good peroration requires some thought. The best way to begin is to look back to the narration. If you return to the beginning, the listeners will perceive that the circle has been closed and the speech must be over. Here are two examples:

- **Yes, it's inevitable that there will be accidents, and that kids will die in playground accidents. But they don't have to. Accidents are preventable, and they don't have to happen at the playground.**
- **Bobby Brady lost his life to a swing, but we can swing into action to save other kids. Let's fix the playground problem.**

Notice that the second example also incorporates an *antithesis*, a sentence with a reversal of elements (from *life/swing* to *swing/action*), which often is an effective way to end a speech. (Chapter 8 has more about how to write an antithesis.)

The three parts of a speech—introduction, body, and conclusion—form the skeleton that supports all the information and arguments you will want to present. Mastering this level of structure will help to make you a confident and effective speaker.

Let's turn now to the basic elements of organization you can choose for the body of your speech and advantages and disadvantages of each one.

MindTap®

Watch a video, and do an interactive activity.

PATTERNS OF ORGANIZATION

Some speeches, such as a eulogy or a commencement address, follow patterns that we will discuss in Chapter 13. For other speeches, you can choose from a variety of organization patterns to fit your purpose, the subject matter, and the audience.

A speech isn't just a set of boxes into which you put information. It's an attempt to connect with the audience. So patterns of organization are often patterns of argument. Even in an informative speech, you are arguing in a sense, because you are trying to relate information to the audience and make a case about the best way to understand it. Making choices about organization means making choices about how best to present your case or your information. The organizational structures we describe in the next section will help pull your points together and show the relationships between them in a different way.

Your choice of organizational pattern will make a difference not only in the way you present your case to your audience but also in the way your audience thinks about your topic and responds to your conclusion. We'll look at five basic organizational patterns—chronological, spatial, cause–effect, problem–solution, and topical—and their advantages and potential drawbacks.

Chronological

The **chronological pattern** orders ideas and arguments in a time-related sequence. The three possibilities are: historical, past–present-future, and step by step.

chronological pattern Time-related sequence of points.

Historical Development   With a historical pattern, you can explain the chronology of a series of events, such as this:

Topic: The History of Recess in Elementary Education

  I. The one-room schoolhouse
  II. The 20th-century elementary school: teeter-totters and rocket ships
  III. The 1990s: revolution in surfaces

Past–Present–Future   Start with what happened or conditions in the past, describe the present, and then say what the future will, or should, be like. This can be an alternative to a problem–solution organization, especially if you're not trying to get the audience to take a specific action but only to get them to agree with the basis for action.

Topic: From the 1950s to the 2000s: How Kids Play Outside

  I. 1950s: Running and biking
  II. 1990s: Skating and blading
  III. 2020: Toys of the future

Step-by-Step   Explain the various parts of a process in sequence. For example, if you want to criticize the voting system, you might describe the process of voting (how things get on the ballot, how ballots get printed, how voters are registered). This will allow you to place your criticisms of the process in a framework that will be easy for the audience to remember and understand.

The following outline breaks down the way kids move as they grow, from babies' beginnings of locomotion to how young children play outside. Even though the main heads are parts of the process, the speech is basically chronological, because the process changes through time.

Topic: Play and Physical Exercise

  I. Crawling/Toddling
    A. New babies
    B. 6–12 months

  II. Walking

    A. 1-year-olds
    B. 2-year-olds

III. Swinging
    A. Backyard toys
    B. Playground toys

Advantages   Chronological ordering helps to convey a strong narrative for your speech by connecting events over time. It may add to your ethos as a speaker by demonstrating your grasp of your topic area, whether history or child development. Chronological orderings also tend to be easy to remember, and they give the audience an easy-to-grasp and intuitive framework for your speech.

Disadvantages   Sometimes chronological orderings can be dull. They might make you seem to be less interested in what can be done today and more interested in things that have gone before. Be careful not to get too mired down in the minute details of history or descriptions of the present day. Instead, remember that the audience members want to do something with the information you give them, and limit the historical facts to the facts that help them understand the topic and decide what they think about it, or what to do about it in the future.

Spatial

spatial pattern Organization of points by location.

A **spatial pattern** organizes points by location in space. Because most people easily follow and remember visual information, spatial organizations are extremely effective. The space can be global, local, or personal.

Geography   You can specify geographic areas that will be the points of your speech. Be sure they're familiar enough so the audience can easily imagine them.

    East–Midwest–West
    urban–rural–suburban
    city–state–national

Familiar locations   If you were explaining student involvement on your campus, you might organize your information around the *buildings* that represent opportunities for students to be active. You might talk about the kinds of activities that go on at the student union and other places where people meet. Because everyone in your audience will have a mental picture of these places, your points will be easy to remember.

    Student involvement at our university
    1. **In the residence halls**
    2. **In the student union**
    3. **In town**

Physical Parts   If you're talking about computer etiquette, you might organize your speech around the keys on the keyboard: "The keys to good email are the Send key and the Delete key."

Head-to-toe is another form of spatial organization. For example, you could structure a speech on the benefits of yoga by listing the mental benefits of controlled breathing and meditation and then move on to improved heart rate, increased flexibility, stamina, better posture, and so on.

    Yoga and your health
    I. **Joints and muscles**
    II. **Lungs**
    III. **Brain**

Advantages   Spatial ordering helps your audience members remember elements of your speech by connecting your points to locations they might know and experiences they share. It adds to your speech's effectiveness by inviting your audience to mentally picture the points you are making.

Disadvantages   You have to make sure that the spatial organization will maintain the audience's interest. Not everyone will be interested in a regional breakdown of a public policy problem, for instance. Avoid spatial ordering if you have to stretch your material too far to match the space you're talking about. Other potential drawbacks are the opinions the audience has of the locations you mention and lack of familiarity with the locations.

Cause and Effect

The **cause-and-effect pattern** identifies the origins or causes of a condition, and then the ways in which it manifests itself. With a cause–effect argument, you can establish why something happens so you can talk about changing it. Linking cause and effect is a good idea if, for instance, you're trying to show that there are problematic results of an ordinary action, such as e-waste caused by frequent purchases of new smartphones.

cause-and-effect pattern Organization of points describing the origins and then the symptoms of a condition.

Organizing by cause and effect is well suited to speeches aimed at understanding, agreement, or enlightenment rather than overt action. For example, if you're talking about the problem of drug abuse, you could try to establish an argument like this:

> **Decreases in government spending on social programs, housing, job training, and support for education (cause)** *have resulted* **(effect) in an increase in drug use and abuse, particularly among lower-income people.**

Or you could create an argument outlined like this:

> **Laws that allow licensed citizens to carry a weapon ("conceal-carry laws") cause an increase in accidental shootings.**
> **I. Carrying a hidden gun**
>   **A. With/without a license**
>   **B. With/without training**
> **II. Increased shootings**
>   **A. Accidental discharges**
>   **B. Mistaken discharges**
>   **C. Discharge during a crime**

This argument is interesting, in that it's possible to argue a different cause–effect argument ("conceal-carry laws reduce crime"), which isn't quite the opposite argument but is evidence for the opposite conclusion about whether we should have these laws.

Advantages   The cause-and-effect pattern is effective because it helps your audience understand the practices and decisions that have led to the situation you're addressing, so it has some of the advantages of historical organization without the risk of getting lost in the history. If listeners are likely to feel powerless to address the circumstances you're pointing out in your speech, identifying the causes can show them how they can take action. Cause-and-effect speeches also help your audience remember the content of your speech, because when the cause and the effect are linked, they are both easier to recall.

Disadvantages   Sometimes audiences resist cause-and-effect thinking. They might disagree on the causes or believe the situation is more complex than the picture you're painting. Speakers also may mistakenly fix on elaborate descriptions of a cause, losing sight of the larger picture. Also, if the causes of a problem are well entrenched, audience members may think there is little they can do to change things.

Globe Photos/ZUMAPRESS/Newscom

James Brady, despite having been paralyzed by a gunshot during the assassination attempt on President Reagan in 1981, spoke often about the problems of guns in society. Would you expect his speeches to have a cause–effect pattern?

Problem-Solution

problem-solution pattern Organization of points that describes a problem and then suggesting a solution and audience action.

The **problem–solution pattern** allows the speaker to examine the symptoms of the problem, suggest a solution, and then propose what the audience can do to get involved. Speakers use this type of organization to advocate new policy or a specific course of action. The justification for the change must be strong enough to support the action called for. Figure 7.3 is an outline for a speech about the problem of bullying gay kids and possible solutions.

Advantages Once you have identified and framed the problem, you may not have to do much work to convince your audience because our natural response to an identified problem is to call for a solution. Problem–solution speeches are persuasive because if you can get the audience members to agree with you about the problem, it's relatively easy to lead them to a solution. This organization is good for motivating action. It also has the virtue of being relatively simple organizationally, so it's easy for you to remember and to sum up for your audience.

Drawbacks The problem–solution speech can seem simplistic, and if the audience members disagree with you about the nature and extent of the problem, they may be hostile to your solution. Conversely, audience members who agree with you about the problem might disagree with you about the solution. Finally, the problem–solution speech can be tricky for the same reason that it is persuasive: It demands a call to action, and sometimes audiences are put off if they feel manipulated or forced into agreeing with you.

Topical

topical pattern Speech organization that relates points to the topic, such as part-to-whole, types, or reasons.

The basis of the **topical pattern** of organization is only that the points have a relationship to the topic. This is the pattern used most frequently but also is one of the most difficult patterns because its success depends on the range and limitations of the subject, the purpose of the speech, and the characteristics of the audience.

The topical pattern is not necessarily a random list. Here are some types of topical patterns:

I. Introduction

A **Narration:** "Boys will be boys." "That's so gay." "Sticks and stones can break my bones, but words will never hurt me." What do all these phrases have in common? All point to attitudes contributing to problem of lesbian, gay, bisexual, transgender, queer (LGBTQ) bullying and violence.

B **Thesis:** LGBTQ bullying is a widespread problem that affects all of us.

C **Preview:** We'll discuss today the problems of bullying and some easy solutions we can all do to prevent it.

II. Body

A **Problem**

1. LGBTQ bullying is increasing

   a. Lots more incidents

      i. Verbal

      ii. Physical

   b. Incidents happening all over country; also locally

2. Causes societal problems

   a. Dropouts

   b. Problems at work

   c. Depression

   d. Suicides

B. **Solution**

1. Awareness; stand up against injustice

   a. Speak out

   b. Report incidents (many schools have ways to report incidents. UWM's is http://hatebias.uwm.edu)

2. Be a straight ally

   a. As in the civil rights movement, didn't have to be part of the group in order to participate.

   b. Martin Luther King, Jr.: Injustice against one is an injustice against all.

   c. Stand in solidarity against bullying/violence.

   d. Today I'm coming out as straight ally.

3. Lobby for change

   a. Congress members to step up anti-bullying campaigns.

   b. Local school boards to implement anti-LGBTQ violence into their anti-bullying campaigns.

FIGURE 7.3
Outline for problem–solution speech

© Cengage Learning

Part-to-whole: The points add up to the argument for the thesis.

Gun control is wrong because it's unconstitutional + ineffective + dangerous.

Types: The points give two or three types of examples related to the thesis.

Three types of academic dishonesty plague universities: collaboration, fabrication, and plagiarism.

Reasons: Each point is a smaller argument that supports the larger point.

There are two valid reasons for going to war: to protect our country and to protect other countries.

Advantages Topical organization is always appropriate to your topic area. It derives from the research you did and directly frames and organizes the content you have worked on. It also builds your ethos as a speaker, because it showcases your research and thus conveys the sense that you know what you are talking about.

Drawbacks Topical organization asks the most from your audiences, because they are not as close to or as invested in the materials as you are, so they have to work harder to engage with and remember an organization scheme that is not immediately or intuitively apparent. For them to remember your content or be motivated to act, you will have to keep things interesting.

MONROE'S MOTIVATED SEQUENCE

The Monroe's Motivated Sequence was developed by Alan Monroe in the Speech Department at Purdue University in the late 1930s. It combines parts of other organizational patterns in an explicitly persuasive structure. The sequence is an elaborated version of the problem–solution pattern, with a tight focus on the audience at each of the five steps. The basic steps of the Monroe's Motivated Sequence are:

1. Attention
2. Need
3. Satisfaction
4. Visualization
5. Action

Some people believe that this very pattern was adapted in early television advertising, which was adept at using a *attention* ("Look at that dirty mess on the carpet!") to set up the *need* ("My carpets are a mess—what should I do?"), allowing for the *satisfaction* (showing the product and explaining how it works), leading to the *visualization* ("Look—the spots are gone!"), and *action* ("Buy this product today!"). Let's look at each of the steps of the sequence and what choices they provide for you.

Helping Your Audience To Do Something

One of the insights that psychologists have demonstrated recently is that human beings are more likely to change their behaviors and beliefs if we think we can do something meaningful to engage or deal with a problem. It turns out that if someone makes a case for change but we don't think we can do much to really bring about change, human beings aren't motivated to act, or even to change our beliefs. But if we think that by changing our thoughts or actions, we can change a state of affairs, we're more likely not only to buy into, and not only decisively change, our beliefs but to actually recruit others to do the same. The psychological term for this phenomena is *self-efficacy:* When we think it makes a difference to think or act

Attention

This step has many of the functions typical of an introduction (and you should add a thesis and preview to it). The attention step is something—image (literal or painted in words), a statistic, a rhetorical question, a story—that will get the attention of this specific audience. What gets attention? Something that either relates to the audience members' desire or goal ("Did you know that you—anybody—can live to be 100 years old?") or runs against their expectations ("You can make more with a college degree, but did you know how much more? Twice as much!").[2] Your attention getting devices should be cut from the same cloth as the rest of your speech, blending in seamlessly. Just as you shouldn't start a speech with an irrelevant joke just because it's funny, you have to find the story, image, or statistic that is interesting and startling *and* relevant to your topic.

Need

The need corresponds to the "problem" section of the speech. This is where you show what's wrong, or lacking, in the way things are. You're trying emphasize (accurately and with sources) the degree to which things are bad, and how the scope of the populations affected. You don't have to state it in these words, but this is the section where you try to answer the question "What we need is. . . ." You can focus on the consequences of not making a change, and hopefully you can show how that affects the audience (among others) directly. Using vivid examples and illustrations, try to make your audience feel some negative emotions (those you'll flip over later in the speech): outrage, pity, discomfort, righteous anger, and whatever seems appropriate to your topic. In this section of the speech, you also may allude briefly to the cause of the problem (which creates the need), but don't spend too much time on it, because the motivated sequence is not as appropriate to a setting where the cause is seriously in dispute.

Satisfaction

Here is where you offer the solution—the policy or course of action that will meet the need. In this section of this speech, you should explain clearly and concisely what will meet the need you established in the previous section, invoking whatever facts, research, and argument you can. You should be sure that the policy satisfies the need theoretically ("Logically, this should reduce the problem because . . .") and also factually ("Here are some studies suggesting that this approach has worked in the past"). You'll have to balance enough specifics to be plausible without overloading the audience with detailed; "streamlined" is a good goal in this speech format.

Visualization

This is the part of the speech that really corresponds, rhetorically, to the *need* step: You've told how the world looks when the need is unmet, so how will the world look when the need is met? The motivational part of the speech comes from that contrast, so here you have to paint a vivid picture. You can approach this task in three ways. First, you can do it *positively*, describing all the good things that will be true if the solution is adopted. Second, you can paint this picture *negatively*, outlining the horrors that will follow from not adopting the solution. Finally, you can use the contrast method, in which you systemically contrast the positive and negative pictures (somewhat like the before-and after pictures in weight-loss ads). This is a bit trickier: You want to have the points relatively balanced, so you can't let this section go on too long. But swiftly summarizing the difference can be effective in making the audience think that the change is worth it.

Action

The Monroe's Motivated Sequence works best when an immediate concrete action can create satisfaction. If you started out with the statement, "Climate change is horrifying!" that statement may be true, but no single immediate action will create a change that meets the need. You have to describe the problem or need in such a way that you can give (at least in part) a direct solution. The action step is where you provide that solution. It's also the "conclusion" of this speech, which makes sense because the point of a speech organized around the Monroe's Motivated Sequence is to motivate the audience directly to action. So you need to make clear the action that the audience should take, and how to go about it. You can add, in quotations, endorsements of the action from famous people. Or you can declare that you have done, or will be doing, the action. You also can set up the conditions for people to take an action ("Here's the email address of our representative . . ." or "I'm passing around a petition for people to sign). The more you can do to enable the action, through information or other means, the more likely people will be to do it.

Advantages   If you have a concrete topic in mind, and you want to give a persuasive speech on the topic, the Monroe Motivated Sequence is a good fit. It builds in a logical order and guides you in filling out the points in ways that are most persuasive. The Sequence is great for getting you to think about your topic in a visual, concrete way.

Disadvantages   The Sequence isn't best for every persuasive topic. If you're looking to raise awareness about a topic or seeking a general change in attitudes rather than looking for a specific action, this isn't your best choice. The things that work well about the Sequence don't lend themselves to broad topics or topics that don't have a concrete here-and-now action to go with them.

Combination

You can combine different organizational patterns within one speech, using patterns to develop your subpoints that are different from those you used in the main outline; they don't have to echo the structure of the main outline. For example, in a problem–solution speech, the first main point might be historical, and the second point might be spatial.

Here's an example with two main points that combines cause–effect and problem solution for the body of the speech. Note how transitions guide the listener through this complex structure.

Cause–effect leading to *problem solution:*

Kids watch lots of TV.
Therefore,
they aren't developing their reading skills.
This is a problem because
they will be the underemployed of tomorrow.
To remedy this,
parents should limit viewing time.

This is a common combination structure that allows you to urge a certain solution after establishing its cause.

Advantages   A combination of formats puts you in control of what you want to say and how you want to say it. You can draft your speech in the way that is most fitting for your audience and your topic.

Disadvantages   A combination approach can ask too much of the speaker and the audience. You have to manage more elements in your speech, and with each new organizational element, the audience can lose track of the structure of your speech. Combination speeches require more time to set up and deliver, so you either have to give a longer speech or cut details that might be important.

Because audience members won't immediately recognize the structure of a combination speech, the members of your audience might be a little more skeptical about your content than they would be otherwise. If you choose this approach, be careful not to make the structure too complex: You might ask yourself how you would take notes on this speech if you were to hear it for the first time and, further, whether you could reproduce an outline of this speech from memory. If you wouldn't feel comfortable doing this, the structure of your speech might be too complex. Keep in mind that your goal is not just to present information but, instead, to connect with your listeners by making the contents of your speech digestible and persuasive.

CHOOSING AN ORGANIZATIONAL PATTERN FOR YOUR TOPIC   TRY IT!

Think about one of your favorite topics, perhaps even from a speech you've already given. Make an outline or quickly reconstruct your original one.

Now imagine that speech in at least two other organizational patterns.

- How would you fit the speech into each of the new patterns?
- How would it change the content and character of the speech to organize it differently?
- What choices would you have to make in redrafting the speech?
- With each of the new patterns, is it a better or worse speech?

Many of your speeches can be organized in different ways. If you always keep the other possibilities in mind, you will be able to recognize what your current organization pattern is built to maximize, and you can focus all your choices on making the best elements of that organizational schema work for you.

Joe Scarnici/Getty Images

Can good organization solve every problem for a speaker like Anderson Cooper?

Choosing the Order of Points: Primacy vs. Recency

In some organizational patterns, it's obvious which points should come first and which should come last. In a problem–solution speech, the problem has to come before the solution. In chronological speeches the points have to move forward or backward in time. In spatial and topical organizations, however, you have a choice to put the points in whatever order you like—but which one?

primacy Organization that places the strongest arguments first to show their importance.

recency The organization that places the strongest argument last so the audience will remember them.

This choice depends on which characteristic is most important for your speech: **primacy**, which means putting your strongest arguments first to show their importance, or **recency**, which puts the strongest arguments last so they will be the most recent in the audiences' memory. The traditional answer favors recency: Your speech should build toward the strongest arguments and the most salient and important facts or ideas.

[handwritten: first / last]

The only time you wouldn't put your best or most important material last is when you think you may have a problem with an audience assumption requiring counterinformation or a counterargument. For example, if you were advocating for a conceal-carry law, your strongest argument would be that people are safer. But because the main fear people have about concealed weapons is that they may get hurt, your audience might not be listening carefully until you establish, in the first point, your evidence that the average person is safer in a community that has a conceal-carry law.

ARRANGING YOUR SUPPORTING MATERIALS

Not only do you have to decide the pattern for your main points, but you also have to figure out where to put the facts, figures, quotations, and other supporting materials you'll be using as evidence for your arguments. Obviously, supporting materials should appear with the claims they're supporting, but here's more specific advice, in the form of five principles, to guide you in figuring out the best places for evidence of various kinds in your speech.

- *Highlight your best quotations, facts, figures, and research information in a prominent place.* Inexperienced speakers sometimes bury their most compelling evidence somewhere in the middle of their speech—the place where audiences often tend to pay less attention. If you have a really good quotation or fact, don't be afraid to highlight it in your *introduction or conclusion,* as long as you refer to it with the appropriate point in the body of your speech. If you decide you must put it in the body, at least place it early and in one of your main points.

- **Avoid long strings of the same type of evidence.** Audiences tend to tune out long lists of facts, statistics, or quotations. The more similar types of evidence you put together, the less effect will any one of them have.

- **Follow numbers or data-heavy evidence with an explanation that helps the audience interpret them.** Often audiences do not know what to do with numbers or statistics (such as social scientific research) or don't immediately understand the implications of your evidence. Providing a simple explanation after numbers or other raw data can assist the audience in drawing appropriate conclusions. If you're pointing out that the average college student spends 1.84 hours in front of a computer for gaming purposes each day, you can put the statistic in perspective by adding, "That means almost 7.5% of your waking time is spent on gaming."

- **Vary the types of evidence you use.** A speech with quotations from experts, statistics, personal narratives, and historical facts is more compelling than a speech that cites only one kind of evidence. So be sure to put multiple types of evidence into each of the sections of your speech. For instance, you could cite the number of drivers in fatal accidents who were texting, you could quote someone who was injured in such an accident, and you could explain a study on the psychology of attention that shows how distraction actually happens.

- **Don't be afraid to give the opposition a fair hearing.** If you found great numbers, quotations, or other materials that support *counterarguments* against your position, quote them in your speech. Take this opportunity to frame the debate for the audience. This will assure your audience that you're familiar with opposing arguments and ready to address them head on. Keep in mind that your citation of opposing positions should be brief, fair, and to the point.

For an overview of your main organizational pattern, the order of points, and the integration of supporting materials, we now will cover outlining, which will help you immeasurably.

OUTLINING

An outline is a way of organizing knowledge, both for you and for your audience. Your outline is midway between your research and the speech that you will give, and it helps you improve both. An outline creates a picture of your speech's *structure.*

First, it helps to objectify the speech. Getting your speech down on paper makes it easier for you to examine it for flaws in organization, in assumptions you've made about the audience, or in your line of reasoning. Now you can "eyeball" the speech to evaluate its tightness and structure:

Check for tightness

- Is all material related to the purpose of the speech?
- Is all necessary supporting material included?
- Is all unnecessary material taken out?

Check the structure

- **Balance:** Are all main points roughly the same size?
- **Completeness:** Is anything missing?
- **Logic:** Is the argument clear and relevant?

Second, an outline can serve as a memory aid through visualization. If you can see the structure of the speech, like a picture, it's easier to remember it.

Third, an outline is easier to revise and rearrange than a fully written-out manuscript of the speech.

Finally, for most speeches, you'll be speaking from notes rather than a full manuscript. So an outline, which contains the "bones" of a speech, gives you a perfect starting place for putting your notes together.

Outline Structure

Unless you're doing a manuscript speech, when you begin writing and revising your speech, your outline *is* your speech. As you revise the outline, you're revising the speech. What does a good outline look like? First, it has to *look* like an outline: It should be as short as you can make it and still include all your points and evidence. (Your instructor may have specific requirements for outlines, especially whether they are full-sentence or keyword outlines.) The structure of a speech has to be obvious at a glance. The *shape* of the outline lets you see the shape of the speech—the forest and not just the trees.

The outline of the body is the most important part. You don't need as much structural detail for the introduction and conclusion, though you may want to fill these in as you get closer to your time of speaking. .

coordinate points Points at the same level in an outline.

Outlines have two kinds of points. **Coordinate points** are points at the same hierarchical level. For instance, these two are coordinate points:

I. Good students
II. Weak students

subordinate points Points supporting a main point.

Subordinate points are one level down from main points; you will always have at least two subordinate points below any one of your main points. For example, here are the two coordinate points again, this time with two subordinate points each:

I. Good students
   A. Those who study
   B. Those who seek the help they need

II. Poor students
   C. Those who hope for the best
   D. Those who can't get their acts together

Notice that every hierarchical level in the outline is indicated in *two* ways: with a different *coordinate symbol* (the type of letter or number we use for each level), and with a different *indent* (each level is indented more than the level above).

Preparation and Delivery Outlines

Because you usually will be speaking extemporaneously (see Chapter 9), your outline will substitute, during the speech preparation process, for a full manuscript. A first version of your outline will serves as your "blackboard" for developing and refining ideas; a final version will be turned in; and another version will go on your cards.

For an extemporaneous speech, "writing" is mostly a metaphor, because it's typically counterproductive to actually write out a manuscript. If you write out the sentences, you may

Some speakers help the audience by showing portions of their outlines as slides or other visuals—especially effective in long speeches.

Dennis MacDonald/Alamy

struggle to recall them when you're speaking from an outline or some notecards. It's best to write only short phrases that will remind you of what you want to say. So until you get to put the finishing touches on certain stylistic elements, "writing" means putting ideas and arguments into a form that you can look at and evaluate, which usually means on paper or in a computer file that you can print.

During the process of preparation, you can use outlines in several different ways. First, you'll need a *working,* or *research, outline.* This is basically a best guess of what your speech is going to look like, and it will evolve all the way through your preparation process. As you do more reading and find out more about your topic—and think through your audience's assumptions and expectations—this outline will change frequently. That's good. Think of this process as a loop: Your research strategy depends on the topic, but once you've done your research, your outline will change. That new outline generates new research questions, and so on, until you think you've got it right.

In addition, for the extemporaneous speeches you'll usually be giving, you'll be speaking from an outline, so you have to be able to put together an outline that meets your needs for delivering your speech. You should consider several factors:

- Is the print large enough for you to read?
- Have you used different fonts, colors, or a highlighter to distinguish different sections of the outline, to help you find your place when you look down?
- Does the page or cards have enough white space to make the outline easy to follow?
- Have you kept your outline minimal, except for the few places where you have a quotation or a line to read word for word?

Summary

Organization is a critical element in the success of your speech. Your choices in arranging your materials have real consequences for the persuasive value of your speech, the listeners' ability to remember it, and their motivation to implement the changes in practice, worldview, or opinion that you advocate. Effective organization requires you to understand the functions

MindTap®

Reflect, personalize, and apply what you've learned with a Speech Simulation.

and elements of the three mains parts of a speech: the introduction, the body, and the conclusion. You'll have to master the various patterns of organization for the body, and add transitions, internal previews, and supporting material to them. Finally, you'll also have to become a proficient outliner, creating representations of your speech that will help you refine and deliver it.

Questions for Review

1. What are the basic parts of a speech? What role does each of them play in helping your audience to connect with your material?
2. What is a transition? What makes a transition effective? Why are good transitions so important in a speech?
3. Compare and contrast the patterns of organization for the body of a speech.
4. What are some ways to order the main points in a speech, especially in topical organization? What are the advantages and disadvantages of the different orderings?
5. What role does outlining play in composing a good speech? What are the best techniques to use?

Questions for Discussion

1. Think of a speech you've heard that seemed to lack a logical order or structure. How did you respond to it? What difference does a good organizational pattern make in an audience's ability to engage a speech?
2. How might the ineffective organization of a speech affect the speaker's ethos, the credibility of his or her arguments, or the persuasiveness of the speech? Why?
3. What organizational pattern do you prefer for speeches? Why?
4. Go to an Internet video site and take a look at either a presidential speech from the last 20 years or a TED Talk (www.ted.com/talks). Try to take notes and identify the organizational pattern. Is it similar to one we've outlined in this chapter? How effective is it?

Key Concepts   MindTap®

Practice defining the chapter's terms by using online flashcards.

body	organization	review
cause-and-effect pattern	peroration	spatial pattern
chronological pattern	preview	subordinate points
conclusion	primacy	Sunday feature
coordinate points	problem–solution pattern	topical pattern
introduction	recency	transitions
inverted pyramid	restatement of the thesis	

PART 3 PRESENTING A GREAT SPEECH

CHAPTER **8** Verbal Style

CHAPTER **9** Delivery

CHAPTER **10** Presentation Aids

DrAfter123/Getty Images

Bob Daemmrich/Alamy

LEARNING OBJECTIVES

- Justify the importance of language that is concrete, lively, and respectful
- Differentiate figures and tropes
- Explain the figures of repetition and contrast, and construct your own
- Explain the tropes of comparison, substitution, exaggeration, and voice, and construct your own
- Employ principles for matching verbal style to the topic and the occasion

CHAPTER OUTLINE

- Introduction: What Is Style, and Why Does It Matter?
- Characteristics of Effective Style
- Classifying Verbal Style: Figures and Tropes
- Figures
- Tropes
- Matching the Style to the Topic and the Occasion

Sierra wants to give a speech about sports. She has some great ideas about the role of sports in modern society and has done the research to make her points. But she has a problem: There is serious competition for her speech—sports! Sports, in-person and televised, are exciting, and she knows that's why people like sports so much. But that means they won't be interested in a bunch of dry arguments and data about sports. So Sierra has a public speaking challenge: How can she give a sports talk that will be nearly as exciting as the real thing? Sierra has to make the right choices about verbal style.

Overview

Speakers often worry about the way they say words—which is important (note that delivery is the subject of the next chapter). But the words you choose to say are just as, or more, important. In ordinary life, we don't think about our words too much; we just talk. Yet, when we want our words to have impact, we should choose them carefully. In addition, we have to take responsibility for our words, and words sometimes can be hurtful or offensive. In a public speaking situation, when we expect people to remember our words and take them seriously, we will have to spend more time thinking about them and choosing them.

MindTap®

Start with a warm-up activity about Sierra's speech, and review the chapter's Learning Objectives.

INTRODUCTION: WHAT IS STYLE, AND WHY DOES IT MATTER?

Now that you have figured out the basic thrust of what you want to say and how you want to organize and support it, the next challenge is to figure out exactly how to express the ideas you want to convey—in other words, the considerations of **style**, the wording choices you will make to achieve the goals of your speech.

This chapter will give you a set of stylistic techniques for making word choices that you can integrate into your speeches. We can't tell you how to phrase *everything* in your speech, because so much about phrasing is unique to you as a speaker and to the audience you are addressing. But we can offer a number of tried-and-true stylistic forms that have been used effectively in great speeches. In the next chapter, we'll complete our discussion of delivery by discussing the nonverbal parts of speaking; of course, there is sense in which that is a kind of "style," but for this chapter (and this book), "style" means the choice of words and use of language.

MindTap®

Read, highlight, and take notes online.

style Word choices made to achieve the goals of a speech.

Style exploits one of the most powerful features of language—that there are many different ways of saying the same thing. For instance, you could say, "It's hot outside, and I'm tired." Or you might say, "It's an oven outside, and I'm beat." Or perhaps you like more formal expressions: "Oh, this insufferable heat—it's left me feeling fatigued." If you try, you probably could come up with dozens of different ways of saying the same thing.

Expressing your thoughts in words is an art of making choices. You have choices about how you say what you want to say, and these choices are important because different choices can convey different impressions about your topic. Striking just the right verbal style for your topic and the occasion will help you achieve your speaking goals. Perhaps you want to evoke a straightforward informational tone; perhaps you want to convey some particularly significant material in a playful and even artful way. Whatever you want to achieve, the style you choose matters.[1]

CHARACTERISTICS OF EFFECTIVE STYLE

No matter how wonderful a speaker's delivery may be, if she begins her speech, "La oss taler i dag om problemet med nettkriminalitet," you won't have any idea that this is a speech about cybercrime—unless you speak Norwegian. No amount of work on topic choice, organizational patterns, or delivery can make up that gap: Language matters. Language matters in another important respect: The word choices that you make in expressing yourself also define the character of your ideas for your audience. Language matters not only in being understood, but also in being interesting, compelling, and in convincing your audience that you're worth listening to.

The study of verbal style, how to choose and use the right words, is central to communicating effectively. The second part of this chapter will discuss how you can choose words to achieve your communication goals, but, first, we will cover the basics. To be an effective speaker, you will have to use language that is concrete and lively, reduces abstraction and makes ideas come alive for listeners, and is respectful and doesn't unintentionally exclude some audience members. We'll talk about each of these characteristics in turn.

Speaking in Images

Evoking strong images is a crucial persuasive technique. Why say, "It was hot outside" when you can say, "It was like an oven outside—if you cracked an egg on the pavement, you could stand there and watch it sizzle on the hot asphalt." New evidence in cognitive science gives us reason to prefer the second formulation over the first. When you describe a vivid visually rich image, your audience will be able to literally imagine seeing the egg frying on the pavement, and this is much more effective than saying that it's hot outside. Why? Well, studies in cognition now say that when people can call up a visual image of a thing, they are engaging your content in two distinct ways: They're both calling up the idea of "hot" (they can recall a time when they were hot), and they can picture the egg frying on the pavement.

This is what cognitive scientists call "multi-modal" engagement. Instead of just relying on the concept "hot," your audience can recall both the physical sensation of being extremely hot, and can call up the visual image of the egg frying on the pavement. This multi-modal engagement, which activates more parts of the brain than just the idea of "hot," helps your audience to engage your content in at least three distinct ways: the idea, the feeling, and the visual image. Engaging lots of different brain functions is a good way to get your audience to bring to bear ideas, images, and experiences, to really experience an idea in more direct ways than just the concept. If you want to create conditions for maximum persuasion, think about the ways that what you are saying can evoke ideas, experiences, and images that engage the audience with your content.

For more information see:

Elizabeth El Refaie, Reconsidering "image metaphor" in the light of perceptual simulation theory, *Metaphor and Symbol*, 30(1), 2015.

Concrete and Lively Language

Holding the interest of the audience and making yourself understood depends, to a large extent, on making abstract ideas and relationships concrete so the audience can more clearly imagine what you're talking about. When people complain that a speech was "dry," they usually mean that the material was presented in a way that was abstract and theoretical rather than concrete and vivid. Concepts, numbers, ideas, and arguments couched in language that creates a picture in audience members' mind become almost as visual as a movie, and the speech, in turn, is more interesting.

Painting images with words—detailed, three-dimensional, persuasively real images—is a skill you can learn. For instance, compare these two sentences. Which one creates a picture in your mind?

1. He cut it up.
2. Swiftly and silently, Jim hacked the watermelon into small pieces.

Clearly, sentence 2 provides much more detail than sentence 1 does. The mental images that audience members construct from sentence 2 would be more similar than their mental images from sentence 1.

If you want to get people's attention about sports, you might try:

Sports are very exciting, with competition as well as highs and lows.

This isn't really interesting. You might think you knew it already, so what's the point? Sierra faces this problem at the beginning of her speech, and here's how she solves it:

It's full of adrenaline rushes, blood, sweat, tears, cheers, pain, pleasure, joy, and everything in between. Whether it's the roar of the crowd, the swish of the basket, the crack of the bat, or the sound of the buzzer, it's something that we're all familiar with despite the heartbreaks and gut-wrenching defeats. We can never let go of one of the greatest things in the world: sports.

This language is exciting, full of images, motion, and a pleasing rhythm. This is the start to a speech that the audience will want to continue to hear. The language of public speaking is not the same as the language of everyday chitchat. Using language that departs somewhat from everyday speech, while remaining appropriate to your audience, makes the occasion special and can inspire listeners to pay closer attention.

Language that is interesting and lively is also easier to remember. Because self-persuasion is the best persuasion, the audience members must remember what you've said so they can mull it over later. Dry and abstract language won't help them do this. You must turn people's *ears* into *eyes* so they will "see" what they're hearing.

How could you make each of the following sentences more concrete and vivid?

- We should do something about immigration.
- U.S. consumers have a responsibility to reduce their environmental impact.
- Better nutrition is in everyone's best interest.

Respectful Language

Because public speaking is designed with an audience—and a public—in mind, you have to speak in way that includes as many people as possible. You shouldn't, deliberately or accidently, make any audience members feel excluded by using language they find disrespectful. Off-color language and sexist and racist language can create disrespect and exclusion.

Off-Color Language Is it ever OK to use foul language? Of course, you can legally say whatever you like. But is it rhetorically smart to do so? In the vast majority of cases, you should avoid it.

The usual argument offered for using off-color language is that it helps speakers to convey the depth of emotion they feel about a topic or to bring in a bit of pathos they wouldn't be able to convey otherwise. It's true that using, say, a four-letter word to describe a bad situation conveys a very different meaning than saying that it's "disappointing." But swearing almost always is a bad choice, for three reasons.

First, you can't know in advance the extent to which rude epithets might undermine your credibility with your audience members or get in the way of their hearing your argument. In general, the more you deviate from the speaking norms your specific audience expects, the more likely you will be to create unintended resistance.

Second, when we speak in public, we model how we think people *ought* to speak in public. What if audience members were to go away from your speech persuaded that foul language was the best way to convey the emotional frame of your topic? If they did, they might not all use the same careful judgments that you did in coming to your word choices, and the quality of public discourse would decline.

Third, many people see the use of foul language as a sign of disrespect toward the audience. As a result, it might make it difficult for you to build the kind of ethical relationship with your audience that you would like to have.

Sexist and Racist Language Our language carries assumptions and implications. We have to be sensitive to whether the assumptions of the words we use are respectful to everyone in our audience. For example, if you talk about "manpower" in your speech, it seems to imply that women aren't able to work or be productive, whereas talking about the "labor force" carries no such implication. Why not skip the implication? You don't believe it anyway. The same reasoning applies to outdated terms such as *fireman* and *policeman*, for which you should substitute *firefighter* and *police officer*. Just as you wouldn't use *boys* to refer to a group of college men, you shouldn't refer to female adults as *girls*. In some parts of the United States, *guys* is used in a gender-neutral way, so "you guys" can refer to both men and women, but you probably should avoid it in a speech, to avoid any misunderstanding.

Racist language includes disrespectful terms for races or ethnicities and common expressions that use the name of an ethnic or racial group in a derogatory way. Generalizations about a group of people also are unacceptable. When a speaker says, "All _____ people are talented in music," the speaker may mean it to be a compliment, but this statement stereotypes people and denies their individuality.

Language that reduces individuals to a single characteristic is also disrespectful. When you talk about "the deaf" or "the blind" or "AIDS victims," you've taken one characteristic and

Chris Rock is one of the comedians who use four-letter words for humor, but what works late at night in a comedy club isn't appropriate in public speaking situations.

the essence of a group of people. Perhaps that characteristic is relevant to your speech, but people are much more than their disabilities or illnesses, and most prefer to be acknowledged as "people who are blind or have a visual impairment" rather than just "the blind." Although some people believe that referring to "the gays" is acceptable, talking about the "gay community" is a more inclusive and respectful choice.

However, you use the techniques of verbal style discussed below to make your speech exciting and memorable, begin by striving to use language that is concrete, lively, and respectful to your audience.

CLASSIFYING VERBAL STYLE: FIGURES AND TROPES

Rhetoricians and linguists have proposed many theories of verbal style and many different systems for categorizing its elements. In this chapter, however, we'll cover just two special forms of speech that are especially useful for public speaking: the **figure**, or a change in the structure of a phrase or sentence that lends an ear-catching quality, and the **trope**, or a change in the way words and concepts are used that give them a new meaning.

figure An ear-catching change in the structure of a phrase or sentence.

You probably already use some figures and tropes in your everyday speech. For instance, only animals have legs and feet, but we routinely refer to "the foot of a mountain" and "the leg of a chair." These common metaphors are a kind of linguistic trope (sometimes called "dead" metaphors because they no longer strike us as metaphors). Some turns of speech, like these familiar images, pass by in conversation without drawing attention to their form, whereas others are uncommon and artful uses of language. This second group is what is important to public speakers.

trope A figure of speech that gives a new meaning for a word or concept.

FIGURES

Your goal in choosing figures for your speech is to use them deliberately to highlight noteworthy content. If you use a figure too frequently, it begins to draw attention to itself rather than to your content, and then it becomes only a distraction for your listeners. But with careful use, figural language can add significant persuasive value to your speech. Two useful types of figures are of repetition and of contrast.

Figures of Repetition

From our earliest days as conversationalists, we learn to avoid structured repetition of words or phrases. If we tell a friend that we're going shopping, for instance, we don't say, "I'm going to buy eggs. I'm going to buy milk. I'm going to buy ketchup." We say, "I'm going to buy eggs, milk, and ketchup." Yet, in public speaking, such repetition, even though it seems redundant, can be used to create structure, lend emphasis, and make words more memorable. A Roman rhetoric textbook, *Rhetorica ad Herennium,* noted that speakers who repeat words and phrases do so not because they are at a loss for words; instead, they are creating something powerful and beautiful: "For there inheres in the repetition an elegance which the ear can distinguish more easily than words can explain."[2]

The following example repeats the phrase, "It takes…," giving both emphasis and structure to the passage:

> It takes no compromising to give people their rights. It takes no money to respect the individual. It takes no survey to remove repressions.
>
> —Harvey Milk, campaign speech for San Francisco Board of Supervisors, 1973. The works of Harvey Milk are owned by L. Stuart Milk and are used for the benefit of the Harvey Milk Foundation.

FAQ *Can I use too much repetition?*

Some of the most memorable speeches in U.S. history rely on repetition. For example, Martin Luther King's "I Have a Dream" speech uses the word *dream* at least eight times. But one of the keys to effective repetition is to cluster repetitions in specific parts of the speech. Such a cluster, which may draw on a theme from earlier in the speech, gives the word or phrase more impact than if it were repeated throughout the whole speech.

You can repeat words, phrases, or sounds effectively, and at the beginning, middle, or end of sentences. Repeating initial sounds is called *alliteration* ("Peter Piper picked a peck of pickled peppers"). Repeating final sounds is called *rhyme* ("Hickory, dickory dock, the mouse ran up the clock"). Both of these repetitions of sounds are more common in poetry and song than in public speaking, which more often uses repeated words and phrases. Let's look at a couple figures of repetition.

Grammatical Repetition Almost everyone knows the final words of President Abraham Lincoln's Gettysburg Address:

> … this government *of the people, by the people, for the people,* shall not perish from the earth.

grammatical repetition
The use of two or more phrases with the same grammatical structure.

Because the phrases in italics have the same grammatical structure (in this case, preposition + definite article + noun), we call this **grammatical repetition**.

Another famous example of grammatical repetition is the message Julius Caesar sent to the Roman Senate (in Latin, of course) in 47 BC to announce the results of a battle he fought in Turkey:

> Veni, vidi, vici. ("I came, I saw, I conquered.")

Here, Caesar gave us three complete sentences with the structure of *I* + verb. It not only is an economical expression but also a memorable one (in the original Latin, it also is an alliteration).

Another example, this time from Martin Luther King, Jr., is:

> You have been the veterans of creative suffering. Continue to work with the faith that unearned suffering is redemptive. Go back to Mississippi, go back to Alabama, go back to South Carolina, go back to Georgia, go back to Louisiana, go back to the slums and ghettos of our northern cities, knowing that somehow this situation can and will be changed.

Martin Luther King Jr.'s famous 1963 "Address to the March on Washington" speech is commonly known as the "I Have a Dream" speech because of his repeated use of that phrase. Why does Dr. King use so much repetition in this speech?

Go back to + (place) is repeated six times, creating speed and force to King's call for civil rights workers to take action, and the emotion is impossible to ignore if you listen to a recording of the "I Have a Dream" speech. This type of repetition is powerful and allows you to focus on either the phrase that is repeated or the complement to that phrase.

Progression **Progression** uses repetition to create a sense of movement. The effect of progression should be that of moving, rung by rung, up a ladder, drawing the listener forward to a conclusion. The following progression became popular during the 2008 U.S. presidential election:[3]

progression Grammatical repetition that creates a sense of movement.

> Rosa sat so that Martin could walk,
> Martin walked so that Barack could run,
> Barack ran so that our children could fly.

Generally, progression leaves the most important item until the end and builds to the word or point you want the audience to remember.

> All this will not be finished in the first 100 days. Nor will it be finished in the first 1,000 days, nor in the life of this administration, nor perhaps in our lifetime on this planet.
> —John F. Kennedy, inaugural address, January 20, 1961

Some possible progressions include the following:

Minutes → hours → days
Great → greater → greatest
Local → state → Federal
Low → middle → high
Bad → worse → worst

Legendary primatologist Jane Goodall said, "Only if we understand, can we care. Only if we care, we will help. Only if we help, we shall be saved."

You also can use progression to structure the points of your speech, so the preview itself will be a progression. For example, if your thesis were "Taxation is unjust," structuring your argument as a progression might yield this argument:

If taxation is unjust for the federal government, it is unjust for a state, and if unjust for a state, it is unjust for our town.

Like repetition, progression uses ordinary words and their normal meanings, but it arranges them to create a striking and memorable effect. You can use these figures to create emphasis for points you are trying to make.

Figures of Contrast

Think about the difference between these two sentences:

> It's often hard for people to change their cultural assumptions, even when they make major geographical and sociological moves.

> You can take the boy out of the country, but you can't take the country out of the boy.

These two sentences have much the same meaning; the difference is in the choice and arrangement of the words. The second version makes the contrast clear and memorable. You can use contrast in several different ways. Let's look at antithesis and a couple of its variations.

antithesis The use of two contrasting or opposing words or meanings.

Antithesis **Antithesis** means putting opposites together by creating a sentence with two contrasting or opposing parts. Here's a famous example:

> One small step for a man; one giant leap for mankind.
> —Neil Armstrong, as he set foot on the moon, July 21, 1969

By putting the contrast of ideas into the structure of the sentence, antithesis makes the point in more than one dimension. Consider this example from Richard Nixon's eulogy for Senator Everett Dirksen in 1969; it's part of Nixon's argument that Dirksen was an outstanding politician:

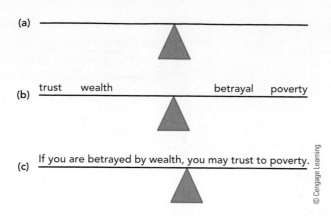

FIGURE 8.1
Constructing an antithesis on a scale

(a)

(b) trust   wealth   betrayal   poverty

(c) If you are betrayed by wealth, you may trust to poverty.

© Cengage Learning

> A politician knows how to make the process of democracy work and loves the intricate workings of the democratic system. A politician knows not only how to count votes but how to make his vote _____.

Because you can easily guess what the last word of this passage must have been, you know that you, like the audience, were following the structure of the sentences, and listening/reading closely.

Consider the final sentence of this passage from a speech by Carrie Chapman Catt, a leading advocate of women's suffrage, to Congress in 1917 on why women should have the vote:

> If parties prefer to postpone action longer and thus do battle with this idea, they challenge the inevitable. The idea will not perish; the party which opposes it may.

The antithesis fills out the meaning of *inevitable* from the previous sentence in a clear and compelling way.

You might think that only someone with poetic abilities could write this way. Not true. Anyone can come up with effective antitheses in a few minutes. When you compose an antithesis, don't try to write it from beginning to end. Instead, start by thinking about a couple of ideas that are crucial to the argument or point you're trying to make. Then try this: Draw a line, and put an arrow in the middle to serve as the fulcrum of your scale (see Figure 8.1).

If your ideas were about trust and money, think about their opposites: trust/betrayal and wealth/poverty. Put the opposing words on either side of the fulcrum in Figure 8.1. Then play around with the words to shape them into phrases. In Figure 8.1, it seemed that reversing the order of the concepts worked better. In a speech whose theme is "money can't buy happiness," this might be an effective way to make the point.

Try to keep about the same number of words and syllables on each side of the fulcrum. Charles Dickens did this in a famous antithesis that begins *A Tale of Two Cities* (see Figure 8.2).

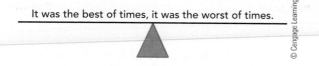

It was the best of times, it was the worst of times.

© Cengage Learning

FIGURE 8.2
Antithesis from *A Tale of Two Cities*

The basic way to create the opposition in an antithesis is to use words with opposite meanings, such as *best* and *worst*. The plain double antithesis and the double-reverse antithesis are slightly more complex ways to structure an antithesis.

Figures of contrast work best if you stick to a few rules:

- Keep the contrasting figures compact—that is, relatively close together and preferably in the same phrase.
- Use contrast sparingly—saving it for important points. You wouldn't, for example, use a contrasting construction in a transition ("Now, the first point, as opposed to the second. . .").
- Look for real opposites—contrast works best when it is stark. Don't try to force an opposition between things that are not actually opposites.

plain double antithesis Two pairs of contrasting words.

Plain Double Antithesis

In **plain double antithesis**, the contrast is double, between two or more pairs of terms, such as between *all* and *none,* between *virtues* and *vices,* and between *dislike* and *admire* in this example:

> He has all the virtues I dislike and none of the vices I admire.
> —Winston Churchill, describing a political opponent

Here are a couple of other examples:

> [We have] made the most difference in people's lives when we've led not by polls, but by principle; not by calculation, but by conviction.
> —Barack Obama, op-ed, *Des Moines Register,* November 27, 2007

> Extremism in defense of liberty is no vice, moderation in the pursuit of justice is no virtue.
> —Barry Goldwater, accepting the Republican Party's nomination for president, 1964

The double-antithesis has all the virtues of the simple antithesis, but it allows you to put more ideas in play.

Double-Reverse Antithesis

A **double-reverse antithesis** achieves opposition by reversing the order of key words to create the opposite meaning, and has an AB-BA structure.

double-reverse antithesis Key words repeated in reverse order.

> Let us never negotiate out of fear, but let us never fear to negotiate.
> —John F. Kennedy, inaugural address, January 20, 1961

> A pessimist sees the difficulty in every opportunity; an optimist sees the opportunity in every difficulty.
> —Winston Churchill

> When the going gets tough, the tough get going.
> —Joseph P. Kennedy

Double-reverse antitheses are somewhat more difficult to compose than the other types, but they are memorable. This is why they get used in advertising jingles.

Aristotle claimed that "popularity of style is mainly due to antithesis," and he was certainly right that antitheses are impressive and memorable. They are especially useful in your peroration (see Chapter 7), where they can help you end your speech clearly and definitely. Because you, as a listener, usually can predict the end of an antithesis after hearing the first half, you're anticipating the end, and it's clear that the speaker means to be absolutely done.

TRY IT! | **RECOGNIZING FIGURES OF REPETITION AND CONTRAST**

Almost everyone knows about Abraham Lincoln's Gettysburg Address, delivered on a battlefield in Pennsylvania after a Civil War battle in which many thousands of soldiers died. Most people find the speech to be powerful, but they're not sure why. The reason might be Lincoln's skill with figures of speech. Find out for yourself. Here's the text of Lincoln's speech. See how many figures of repetition and contrast you can find in it.

Fourscore and seven years ago our fathers brought forth on this continent a new nation, conceived in liberty and dedicated to the proposition that all men are created equal.

Now we are engaged in a great civil war, testing whether that nation or any nation so conceived and so dedicated can long endure. We are met on a great battlefield of that war. We have come to dedicate a portion of that field as a final resting-place for those who here gave their lives that that nation might live. It is altogether fitting and proper that we should do this.

But, in a larger sense, we cannot dedicate, we cannot consecrate, we cannot hallow this ground. The brave men, living and dead who struggled here have consecrated it far above our poor power to add or detract. The world will little note nor long remember what we say here, but it can never forget what they did here. It is for us the living rather to be dedicated here to the unfinished work which they who fought here have thus far so nobly advanced. It is rather for us to be here dedicated to the great task remaining before us—that from these honored dead we take increased devotion to that cause for which they gave the last full measure of devotion—that we here highly resolve that these dead shall not have died in vain, that this nation under God shall have a new birth of freedom, and that government of the people, by the people, for the people shall not perish from the earth.

How hard was it to find these figures? Do you think they helped to make the speech powerful and memorable? Which ones would you personally change?

TROPES

Tropes are words or phrases that we use to convey a message other than their usual, literal meaning. As we pointed out earlier, you may not realize it, but you use tropes in your daily speech. The challenge for your public speaking is to choose tropes that serve your purpose and are understandable to the audience.

Tropes are surprisingly easy to create and use, and they're highly effective with audiences. Tropes can serve several purposes in your speech, including comparison, substitution, and exaggeration (see Table 8.1). We'll begin with the comparative tropes, metaphor and simile, and then move to the tropes of substitution (metonymy), exaggeration, and voice.

FAQ *Why is it called a "trope"?*

Trope derives from the Greek word *tropos*, which means "turn." A trope is a turn of meaning that is somehow meaningful to the audience. If you "turn a phrase" to say something in an indirect but artful way, you have used a trope.

Advice for Being More Charismatic

One of the most difficult things in training public speakers has been, until recently, teaching people how to be more charismatic. If you ask people how to be more charismatic, they often respond with mostly useless advice: Be more confident, own the room, and so on. Being charismatic, confident, or "owning the room" are not things that speakers can decide to do on a whim. If people already knew how to be more charismatic or how to appear more confident, they wouldn't need this advice. Being charismatic or confident are the products of specific choices; they are the culmination of things that the speaker actually does, as opposed to being things that a speaker can just decide to be.

Scholars who are interested in leadership have started to ask exactly what choices make a person appear more charismatic, and their findings have been extremely interesting. One of the essential things in projecting leadership and, therefore, charisma is to employ some of the tropes discussed in this chapter. Specifically, researchers have found that employing a central explanatory metaphor or analogy tends to make audiences perceive a speaker as more charismatic.

In the research, employing a central explanatory metaphor not only increased the perception that speakers knew what they were talking about, but also increased the tendency of speakers to talk about values, and made the content of the speech more accessible to the audience: Whereas a direct claim that was rooted in the idea behind a content may have fallen flat, a metaphor that explained and imparted value-based content to a claim was found to engage the audience and to make the underlying values of the speaker more accessible. If you want to be more charismatic, you should organize your speech around one or more central metaphors. Your audience will think better of you and the claims you make.

For more information see:

John Antonakis, Marika Fenley, & Sue Liechti, Learning charisma, *Harvard Business Review*, June 2012, https://hbr.org/2012/06/learning-charisma-2

Tropes of Comparison: Metaphor and Simile

Every time you get up to speak, you're telling the audience members something they don't know already. How can you help them to understand? You'll have to start with things they do know and lead them into the new information. Tropes of comparison are a great way to accomplish this, because they allow you to compare the unfamiliar to the familiar.

metaphor A word or phrase applied to something in a way that is not literally true.

Metaphor A **metaphor** is an assertion that isn't literally true but is still understandable. In essence, it is a comparison that doesn't use the word *like* or *as*, and it is a particularly important trope. When you say of a favorite football player, "Oh, he's a monster," you don't mean it literally (he's a human being, not a monster); you mean it metaphorically (he's a really large, intense, tough player). Metaphors borrow a meaning or association from one context and import it to another. Although what you've said isn't literally true, it invites the listener to transfer meaning from *monster* to the football player.

Table 8.1 Types of Tropes and Their Functions

Comparison	Exaggeration
Metaphor	Understatement
Simile	Overstatement
Substitution	**Voice**
Metonymy	Personification

Metaphors can make unfamiliar things familiar. For instance, you could say,

College basketball teams are the minor leagues of professional basketball.

This isn't literally true, because professional teams don't fund or control college teams, but the metaphor points out the structural similarity in the relationship between student athletes and professional teams.

Metaphors also can simplify complicated things. The statement "Your body is a machine, so it needs regular maintenance in the form of checkups" lets your audience members apply their knowledge about cars to health issues. Metaphors are so common that you may not realize how often you use them. Knowing how to create or find good metaphors for a given speech is the challenge.

Continuing the example of the speech about blood donation from Chapter 1, here are some sample metaphors:

Turn on the light for someone without hope—give blood.
Donating blood opens the door to hope.
Blood is life.
Giving your blood is giving yourself.
That little tube is a lifeline to others.

Notice that metaphors can clarify what you're doing when you give blood ("blood is life"), or they can express the benefits of giving blood ("opens the door to hope"). Which you choose depends on the point you're trying to make in your speech.

Sometimes entire speeches can even be structured around a metaphor: If the audience members understand and remember the metaphor, they will understand and remember the entire speech. For example, suppose you're talking about educational reform, particularly for underachieving students, and your points consist of the needs to improve home life, classroom facilities, and after-school activities. You might choose the metaphor of an ailing tree: What could we do to improve it? First, we'd look at the roots, the part we can't see (home life), and be sure the soil was properly balanced (appropriate opportunities at home). Then, we'd attend to the trunk of the tree (the classroom) and make sure it was whole and pest-free (good facilities and no distracting students). Finally, we'd look at the leaves (after-school programs) and make sure they were healthy and able to nurture the rest of the tree (extracurricular opportunities that enhance the rest of the educational process).

Although it's not always possible find an appropriate controlling metaphor for an entire speech, it's often worth the effort. Just make sure that all the parts fit. (If the metaphor falls apart or contradicts itself at some point, it's like a flat note for a singer and can spoil the audience's impression of your speech.) Also make sure the metaphor isn't so strange or obscure that you'll confuse the audience.

Simile A **simile** is an explicit comparison between two things, using the word *like* or *as* to connect them. Less subtle and complex than metaphors, similes are most useful when you're trying to help the audience members immediately see the clear relationship between something they know about—for instance, "beating your head against the wall"—and a new or unexplored idea or experience—"taking a math class too advanced for you." The simile could be, "Taking a math class too advanced for you is like beating your head against the wall." Clearly, taking this class is going to prove painful and frustrating.

Similes are related to metaphors, yet they can be more precise, because they make the terms of a connection explicit: One thing is like or can be understood "as" (in explicit connection to) another thing. Because the connection is explicit in a simile, you can fill out the similarity as specifically as you need to, helping you make your point clearly. Compare these examples of similes about blood donation to the examples of metaphors about blood donation in the previous section:

simile An explicit comparison that uses *like* or *as* to connect two things.

Giving blood is like making a deposit in a bank.
Giving blood is as important as giving time or money.

Similes also are useful when the object of comparison has parts you can use to explain aspects of the main idea. Here's a simile for a speech about changing our diets:

> Your body is like a machine: You take fuel in, you produce heat and do work, and you produce waste products. We need to look at the kinds of "fuels" we use and how efficient they are for our "machines."

Similes can be useful because they are familiar, but if they are trite or clichéd, they may not make a strong impression on the audience. Like a stone worn smooth from long handling, familiar similes no longer create much mental friction. If you've heard it a lot, you often just don't hear it. Here are some classic similes that you probably should avoid in favor of something fresh:

brave as a lion
blind as a bat
busy as a bee
cold as ice
dry as a bone
pretty as a picture
quiet as a mouse

sick as a dog
silent as the grave
gentle as a lamb
good as gold
hard as nails
strong as an ox
sweet as honey

TRY IT! Using the blood donation example as a model, design a metaphor that is appropriate for the topic of your next speech.

- Now, take that metaphor and reframe it as a simile.
- Which of the two is more effective for your purposes?
- Which is more powerful?
- Why?

The Trope of Substitution: Metonymy

metonymy An expression that substitutes a part or a property for the whole.

Metonymy (pronounced *meh-TAHN-ah-mee*) is an expression that substitutes a part for the whole, or a property of something for the thing itself. An example is a television executive saying, "We need to double the eyeballs in this timeslot." Obviously, the programmer is talking about viewers, not actual eyeballs, but substituting the relevant part of the viewers' anatomy creates metonymy.

Metonymy not only is a kind of shorthand, but it also directs listeners' attention in some way. The eyes are particularly important to television watchers. Historically, the metonymy in which sailors are called "hands" ("All hands on deck!") is rooted in the days when ships were controlled by ropes, which the sailors worked with their hands. Journalists sometimes refer to infantry soldiers as "boots on the ground," because traditionally the infantry advanced on foot.

How could metonymy help a speech about blood donation? Suppose your argument is that giving blood is a small inconvenience that has a huge positive impact. To sum up that argument in a memorable way, you could use metonymy:

> That tiny pain can save a life.
> Every bare arm saves a life.
> Blood donation is community in a pint-sized bag.

In each of these examples, some feature of the experience of blood donation stands in for the larger meaning of giving blood.

Jackie Chan isn't a native speaker of English, though he speaks it well. Does his accent matter in his ability to employ verbal style effectively?

Tropes of Exaggeration: Overstatement and Understatement

Another way to get your point across is by using overstatement and understatement. **Hyperbole** is an overstatement, a claim so over the top that it obviously isn't true:

I have a million things to do today.

Litotes (pronounced *li-TOE-tees*) is an understatement, expressing something in a way that obviously is out of proportion with the facts.

The United States has just a small army.

Hyperbole and litotes are both means of ironic exaggeration that put a particular perspective on an event. Litotes usually includes a kind of reversal, in which the understatement emphasizes the magnitude of the truth without making the speaker seem overly passionate or concerned; the audience gets to draw the conclusion.

Here are examples of litotes and hyperbole about blood donation:

Giving blood takes just a second.
A drop of blood from you can do an ocean of good for someone else.

These tropes put the experience of blood donation in perspective, highlighting how a small sacrifice can yield an important result.

The Trope of Voice: Personification

Personification is the process of giving human qualities to abstract or inanimate objects, allowing them to speak, feel, or think.

The cost of this school building speaks volumes about its importance to the community.

hyperbole Extreme overstatement that obviously is untrue.

litotes An exaggerated understatement that obviously is untrue.

personification Human qualities ascribed to an abstract or inanimate object.

Personification is an effective way to position an argument or point of view by shifting from the actual speaker to an imaginary one. For example, if a speaker on a Civil War topic wants to avoid seeming partisan, she might attribute certain arguments to the locations themselves.

The battlefields speak to us eloquently. They ask us to consider the meaning of disagreement, and sacrifice, in a democracy.

If you were going to make an argument about the impact of blood donation, you could give agency to the blood or illustrate that without donations, people won't get the surgeries they need:

Your blood might go out and save a life.
All these empty hospital beds whisper, "Where were the blood donors?"

Thanks to modern film animation techniques, talking objects are familiar, and speakers should make creative use of them.

MATCHING THE STYLE TO THE TOPIC AND THE OCCASION

In this chapter we've given you many new choices about language. Making these choices requires you to consider how to coordinate them with your goal, with the occasion, and with the topic. For example, if your speech is about an everyday topic, your style should be simple—reserving metaphors and examples for difficult concepts. You wouldn't, for example, talk about the "tyranny" of cilantro-haters or the "bloody massacre" of class registration. But if you're talking about a subject with a legitimate emotional charge, you might use a more elaborate style. No one should give a speech about a massacre and say that it was "kind of a bummer."

Similarly, your style should fit the occasion and the audience. If you're giving a toast in front of a crowd of college friends at a wedding, you'll have to strike a balance between the customary ribbing, old stories, and something sweet (often metaphorical) about love. If you're giving a pitch at a business meeting, you wouldn't use too much figurative language, and only if it relates to your goal. For example, you might use a poker metaphor to invite someone to "double down" on an investment, but you likely wouldn't talk about how an investment made your "heart take wing." (We'll discuss special-occasion speeches like these in Chapter 13.)

As you think about language and your speech, remember: Novelty is like salt; a little goes a long way. If every sentence is overwhelmingly interesting, the audience will burn out and probably stop listening well. Use figures to highlight your most important points, the ones you absolutely want the audience to walk away remembering. Look through your speech and ask yourself, "If they remember only two things, what would I want the two things to be?" Figures are helpful when you move from one idea or point to another—as transitions and in the introduction, conclusion, or anywhere you're trying to draw attention to main ideas and relationships.

The speeches you give in class will be designed primarily to inform your audiences about something important or interesting to you or to persuade them to get on board with a policy or other course of action. As a result, although you have some room to use strongly figured language, you will have to pick your places. For example, stylistic figures work well in stories that serve as an example of a larger issue and in your call for action.

Summary

Language matters. Choosing the right words is a choice about style, even more than delivery is. Although no secret verbal jiu-jitsu can enable you to persuade people by just choosing the right words, presenting your arguments in smart, compelling language helps to make you an effective speaker and communicator. Excellent speakers start by ensuring that their language choices are as concrete, vivid, and respectful as possible. They then go on to look for places in their speeches where they can arrange words (as *figures*) to make a point or use a turn of phrase (a *trope*) to enable the audience to see their point. All of these choices have to be made *appropriately*, taking into account the audience, the occasion, and the topic.

Having good ideas and good arguments in your speech is necessary, but people are not simply data-processing units. The way you use language to convey an idea makes a big difference in how your audience will receive your ideas. Stylistic choices can be difficult, but the most important thing for good style is to think about your choices and to select wisely.

Questions for Review

1. What is style? How do the choices you make about language influence your audience's reception of your ideas?
2. What are the different types of figures?
3. To what uses can tropes be put? Give examples.
4. Give an example showing how you would integrate tropes and figures into a speech.
5. What should guide your choices in using tropes, figures, and other stylistic elements in your speech?

Questions for Discussion

1. Can someone use too many tropes and figures? How would you tell whether a speech is over the top?
2. Which kind of trope seems to be the most common, in everything from famous speakers to advertising jingles? Why do you think it's so popular?
3. Take a simple statement such as, "This course is difficult." Now invent as many different ways of saying it as you can. Which of the ways that you invented might be effective in a speech? Which would not? Why?
4. Go to www.americanrhetoric.com and select a speech. Choose one section of the speech (the introduction, conclusion, or a specific argument) and list all the tropes and figures you find. Then write a brief paragraph explaining which ones served the speaker's purpose and which ones didn't. Compare your results with your classmates.

Key Concepts   MindTap®

Practice defining the chapter's terms by using online flashcards.

antithesis	litotes	progression
double-reverse antithesis	metonymy	simile
figure	metaphor	style
grammatical repetition	personification	trope
hyperbole	plain double antithesis	

CHAPTER 9 DELIVERY

LEARNING OBJECTIVES

- Differentiate talking and speaking
- Explain the techniques for creating focus and energy from anxiety
- Compare the different types of delivery and connect them to appropriate situations
- Demonstrate the principles of good vocal delivery
- Demonstrate the principles of good physical delivery
- Choose the best ways to practice your speech
- Employ methods for engaging audience questions
- Practice the kinds of cooperation and coordination required for group presentations

CHAPTER OUTLINE

- Introduction: Stand and Deliver
- Speaking or Talking?
- Creating Focus and Energy from Your Anxiety
- Types of Preparation and Delivery
- Types of Speaking Aids
- Using Your Voice Effectively
- Using Your Body Effectively
- Communicating Credibility
- How to Practice Delivering Your Speech
- Answering Questions from the Audience
- Group Presentations

Zadie wanted to give a speech about a job she had during her first year in college, working at an ice cream place. She had some amusing and enlightening experiences to relate. It all looked great on paper—but then the speech fell flat. The writing still seemed fine to her, so she wondered if delivery could make a difference: Could she have made a really great speech not-so-great with weak delivery? What should she have done differently?

Overview

What seems scariest or most difficult about public speaking for most people is the performance—actually getting up to speak. The hard work, described in the previous eight chapters, really comes before you get up to speak. Moreover, having a well-organized speech that you care about and that is properly adapted to your audience will make you more comfortable. It's actually one of the best things you can do to improve your delivery experience. But you can learn reliable methods for improving delivery, moderating fear, and preparing to speak. We'll examine them in this chapter, starting with strategies for dealing with your anxiety, then moving to the different types of delivery. After that, we'll look at how to use your voice and your body effectively and how to communicate credibility. The chapter concludes by discussing the most effective ways to practice your speech and how to handle audience questions.

© 2017 Cengage Learning

MindTap®

Start with a warm-up activity about Zadie and how delivery matters, and review the chapter's Learning Objectives.

INTRODUCTION: STAND AND DELIVER

So far in this book, we've discussed the choices that go into creating a good speech. We've discussed how you should think about your audience and the purpose of your speech, how you can organize your speech, how you should support your arguments, and how to choose the best way to say what you want to say. Now we're ready to discuss how to actually stand up and give your speech.

Delivery is one of the most rewarding, and for some the most challenging, part of the public speaking process. But like all the other parts, delivery depends on some basic choices. Although doing all the work necessary to put together a good speech improves your chances

MindTap®

Read, highlight, and take notes online.

of giving a successful speech, the way you deliver it—your choices and your practices in giving the speech—matters to the way your audience receives it.

For evidence of this, think of Martin Luther King, Jr.'s famous "I Have a Dream" speech. Here's the conclusion from that speech:

> When we allow freedom ring, when we let it ring from every village and every hamlet, from every state and every city, we will be able to speed up that day when all of God's children, black men and white men, Jews and Gentiles, Protestants and Catholics, will be able to join hands and sing in the words of the old Negro spiritual, "Free at last, free at last! Thank God Almighty, we are free at last!"

If you listen to this speech (available in many places online), you will notice a number of things about how Dr. King delivers the speech. First, you might observe how crisply and distinctly he delivers each of the words. Note also how effective he is in using the pace and tone of his voice to emphasize certain words: Anyone who transcribes the speech knows exactly where to put the exclamation points ("Free at last!"), and no listener can doubt the importance to Dr. King that *all* of "God's children" be free.

But imagine someone else giving the same speech under entirely different circumstances, a disheveled speaker who stands in front of an audience, fumbling with his notes. Speaking in a mumbling monotone, he inserts excess words and awkward pauses:

> **When we . . . um . . . [pause] allow freedom, you know [scratches cheek] . . . like, to ring, from every village, and every hamlet, and from every state and . . . uh, every, um . . . city . . .**

We don't have to butcher Martin Luther King's great speech any further to make the point: The way a speaker delivers a message makes a big difference in the way an audience responds to it, and even the most skillfully drafted speeches about the most crucial topics can fall flat if the speaker doesn't pay attention to the finer points of delivery.

SPEAKING OR TALKING?

What are the obstacles to good delivery? The first is that you may not have been trained to deliver a public speech. Good public speaking is the result of practice and training. In the course of this chapter, we will provide some important tips for practicing and delivering a good public speech.

The second, but perhaps more significant, obstacle is anxiety about public speaking. Jerry Seinfeld once said:

> According to most studies, people's number one fear is public speaking. Number two is death. Death is number two. Does that sound right? This means to the average person, if you go to a funeral, you're better off in the casket than doing the eulogy.[1]

It's commonplace that some people fear public speaking more than anything else. Yet, as long as the label "public speaking" is not attached to the event or occasion, most of us are really quite comfortable talking in public. You usually spend much of each day talking to other people, and you take for granted your ability to do this. Consider, for instance, how often you do the following:

- Order a complicated coffee drink, making yourself clear, while others in line watch and listen.
- Speak up in a class, with the rest of the class listening.
- Give directions to someone who stops you on the street.

- Deal with an irate customer at your workplace.
- Persuade your mechanic to fix your car just a little bit sooner.

Each of these events is, in a sense, a kind of public speech. You decide (perhaps subconsciously) what you're trying to do, note who the audience members are, and then say the right words, with the right look on your face, in the right tone of voice. You're so good at this everyday communication (because you've been doing it for years) that you tend to think it's easy and that it's natural rather than a learned skill. But it's the result of years of practice ever since you were young, learning to interact with others.

Anyone who has traveled abroad and spent time in other cultures soon realizes that successful communication does not require just saying the words of the other language but also embedding them in the performance. Greeting a shopkeeper in France doesn't mean merely saying the word *bonjour* ("good day/hello") but saying it in the right upward intonation, eyebrows up, but without actually smiling—learning to *perform* the greeting that native speakers give without thinking.

The point of public speaking training is to *extend* and *enlarge* your communication performance skills, not to create them from scratch. You're already a much better communicator than you probably realize, and in working on your public speaking, you're building on years of resources and skills that you've developed. What makes some people nervous about public speaking is thinking that it's different from everyday communication that takes years of study and practice to do so competently. Of course, being a *great* speaker takes years of practice, but being a good and effective speaker is within everyone's ability. We'll turn next to the main obstacle: anxiety.

CREATING FOCUS AND ENERGY FROM YOUR ANXIETY

The biggest concern for most speakers is anxiety about speaking. How can you deal with it? How can you overcome it to create a focus for yourself and communicate energy to the audience? Here are some effective strategies that will start to work for you right away.

1. **Remember—we are all in the same boat.**
   Keep in mind that almost everyone is anxious when they speak, even the most seasoned speakers. But no one has ever died from public speaking anxiety. You'll get through it! Take comfort in knowing that you and your fellow classmates are all negotiating some nervousness in speaking. You can work together to create a supportive atmosphere for everyone. This means not only that you each need to think about how you will speak in front of others but also that you all need to work on being charitable and responsive audience members.

2. **Manage your expectations.**
   One of the reasons that people fret so much about public speaking anxiety is that they secretly think they can eliminate all of their anxiety. This is unlikely, so the most productive mind-set is to go into a speaking situation accepting that you'll be nervous and that being nervous is OK. The question for you is not "Will I be nervous?" or "How can I control my feelings?" but, rather, "How can I respond to my nervousness productively?"

3. **Recognize that nerves make you a *better* speaker.**
   Nervousness is a good thing, because it means that you care about what the audience thinks. If you didn't care, you wouldn't be nervous. And you'd be a boring speaker, because you'd be speaking only to please yourself. Instead of aiming to be entirely without nerves or completely comfortable, try to turn your nerves into energy. That way, nerves often look like excitement and enthusiasm to the audience. How do you

"Breathe. Speak well. Leave them breathless."

Cartoonresource/Shutterstock.com

do this? By not reacting to your nerves. For many people, feeling nervous (flushed face, quicker breathing, thumping heartbeat) starts a cycle: nervous, nervous about being nervous, nervous about being nervous about being nervous, and so on. Instead, your strategy should be to notice your nerves and then turn your attention, calmly and deliberately, back to speaking. That little bit of nervous energy is still there, and the audience may notice it, but you are in control and communicating.

4. **Keep in mind that you don't look as nervous as you feel.**

    Few people are stunningly articulate and at ease when they are in front of an audience for the first time. But looking nervous and feeling nervous are two different things. Though you may feel like a bundle of nerves, this isn't what the audience members see. They see a person who would like to do a good job of giving a speech and who is attempting to impart useful information to them. So take comfort in knowing that your feeling of nervousness is nearly all subjective and not what the audience is perceiving about you as you speak.

5. **Strive to see the bigger picture.**

    Public speaking is a learning process. Every time you speak in front of an audience, you're in the *process* of learning to speak more effectively. This means that you should be easy on yourself when you don't give a perfect speech. Instead of focusing on your shortcomings, focus on what you can do better next time.

6. **Remember that your topic is more important than your nerves.**

    Presumably, you have picked a topic that is important to you, one that you believe should be important to your audience as well. Recognize that what you want to say is the main thing. To help your motivation trump your nerves, recognize that what you're saying trumps the nerves you may feel.

7. **Practice!**

    As with any other skill, practice can help you get through the tough points in your speech. You can practice in two ways: (1) Running through the speech in your mind, ask yourself what parts are potentially difficult, and focus your practice efforts on these parts; and (2) give the speech in front of a friend or family member. This not only will give you a chance to gain some valuable feedback but also will help you get used to speaking in front of other people. "How to Practice Delivering Your Speech," discussed later in this chapter, offers additional recommendations.

8. **Let your preparation speak for you.**

    If you're giving an unprepared speech off the cuff, you have reason to feel unsure of yourself. If, however, you put in the work required to draft a well-ordered, coherent speech, you can rely on your notes and the concepts you've organized as supports to get you through any nervous moments. If you have a well-conceived outline and central concept for your speech, it will be easy to pick up the flow even if you get lost or stumble.

9. **Visualize your success and believe in it.**

    Many times, before the speech, speakers will get lost in daydreams about screwing up and feeling humiliated. Not only are these worries unlikely to come true, but they make it harder for you to deal with your natural and useful nervousness. Instead, visualize a successful speech, in which you feel nervous but move past it to a great performance.

10. **Remember—the audience is on your side.**

    No one wants to hear a bad speech. The audience actually is hoping for a great one. But envision an audience of people you are comfortable with (regardless of who is really sitting there) and act as if you are giving the speech to them. This can help you manage any anxiety about whether the audience is friendly. Trust yourself and trust your audience. Keep in mind that audiences don't want to see speakers fail. Audience members want you to succeed, especially because they have been or will be in the same position soon.

11. **Act "as if."**

    If all else fails, keep in mind that it's not how you feel but, rather, how you act that dictates the success of your performance. As the saying goes, "Fake it until you make it." You don't have to *feel* calm; you just have to get through the speech. So the best thing you can do is to act as if you *belong* in front of that room. This also will convey a sense of authority that will make you feel better.

TYPES OF PREPARATION AND DELIVERY

The most obvious difference between conversational communication and public speaking is that people typically prepare carefully for public speaking—both for the content and the performance—whereas conversation seems to happen without our even thinking about it. Speakers can choose among several methods to prepare for performance, each with its strengths and weaknesses. Different methods of preparation will put different demands on your delivery.

Speaking From Memory

In a **speech from memory**, the speaker writes out the text of the speech and then memorizes it. Speakers in antiquity used this technique a great deal—in classical Greek and

speech from memory
A speech that is written out, memorized, then delivered.

Roman education, students memorized enormous chunks of text—but hardly anyone does this anymore. Why? Because it's difficult, and there's not much need for it. With the development of books and computers (and the teleprompter), we no longer have to memorize the texts we want to remember.

For the *appearance* of spontaneity, you can't beat speaking from memory—*if* you have the gift of making a rehearsed speech sound spontaneous. But memorization is a lot of work, and you run the risk of forgetting your material, getting lost, or sounding rehearsed and mechanical. Speaking from memory comes close to acting and is the mode of performance farthest from daily conversation.

Speaking From Manuscript

manuscript speech
A speech that is written out
and read to the audience.

For a **manuscript speech**, the speaker writes out the text, then reads it to the audience. Although this is a common method and easier than memorization, it still requires a great deal of skill. Many speeches that aren't written by professional speechwriters aren't designed to be read aloud, and many people read aloud poorly enough that the audience is left wondering, "Why couldn't this speaker give me the text and let me read it myself?"

Many politicians use the manuscript delivery technique by reading from a teleprompter, which shows them an electronic text at eye level. The teleprompter enables them to read without ever looking down, giving an impression of being natural, which also may be the result of long practice.

Some new speakers convince themselves that a manuscript will solve their performance problems and reduce their anxiety. That's possible, but these speakers often stare at their manuscript, reading in a robotic monotone and never looking at the audience. They may *say* they're less nervous, but it's hard to believe that from looking at them.

Extemporaneous Speaking

extemporaneous speech
A speech delivered from
written notes or an outline.

In an **extemporaneous speech** the speaker relies on limited notes and supplies the specific words and sentences as he or she speaks. If the speaker were to deliver the same speech again,

President Ronald Reagan was famous for his ability to read from a text, yet making it sound as if he were thinking up the words in the moment. How difficult would this skill be to acquire?

Ronald Reagan Library/Archive Photos/Getty Images

the words would be slightly different. Extemporaneous speaking is the most common type of formal speaking that you will do and, therefore, the most important type for you to learn.

Preparation for extemporaneous speaking can be highly individual. Some people can speak from just a list of words (their topics); others prefer a detailed outline; and still others use something between the two. Even with notes, however, you may well write out certain parts of the speech. If you have a really great metaphor or antithesis, you should write it out word for word, because the exact words matter. Many people also like to write out the first and last couple of sentences of their speech because it helps them in the places where they're most likely to be nervous or unsure.

Impromptu Speaking

Impromptu speaking means speaking with little or no preparation, off the top of your head. You already use it every time you're called on in class or in a meeting, and it's not as difficult to do in a public speaking situation as you might think. Many moments in your work career (from the job interview onward) will be impromptu or have impromptu components.

In impromptu speaking, you use the same skills of organization and argument that you would in a normal speech, but you have to plan the structure rapidly in your head instead of preparing it ahead of time. The more experience you have in speaking, the more likely you will have a stock of arguments, anecdotes, and even evidence that you can bring out on the spot.

impromptu speaking
A speech delivered on the spot, without preparation.

ARE YOU A BETTER READER OR SPEAKER? TRY IT!

If you have access to a video camera or a video-enabled computer, try the following exercise:

- Deliver a three-minute chunk of your speech from a manuscript. Now try to deliver the same chunk from notecards, and then from memory.
- Track the differences you notice as you give the speech using each method.
- Watch the video of each delivery. How did your impressions of your own performance match up with the video? What does this exercise tell you about the process of speaking?

Staying on Time

"There was never a speech too short" is an old saying about good public speaking. As the quip ironically reminds us, many speakers go on longer than they should.

Staying within your time limit is a necessary skill for competent, ethical speaking. It demonstrates your respect for your audience's time and that of any other speakers on the program, as well as your accurate understanding of the speaking occasion or context. Audiences have little patience with speakers who abuse their time, and have trouble paying attention to such speakers. In many situations, you'll have a set amount of time in which to speak, and if you go over that limit, you'll be unpopular with your audience or even cut off before you can finish!

If you've designed your speech carefully and practiced it consistently, it's usually not too hard to give it within a minute of the allotted time, but you have to be aware if you're going too quickly or too slowly so you can adjust your pace and avoid going over time. In many speaking situations, either you'll be cut off when your time is up or you'll step on someone else's speaking time, a clear violation of the Golden Rule. It makes sense to have someone give you time signals (holding up fingers or cards with numbers) to show you, in countdown style, how much time you have left in the speech. Once you've practiced this way for a while, it's easy to stay in control of how long you speak.

Each preparation method has its own dangers for straying beyond the time limit. If you're using a manuscript or have memorized a manuscript, you're likely to be consistent in your timing, but there's always the chance that you'll speak more quickly, or more slowly, in the real speech than in practice. In impromptu speaking, you probably should be looking at a clock, because you're creating the speech as you go along, and you may have to edit on the fly to stay within your allotted time. The biggest difficulty comes with the most common preparation method—extemporaneous speaking. Because you're speaking only from notes and previous preparation, your speech easily can go too short or too long. But if you prepare carefully and practice in all the ways suggested later in this chapter, you should be able to control the length very well.

TYPES OF SPEAKING AIDS

Unless you're giving a memorized speech, you'll have to think about what kind of speaking aids to help you keep track of what you plan to say. Each type of aid has advantages and disadvantages. In some cases the choice is a matter of preference, but in other cases you may be forced into a certain choice by the situation. Remember, however, that you still have to *know* and *remember your* speech. Speaking aids just help you stay on track.

If, as is almost always the case, you're giving an extemporaneous speech, you have some choices about your performance aids:

- You can make a printed outline on 8.5" × 11" paper, using a large enough font with enough white space on the page that it's easy to read. The disadvantage is that you're stuck at the podium, because it's difficult to carry around a floppy piece of paper and consult it effectively.
- If you're going to walk around, your notes or outline printed on 4" × 6" or 5" × 8" cards is effective. You can hold the cards in your hand, walk around with them, gesture with them, and put them down if needed. Like the outline on a sheet of paper, the words on the cards have to be large enough to read easily.

Your next choice is what to put on the cards or notes. You should start with your outline (see Chapter 7). It reflects all of your research and thinking, so you usually will need just a word or phrase ("Facts about student loans") to help you recall what point comes next. In addition, the more you practice, the less elaborate your speaking outline will need to be.

Some things should be written out word for word in your speaking notes:

- Because *quotations* are someone else's words, you have to get them exactly right.
- If you're giving the audience *quantitative information*, you'll want to be sure that you get the numbers straight.
- The *names of the sources that you refer to;* for example, *the names of scholarly journals* can be long and complicated (for example, *Transactions of the American Entomological Society*, a journal about insects).
- If you have taken the trouble to create a wonderful antithesis or other figure, you must get the exact wording to have the full effect.

You also may want to customize your cards and notes to improve your delivery. After you print your speaking outline, you can write in delivery notes to yourself ("Breathe!" "Look up"). Or you can use highlighters or color print to symbolize different delivery reminders. For example, a green dot might mean "Breathe!" and a blue dot might mean "Look at the audience." You'll get used to your own system as you practice.

Some speakers use colors to guide them through a complicated outline. For example, main points are blue, subpoints are green, and citations are orange. Then, when you glance down at the card, your eye is drawn immediately to where you want to be in the speech.

Using notes on cards or paper can help you keep track of what you want to say.

If you're giving a manuscript speech and don't have a teleprompter, you'll have to read from a set of printed pages you bring with you. Make sure that the font size is large enough to read easily at a glance without squinting or bending your head toward the text. Most professionals double-space their "reading" manuscript so their eyes can find their place on the page more readily. These scripts commonly are printed entirely in uppercase, though some people find all capitals harder to read.

The most commonly used presentation aid consists of PowerPoint slides, which can be a blessing or a curse (see Chapter 10). Although they are intended to help the audience follow the presentation, you also can think of them as a set of extemporaneous notes for yourself as speaker. If you know your material well, the slides may be the only the reminder you need. You also can print the slides for yourself and add delivery notes to them (either by hand or in the Notes panel), just as you would your cards or outline.

USING YOUR VOICE EFFECTIVELY

Your voice is your most supple and important performance instrument. The vibrant richness of the spoken word gives us the ability as speakers to create emphasis and shape meaning. The aspects of your voice that you can control during speaking are volume, speed, articulation, and inflection. Let's see what each one adds to your delivery.

Volume

If you can't be heard, your speech won't be effective. Your voice has to be loud enough for the room, but not overpowering. (Most aspects of delivery are about finding the golden mean between extremes.) You will encounter mainly three sizes of rooms that affect volume considerations:

1. *About 5 to 10 people in a small room.* In this case, a natural conversational voice will be fine, or maybe a bit louder than normal to catch people's attention. Using a "big voice" in this setting will be distracting.

Exactostock/SuperStock

A lapel mic allows you to amplify your voice while giving you the freedom to move around in the front of the audience.

2. *About 10 to 50 people in a larger room.* In this case, you will have to speak up and create more volume than normal. You're still close to conversational delivery, but you have to spēak loudly enough so people in the back can hear you. You may have to slow your pace a bit to achieve this (see the discussion of speed, in the next section).

3. *More than 50 people in a big room or auditorium.* Here you face a choice. The best option is to use a microphone (or a lapel mic, if one is available). The other option is to shout without sounding like you're shouting. With a little practice, this isn't too difficult. You'll have to slow down and insert enough pauses to give yourself breathing breaks. It's best to write speeches for this setting in shorter sentences and phrases. (Campaign speeches typically use this strategy.)

To turn up the volume of your voice in the larger settings, *relax*. Try not to tighten your throat or put any stress on the muscles there; it's common for your voice to strain as you "speak up" through vocal tension. Unlike the muscles in your body, your vocal folds (or "cords"—they actually aren't muscles but, rather, bands of tissue in your larynx that vibrate to produce sound) work best when at ease. Like a singer, your throat should be relaxed. Your voice works like a trumpet or clarinet: The sound coming out of it doesn't get louder because you tighten your lips (or fingers) but, instead, because you increase the air pressure going through it.

You can increase the air pressure going through your throat by taking deep breaths, and by taking in and pushing out air using the muscles below your ribcage. If your breathing is shallow (just your collarbone is going up and down, known as "clavicular breathing"), you can't push enough air to gain volume. Think of planting your feet flat on the floor and pushing

FIGURE 9.1
The diaphragm

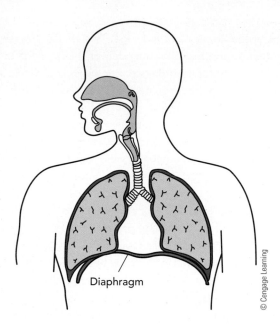

Diaphragm

your voice out from your diaphragm, the muscle that stretches across the bottom of your rib cage (see Figure 9.1), rather than from your throat. That will require breaths that seem to go all the way down to your stomach and lower abdomen, or you won't be sufficiently activating your diaphragm.

For a more public-sized voice, the sound also has to resonate sufficiently through your head. Your voice sounds best when it resonates normally—through your sinuses. The Try It! box tells you how to find out whether you're resonating.

TEST YOUR RESONANCE **TRY IT!**

You can test your resonance by laying your hand lightly on top of your head while you increase your volume. As you get louder, you should feel the vowels in your speech vibrate slightly up top. If you don't feel this, keep experimenting until you can. Your voice will be richer and stronger for it.

Speed

Some people speak quickly, but we can still understand them. Others speak a bit slowly, but we can understand them as well. So there isn't one perfect pace, but people have to be able to understand you. As you practice, you should get regular feedback about whether your speech allows you to be understood.

REMIX

Words Per Minute

One of the most common pieces of advice about speed of public speaking is that you should speak just below conversational rate. Normal conversational rate is somewhere around 110 to 150 words per minute for the average American, so most of the advice to speak just below your normal conversational rate would, at a minimum, put you at the low end of this range. This advice is reasonable: Often, speakers are so amped up to speak that they deliver their speech at a significant clip, which can be off-putting for an audience. People who give this advice also are worried that audiences can't digest arguments or ideas as well if they are delivered at a blistering rate of speed.

But what do the data say? One place to look is contemporary neuroscience. In the journal *Brain and Language*, neuroscientists Jonathan Peelle and Corey McMillan used brain imaging to look at how humans process rapid complex speech. What they found was that humans have a much higher capacity for processing rapid speech than we first realized, and that, interestingly, when speech was a bit too rapid and complex for normal processing, the listeners usually compensated by recruiting areas of the brain not used primarily for language processing to unpack dense messages.

This doesn't mean, of course, that you should speak as quickly as you can, nor does it mean that speaking quickly is intrinsically better. Some data suggest that a slightly higher than conversational rate of delivery creates an impression of competence and intelligence. But other data suggest that a slightly higher than normal rate can, under certain circumstances, make a speaker look either anxious or, worse, like a fast-talking manipulator.

The point, as in all speech settings, is this: Your rate of speed at any point in a speech should reflect a conscious choice to signal something (excitement, passion, deliberation, and care, for instance), and you need to think carefully about how your rate of speech helps to solidify the impressions you are attempting to produce. Similarly, regardless of how quickly or slowly you're speaking, you have to maintain good discipline in pausing, articulating, emphasizing, and so on.

For more information, see:
Jonathan Peelle & Corey McMillan, Dissociable patterns of brain activity during comprehension of rapid and syntactically complex speech: Evidence from fMRI, *Brain and Language*, 2004, 91:315–325.

If you speak too fast, it all runs together. If you speak too slowly or with too many long pauses, the audience loses the thread of your thought. For most people, the best pace for public speaking is just a bit slower than their normal pace, because this allows for clear articulation (see the next section).

If you're in a setting with a microphone, you may have to adjust your pace to accommodate the amplification. The larger room, the longer it seems to take for your amplified voice to reach the back, so words that are clear to the front-row audience seem mushed together and hard to understand in the back row. You'll have to practice to get used to the slower pace and pauses with a microphone in a larger room.

Articulation

articulation The clarity with which words are pronounced.

Articulation is the clarity with which you pronounce the sounds in words and make them distinct and intelligible. If you don't articulate clearly enough, people may miss or mishear words or phrases in your speech because they can't back up your speech in a DVR or CD and listen again. They'll just be lost.

You also can go wrong by overenunciating—pronouncing sounds that aren't normally pronounced in English (linguists call this "hypercorrectness"). For instance, *often* usually is pronounced "offen"; the *t* is silent. Some speakers who are trying too hard to articulate will add the *t* sound, thinking that this is somehow more correct. Similarly, some clusters of words run together when spoken. Creating a distinct gap between the words in the phrase "an hour" sounds strange. Not only does it make listeners work harder, but overenunciation also can be irritating and make the speaker sound pretentious.

Good speakers find a middle ground between the extremes. Ideally, your articulation will be a bit more crisp than usual, stepped up a notch so people in the back row will catch it as clearly as those in the front row.

Inflection

Inflection is the emphasis you put on words to shape meaning for the listener. As you say a sentence aloud, you naturally speed up and slow down, become louder and softer. You shape sentences with your voice the way a singer shapes a musical phrase. When people complain that a speech is in monotone, what's missing is *inflection*; the speaker has failed to make the speech rise and fall and, in effect, to be more musical.

Try an experiment with a famous phrase from the end of the Gettysburg Address, given by Abraham Lincoln during the Civil War:

> …that this nation, under God, shall have a new birth of freedom—and that government of the people, by the people, for the people, shall not perish from the earth.

Most people today read the phrase in the following way, emphasizing the italicized words:

of the people, by the people, for the people

What if you were to read it the way Lincoln read it, with the emphasis on the nouns instead of the prepositions?[2]

of the *people*, by the *people*, for the *people*

The difference is huge. Instead of being about abstract relations ("of . . . by . . . for"), the phrase now drives home a central point of Lincoln's political philosophy—that democracy is a form of governing in which the government serves the people even as they create it.

Now try reading this sentence (from Lincoln's second inaugural address) aloud; Lincoln was trying to urge the worn-torn country to unite:

> A house divided against itself cannot stand.

When you stress a word, it creates either *focus* or *contrast*. **Focus** signals that, of all the words in the sentence, *this* particular word tells you what the sentence is about, the relevant context for the sentence. **Contrast** helps to establish what the sentence *isn't* about.

A *house* divided against itself cannot stand.

Contrast: But something else could stand.

A house *divided* against itself cannot stand.

Focus: This sentence is about division.

A house divided against *itself* cannot stand.

Contrast: But divided against something else, it could stand.

A house divided against itself *cannot* stand.

Contrast: Being divided is linked to the impossibility of standing.

If you try out all the various possibilities of stress in this sentence, the one that best matches Lincoln's meaning in the speech is the stress on both *cannot* and *divided*. Obviously, you won't work this hard for every sentence in a speech, but for significant ones, and maybe quotations, it's worth your trouble.

Because people sometimes lose their natural inflections and fall into a monotone when they're nervous, practice is your best friend for speech performance. For key sentences in your

inflection Verbal emphasis on certain words to reinforce meaning.

focus Verbal emphasis on a word, signaling that it is the key to a sentence's meaning.

contrast Verbal emphasis on a word, signaling an opposition.

speech, try out different inflections and see how they sound, both to you and to your practice audience. Mark your notes or cards with emphasis if it helps you remember. You need to get used to the sound of your voice at public volume *and* inflecting.

HOW TO NOT GIVE A GOOD SPEECH

Grab some video equipment (even a smartphone) or a patient friend and deliver a small segment of your speech trying to use the most effective rate, volume, inflection, and articulation.

Now try to give the same speech segment quickly, or in a monotone, or while overarticulating.

- What do you notice about how easy or difficult it is to listen to you in each of these cases?
- Which of these vocal qualities is already a strength for you, and which do you need to work on?

USING YOUR BODY EFFECTIVELY

In addition to using your voice effectively, three things to think about for physical delivery are: standing, walking, and gesturing. Standing is necessary because that's what you do while you speak; walking can make a difference because a little bit of movement is interesting and can help the audience follow your speech; gesturing allows you to be both expressive and focused.

Standing

Standing before an audience isn't the same experience as standing at a bus stop. You don't want to stand at attention, but you'll want to consciously choose to present yourself in the best possible posture, which can improve your delivery and prevent distracting motions. You'll look—and feel—more confident if you practice the following suggestions:

- *Stand straight:* Keep your back straight and tall as you stand before the audience. This stance both confers and conveys self-confidence and helps you better project your speaking voice, as we've just discussed. Don't stoop to see your cards on the podium; if you hold them about chest high, you'll be able to see them easily. (This is also a good strategy when the podium is too low or too high for you or you elect not to use it.) Establish your stance as you step up to begin your speech, and remain conscious of your posture as you continue your presentation. Correct your position quietly if you sense that you're slouching.
- *Keep your chin up and shoulders down:* It's easier to breathe (and therefore to speak) and to see the audience when you lift your chin slightly. The most common delivery problem is not making eye contact (see below). If your chin is on your chest, you won't be able to see the audience even if you remember to look, so keep your shoulders slightly back and down.
- *Settle your weight on both feet:* If your weight isn't distributed evenly over both feet, you not only will throw off your posture, but you risk letting your free foot do unexpected things such as unconsciously wiggling, tapping, or shuffling. You also might start to shift back and forth or side to side—something many people do when they're nervous. These motions are distracting to the audience, even if you aren't aware that you're doing them. Keeping your weight firmly on both feet is the best way to avoid such problems.

Former NBA standout Yao Ming speaks often about U.S.–China relations. Does his height work for or against him as a speaker?

Walking

Though you'll be making a conscious effort to stand tall and keep your weight on both feet, you needn't feel nailed to the spot. Unless you're speaking into a fixed microphone, you should feel free to move around a bit, in a way that feels natural to you. Not only will this help relax your muscles, which is useful in reducing nervousness, but it also will keep the audience's attention on you and add visual interest to your presentation. Coming out from behind the podium (if you can) brings you physically and psychologically closer to the audience, too, which can help you get across your important points. As you probably can guess, there's a happy medium between standing stiffly in place and moving around too much. How do you find it? Read on.

- *Avoid pacing:* Walk purposefully; don't keep walking back and forth, back and forth. You can even return to the podium occasionally and stay still to be sure you aren't overdoing it. And you needn't walk far; a few steps in either direction will be enough to keep the audience's eyes on you. Walk at your normal pace, or a bit slower; there's no need to rush. Audiences find too much movement, as well as rhythmic movement and pacing, annoying.

- *Don't trip yourself:* When you do walk, put one foot straight in front of the other. Don't cross your feet and risk tripping yourself. Because your main attention is elsewhere, you should limit the chances of making a silly mistake.

- *Face the front:* No matter where or how far or when you walk about, avoid turning your back to the audience, especially while you're actually speaking. If you're using visual aids (see Chapter 10), you may have to turn away from the audience briefly to set up your visuals or point to something, but generally you should face the audience from beginning to end.

- *Move with your speech transitions:* The transitions, or "joints," in your speech are the best times for you to move around, because pausing to take a couple of steps and then starting again signals to the audience, "We're on a new point now."

- *Move from front to back to front:* Generally, in whatever space is available to move around as you speak, you should start out toward the front, move to the back and sides during your speech's transitions, and return to the front for the conclusion (returning to your physical starting point visually parallels the way your conclusion recalls the thesis, and your peroration recalls the narration).

Using Gestures

Gesturing is highly individual. Some people move their hands a lot when they speak, and some don't; some people come from cultural backgrounds that value a lot of gesturing, and others don't. The best choice for you, in public speaking, is to be yourself—be natural. If you normally don't gesture much but try to do so during a speech, your gestures probably will look robotic and strange. If you naturally gesture quite a bit and try to hold still, you'll look like you're *trying* not to gesture and the audience will notice it. If the audience is paying attention to whether you're gesturing or not instead of listening to you, it defeats your purpose in speaking.

Hands are extremely expressive, and you've spent a lifetime learning to use yours. The only reason you have to think about gesturing is to adapt what you normally do to the public speaking situation. The basic rule is that your hands should either be at your sides, hanging naturally, or in front of you, between your shoulders and waist. If you're holding cards, they should be about chest high so you can see them without stretching your neck to look down.

Pants and jacket pockets can be a problem, especially for men. If your hands are in your pockets, they're still visible to the audience, along with all the stuff in your pocket—the loose change, the thumb drive, the car keys, the sunglasses, the pack of gum. Some speakers play with these items when they're nervous, and if you do, the jingling and movement will be distracting to your audience. A little formality is in order here, because you should appear more focused and engaged.

Your hands should be in front of you, not behind your back or covering your groin (like a "fig leaf"). Keep them between your shoulders and waist, and use whatever movement is natural to you. Intentionally illustrative gestures, such as holding up two fingers for "two options" or pointing upward for "inflated prices," often look contrived and can be distracting. Unless you're a skilled and experienced performer who has learned to make practiced gestures look natural, you should trust your own good sense and communication ability, and not try too hard. If you're focused on the audience and engaged in communicating, your natural gestures will be appropriate and effective.

COMMUNICATING CREDIBILITY

How do your delivery skills help to project your credibility? Essentially, you're asking the audience members to make a judgment that you're engaged enough with them so they will make the effort to engage you and your ideas. You can signal your engagement in two significant ways: through eye contact and through appropriate dress.

Making Eye Contact

eye contact Meeting the gaze of people in your audience.

Eye contact is a normal part of our every-day communication. Actually, it's so important in a casual conversation that if you don't make good eye contact, you may seem shifty or untrustworthy. That same judgment may be made about speakers who don't look at their audiences. (Obviously, this doesn't apply to speakers who are blind or visually impaired.) When you're nervous and thinking hard about what to say, you may not focus on eye contact, so it's best to make it a habit.

- *Begin your speech with a pause and eye contact:* It's not effective to begin speaking while looking at your notes or cards, even though when you're nervous that's where you want to look. Staring down seems to communicate to the audience members that you don't want to be speaking—or at least not in front of them. Maybe you actually feel that way, but the best antidote to that feeling is to act as if it weren't true. Before you begin speaking, take a deep breath, look around the room, and make eye contact with the people looking at you.

Actor Mark Ruffalo, speaking out against the natural gas-drilling practice known as hydrofracking, successfully uses natural gestures and eye contact.

- *Make actual eye contact:* Keep your chin up, look at the audience members—and look them in the eyes. Yes, they can tell if you aren't. Looking over their heads or at their shoes makes a poor impression. If you make a habit of looking people in the eye, it will become effortless.
- *Sweep the room:* Look at everybody by scanning the room side to side and back to front. Sometimes it's helpful to seek out the faces of those wonderful audience members who look like they care about what you're saying; they're smiling and nodding and giving you the feedback you need. If you find one person like this in each quarter of the room, take turns talking to each of them and looking briefly at the people in between as you shift your gaze. Try not to stare at any one audience member; instead, share your gaze around the room so everyone feels included in your speech.

Choosing Your Appearance

Your **appropriate clothes** and the way you present yourself will depend on the occasion on which you are speaking. A funeral or wedding may require you to be dressed formally, whereas jeans and a clean T-shirt might be acceptable at a neighborhood meeting or the school board. In general, you want your clothes to attract as little attention as possible, so your words speak more loudly than your appearance. That doesn't mean that you have to dress in a bland or dowdy way. It means that in each speaking context, you shouldn't stand out from others simply because of your clothes. Instead, you should shine because of how smart and compelling your speaking is.

appropriate clothes Appearance that fits the occasion and adds to your credibility.

In particular, overtly sexy clothes don't help speakers communicate effectively. A tight T-shirt on a muscular guy or a seriously short skirt on an attractive woman may look good, but may create a problem in the public speaking context if the clothes attract more attention than the speaker's words.

In general, professional clothing choices are clothes that are neat and clean and don't attract much attention, allowing the audience to focus on what's being said. As a speaker, you want to be taken seriously for your words.

Some clothing choices aren't functional for speakers. You'll want to wear reasonably comfortable clothes that you don't have to worry about. High heels can make you more likely to trip; heavy shoes may thud across a stage. Anything that jangles or dangles (such as loose or heavy jewelry, ornamental zippers, and so on) is likely to be distracting, especially if the sound will be picked up by a microphone.

It goes without saying that you shouldn't be chewing gum while speaking. Traditionally, it's impolite to wear a hat while speaking. Just as important, a ball cap covers your face when you look down at your cards, or even at the front row.

HOW TO PRACTICE DELIVERING YOUR SPEECH

Rehearsal is necessary for every speaker and every setting. Quite simply, practice helps you gain confidence, which in turn helps you focus on and engage with the audience instead of with your nerves. It also allows you to edit and refine your speech and to see which parts work and which don't.

Sometimes, speakers think that unless they have a word-for-word manuscript, they can't really practice, so they'll just have to wing it. This isn't the case at all. Extemporaneous speeches do get better and better with practice from speaking notes; you might use slightly different words each time, but you get better and better at communicating your points.

When people get nervous, they tend to lose their conscious focus and go on autopilot. If you have practiced your speech, you already know what you want to say and how you want to say it, so you'll be fine. (But you may not remember much about it afterward!) People get stuck only when they're nervous *and* trying to give their speech for the first or second time. Here are some tips for effective practice sessions.

Practice, All the Way Through, at Least Four Times

You should practice your speech all the way through, at an absolute minimum, four times. The first and possibly the second times, your delivery might be shaky, but don't worry. You will have at least two more opportunities to improve your speech as you get more comfortable with it. At first, you may depend a lot on your cards and notes. In your later practices, as you get better, you can focus on voice and eye contact and ask your practice audience (discussed in the next section) for feedback on things you've worked on since the first practice. You'll be amazed at how much less effort and how much more control comes with repeated practice.

Sitting at a desk or in a chair, looking at your cards, and muttering the speech under your breath don't exactly count as practice. They aren't close enough to actual speaking to do you much good. It might help you memorize your points a little better, but to be as comfortable as possible and do a good job in your actual speech, you will have to approximate actually giving it, standing up, speaking from your notes or cards, with a few people present, and using whatever technology you'll be using in your speech.

Practice in Front of an Audience

Most people find that practicing in front of a mirror does more harm than good because it tends to make you focus on how you look rather than on what you're saying. Experienced speakers may find the mirror helpful for fixing small problems in their delivery, but beginning speakers usually have bigger goals for their practice sessions than just a few minor fixes.

Practice by *talking to* somebody, not thinking about yourself. The speech is for audience members; if you focus on them, you won't be as likely to think, "Geez, how am I doing?" and make yourself nervous. Instead of using a mirror, therefore, practice in front of a couple of trusted friends, classmates, or family members. Ahead of time, ask your practice audience to be ready to give you specific feedback about your content and delivery. And have one of your practice audience members give you time signals each time.

How you choose the people in your practice audience depends on what you want your practice sessions to achieve. If you want your rehearsals to be as comfortable as possible, invite people with whom you don't feel any nervousness. If you want to get used to feeling a bit nervous and practice dealing with that, you might invite people who will make you a little nervous—whether those are friends who will give critical feedback or relative strangers, such as classmates. This second strategy is usually more effective, because performing smoothly when you're nervous is a skill you need.

If you can't find people who can help you for a few minutes by listening to you practice your speech, rehearse at least a couple of times in front of a wall or in an empty room, and imagine the presence of the audience. But make every effort to provide yourself with a live audience for at least two or three of your sessions.

Practice Making Mistakes

Everybody makes mistakes in speaking, all way from a slightly mispronounced word, to mixing up the order of points, to becoming completely blocked and forgetting the topic of the speech for just a moment (that last mistake happens to even highly experienced speaking teachers). Such mistakes are going to happen during practice, and how well you deal with them during practice will determine how well you will deal with them in your speech.

[handwritten: mistakes will happen, depends on how you deal wit them]

If you slip up, stop and take a deep breath, pause a moment to compose yourself, and begin again when you're ready. The pause may seem like an eternity to you, but it's brief from the audience's perspective. If you don't pause and get your bearings, you might rush ahead and make the situation worse.

It's best not to comment on your own speaking ("Wow, that was stupid!"). It attracts attention to something the audience members might not even realize was an error, because they didn't prepare your speech and haven't seen your outline. You've seen television broadcasters make mistakes many times, but you don't really notice because they respond so professionally: "Back in 1988—sorry, 1998—a large company founded by. . . ."

Paying too much attention to the little hesitations, stumbles, and stutters—which happen almost every time we speak anyway—can cause a speaker to lose focus on the audience. Instead, simply move on. Even the most experienced speakers occasionally trip over their words. What matters is how you respond to these minor stumbles, and that's something you have complete control over.

Breathe, Breathe, Breathe

Stage fright can disrupt your breathing, and if you can't breathe, you can't speak. So as you practice your speech, if you find that you can get to the second point without taking a breath, you'll be out of breath. It's a good idea to mark your cards with reminders to breathe every point or so. If you find your breath coming in shallow gasps, try to slow down and breathe from your diaphragm rather than your upper chest, taking fewer but deeper breaths. Again, you can practice proper breathing as you practice your speech.

ANSWERING QUESTIONS FROM THE AUDIENCE

In many situations, you'll have a chance to take questions from the audience and, thus, extend your speech into an actual conversation. The opportunity to enter into dialogue with your audience is wonderful, and you should make the most of it. Here are some ways to prepare for and manage the process of taking questions from the audience.

Chelsea Clinton has been in the public eye since her father started running for President. What kinds of questions has she had to answer?

Anticipating Questions

Here are several strategies for anticipating the questions you might receive.

- Think about where you struggled with the topic when you were developing the speech. Go back through your notes. Does something jump out on which you spent a disproportionate amount of time? If it was difficult for you, it probably will be difficult for your audience as well.
- If you're working with technical material, expect to be asked to repeat or amplify complicated concepts or numbers. If you had a slide with a chart or diagram up for a minute or less, be prepared to put it back up.
- Think about the specific strategic decisions you made in putting your speech together. You had only a certain amount of time for your speech, so you had to decide which topics to focus on and which to treat more superficially. You can expect questions on those topics, asking you to expand and deepen them.
- At your practice sessions, ask the audience for questions.

Interpreting the Questions

When you get questions, the first rule is to slow down and take your time. You won't give a good answer if you don't fully understand the question.

Make sure that you understand what the person is asking. The best way to do this is to use the active-listening technique of restating the question: "So it sounds like you're asking if I think we should eliminate government-funded student loan programs. Is that right?" If the asker doesn't agree, go back and forth until you've got it.

Before you answer, think briefly about the question-behind-the-question. In many cases, the question asked is a cover for the person's real concern. If your answer can address that concern, you'll do a better job of answering the question. So, to take the previous example, a question about canceling loan programs might conceal the question, "How am I supposed to pay for college if you take those programs away?" If you weren't advocating elimination of these programs, you can correct that perception and address the question-behind-the-question. If you were advocating elimination, you not only can restate your point, but you also can address this concern.

The basic point is to take your time and be sure you understand the question before you jump in with answers that could just increase confusion.

Giving Your Answers

When you begin answering questions, here are some easy tips that will make you more successful.

- *The question is public, and so is the answer.* Just as the question was addressed to the entire room, your answer should be as well. Look directly at the questioner while clarifying the question, but then look around the room as you would normally during a speech. This helps to prevent the exchange from becoming personal.

- *Respond to all questions as friendly questions.* Even if the tone of voice or manner of expression might lead you to think otherwise, treat all questions as friendly and helpful. Thank the questioner, and as much as you can, praise the question ("That's a great question," "You make a really interesting point," "That's very helpful, thanks"). This isn't mere politeness. All questions are helpful. If somebody has a question, it means that as a communicator, you did your job well, because that person is engaged enough to want to continue the dialogue.

- *You don't need to have all the answers.* If you don't know something, say you don't know. Be generous in praising questions that advance the public dialogue even further.

- *Answer questions, not speeches.* In public settings, there always seem to be people who use the question period to make speeches on their favorite topics, whether relevant to your speech or not. Don't twist yourself into a pretzel trying to make a speech into a question. Simply thank the person for the interesting insight and call on the next person.

- *Focus.* Many times, questions that are asked with sincerity and goodwill lead you away from your topic. Sometimes that's OK, but sometimes it takes away time from the more pertinent questions that others want to ask. You usually will have to "referee" this yourself, but it's not too difficult. If the question doesn't seem to lead anywhere for your audience and topic, you might say something like "That's a really interesting point, and I'd like to talk to you about it afterward." Or, if you think you can make a connection, especially to a question-behind-the-question, you could say, "I'm not sure if this is what you're getting at, but here's what my argument would be about your point," and then go on to reiterate or expand on a point you've already made.

MindTap®

Watch a video, and do an interactive activity.

Sharing a dialogue with an audience that has engaged you and cares about your topic—even if some members disagree with you—is one of the most satisfying and important parts of giving a public speech.

Vocal Fry

The many small choices that make up your speaking style are one of the most difficult things to address in a textbook. We can encourage you to be clear and articulate, to employ appropriate volume and pacing, but nothing substitutes for direct feedback. Of course, you will receive such feedback from your teachers and peers about your speaking style, and you should listen and respond to it carefully.

Scholars who study speaking patterns have noticed a few trends about people under age 30 that we might address here. One of the most interesting new speech patterns involves what is called "vocal fry," the tendency for people to end a sentence or a thought by dropping their pitch and adding a bit of a creaky vibration to the tenor of their voice. This is a common pattern, especially among young, educated, upwardly mobile women.

Anderson, Klofstad, Venkatachalam and Mayhew (in the video link on MindTap) found that the presence of vocal fry in a speech lessened the audience's perception of the speaker's credibility. The paper that presents their research (cited below) also shows that vocal fry has a negative impact on workplace performance, particularly for female speakers—though a small amount of evidence has shown that the effects of vocal fry are not as negative as the Anderson, Klofstad, Venkatachalam, and Mayhew study suggests.

The bottom line is that you should be attentive to any speech patterns that stand out to an audience, and you not only should think about but also ask your teacher and peers about the effects of these patterns. If you develop an awareness of your speech patterns and understand their effects, you can make more intentional choices about how and under what conditions to employ or deviate from your normal patterns.

For more information see:

Rindy Anderson, Casey Klofstad, William Mayew, and Mohan Venkatachalam, Vocal fry may undermine the success of young women in the labor market (May 28, 2014), *PLOS ONE 9* (5): e97506, http://journals.plos.org/plosone/article?id=10.1371/journal.pone.0097506

GROUP PRESENTATIONS

group presentation A coordinated report by two to six people about their group's research or creative work.

A **group presentation** is made by two to six speakers. Often the group has been doing research or creative work and the members decide to present it together. In a group presentation like this, let's assume that you're going to use all the best public speaking skills you've learned through this book: making choices about content, organization, language, and delivery; thinking carefully about audience; and so on. Let's also assume your fellow speakers have done their homework and are good speakers, too. Now what? Even if you are a fantastic presenter, you're still left with the challenge of coordinating everything you want to achieve with the other people with whom you'll be presenting.

A group has to work hard to make sure it's a *group* presentation, not just a bunch of people all standing up at the same time. What's the difference? An effective group presentation maximizes the skills of the presenters so it adds up to much more than just a string of good speeches. It presents a consistent set of ideas and arguments in a compelling way, it's seamless, and the audience doesn't even notice the work that went into coordinating it.

A weak group presentation is awkward and chaotic; no one is sure who is speaking, what each speaker has to do with the others, where the presentation is going, or what its point is. Here's the danger: Even if everyone is individually a good speaker, the group presentation can still crash and burn.

The keys to excellent group work are *cooperation* and *coordination*. By cooperation, we mean the collaboration that goes into preparing the presentation. Coordination means using effective techniques for managing multiple speakers, and perhaps technologies, in the presentation itself. Because you're not in sole control of the presentation, these strategies must be added to the skills you've mastered for preparing effective informative speeches. Let's look at each in turn.

Cooperation

Even if the speakers are skilled and knowledgeable, the success of a group presentation depends on what happens during the preparation phase. The biggest mistake your group can make is to say, "Let's all go off and prepare, and we'll put the pieces together on the day." That's a recipe for disaster. Why? Suppose your group was putting together a meal and each person was to make one part—the appetizer, the soup, the main course, dessert, and so on. Without cooperation, what happens? The appetizer is chicken wings, the soup is chicken noodle, the main course is roast chicken, and…you get the idea. Even if each dish were well prepared, it's a disappointing and unsatisfactory meal.

Planning   In putting together a meal—or a group presentation—the key is planning. The group has to sketch out the parts in advance and make sure they fit together in a satisfying way. First, members have to agree on a topic and purpose: What will we be talking about, and what do we want to accomplish? You might be doing a class project requiring a presentation, or speaking at a sales meeting, or presenting your designs for a better mousetrap to an engineering firm, or outlining to the city council why a new park is needed and where it should be built.

Even when group members work on their own, they should make choices consistent with the common topic and purpose. Of course, in choosing your group's topic and purpose, you'll want to think about all the usual things: relevance to the audience, situation constraints (time, technology), and so on.

FAQ *It seems like a lot of work. Are there any advantages to group presentations?*

Yes, there are advantages; the work you put in can pay off for all of you.

- Each person has strengths and weaknesses, and you can set up the group presentation to take advantage of everyone's strengths.
- When it is well done, the transition between speakers keeps the audience's interest.
- The transition between speakers creates a sense of forward movement in the presentation.
- Members can support each other, and camaraderie can help reduce nerves—you're not alone up there.
- During the question and answer period, you have the advantage of more knowledge and expertise in answering questions.

© Directphoto.org/Alamy

The challenge for each speaker in group presentations is to make a contribution that will allow the group to be outstanding and effective.

Division of Labor Next, divide up the work. You probably shouldn't expect that everyone will give an individual speech, or it may be hard to stay within the stated timeframe. It's better to assign one or two people—based on their experience, expertise, or willingness—to each take responsibility for one of the parts of the larger presentation, which include:

- research
- themes/arguments
- organization
- slides/technology

Obviously, after members have done some of their work on these areas, the group will want to gather again to share their results and check their progress. Sometimes you'll have to adjust your goals or your methods, and more meetings probably will be advisable as you advance in your task.

High-quality group presentations require a lot of discussion and contact. It's immediately obvious, when you're watching a group, to know whether they put the appropriate amount of time into group preparation and cooperation.

Speaking Times As you divide up the speaking in your presentation, think about how much time each presenter will have. You probably want to try to give everyone roughly equal time; otherwise, it may seem that one speaker or one section is far more important than the others. It's also important to minimize transition and not switch between speakers more often than necessary. For example, changing speakers every two minutes is distracting rather than interesting, and increases the burden of trying to make transitions and keep the presentation coherent.

Coordination

The first step in coordinating a group presentation is to <u>organize</u> the presence of more than one person on the stage. You have to figure out how your presentation will become a single coherent presentation from the group and not a series of little speeches that happen one after another. Obviously, everybody should practice together, but the bigger question is about the "hand-off" between speakers. How do you avoid awkward silence and shuffling, with everyone looking at each other, hoping that somebody remembers what's next? Two methods have proved to be successful: relay presentations and the "master of ceremonies."

relay presentation A group presentation structured as one speech, in which the speakers take one or more of the elements and transition to the next speaker.

Relay Presentations In a **relay presentation**, each person hands off the topic to the next person. You could design your overall presentation as one big speech, with an introduction, a body consisting of two or three points, and a conclusion, then assign each of these sections to a speaker. If you have four people, have the same person present the introduction and conclusion. If you have only three people, have someone present at least two of the points in the body. In this style, the presentation is like a relay race: Each person passes off to the next when finished and then sits down or steps backs.

master of ceremonies (MC) The person who provides the introductions and transitions in a group presentation.

Master of Ceremonies The **master of ceremonies (MC)** is the person who manages the entire presentation, like the conductor of an orchestra who points to each musician or section when it's their turn to play. If you use a master of ceremonies, you can divide up the presentation however you like.

Transitions In the MC style, transitions are easier for the participants, because the MC does them. In the relay style, each person has to make a smooth and clear transition to the next speaker.

In either case, transitions that work must have two things: (1) a really strong preview, and (2) transition notes that are written out in advance. Without a strong preview, the audience will be lost already, and good transitions may help, but will not save the day. Making up transitions on the fly is foolish because no matter how well you know the material, the transitions won't be as strong as if you thought them through beforehand.

Advantages and Disadvantages of Each Method   The relay style is simple and direct and probably takes a little less time, but it requires that each speaker be really good at making the transition to the next one. The MC style requires a little more time, as the MC cuts in to make the transition at the end of each segment, but it allows the rest of the presenters to focus on their specific section.

Delivering the Group Presentation

The many different faces and voices introduce a lot of variety into your group presentation, so it's important to provide continuity that balances it out. Similar structure throughout the presentation will help to keep the audience focused. Make your slides or handouts consistent in style. Organize each section of the presentation in a similar way, and make clear to the audience that you're doing so. If the speakers and their content are tied together stylistically and organizationally, they will create a presentation whose parts are "cut from the same cloth"—meaning that the variety has regularity.

Rehearsing the Group Presentation

A group presentation requires at least three full run-throughs, to check for time, transitions, and coordination. You have to do the whole presentation, with everyone saying his or her bit, or you won't know what's likely to go wrong or how to fix it. Even more than a solo presentation, a group presentation requires you not only to be good at your speech but to coordinate with others as well. So you will have to pay attention not only to the quality of your own performance but also to how it interacts with those of the others.

- Do you go on too long and cut into someone else's time?
- Is someone doing that to you?
- Does some of your material overlap with someone else's?
- Does your part connect to the preceding part in the same way the transition says it does?

These are problems to diagnose and fix at the rehearsal stage.

Whatever technology your group decides to use, be sure to practice with it, too, and make sure everybody in the group knows how to use it. From the laptop to the projector to the slide program, you need to have people back up as well as technology back up to ensure that everything goes well on the day of the presentation.

Summary

Creating a good speech means delivering it in a way that engages the audience in your message. Speaking in public differs from chatting or conversation in significant ways, because it is addressed to more than one or two people. Because of the larger audience, most speakers experience some level of anxiety, which can be turned into focus and energy that will improve their performances. Different kinds of preparation (memory, manuscript, extemporaneous, and impromptu) affect the nature of your delivery. To deliver a speech effectively, you have to understand how to use your voice and body in front of a group and how to create credibility with eye contact and appropriate dress. Delivery improves with practice, which will be most effective if you practice your speech at least four times from beginning to end in front of a practice audience. If you have the opportunity to answer questions from the audience, welcome their engagement and the opportunity for dialogue.

MindTap®

Reflect, personalize, and apply what you've learned.

Questions for Review

1. What is the difference between speaking and talking?
2. What are some techniques for turning anxiety into focus and energy?
3. What makes a speaking voice effective? How is an effective voice produced?
4. How can you use delivery to communicate credibility?
5. Why should you practice? What makes practice effective?
6. What factors should you consider in composing your part of a group presentation?

Questions for Discussion

1. Go to www.ted.com/talks and find two talks that interest you. Compare and contrast the delivery of each. Which one is better? Why?
2. How do the content of a speech, the occasion, and the expectations of an audience factor into delivery choices? Give examples.
3. Why do you get nervous speaking? What is your best technique for managing it?
4. For one of the speeches you chose for Question 1, create a list of five questions that you would expect this speaker to get from the audience. These are not just *your* questions but, rather, questions that you would expect to others to ask. Do you think the speaker could have anticipated most of these questions? Why or why not?
5. What makes group presentations challenging? What makes them rewarding? What are some concrete ways by which to approach your next one differently?

Key Concepts   MindTap®

Practice defining the chapter's terms by using online flashcards.

appropriate clothes	focus	manuscript speech
articulation	group presentation	master of ceremonies
extemporaneous speech	impromptu speaking	relay presentation
eye contact	inflection	speech from memory

Ariel Skelley/Blend Images/Getty Images

LEARNING OBJECTIVES

- Explain the goals of using presentation aids
- Identify the basic principles for employing presentation aids
- Describe the basic elements of composition for the content of presentation aids
- Explain how to employ handouts, posters, charts, and other non-electronic media
- Choose presentations aids for an effective demonstration speech
- Critique the usefulness of various forms of digital media
- Deliver a speech with presentation aids

CHAPTER OUTLINE

- Introduction: Adding Media to Your Message
- Why Use Presentation Aids?
- Principles for Integrating Presentation Aids
- Static Visual Elements
- Moving Images
- Audio
- Non-Electronic Media
- Demonstration Speeches and Presentation Aids
- Presentation Software
- Delivering Your Speech with Presentation Aids

S haura wants to give an informative speech on a topic that reflects her knowledge of biology and also challenges herself with a topic that doesn't sound interesting at first— "gastropods." Slugs. She wants to makes slugs exciting and interesting but also get into some scientific detail about them. Shaura wonders if she can bring something helpful besides words to improve her speech. What about visual aids? She knows that some visual aids are ineffective, so how can she choose those that will enhance her speech?

Overview

This chapter addresses the use of presentation aids— things you use to communicate with the audience other than your voice, gestures, and body language. Presentation aids can be digital or physical, visual or audio, content. Like any element of a good public speech, they require that you make deliberate and responsible choices for engaging your audience. To help you understand these choices, we discuss goals for their use and general principles for integrating presentation aids into your speech. Next, we offer pointers for effective visual and audio elements and for non-electronic media (such as handouts, posters, flip charts, and objects), including a specific section about demonstration speeches using an object. An abundantly illustrated section on presentation software follows. Finally, we offer concrete advice for integrating presentation aids into your speech, rehearsing with them, and developing a backup plan for digital media—all the while maintaining basic public speaking fundamentals.

MindTap®
Start with a warm-up activity about Shaura's speech, and review the chapter's Learning Objectives.

INTRODUCTION: ADDING MEDIA TO YOUR MESSAGE

MindTap®
Read, highlight, and take notes online.

Public speaking is an art with ancient roots, but it also is an art that evolves to meet the demands of changing times. Audiences increasingly expect speakers to present images, videos, and audio clips that allow them to directly experience the objects, events, people, and ideas that make up a speech.

In this chapter, we will describe how to develop and use handouts, objects, posters, charts, presentation software, videos, audio clips, and anything else you might employ to engage the full range of the audience's senses in communicating your message. Your presentation aids—sometimes also called supplemental media—should follow the same principles for public speaking that we have outlined in the other chapters of this book. The choice of whether to use presentation aids and, if so, what kind is determined by your goals for the speech and for the audience, your analysis of the audience that informs your speaking choices, your ethical goals, and the message about your topic that you would like to convey to your audience.

Images, videos, audio clips, and other forms of presentation aids can make the public conversation clearer and increase its impact: For example, *showing* the magnitude of an environmental or a social crisis such as an oil spill or a famine can help to galvanize public action. But these media must be used effectively. Have you ever sat through a presentation in which the speaker simply read his or her digital slides to the audience as if they were a script? Poorly handled visual aids can be an impediment to communicating effectively with an audience.

WHAT GOALS MIGHT PRESENTATION AIDS SERVE FOR MY SPEECH? `TRY IT!`

Think about the speech you are currently working on.

- List the elements that might be strengthened by some kind of presentation aid or supplemental media.
- Next to each element, write the medium that would be most appropriate, and which goal for your speech it might advance.
- Were you able to find a goal for each presentation aid?

WHY USE PRESENTATION AIDS?

Like all the other choices in composing and delivering your speech, your use of **presentation aids** should intentionally advance a specific and well-defined goal. You shouldn't include supplementary media just because it seems like the thing to do. If you lack a defined purpose or goal, presentation aids are likely to either become a crutch or to get in the way of your speech, instead of enhancing its power and influence.

So what are the primary reasons that you might want to integrate supplementary media into your speech? Here are a few you might consider:

- *To help the audience directly experience something you're speaking about.* Hearing or seeing the object, image, process, event, or sound you're discussing can make your audience feel connected to your topic. A presentation aid can help to engage audience members by calling upon more of their senses. For example, your comparison of the musical styles of Beyoncé and Adele would benefit from audio clips of each singer's work.
- *To simplify explanations.* Sometimes, the task of explaining a complex event, idea, object, or process is easier if the audience can see or hear it themselves. For example, a simplified diagram of a nuclear reactor can serve as a reference point for a discussion of its safety features.
- *To increase audience engagement and attention.* When used properly, presentation aids can increase the audience's attention by offering images, text, or sounds to complement your spoken words. For instance, you might begin a presentation about the work of director Alfred Hitchcock by playing a bit of the musical theme from his long-running television show.

> **presentation aids** Media to supplement a speech, including handouts, objects, posters, charts, presentation software, videos, and audio clips.

- *To increase audience retention.* Giving audience members more than one way to engage with your speech increases their ability to follow it and to recall its major points. One study found that the combination of spoken and visual data significantly increased an audience's ability to recall the major points of a speech long after listening to it.[1] For that reason, you might want to graph some before-and-after statistics to illustrate the effect of an increase in the school district's budget for students' reading scores.
- *To increase your credibility.* Effective use of supplemental media can increase your credibility by enhancing the audience's connection with you and your materials and by showcasing your expertise. For instance, one study found that the use of presentation software in a classroom presentation significantly boosted the speaker's credibility with the audience.[2] So your demonstration of yoga poses that improve flexibility would lend authority to your presentation about the benefits of yoga.

If you decide to use presentation aids, eight basic principles can help you maximize their benefits.

PRINCIPLES FOR INTEGRATING PRESENTATION AIDS

Presentation aids that work well for the speaker and the audience do so because the speaker chose them with care and envisioned them as highlighting the best qualities of the speech.

Principle 1: Presentation aids aren't mandatory; use them only when you have a goal in mind and time to prepare them well.

One of your public speaking class requirements may be to incorporate presentation aids, in which case you should find most of this chapter helpful. If you aren't required to use aids, however, you can avoid weakening an otherwise fine presentation by *not* adding poor or distracting aids as merely a crutch to help you get through a speech.

Principle 2: The focus of the presentation is the speaker, not the presentation aid.

You should use the presentation aid, as opposed to it using you. The focus of your speech should be you and not the aids you're using. For example, if you're using presentation software, you might be tempted to read text off the screen as if it were a script, or you might break eye contact with the audience by facing the screen most of the time. Or you might be tempted to simply play your video, letting it make your arguments for you without actively using, engaging, and interpreting its contents. Your speech should not just repeat the content in the presentation aid; the aid should supplement and extend what *you* are saying. You have the job of actively interpreting its relevance and role in your speech.

Principle 3: Presentation aids should invite interaction with the audience, not form a barrier between the audience and the speaker.

Used well, presentation aids allow the audience to see or hear something that confirms what you're saying in your speech. Presentation aids are never an excuse for neglecting public speaking fundamentals: You still need to signpost; you still need to maintain eye contact and adjust your nonverbal behavior; and you still need to build a relationship with your audience by considering their needs and the occasion.

Principle 4: Presentation aids require good composition, just like any other element of a good public speech.

As we'll see in the next section, good composition is clear, uncluttered, topical, and simple (think of the acronym CUTS).

- *Clear:* The supplemental media you choose has to be easy for your audience to see or hear, and easy to digest while you're speaking (or afterward, if it is a handout). A packet with pages in the wrong order is a poor choice for a handout.

- *Uncluttered:* The images or sounds you present should have one specific purpose and be without any accompanying "noise"—that is, without extra visual elements or sounds that interfere with audience members' hearing what you would like them to hear. One large picture is more effective than a collage of small images that are hard to see.
- *Topical:* Your aids should have a direct and readily understood link to your topic or to some significant element of your speech. A photo of the local airport would not be obviously relevant to a speech about the benefits of curbside recycling programs.
- *Simple:* The more streamlined the composition of your presentation aids, the less likely they will get in the way of your speech (see Figure 10.1). As we'll see later in this chapter, some types of information lend themselves better than others to certain kinds of diagrams.

FAQ *Why does composition matter?*

Your choice of elements, and the way you put them together, governs the composition of a presentation aid. Good composition matters because it makes your supplemental media aesthetically pleasing and easy to understand. If you would like to learn more about visual composition, you might start at one of these websites:

- Photo Composition Articles: http://photoinf.com/General/Robert_Berdan/Composition_and_the_Elements_of_Visual_Design.htm
- Digital Storytelling: http://www.hippasus.com/resources/viscomp/index.html
- Composition and Design Principles: http://www.goshen.edu/art/ed/Compose.htm
- The speech you give when convincing a loved one to do something—to enter a long-term relationship

Principle 5: Effective and ethical use of presentation aids ensures that the image, video, or sound clip will be appropriate to the room and the audience.

Video and audio clips should be short, and you should test the volume ahead of time to be sure it's appropriate for the setting. Good public speaking practice also dictates that the aids you use must not be offensive or dangerous. Avoid images in questionable taste, and be more than scrupulous in adhering to rules about the presence of weapons and harmful or illegal substances. A picture, instead of the actual object, can be worth a thousand words.

FIGURE 10.1
Visuals that are designed simply (such as the one on the right, not the one on the left) are easier for your audience to engage.

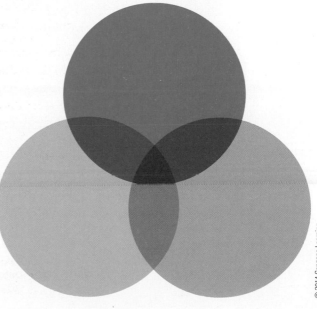

© 2014 Cengage Learning

Principle 6: Supplemental media should solve a problem or deal with a challenge you face in giving your speech.

Your enthusiasm is part of the reason audience members will enjoy listening to you, but when they aren't as familiar with the abstract concepts in your speech as you are—such as in Shaura's challenging topic in the chapter opening—you may need a picture, chart, or other aid to make these concepts seem real and concrete. For example, if you're giving a speech about refugee camps, you can *say* that the conditions in the camp are bad, but if you can show a picture or video that documents these conditions, your claim becomes much more concrete. Suppose you want to make the claim that foreign-aid investments to prevent water scarcity in developing countries can do much good at a relatively low cost. You could read a list of budget numbers,[3] but a pie chart showing the tiny sliver of the federal budget that goes to international affairs would give your audience a more concrete and easily digestible means of grasping a set of potentially complex relationships (see Figure 10.2).

A good presentation aid also can help your audience stay engaged with and better comprehend a long speech or one with complex organization. A handout or some simple slides of your outline can allow people to see the overall structure of your speech, keep better track of your arguments, and visually follow the progression of your points.

Principle 7: Less is more.

Technology's vast capabilities can seduce us into using presentation aids more than we need to. To guard against this, remember that when it comes to supplements for your speech, less is always more. Why use 20 slides if 10 will do? Why use 10 if 5 will suffice? Why show an extended video clip when an excerpt can tell the story? Remember that aids are there to solve problems. Ask of each one: "Is this solving a problem for me? Is there any way I could do without it?" The simpler and more streamlined your presentation, the more compelling you will be as a speaker.

FIGURE 10.2
Simply designed visuals (such as the one on the right, not the one on the left) are easier for your audience to engage.

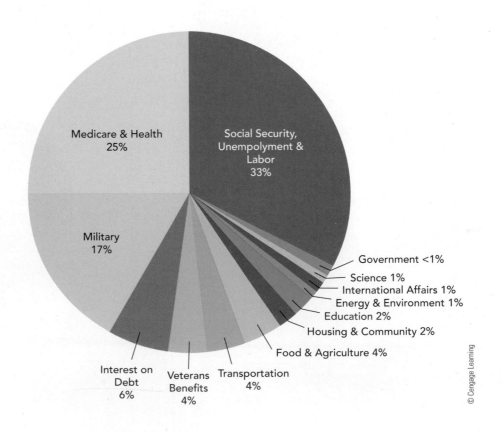

Principle 8: Credit your sources.

As with any element of a public speech, if you borrow an image, photo, graph, chart, or audio or video clip that someone else has made, you must credit the author verbally in your speech, visually on the image itself if possible, and also in the outline or bibliography you hand in if your instructor requires one. By the same token, if you take a picture to use in your speech, be sure to ask anyone who appears prominently in the photo for (written) permission to use it in your speech. And if you create your own graph, chart, or diagram, be sure to document the source of your information properly.

These principles and the goals that underwrite them apply to every presentation aid. Whether you are putting pictures on a poster, drawing graphs on a flip chart, or using presentation software with text and embedded video, you have to make choices regarding the goals you have in mind. Keep the focus of the presentation on your speech, maintain your engagement with the audience, employ good composition and sound ethics, and address specific challenges presented by your topic and your speaking situation. With this foundation in mind, let's look at some of the common elements that appear in different kinds of presentation aids.

MindTap®
Watch a video, and do an interactive activity.

STATIC VISUAL ELEMENTS

Images that don't move—photos, pictures, graphs, diagrams, maps—are effective when carefully tied to the content of your speech, where they can confirm your claims visually.

Pictures and Photos

Whether you're using pictures or photos on a poster, a flip chart, or projecting them on a screen, remember that a picture or a photo has to be topical: It must fulfill a specific purpose that advances your goal. Speakers often are tempted to include visually compelling images even though they are only tangential to their goals, but they should resist the temptation. Pictures and photos also have to be appropriate for your audience and the situation, so, for example, you should avoid images that people might find offensive or difficult to stomach.

Select images that are sized appropriately and have good resolution. The one in the middle here meets these criteria.

Also, photos and pictures are most effective when they demonstrate excellent visual composition. Here are a few simple rules for making sure you get maximum impact from your pictures.

1. *Size and image resolution count.* Pictures, or elements of the picture that you'd like your audience to see, should be large enough to be visible without straining and with good enough image resolution for the image to be clear. If a picture is too small for your purposes, or if enlarging it degrades the quality too much, don't use it.

2. *Choices change the emphasis.* **Cropping** is the process of selecting a portion of an image to draw the viewer's eyes toward the most relevant subject. The main subject should be clearly visible, usually near the center of the frame. Ineffective cropping choices omit important elements or make the image look crowded, for instance. Other choices simply reflect a difference in emphasis that can affect what your audience takes away from the picture. As examples of how cropping choices change the emphasis, see the three versions of a photo of California governor Jerry Brown addressing a conference about climate risks.

3. *Brightness and focus* are important. Use only photos that have an appropriate level of brightness and are in clear focus, so they are easy to see and interesting to look at. If your photo is too dark or blurry, it will be difficult for the audience to get the full benefit from it.

cropping Selecting a portion of an image to focus on the important subject.

Here, California Governor Jerry Brown (right) is addressing the Governor's Conference on Extreme Climate Risks and California's Future at the California Academy of Sciences in San Francisco, seated with Rajendra Pachauri (middle), former chair of the United Nations Intergovernmental Panel on Climate Change, and billionaire philanthropist Richard Branson (left). Although Governor Brown is the one speaking in this photo, he's not in the center. Framing the image this way emphasizes the event, the exchange of ideas on the stage, and the importance of the conversation to the audience.

AP Images/Jeff Chiu

This is the same photo, cropped to put Governor Brown in the center of the image, which de-emphasizes the audience and the occasion. This photo not only focuses on the governor as the speaker but also highlights the intensity of his engagement with his audience and the topic. Although this version of the photo emphasizes different things, it represents another effective choice.

AP Images/Jeff Chiu

Here is one more cropping choice. Even if the goal was to focus on the man sitting in the middle (Dr. Rajendra Pachauri), the scene is cropped a bit too closely, so the viewer may think that some elements of the event are missing and that there's not enough room to comfortably contain the entire shot. This version isn't pleasing to the eye and may distract listeners from the message.

AP Images/Jeff Chiu

Smit/Shutterstock.com

Images that are bright and in crisp focus add impact to your presentation, whereas images that are dark or blurry will detract from your words.

Much more could be said about visual composition, but if you pay attention to size, resolution, cropping, and brightness and focus, you will at least avoid picking photos that distract the audience or that detract from the polish of your presentation.

CROPPING AND FRAMING A PHOTO **TRY IT!**

Find a photo online that you would like to use in a speech, and open it in picture software. Manipulate the frame and size to produce three versions of the image.

- What are the differences among the versions?
- What does each highlight or downplay?
- Which would be most appropriate for a speech about the topic? Why?

FIGURE 10.4

A line graph showing the relationship between hours studying and grade on a test.

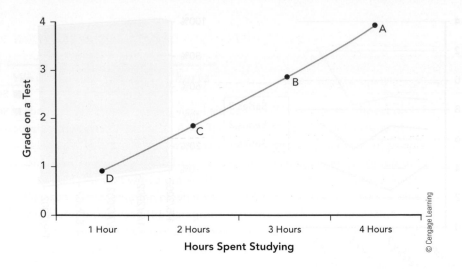

© Cengage Learning

comedy films over the last four decades, a bar graph would allow you to show these trends side by side (Figure 10.5).

Using a **pie chart** is a good way to show the relationship between one data point and its context, or of showing the allocation of a resource such as time, money, or interest. By their nature, pie charts show a whole and the individual components that make up the whole, so they are effective for giving the audience the bigger picture for an individual data point, especially an allocation that's complex or characterized by great disparity. For instance, if you want to show a relationship involving disparity, say, between the amount of time you spend checking email, using social media, fooling around on the Internet, and actually doing research for a term paper on a given night during finals week, you might use a pie chart like the one in Figure 10.6.

pie chart A circular chart that displays numerical information as slices whose sizes are proportional to their value.

FIGURE 10.5

A bar chart showing a hypothetical number of action, horror, and comedy blockbuster films across four decades.

FIGURE 10.6

A pie chart showing hours spent on laptop during finals week.

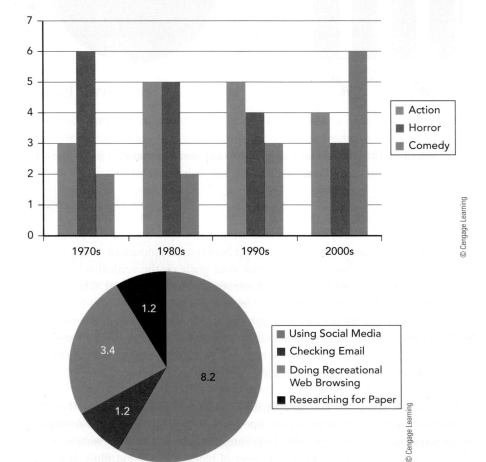

© Cengage Learning

Pick a part of a speech that requires you to use some data. Experiment with representing this data as a line graph, a bar graph, and a pie chart.

- Does the data fit into each of these formats?
- In which format does it make the most sense? Why?
- Which format would be the best choice for presenting this data in your speech? Why?

Pie charts also can show complex allocation of a resource among many different uses. For example, if you were giving an informative speech about the energy usage of the typical U.S. household, you could show a pie chart that breaks down usage into discrete categories, as in Figure 10.7.

Though you could use this chart to show the disparity between space heating and other energy uses, it also demonstrates the broad variety of different kinds of energy use that factor into household energy consumption. This is what makes pie charts useful—they can both show a stark visual representation of relationships between elements of a category and the diversity of the category.

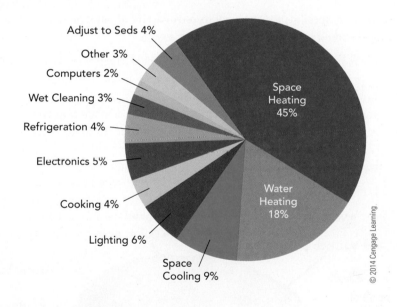

FIGURE 10.7
A pie chart showing residential energy consumption by end use for U.S. households (U.S. Department of Energy, March 2012, "Residential Sector," Chapter 2, Introduction, in *Buildings Energy Data Book*. Retrieved from http://buildingsdatabook.eren.doe.gov/ChapterIntro2.aspx

© 2014 Cengage Learning

Maps and Diagrams

If your speech relies on making a point about geography—for example, if you want to show the geographic distribution of new AIDS cases—or if your speech requires listeners to be familiar with the geography of a place—such as Yellowstone National Park—a good map can add visual impact to your presentation and give your audience a useful point of reference. Maps follow many of the same rules as other static visual images, but they also require you to provide a visual context. Either the map must be large enough for the audience to see the specific geographic area in its context, or you should show other images that provide that context. Yellowstone, for instance, is mostly in Wyoming but also occupies parts of Montana and Idaho, so you would have to show at least these three states in one or more images to provide the park's geographic context. Maps also should be labeled appropriately, with just enough information to support your points and in easily readable form.

diagram A pictorial
representation of the parts of
an object.

A **diagram** is a visual schema that shows, for example, the parts that make up an object, as in Figure 10.8. A diagram is like a <u>map in that it represents spatial relationships</u>, but it shows these relationships in regard to an object, such as a camera or a lawnmower, for instance, as opposed to a place. Like other images, diagrams should be simple enough for the audience to digest in the context of a speech, with both high enough resolution and strong enough contrast to allow the audience to read the image easily.

Text

A number of different kinds of presentation aids can use text, and these include handouts, posters and flip charts, videos, and presentation software. Here are a few tips for using textual elements effectively:

- *Make textual elements clear and easily readable.* If the audience has to strain to read text on a slide, flip chart, or handout, most of the attention goes into deciphering it instead of listening to your speech. All of the text you present should be of a size, color, and font that allows the average viewer in your specific audience to read it easily. And allow plenty of white space around the text for high legibility.
- *Use text sparingly.* The primary focus of your audience's attention should be your speech, not the text in your presentation aid. If the audience has to spend more than 10 to 20 seconds reading, your visual is likely to interfere with your speech.
- *Use text for specific purposes, not as a transcript of your speech.* Text in a presentation aid should have one of a few specific functions:

  — *Summarize or outline.* Bullet points give the audience a visual map of where you are going or emphasize the most important points. An individual bullet point should contain only four or five words.

  — *Highlight a quotation or important phrase.* Remember, however, that text is best used sparingly in visual aids, so keep quotations in presentation aids to about 10 to 12 words. For example, if you were giving a speech about Rwanda and you wanted to show a slide quoting Roméo Dallaire, commander of the UN peacekeeping force

FIGURE 10.8
How many layers of meaning
does this diagram have?

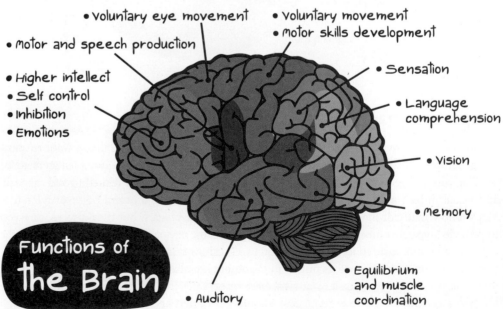

for Rwanda, 1993–1994, on the absence of international media coverage, you might be tempted to show all of the following:

> "The international media initially affected events by their absence. A tree was falling in the forest and no one was there to hear it. Only those of us in Rwanda, it seemed, could hear the sound, because the international media were not there in any appreciable numbers at the outset."

Although you would likely *read* the quotation in its entirety, you would make more effective use of it in your presentation aid if you were to show just this portion:

> "Only those of us in Rwanda …could hear the sound…."

- *Define a central concept or idea.* If there is an argument or point you believe your audience must understand, you can dedicate a slide or a poster to it, but present it in as brief a form as possible.

In short, the guideline for using text in presentation aids is to do the majority of your explanatory work by speaking, not by making the audience read.

MOVING IMAGES

Video, animation, and other moving images can add impact and interest to a presentation. They provide a dynamic visual element that can grab your audience's attention, and they can forge a connection among images that might not be conveyed as effectively through words alone.

Of course, the basic recommendations for any supplemental media apply to moving images. They should follow the principle of CUTS, which we described earlier: They should be clear (free of interference), uncluttered (focusing on the action you want to discuss), topical (supporting of one of your speaking goals), and simple (free of unnecessary elements or information).

It's particularly important for video to be topical and simple. To make sure that a video is truly topical, ask yourself whether it adds to your audience's understanding of your topic. If you can't imagine your audience fully grasping the power, complexity, or detail of what you're saying without the supplemental video, you definitely should show it. If the video doesn't advance the power of your claims, or if showing it doesn't give the audience members something they can't get from your speech alone, there's no reason to show it. Simplicity is important, too, because each element of the video should support the broader point you're making. Extraneous content will distract listeners from your speech.

AUDIO

Audio clips add an extra dimension to your speech, particularly if you're addressing a musical element or quote from a great speaker that you might not be able to do justice to in your own words. Audio, like video, also has to follow the rule of CUTS: clear (able to be easily heard), uncluttered (free of other noise or interference), topical (both directly related to your speech and necessary for making your point), and simple (without excess content).

Now we'll turn to the specific ways you can incorporate static visual elements, moving images, and audio into a presentation aid. We'll start with presentation aids that have been around for a long time—non-electronic aids including handouts, posters, flip charts, and objects, with a special focus on demonstration speeches, which require you to interact with an object. Then we will turn to presentation software, and will conclude the chapter with suggestions about preparation and delivery with presentation aids, especially digital aids.

Not every effective presentation aid requires a power supply. Traditional presentation aids such as handouts, posters, flip charts, and objects actually have a number of advantages over their digital counterparts. They're less likely to cause hiccups in your presentation, such as problems with setup or equipment, and they provide a tangible physical presence on the speaking stage that allows you to give a direct, face-to-face presentation of important contents in your speech.

FAQ *What are the best ways to use a handout?*

A handout is best suited to provide

- a complete outline or a summary,
- an outline for taking notes,
- memorable quotations,
- data that might be cumbersome to present thoroughly in a speech, and
- reference to more resources for understanding your topic.

To Handout or Not To Handout

Evidence supports the idea that a handout can be a good tool for helping your audience remember your speech. For example, one study found that both telling and showing the audience something (using a handout to do the showing) helped an audience remember more of the content of a speech to a significant extent: By "telling" alone, 10% of an audience had significant recall after three days; by "showing," 35% had significant recall; and by "telling and showing," 65% of an audience had significant recall. So, clearly a handout can help drive your message home.

The problem, of course, is that handouts can be risky because if they're too complex, they can distract your audience. The audience members might bury their noses in the handout and, as a result, won't focus as intently on what you have to say. To avoid this effect, you may choose to hold onto a handout until the end of a speech, but if you do that, you're also missing the opportunity to "show" the audience what you're talking about.

Whatever choice you make in regard to handouts, a study by Burt Pryor and his colleagues has an interesting suggestion. Their study on handouts and information processing showed that the effect of a handout can be neutral to negative if the handout simply repeats the points the speaker is making. Repetition, they argue, can have a strange tendency to make an audience more resistant to a message. But, based on their study, they argue that if a handout contains significant information and/or messaging not treated directly in the speech, the handout tends to create a more positive impression of a speaker's claims.

So, if you do use a handout, make sure that it imparts some value other than recapping what you're saying already in the speech, and make sure that you construct it using the principles in this chapter. If you're wise, you can make a handout work for you by using it to present information that you otherwise wouldn't have the time or inclination to explain. As with all visual aids, handouts have to work for you, and they shouldn't ever become a substitute for well-delivered speech content. Used wisely, though, a handout can be a beneficial supplement to and support for your core message.

For more information see:

Burt Pryor, Jeff Butler, Aaron Boyson, and Rufus Barfield, "Effects of distributing 'handouts' during a speech on receiver's inferred information processing," *Perceptual and Motor Skills*, 89(1), August 1999, pp. 145–150.

Handouts

If you decide to use a handout, your first decision will be when to distribute it. One school of thought argues that you shouldn't hand out anything that might distract the audience while you're speaking. Handouts can be useful, but they also give the audience members something to read or even doodle on instead of paying attention to your speech. The other school of thought holds that a handout can provide your audience members with valuable resources, such as an outline they can follow or quotations you refer to in your speech. In addition, a handout can be a nice takeaway for audience members, allowing them to engage your speech by reviewing your points or looking at some of the sources you cited.

Like any decision about a speech, you can make the correct decisions about handouts only in the context of your overarching goals. Most of the time, the risk of distributing a handout outweighs the benefit, especially if you believe the primary goal of a speech is to have a conversation with the audience. But if your speech requires an audience to read and engage with a somewhat complex quotation or text—for instance, if you're giving a speech about why Martin Luther King, Jr.'s "I Have a Dream" is such a great speech—it may be worth the risk to provide the audience with a few portions of the speech on a handout for both you and the audience to refer to in the course of your speech.

If you do choose to employ a handout, and regardless of when you decide to distribute it, a few tips can help ensure its effectiveness. First, following the principles of visual use of text that we established earlier, a good handout should have lots of white space. If it's too dense with text, it almost certainly will distract audience members during your presentation because they're working so hard to read it. Second, the handout has to align closely with your purpose and omit extraneous information.

Posters and Flip Charts

Posters and flip charts can add power and clarity to a presentation by giving the audience images or text to connect with during the course of the speech. These aids are easy to set up and risk none of digital media's equipment failures.

Posters should be placed in a readily visible position near the center of the speaking area—which means that they're not well suited to a large room or audience. Follow the basic principles for display of any visual media by making posters large enough to be easily seen by the entire audience, to be visually interesting and relevant to your topic, and not to be so complex that the audience will have to work hard to digest them. Posters usually should contain one major theme or support one major point in the speech, rather than a series of images or a significant amount of text. If you'd like to present multiple images supporting independent points, or if you want text that accompanies multiple points in your speech, consider using a number of posters. A series of posters can tell a linear story or showcase orientation points for the individual elements of a speech.

Another way to achieve this effect is to use a flip chart. The flip chart is also a low-tech way to control what the audience is seeing, but it can be difficult and sometimes expensive to make a set of flip charts (or even a poster) large enough for a medium-sized audience to see comfortably.

Objects

If you'd like to talk about an object or something you do with an object, you could simply describe the object, you could show a picture of it, or, if the object is portable and appropriate for the speaking situation, you could bring it and show it directly to the audience. There are limits (you shouldn't bring anything that is dangerous, offensive, or against the law or campus rules), but any object that is small enough for you to bring in and large enough to be seen by an audience is worth considering as a presentation aid.

Of course, the object must help to meet one of your speaking goals. Ordinary items that everyone is familiar with are unlikely to hold audience interest or tell listeners anything new. For instance, a plain piece of paper isn't a good presentation aid—unless you're giving a speech about how to fold it into an origami swan.

Using an object as a presentation aid has some risks that you should recognize and try to counteract. One tendency is to play with the object as you are speaking. This is distracting and will draw the audience's attention from your speech. Manipulate or gesture toward the object only when there is a good reason to do so—for example, if you're pointing out the fine craftsmanship of a handwoven basket or talking the audience through the steps of a process such as how to blend oil paint on canvas. Having a table to place the object on while you're not referring to it will help you avoid playing with it. Second, you may be tempted to look at the object as you're speaking. Of course, you should glance at it occasionally, but it shouldn't become an excuse for you to lose regular eye contact with the audience.

DEMONSTRATION SPEECHES AND PRESENTATION AIDS

demonstration speech
An informative speech about an object or a process that uses a physical object as a presentation aid.

Let's discuss demonstration speeches in a bit more depth before moving on. A **demonstration speech** is a specific type of informative speech, and most of the techniques for giving an informative speech about an object or process apply to demonstration speeches (see Chapter 11). The added wrinkle for a demonstration speech is that you're also presenting a tangible physical object to the audience as a presentation aid.

The risks to avoid in demonstration speeches are using the object as a crutch or talking to it instead of talking to the audience *about* it. To avoid this danger, organize your speech to achieve the following goals:

- *Introduce the object.* Say what the object is and where it is from. For instance, use a movie prop from a classic film.
- *Give some background on the object.* Describe how it is made, how old it is if its age is relevant, how you came to have it, and any other interesting background about it. Perhaps you bought the prop on eBay and the film's stars all autographed it.
- *Talk about what makes the object unique and relevant.* This is the heart of your demonstration. What does the object do, and how? Why are you showing it? What makes it noteworthy enough for a speech? What makes it interesting to the audience? Your movie prop might be one of a kind; it might have appeared in an iconic scene in the film; or maybe it has inspired you to pursue a career in set design.
- *If you are speaking about a process using the object*, describe the steps in the process one by one, and indicate or demonstrate, if possible, how the object is part of the process. If you are describing how to re-pot a houseplant, for instance, you could first demonstrate how to use a trowel to loosen the plant in its current pot.
- *Conclude your speech by recapping* why the object is speechworthy and why you chose to present it.

If you follow these suggestions, use good presentation-aid technique, and keep in mind the elements of informative speaking from Chapter 11, you will be well prepared to give an effective demonstrative speech.

PRESENTATION SOFTWARE

Presentation software such as PowerPoint, Keynote, and Prezi can serve as powerful supplements to a speech, unless the speaker is simply reading the slides to the audience. The two basic kinds of presentation software are spatial mapping and slide-based. **Spatial mapping software** creates a large idea map of your presentation (see Figure 4.3 in Chapter 4 for an example of an idea map) and allows you to move between various elements of the map as you present. **Slide-based presentation software** moves in a sequence from one image or slide to the next.

Whichever kind of presentation software you are using, the CUTS principle still applies. Each individual slide or part of your spatial map has to be *clear* enough and large enough for the whole audience to see easily. Each slide should be *uncluttered*, presenting only one theme at a time with the fewest possible images and text elements. Every element should be *topical*—directly related to and necessary for your speech. Finally, each slide should be *simple*, so it can be digested with little effort.

Prezi, available in a free academic version at www.prezi.com, is spatial mapping software for creating a "map" or structure of your ideas and arguments. You can move around it and zoom in just by clicking the mouse. The size of the circles in your map indicates the relative importance of the topics, and circles that touch each other indicate topics that are related, as Figure 10.9 shows. Not only do they display information to the audience about your specific points (the cost of various curriculum options, in Figure 10.9a), but they also showcase the organization of those points (Figure 10.9b) and allow you to zoom in on the images (Figure 10.9c) as you move through your presentation.

PowerPoint, Keynote, and other slide-based software packages offer a platform for giving your audience a multimedia experience. You can integrate audio, video, images, and text to engage your audience through multiple senses. Edward Tufte, an emeritus professor of political science, statistics, and computer science at Yale, known for his work on the presentation of visual information,[4] cautions against letting the slides control the speaker (and, thus, the audience). The problem is that slides are linear and allow the speaker to move through the material in only one direction.

You can avoid this problem by following a few simple principles, some of which we have already outlined.

- *Make your presentation image rich, as opposed to being text-rich.* Using an image-heavy presentation forces you to interpret and contextualize the images for the audience, as opposed to reading aloud a series of lists.
- *Make sure each slide is absolutely necessary for the audience to understand what you're saying.* Don't feel pressured to include a slide or bullet point for every element of your speech. Use slides sparingly, only when they are necessary to help the audience understand a point.
- *Remember that fewer slides are better.* Speakers sometimes create huge presentations and then feel compelled to speed up their speech or shorten their explanations to get through the slides. Because you, not your slides, are the focus of your speech, you should select the fewest slides possible to maximize your speech time.
- *Don't leave slides up when you're not talking about them.* If you use slides sparingly and only for a specific purpose, you'll find a good bit of time in your speech when you're not talking about anything that's on the screen. Cut in a number of blank slides so when you aren't talking about text or image on a slide, the screen is dormant and doesn't distract the audience from you.

Figure 10.10 demonstrates a number of additional points to consider when composing slide-based presentations, especially when they contain text-heavy elements.

spatial mapping software Presentation software that creates an idea map.

slide-based presentation software Presentation software that allows images or slides to move in a sequence from one to the next.

FIGURE 10.9
Slides in Prezi and other presentation software programs can communicate multiple kinds of information.

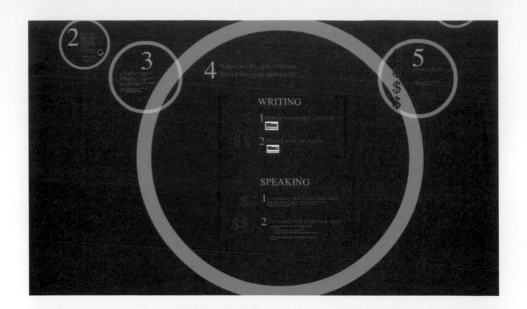

PowerPoint:
Slide Structure – Bad

- This page contains too many words for a presentation slide. It is not written in point form, making it difficult both for your audience to read and for you to present each point. Although there are exactly the same number of points on this slide as the previous slide, it looks much more complicated. In short, your audience will spend too much time trying to read this paragraph instead of listening to you.

© Cengage Learning

FIGURE 10.10A
DON'T have all text and no structure.

PowerPoint:
Slide Structure – Good

- Write in point form, not complete sentences
- Include 4–5 points per slide maximum
- Avoid wordiness: use key words and phrases only

© Cengage Learning

FIGURE 10.10B
DO have clear, simple structure on your slides.

PowerPoint:
Slide Structure – Bad

- Do not use distracting animation
- Do not go overboard with the animation
- Be consistent with the animation that you use

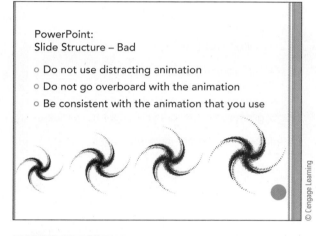

© Cengage Learning

FIGURE 10.10C
DON'T use distracting animation.

PowerPoint:
Fonts – Good

- Use at least a **32**-point font
- Use different size fonts for main points and secondary points
  - This font is **28**-point, the main point font is **32**-point, and the title font is **36**-point
- Use a standard font like Times New Roman or Arial

© Cengage Learning

FIGURE 10.10D
DO use simple, clear text.

PowerPoint:
Fonts – Bad

- If you use a small font, your audience won't be able to read what you have written. This is a 12-point font.
- CAPITALIZE ONLY WHEN NECESSARY. IT IS DIFFICULT TO READ TEXT IN ALL CAPS
- Don't use a complicated font, they are hard to read

© Cengage Learning

FIGURE 10.10E
DON'T use small or hard-to-read fonts.

PowerPoint:
Color – Good

- Use a color of font that contrasts sharply with the background
  Ex: blue or black font on white background
- Use color to reinforce the logic of your structure
  Ex: light blue title versus dark blue text
- Use color to emphasize a point
  But only use this occasionally

© Cengage Learning

FIGURE 10.10F
DO keep color simple and functional.

FIGURE 10.10
Continued

PowerPoint:
Color – Bad

○ Don't use a font color that does not contrast
with the background color-it's hard to read

○ Using color for decoration is distracting and
annoying.

○ Don't use a different color for each point

○ Don't use a different color for secondary points

○ Trying to be creative with color is also bad

FIGURE 10.10G
DON'T use color excessively.

PowerPoint:
Background – Good

○ Use backgrounds such as this one that are
attractive but simple

○ Use backgrounds which are light

○ Use the same background consistently
throughout your presentation

FIGURE 10.10H
DO use simple and readable backgrounds.

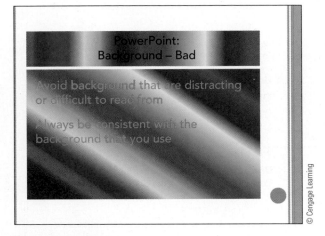

PowerPoint:
Background – Bad

Avoid background that are distracting
or difficult to read from

Always be consistent with the
background that you use

FIGURE 10.10I
DON'T use backgrounds that overpower the text.

PowerPoint:
Spelling and Grammar

○ Proof your slides for
• speling mistakes
• the use of repeated words
• grammatical errors you might have make

○ U cant use txt spelling 4 ur slides.

FIGURE 10.10J
DO proofread your slides.

FIGURE 10.10
Do's and Don'ts for Composing Slides

DELIVERING YOUR SPEECH WITH PRESENTATION AIDS

Finally, here's how to ensure that your presentation aids are supporting your speech rather than overpowering you as the speaker.

- *Always rehearse.* Perhaps even more than other public speeches, a speech with presentation aids requires rehearsal. Rehearsing will increase your confidence; allow you to check and make sure your aids are clear, uncluttered, topical, and simple; and give you enough familiarity with them to maintain eye contact with the audience. Rehearsing also enables you to work on timing, to make sure you move smoothly from speech content to presentation aid and back again while staying within your time limit.

- *Remember that your aids are not self-interpreting.* Avoid falling into the trap of thinking that when you show something, you don't have to explain it. Whether it is your grandfather's violin or a line graph of changing population demographics, any visual or audio element requires (1) an explanation of what it is, (2) some sense of where you got it, and (3) a statement of what it means and why it's important to your audience.

- **Maintain eye contact.** It is often tempting to look at your visual aid, or worst of all, to turn your back on the audience to look at a screen. Avoid hiding behind your technology. No matter how nervous or insecure you feel, you're more interesting and a better communicator than your presentation aids.

Preparing to Use Digital Media

Digital media, when used effectively, can add a powerfully dynamic element to your presentation. Equipment that doesn't work can sabotage your planned speech. No matter what media you are using, these preparatory steps will help you minimize that risk:

- Make sure that the room contains the proper equipment for your needs, and that you will have access to it before your speech so you don't waste valuable speech time setting up.
- Make sure that the available equipment will work with your presentation aid. For example, check to see if there's a DVD player if you have a DVD; if there's a dedicated computer for using presentation software, confirm that the computer has the proper presentation software; and if you're using a laptop, make sure that your hardware is compatible with the projector.
- Make sure that the room can be appropriately configured for your supplemental media. Can you dim the lights comfortably so the audience can see your slides? Can the chairs be moved so everyone can see the screen? Can you set speakers to a sufficient volume for your audience to hear?
- If you're going to play a video or an audio clip, familiarize yourself with the controls of the video or audio player you'll be using, and preset and cue up as much as possible ahead of time.

Getting access to the room ahead of time will help you head off many problems that could interfere with your presentation aids.

Developing a Backup Plan for Digital Media

The only surefire way to protect yourself from the ever-present possibility that your presentation aids will fail is to have a powerful, well-constructed speech that you can present without them. But there also *are* things you can do to recover when you have a digital meltdown.

- You can copy your slides to distribute them as hard copies later.
- You can use a web-based presentation program so, as long as you have Internet access, you can show at least the major visual elements.
- You can bring your presentation on a thumb drive in case you don't have Internet access.

Plan each time as if the worst that *can* happen *will* happen. And remember, if you focus on and hone your speaking skills, you can be fantastic even during a power failure.

Summary

Proper use of presentation aids or supplemental media allows you to make complex points simpler, engage more of the audience's senses, and demonstrate objects and processes that are difficult to describe with words alone. These aids are effective only when they assist you in the larger task of giving an effective speech. As a responsible speaker, you must make deliberate and ethical choices for engaging your audience, guided by the goals you want to achieve with

MindTap®

Reflect, personalize, and apply what you've learned.

your audience and the principles for good use of supplemental media. Whether you are using a simple poster or the most sophisticated digital media, make sure that each one achieves a concrete purpose, follows good design principles, and supports you as a speaker instead of displacing you in the audience's attention.

Questions for Review

1. What are the basic principles for effective use of visual presentation elements?
2. What kinds of problems can presentation aids help to solve? What problems can they create?
3. What does "less is more" mean in the context of presentation aids?
4. What does CUTS stand for, and why is it important?
5. List three do's and three don'ts for PowerPoint slides.

Questions for Discussion

1. What kinds of speeches require presentation aids? What kinds of presentation aids help in digesting a speech?
2. What is the difference between a presentation aid that supports a speech and one that substitutes for the speech?
3. Describe the best use of presentation aids that you have seen. Can you think of the worst? What made the difference?

Key Concepts   MindTap®

Practice defining the chapter's terms by using online flashcards.

bar graph	diagram	presentation aids
chart	graph	slide-based presentation
cropping	line graph	spatial mapping
demonstration speech	pie chart	

PART 4 KINDS OF SPEECHES

CHAPTER **11** Informative Speaking

CHAPTER **12** Being Persuasive

CHAPTER **13** Special Types of Speeches and Presentations

DrAfter123/Getty Images

11 INFORMATIVE SPEAKING

AP Images/Gillian Jones

LEARNING OBJECTIVES

- Analyze the goals of informative speaking
- Outline the responsibilities of informative speakers
- Choose appropriate topics for informative speeches
- Master the techniques of informative speaking
- Make effective choices of supporting materials, organizational pattern, and terminology
- Describe the benefits of alternate informative speaking formats TED and PechaKucha

CHAPTER OUTLINE

- Introduction: Telling It Like It Is
- Goals of Informative Speaking
- Responsibilities of the Informative Speaker
- Topics for Informative Speeches
- Techniques of Informative Speaking
- Choices That Make Information Effective
- Alternative Speech Formats

Katie likes math. But she knows that this fondness isn't universal, even among those who are good at it. So after choosing to give an informative speech on the number *pi*, she has to confront some serious questions. First, does she know enough to give the speech? *What* does she have to know? Theory, history, philosophy? *Why* would the audience care about any of this? Katie has a lot of questions about how to get information, and how to communicate it effectively.

Overview

This chapter introduces you to informative speaking. Unlike a persuasive speech (Chapter 12), in which your goal is to move an audience to action, your aim in an **informative speech** is to provide your audience with a basic factual understanding of your topic. First, we will discuss the goal of an informative speech, which is to communicate new information—that is, facts and data—to your audience about your topic. You might use this information to encourage the audience to develop a new perspective on the topic or to elicit positive or negative feelings about it. Next, we will address the responsibilities of informative speech, highlighting the ways that your choices can make a difference in how your audience will understand and relate to your topics. Then we will provide you with some pointers for picking a good informative topic. Finally, we will discuss the kinds of techniques that you can use to give a good informative speech, highlighting the kinds of choices you will have to make in creating an effective informative speech.

MindTap®
Start with a warm-up activity about Katie's speech, and review the chapter's Learning Objectives.

informative speech A speech that provides an audience with facts and data about a topic so that they will understand it.

INTRODUCTION: TELLING IT LIKE IT IS

Not all instances of speech aim at changing the behavior or opinions of the audience. A speaker might simply want to give an audience members some helpful information that contributes to their understanding of an object, process, or event. For example, a student might listen to a speech at the orientation about how to fill out a student aid form, or might give a speech to educate other students about a student organization. In other words, sometimes

MindTap®
Read, highlight, and take notes online.

speakers speak to convey information about a topic, not to persuade the audience to do something with the information.

Nevertheless, the information that you convey to your audience members could influence their decisions in the future. Each of us is confronted with a number of choices in day-to-day life: What should I have for lunch? Should I see the doctor about this cough? Should I follow a budget? Whom should I vote for? If we are making these decisions reflectively—if we are actively thinking and informing ourselves about them and perhaps even discussing them with others—we are deciding on the basis of the best information available to us.

Thus, we navigate our worlds largely on the basis of the stock of information we have accumulated. So, for example, when you decide what to eat for lunch, you have to make a number of information-based decisions: Are you eating for health, convenience, or value, or are you looking for the tastiest meal you can find? Once you decide what drives your choice for lunch, you refer to other information that helps you achieve the goal. For example, if you are eating for value, you have to know who offers the cheapest lunch deal around. The same holds true for bigger decisions, such as whom you should vote for: You have to find out which candidates best represent your interests and concerns.

Informative speaking is essential because it adds to the audience's available information, and even if your topic seems minor, it may be useful to some of your audience members. Maybe your speech about how to eat a balanced diet will influence their eating choices, helping them to create good eating habits. Perhaps a speech on how to prepare a budget will influence them to take better care of their money. Or a speech on how to buy a good car might help some members save money and buy a safer vehicle.

Whatever the topic, the information you convey to your audience members can affect their future choices. For this reason, think carefully about your choices in presenting information to your audience. A clear, concise, well-researched, and well-delivered speech can be a valuable asset to your listeners. A speech that is difficult to follow or contains inaccurate information might lead your audience to make some poor or ill-informed choices.

Better choices in informative speaking improve the collective decision-making capacity of your audience. As a result, informative speech can play a significant, if indirect, role in healthy personal, and even civic, deliberation. So the goal of informative speaking is to figure out how to best present good information to your audience.

To help you focus on the kinds of choices you'll make in contributing to better decision-making through informative speaking, we begin by looking at the three goals of an informative speech.

GOALS OF INFORMATIVE SPEAKING

In contrast to persuasive speech, which calls for the audience to take action (to be discussed in Chapter 12), your goal in an informative speech is to convey information (facts and data) about your topic. Though an informative speech may change the way the audience thinks about or takes action on a topic, your primary aim is to deliver information as impartially as possible. You have three approaches to choose from:

1. helping your audience encounter and process new information,
2. providing the audience with a new perspective on the topic, or
3. eliciting positive or negative feelings about the information.

The first goal, presenting new information, depends on choices you make about clarity and starting with

FAQ Why call it "informative?"

The word *informative* comes from the Latin word *informare*, which means "to shape, form, train, instruct, or educate." To inform someone is thus to "shape, form, train, instruct, or educate" someone about the topic.

common ground. The second and third goals (new perspectives and feelings about the topic) depend on choices you make to help the audience connect the breadth of information you present with a set of concepts, organizing principles, or feelings. Though any informative speech may have more than one of the goals that follow, all informative speeches will have at least one of them.

Present New Information

One of the primary goals of an informative speech is to *help your audience encounter and understand new information.* You'll want to present your informative speech in a way that best helps the audience digest the information, because the more readily your audience members can assimilate the information, the more useful this information can be for them.

Your audience members probably will have many different orientations in regard to your topic. Some may think they have already heard just about everything there is to know about your topic. Others may have no interest in, or no frame of reference for, your topic. A good informative speech addresses both of these segments of the audience (and the people in between) by starting from a common base of knowledge about the topic and then adding specific new facts and data about it. So, for example, you might begin a speech about political advertising by saying:

> **We've all seen political commercials around election time. Candidates are always trying their hardest to get their messages out to voters. But did you know that candidates are increasingly turning to highly targeted Internet advertising strategies that help them tailor their messages toward ever more specific segments of the population?**

Beginning with a recognizable starting point and then increasing your audience's understanding of the issue is appropriate for both the well-informed and the less-informed members of your audience.

Now, take a look at how the following passage from another informative speech delivers new information:

> **One of the choices people most commonly make when they become interested in controlling their weight is to substitute sugar-free foods for sugary foods. We all know that if you want to lose weight, you should limit your calorie intake. Artificial sweeteners allow us to do that without giving up our afternoon soda, our favorite candy, or a little treat after dinner. But did you know there is strong evidence that artificial sweeteners actually make it harder to lose weight? Researchers at the University of Texas Health Sciences Center at San Antonio found that artificial sweeteners cause us to underestimate the calorie content of the other foods we are eating.[1] So, even though a diet soft drink will help you avoid the calories you might have consumed if you were to drink its sugary counterpart, the net effect of consuming such drinks might be to increase your overall calorie count.**

This passage begins with a bit of conventional wisdom ("One of the choices people most commonly make . . .") and then poses a question ("But did you know . . ."). Research about the topic follows that setup.

So what makes this passage effective? People like the novelty of new information, and they usually appreciate the surprise value of information that upsets conventional wisdom. This strategy will help you gain and hold the audience members' attention. Whether they are accepting or a bit skeptical, they probably will listen to your supporting evidence and information more closely when they believe you're telling them something new and potentially interesting.

Journalist Michael Pollan has written and spoken widely about nutrition science and theories of healthy eating. What challenges does he face in talking to the public about the complexity of nutritional research?

David Kamerman/Boston Globe/Getty Images

If the information isn't new or interesting for audience members, they may tune you out. If they have reason to doubt that the new information is credible, they may not be willing to follow you to your conclusion.

Finally, sometimes the value of a good informative speech lies in the way it helps audience members organize information they *already* know. For example, most students have heard plenty of advice about job searches, and most have some experience of their own, but a speech titled "Twelve Tips for Handling a Job Search Online" can help them assemble familiar information into a concise, usable strategy.

Provide New Perspectives

A second goal of informative speaking is to *encourage listeners to adopt a new perspective* on the information you're presenting, understanding it in a new way. The way you choose to frame your content gives your audience members a new context or reference point for understanding their relationship to it.

Context creates a perspective that makes the information clear. For example, humor can be a good way of looking at the relationship between advertising and politics: "You're already familiar with political advertising—we all see a lot of it on TV and billboards—but I'd like to explain just how funny it can be." Contextualizing information provides a standpoint for viewing your topic, helps you organize your content around a memorable central theme, and helps your audience link the various elements of your speech to it.

Strategies that help an audience think in a new way about familiar facts can be effective. Consider this introduction for an informative speech:

> **According to the Centers for Disease Control and Prevention, 67% of U.S. adults over the age of 20 are overweight.[2] With so many people struggling with their weight, perhaps it's not surprising that market research conducted by General Nutrition Centers showed that 38% of the people who make New Year's resolutions resolved to lose weight in the coming year.[3] We often think of weight loss as a personal problem with important implications for our well-being, and the solution for each of us to be healthier is to exercise more and eat better.**

Without question, carrying extra weight can have significant implications for an individual's length and quality of life. But the collective size of our waistlines also has fairly significant implications for the public at large. For example, obesity exerts dramatic effects on the cost of health care. To show why this is the case, we might start with some estimates about the relationship between obesity and health care spending. According to former Surgeon General Regina Benjamin, obesity and the health problems associated with it reduce annual productivity by 200 to 440 dollars per person, resulting in a massive loss in economic productivity.[4]

This isn't a persuasive speech, because it doesn't say that the audience members *should* view obesity as a public health problem, but it asserts that it's an interesting topic because they *could*. Yet, as the excerpt shows, it does introduce the audience to a new way of thinking about the problem. Its goal is to inform the audience members and shape their viewpoint by connecting information they already know—that the United States has an obesity problem—to another set of facts with which they probably are also familiar—that the United States has a problem with the high cost of health care.

Should vs could

Choosing the new-perspective strategy has a number of benefits. First, it organizes the facts in the speech around a set of central themes, so it makes it easy for the audience to engage, digest, and remember the individual elements of your speech. Second, though the strategy is not explicitly persuasive, it allows you to shape how your audience will understand the facts. Thus, this strategy adds to the stock of useful public knowledge without explicitly calling for a specific change. Third, the strategy is interesting for audience members because it can reveal new ways of thinking about familiar facts and ideas and show new connections between them.

Generate Positive or Negative Feelings

Another goal of informative speaking is to tie the elements of your speech to the attitudes or feelings that you want the audience to hold about the topic. Although an informative speech, by definition, doesn't seek to persuade the audience to adopt any specific course of action, it

Bill Gates, founder of Microsoft and co-chair of the Bill and Melinda Gates Foundation, talks about the Ebola crisis in West Africa during the Politico "Lessons from Leaders" series at the Bank of America offices on September 29, 2014, in Washington, DC. What are some of Gates' biggest challenges in talking about a disease such as Ebola?

Chip Somodevilla/Getty Images

Table 6.1 Some Positive and Negative Synonyms	
Positive	Negative
tidy	obsessive
self-confident	arrogant
dynamic	chaotic
innovative	unproven
cost-effective	stingy
voluptuous	fat
creative	weird
thrifty	cheap
prudent	selfish

does have a set of guiding principles that tie it together. If you provide this by organizing your informative speech around a central theme, you also can arrange its elements around a central set of positive or negative attitudes or feelings.

Consider the difference between saying a coworker is "assertive" and saying he is "bossy." These terms are not very different in meaning, but they do convey very different judgments about the person described. Assertiveness is often a helpful trait at work, but employees don't want someone to be bossy. Wording and other stylistic choices (discussed in Chapter 8) can influence the way an audience understands an informative speech without changing the basic content of the information presented. For instance, you could choose to describe your coworker as "achievement-oriented" without commenting on his assertiveness or bossiness at all. Decisions like this help to create negative or positive feelings in your listeners about the topic of your speech.

For more examples of positively and negatively charged terms, take a look at Table 6.1, and remember that your wording choices are part of your larger strategy to convey information to your audience in an engaging, memorable, and helpful way.

Just keep in mind that if the speech is to remain an informative speech, you can't call for a specific change in thinking or action. However, there is a world of difference between claims that political advertising "extends" or that it "erodes" public discourse. Both are informational claims, and you could present facts that support either one. Although both sides may be valid, the informative goal you select to configure your speech—whether concept, perspective, or attitude—determines how you will present the facts.

How to Choose an Informative Goal

Though any informative speech may have more than one goal, let's consider some examples of how choosing the different informative goals will change the nature of your speech, as well as how you might compose a speech for each goal.

Let's look at the choices you might make in selecting information about obesity in our hypothetical speech. Imagine you're trying to convey the idea that obesity is a significant public health problem and your goal is to inform the audience of this problem but you're worried that people have heard this so often it doesn't seem to register with them. Let's say the basic piece of information you want to convey is: "67% of U.S. adults are overweight." You could introduce this fact in a number of ways, and each option will make your audience think about it in a different way. As we saw in Chapter 3, to make the right choice, you first need to know your audience.

If you guess your audience members won't think obesity is a significant public health problem because they're mostly young and healthy and they're generally uninterested in public health issues, you could try to create concern by choosing "shock language":

The United States is drowning in a sea of fat: More than two of every three citizens are overweight. Even though you might be perfectly healthy, the massive burden that obesity puts on our medical system can significantly damage your ability to get reasonably priced health care.

"Drowning in a sea of fat" is evocative and emotive language: It implies negative feelings about the obesity epidemic.

However, if you aren't interested in shock value, or if you believe your audience might think you're overselling the relevance of your information, you could choose a straightforward presentation of the facts:

According to the Centers for Disease Control and Prevention, 67% of U.S. adults carry excess body weight.

But what if a neutral presentation of facts won't engage your audience members and a dramatic "sea of fat" approach will turn them off? Then you might solicit the audience's goodwill with a more empathetic approach. You could personalize the presentation and address your listeners' potential resistance before offering the statistic:

Almost all of us have worried about our waistlines at some point in our lives. I know I have. Before we start to feel guilty about our weight, though, we can take comfort from the fact that none of us is alone: Almost 70% of U.S. adults struggle with maintaining a healthy body weight.

The statement that the speaker and almost everyone else has or has had a weight problem might help eliminate the audience's resistance to hearing that obesity is an epidemic because it avoids judgment and it describes excess body weight in neutral terms (as opposed to negatively charged terms such as "fat") and as a problem for many people. This version avoids a potentially negative emotional appeal, and it might be a bit easier for some audiences to accept.

© 2017 Cengage Learning

MindTap®
Watch a video, and do an interactive activity.

RE-DOING OBESITY   TRY IT!

What other approaches to an informative speech about obesity speech could you imagine?

- Describe at least two different approaches that an informative speech could take about the topic.
- How would you attempt to create positive or negative feelings about the topic in each of those two speeches?
- What role could positive feeling play in making a topic like obesity relevant?

RESPONSIBILITIES OF THE INFORMATIVE SPEAKER

Informative speaking often seems to be a neutral type of speech, just conveying information. But as the preceding section demonstrates, you make choices in an informative speech, and those choices present information from different perspectives, so informative speeches are not necessarily neutral. Because we make choices about what to say in an informative speech, we should take responsibility for those choices.

Newspapers, television, and Internet news sites present themselves as places that give the facts and allow you, the viewer, to decide what to think. But no reporting is ever truly unbiased, because to report something is to create a picture of an event—whether in 30 seconds of news video or a few hundred words on a page or screen—and that picture is incomplete. Presenting a fact also means choosing what to say, how to say it, and what to leave out. These choices result in a specific view of the facts. For instance, one report might simply say that a suspect in last night's robbery and shooting has been apprehended, while another identifies the suspect by gender, race, and age. Based on which report they read or hear, the audience will have different feelings about the suspect.

When you deliver an informative speech, you have choices about which information to include, how to organize your speech, and how to deliver it. These choices imply responsibilities: You may be the primary source of information on your topic for an audience member. Thus, like a responsible journalist, you should present your speech in a way that gives your audience the best chance to learn from the information. At the end of your talk, the listeners should know something worthwhile about your topic that they didn't know before.

So what are the responsibilities of an informative speaker?

- To do the necessary research to find relevant and credible information
- To present to the audience the essential facts about your topic in a way that is factually correct and true to the research you have done
- To present the facts in a clear and accessible manner
- To provide the audience members with an organized presentation of these facts that they can digest, engage, and remember
- To provide information that is useful and relevant to your audience members, with the goal of improving their decision-making.

To fulfill these responsibilities, keep the following principles in mind as you compose your speech:

1. **The facts don't speak for themselves.** "Here's all the stuff I found in my research," or a jumble of disconnected facts, is an ineffective approach even when your research is accurate, because it assumes the audience will work to make something meaningful from all the pieces of information. You need to pull the facts together into a coherent picture to provide meaning for your audience.

2. **Relevance matters.** Nothing is more boring than listening to pointless or irrelevant information. To be an engaging and compelling speaker, demonstrate the relevance of your content up front. Remember that relevance also matters when you're deciding which examples to use, because examples that click with one audience might be mystifying to another audience.

3. **Clarity is the result of choices.** Clarity can seem effortless, but a lot of work goes into appearing effortless. Speakers are clear and easy to follow because they make good choices tailored to their audience. A number of techniques can increase your clarity:

   - Use simple, short, direct sentences. This is especially useful when presenting a statistic. For example, instead of saying the tangled, "A majority of experts agree that of the net percentage of return on investment for a dollar in renewable energy technologies is 6%," say, "Experts say that investments in renewable energy generate a 6% return."
   - Break down long lists of facts into individual sentences to give the audience time to follow your claims. For example, instead of saying, "There are three reasons why the parking problem on campus has gotten worse, including an increase in demand, an expansion in permits, and a reduction in spaces," say, "Parking on campus has become more difficult to come by. First, because of increased student

Developing expertise through research is one of the responsibilities of an informative speaker.

Rob Melnychuk /Digital Vision/Getty Images

and employee populations, more people are looking for spots. Second, the parking office has issued more permits than it has in the past, so there are more people looking for parking on any given day. Finally, new construction has eliminated a number of open parking spaces." The enumeration and the additional content make the individual claims clearer and stronger and also afford the audience the chance to process each of them.

The bottom line is that responsible informative speaking requires you to present facts in a clear and organized manner around a central theme or set of themes. It requires concise, direct, and carefully crafted claims, and it requires you to present the facts in your speech in a way that is true to the research that you have done.

FAQ *Do I really need to worry about being boring?*

Yes, you really do. You can be smart and well informed, but if you're boring, the audience isn't listening, so you're wasting everyone's time. The key is to focus on being concrete and vivid in every part of your speech. In Chapter 8, we discussed strategies for making your information come alive for your audience.

TOPICS FOR INFORMATIVE SPEECHES

If you are asked to give an informative speech, you may be able to choose your own topic, and choosing wisely will help you give a better speech. Many topics are easy to explain, and clarifying some topics can make for an interesting informative speech, but other topics may be too ambitious for your audience and your time limit. For example, it might be more manageable to give a general overview of global warming than to focus your speech on the mathematics that underlie climate modeling, especially if you have only a short time to speak with a nontechnical audience. This is not to say that you should dodge difficult topics, but, rather, that you should choose those that are reasonably translatable to, and useful for, your audience in the time you have available.

Informative speeches can be about objects, events, people, processes, or ideas. Here are some suggestions for presenting those topics in interesting ways.

Objects

Sometimes a speech informs the audience about an object or an event—for example, navigational apps for a tablet computer or the mechanical causes of a recent plane crash. Audience members might find an object or event interesting or helpful for these reasons:

- How often they encounter it (every day is more interesting than only sometimes; people go to class every week, but they get married or have surgery rarely)
- The role it plays in their lives (toothbrushes are more important than jellyfish to most people, and yearly checkups with the doctor are important to our health)
- Whether they can profit from knowing more about it (a little knowledge about a car's workings can reduce gasoline bills)

In contrast to a demonstration speech (discussed in Chapter 10), an informative speech about an object or an event doesn't require the subject of your speech to be physically in front of you, so it's important to give the audience a vivid image, painted in words, of the object.

Events

Sometimes events are the center of an informative speech. An audience might find an event interesting or important for these reasons:

- Whether it is a regular event (getting something to eat, going to the dentist) or a milestone event (getting married, getting your first job, attending a funeral).
- The significance of the event: Is it a source of joy, sorrow, pain, or pleasure?
- How knowing the structure and functions of the event can help to make it better or to solve problems.

As with the object speech, the challenge—even more so with an event—is to make to make the topic concrete and visual for the audience.

People

What makes a person an interesting topic for a speech? It could be the person's *accomplishments,* such as winning an event in the Special Olympics, or unusual or admirable *abilities,* such as a command of several foreign languages or acknowledged cooking skills. Or someone might be interesting simply because he or she is already *famous,* like Michelle Obama, or even *infamous,* like the convicted swindler Bernie Madoff.

When speaking about a person, you might want to consider these tips for making your speech relevant and compelling:

- If the person is already well known, seek out new information that your listeners might not know, to hold their interest. What was the person like before he or she became famous? What does he or she do when not in the spotlight? For example, former President Jimmy Carter has worked extensively with Habitat for Humanity, and you could give an informative speech about that organization, focusing on the personal angle of how one does meaningful work *after* being president.
- If the person isn't well known, find a way to convey his or her essence to the audience. Instead of a possibly tedious list of facts, however, begin with the quality,

FAQ *What's the difference between fame and notoriety?*

Fame results from *good* things you've done, whereas notoriety (or "being notorious") results from *bad* things you've done.

characteristic, or achievement of this person that's most relevant to the audience or a way that speaks to your listeners' values, and structure your speech around that. If, for instance, you want to give an informative speech about why you like music so much, you might tell a story about how you fondly remember sitting on the porch and playing the guitar with your late uncle.

An informative speech about a person should include biographical information, but the speech shouldn't be *only* a biography. Your audience members should come away thinking that they know your subject as a person, that they understand what motivated your subject to do great (or terrible) things, and that they might even have some insight into why the person made the life choices that he or she did.

Processes

Giving an informative speech about a process can be challenging, but this type of presentation also can be highly useful or helpful to your audience. The process you choose to speak about might be relatively uncomplicated, such as applying to graduate school, or highly complex, such as the Olympic scoring system for figure skating or how a piece of software gets developed from concept through training of users.

A process might be abstract, such as the process of evolution, or concrete, such as the series of events in an actual case of natural selection. By definition, processes are continuous, so your description must cut that continuous flow into a discrete series of chunks or steps. For example, if you want to give a speech about how to poach an egg perfectly, you might organize the speech into selecting an egg, controlling the water temperature, timing the cooking process, and serving the egg.

Ideas

Sometimes you'll want to talk about an abstract concept: freedom, morality, courage, gender. The more abstract and philosophical your topic, the more challenging it may be to find ways to make it real to your audience. Several strategies can help you:

iStockphoto.com/TheImageArea

iStockphoto.com/Cstbphoto

Yellow Dog Productions/The Image Bank/Getty Images

Informative speeches about people we admire—soldiers (a), firefighters (b), and teachers (c)—allow us to illustrate exemplary values with vivid examples drawn from their lives. What values might these photos illustrate?

A good informative topic gives the audience information that is both new and useful. If the information is not new to the audience in some way, the listeners will be bored. If it is not useful (even if the only use is entertainment or satisfying curiosity), they won't care. A few questions can get you on your way to finding a good topic:

- What are you interested in that others might not know about? What interesting facts have you stumbled across that you think others might profit from or be interested in?
- What do your audience members need to know to improve their everyday lives? What information would be useful to them?
- Can you think of instances where conventional wisdom or common sense about a topic is either wrong or misleading? How could you demonstrate this to an audience?

- *Connect your topic to familiar ideas.* If you connect an abstract idea to a concrete idea that's familiar to the audience, it will be easier for the audience to follow. So, for example, if you want to talk about the federal budget deficit, you might start by talking about setting a personal budget, talking about the implications of overspending, and then connecting these ideas to the broader concept of the budget deficit.
- *Use detailed examples.* If you want to give an informative speech about courage as a character quality, you might start with an example of someone showing courage under fire—for instance, a soldier who braved gunfire to save a wounded comrade. The more detail you provide, the more dramatic and concrete your definition of "courage" will be.
- *Compare two similar cases.* What if you want to give a speech about the idea of justice? It might get boring quickly if you were to just give definitions of justice. But you could start instead by comparing two stories: "Rasheed was an African American teenager who was shot on the street late at night. Amy was a White college woman who was shot on the way home from class. Rasheed's murder went largely unnoticed by the police and media, labeled as yet another casualty in gang warfare. But Amy's murder created a firestorm of police and media activity. The question here is: What is the nature of justice in these two situations? Doesn't justice imply equal treatment for similar circumstances?" Comparing two specific examples provides your audience members with a set of concrete concepts to help them engage and interpret the information.

TECHNIQUES OF INFORMATIVE SPEAKING

What are some specific ways for informative speakers to present the facts surrounding their topics? Defining, describing, and explaining are some concrete techniques you can use to compose an informative speech that achieves your goals in a responsible way.

Defining

definition A statement of the relevant meaning of a word, phrase, or term.

New and unfamiliar terms should be defined for two reasons. First, audiences aren't impressed by technical vocabulary. They just say to themselves, "Doesn't the speaker understand the topic well enough to explain it to me?" Second, a **definition** helps to set up arguments and explanations. So, for example, in the speech about the murders of Amy and Rasheed, the speaker defines justice as similar treatment for similar people, this definition can be used to bring up some of the controversies about justice. For example, should justice be affected by considerations of place and context?

Terms and concepts can be defined in several ways. For example, if you were trying to explain credit hours in a speech about financial aid, you could offer any of the following types of definitions, all of which are correct:

- *Logical* (an abstract definition): A weight assigned to a course grade.
- *Operational* (the concept in practice): The hours your class meets per week.
- *Authority* (based on a rule): The college catalog defines a credit hour as. . . .

- *Negation* (by contrast to something else): Credit hours are not the same as courses, because courses can have anywhere from 1 to 6 credits.
- *By example* (a concrete, relevant instance): You get 3 credit hours for your public speaking course.

Defining is a particularly important strategy in an informative speech, because it can create a theme to organize your reflections.

Definitions, Explanations, and Feelings

What makes a definition good? What makes for a good explanation of a thing? Most of us think that definitions are good because they are accurate or effective in defining the character of a concept or thing. We like definitions if they seem true. By the same token, most of us think that an explanation is good because it mirrors reality or because it contains the appropriate information to help us understand something. An explanation is good if it helps us make sense out of something. The informational content of definitions and explanations alike is undoubtedly important, and all things being equal, it is good that your definitions are true and your explanations are accurate.

But there's another side to definitions and explanations—one that we'd call, in fancy terminology, "affective." Here, "affective" means that we also like definitions and explanations because they make us feel good. They conform with our understandings of the world if they make it more predictable and more intelligible to us. As philosopher J.D. Trout put it, like it or not, good definitions and explanations don't work only because they're true; they also work because they "feel right" or "seem accurate."

What does this mean for you? At a minimum, the subjective element in definitions and explanations means that even when you're giving an informative speech, you must pay attention to the predispositions of your audience members. You have to think about whether your descriptions and definitions will match their experiences. If your definitions and descriptions match their experiences, they are more inclined to buy in to your account. But if your definitions are very different from what your audience members would expect, or if your descriptions are far afield of their experiences, you may have to spend a little more time to get your audience to see what it is that you're saying. As always, think about the character of your choices here, evaluate their implications, and you'll be on firmer ground.

For more information, see:

J.D. Trout, "Scientific explanation and the sense of understanding," *Philosophy of Science*, 69 (June 2002), pp. 212–233.

Describing

Much of your success in informative speaking depends on your ability to describe things—objects, events, people, and ideas—in concrete and memorable terms. Concrete details and mental pictures are two techniques for effective **description**.

description A set of vivid and concrete details that characterize an object, event, person, or idea.

Concrete Details Telling your audience "The economy is in bad shape" is uninventive and bland. If, in contrast, you say "Factories are closing, people are out of work, and some people, like Adam Schmidt of Pleasantville, USA, are struggling to even put food on the table," you are giving a much more detailed and evocative statement of the problem. Vivid

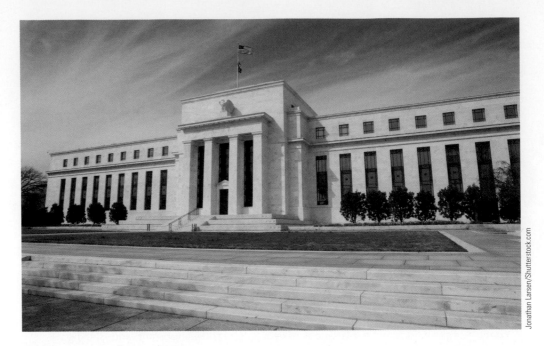

Good speakers create vivid images for audiences. When explaining the functions of the U.S. Federal Reserve, the nation's central bank, pictured here, it's helpful to call upon images of more familiar banks and walk the audience through them.

Jonathan Larsen/Shutterstock.com

and concrete details, such as factory closings and the struggles of an individual citizen, take advantage of the idea, first put forward by ancient rhetoricians, that the mind works by dealing with images.

Mental Pictures   Concrete details in your speech help you create a picture in the mind's eye of audience members. You also can create a mental picture using images they have already seen. Ask them to call up these images and put them together in a way that serves your purpose. If you have a fairly abstract topic, such as how the Federal Reserve sets the discount rate, it helps to suggest an image. You might compare the Fed's "discount window" to a bank window, where people can walk up and deposit or withdraw their money. The Federal Reserve is the "bank," but ordinary people can't walk up to its window; only large banks can. You explain the point with this mental picture:

> Imagine a bank—a tall building, big bronze doors, and lots of marble on the floor—an old-fashioned, really impressive building. But as you walk up to get in line, you notice a sign above you that says, "You Must Be This Tall to Stand in This Line"—and the sign is more than 7 feet off the ground! Suddenly you realize that although this looks like a regular bank, it's not. The vast majority of people aren't even allowed to get in line. It's extremely exclusive, and you'd like to know what kind of services "big" people get at the teller's window.

TRY IT!   **MAKE A MENTAL PICTURE**

Here's a description of a situation: "Poverty has negative health effects."

- What synonyms for *poverty* might you employ? And what are synonyms for *negative* and for *health effects*?
- Create three different versions of this sentence, making the description more engaging.
- Compare these versions with the ones your classmates come up with. Which descriptions are the most engaging? Why? Which, if any, descriptions are overdone? Why?

Detailed, visually evocative explanations not only can make your speech more interesting but also can provide your audience members with specific points, which they can connect with their everyday experience.

Explaining

You can use a number of strategies to explain something complex, including breaking a process or set of events into smaller parts and using analogies and examples. The goal of an **explanation** is to give your audience an easily digestible concept.

Breaking It Down A process or set of events can be broken into smaller units. For example, if you were giving an informative speech about global warming and wanted to explain how carbon emissions increase the net temperature of the earth, you could say, "Increasing carbon dioxide levels absorb heat radiated from the earth's surface," but this might not be entirely clear to everyone in the audience. To make the idea easier to grasp, you might explain it this way:

> Sunlight enters the earth's atmosphere and warms the surface of the planet. The surface then radiates heat back into the atmosphere. As levels of carbon dioxide increase near the surface, however, heat is trapped by the earth's polluted atmosphere. This trapped heat increases the overall temperature of the earth.

By explaining the rise in temperature as a step-by-step process that begins with the arrival of sunlight into earth's atmosphere, you've helped your listeners understand the relationship between the specific claims you have made in the speech, and you have made your evidence (in this case, scientific evidence) more accessible to the audience.

Using Analogies When a process is difficult to grasp, you can try to explain it with an **analogy**. Analogies help audiences understand complex information because they liken the topic to something the listeners already understand. Here's an example:

> Global warming is sometimes referred to as the "greenhouse effect." A greenhouse is a glass structure that a gardener uses to help to keep plants warm during cold months. The glass lets sunlight inside to warm the air and traps the heat the sun generates because glass is a good insulator. Global warming works the same way: Earth's atmosphere allows sunlight in, and the bigger the blanket of carbon dioxide and other gases, the more readily the atmosphere retains the sun's heat.

Using Examples When a complex explanation might be too long or too abstract for your audience or speaking situation, a specific example is often helpful. Imagine that you're giving an informative speech about the collapse of the housing market and you want to explain how the collapse of home values made it difficult for some homeowners to avoid bankruptcy. You could say, "Declining home values made it difficult for some people to refinance their way out of bad loans," but your point might not be immediately clear to an audience. An example could clarify the meaning:

> Martina Case wasn't sure she could afford the $500,000 price tag on the new home she wanted. Her monthly payments would be too high if she would try to finance the purchase using a conventional mortgage loan. A quick-talking loan officer convinced her that she could take out a loan with a low initial

FAQ *Is it always better to use vivid language?*

Only as long as it's in proportion to your topic and goals. To say "It's hot today" is fine, and to say "It's a flaming inferno out there today" helps your audience call up a dramatic vision of heat and identify with it. But if you say "The blazing hot sun sizzled my flesh more intensely than the proverbial fires of Hades," your audience might think you're overdoing it.

explanation A statement or account that makes a process or complex concept clear.

analogy A comparison based on similarities between something familiar and something unfamiliar.

Senator Elizabeth Warren (D-Massachusetts) speaks about raising wages during the forum AFL-CIO National Summit at Gallaudet University in Washington, DC. How does her background as a law professor and scholar both help her and pose challenges for her as a speaker?

interest rate (and, therefore, low initial payments). Sure, the loan's interest rate would double in a few years, and the payments then would skyrocket, but Martina thought she would surely find a way to refinance the loan at a lower interest rate before then, because property values would continue to increase.

But then something devastating happened: The real estate market collapsed. Two years later, Martina's $500,000 home was worth only $325,000. She couldn't afford the payments on the house because the interest rate had gone up; she couldn't refinance because the house was worth less than the amount of the loan she already had on it; and she couldn't sell it without taking a huge loss. Declaring bankruptcy was her only option.

What happened to Martina Case has happened again and again during the past few years as declining home values have made it difficult for homeowners to get out from under bad home loans.

Although this explanation may not be necessary for economically savvy listeners, an example such as this can be helpful for many in the audience because it personalizes an abstract concept and allows the audience to digest the information more easily.

TRY IT! **EXPLANATION TECHNIQUES**

We have suggested breakdowns of complex processes, analogies, and extended examples as three techniques for explaining a complex idea.

- Pick a topic you might like to speak on.
- When should you employ each of these tactics in a speech about that topic?
- How do you decide?

CHOICES THAT MAKE INFORMATION EFFECTIVE

Audience members usually know who an effective informative speaker is. It's someone who is *clear* and *interesting,* who helps us easily understand something new, and who makes us want to know more about it. In addition to the techniques of defining, describing, and explaining, here are several other ways to maximize the clarity and interest of an informative speech:

- Keep things simple.
- Use supporting material well.
- Connect your topic to your audience.
- Organize your presentation to inform and captivate.
- Choose effective language.

Keep It Simple

It's natural to want to share *everything* you know about a topic after you've spent so much time researching it. But you often will have too much information for the time allotted, and you certainly won't want to wash away your audience's interest with a deluge of information.

The more you know, the harder you must work to make sure you're editing your information to suit your purpose and the audience's level of understanding. Some speakers seem to think, "Well, if my audience can't follow along, they'll at least be impressed by how much I know." But audience members are like students: If a teacher is too complex or presenting too much at once, the students get bored and annoyed.

It's better to keep your message and its presentation as simple as possible to meet the information needs of your audience and the situation. Suppose you want to inform your listeners about the three factors you believe have contributed to a reduction in traffic fatalities in your town: increased police enforcement of the ban on cell-phone use while driving, the city council's new public service messages about the hazards of drunk driving, and the addition of traffic lights at several hazardous intersections. Although it might have been fascinating to research, you probably won't have to describe, for instance, the process by which the city council chose a marketing firm to help create its anti-drunk-driving campaign.

Connect Your Topic to Your Audience

How can you best create a relationship between your topic and your audience? First, consider what might make listeners care. What are their needs—for example, money, self-esteem? What are their motivations—success, pride, passion for new experiences? Are they interested in people, high-tech gadgets, nature, or something else?

Some needs are nearly universal: Everyone wants to be healthy, do meaningful work, and have satisfying relationships. Some needs are specific to an audience: Students want better grades and cheaper tuition, whereas parents may want better schools and safer streets. Your informational claims have to take the motives and experiences of your audience into account.

Likewise, in presenting your evidence, you should take your audience's knowledge and experiences into account. A good way to do this is to start with something familiar that is similar in some way to your unfamiliar topic, because people learn new information by relating it to what they know already or experiences they've had already.

If, for instance, you want to inform listeners about the benefits of yoga, you would first ask yourself, "What sorts of activities or experiences similar to yoga might my audience already know about?" Because yoga can enhance health, one possibility would be alternative medicine, which is also believed to improve health. But many people aren't familiar with alternative medicine, so that probably wouldn't be a good angle. The benefits of yoga are both physical and spiritual, so another possibility is to choose to frame yoga as a specific kind of exercise combined with a kind of meditation. Using this framework, you could draw links to other experiences that might illuminate for your listeners what participants claim about the health benefits of yoga.

Use Supporting Material Wisely

supporting material
Research-based examples, analogies, and explanations.

A big part of any informative speech is to use the **supporting material** you discovered in your research—examples, analogies, and other kinds of explanatory information. How can you make the best use of this material in shaping an effective informative speech? (Chapter 10 covered presentation aids and visuals, another kind of supporting material.)

Don't Overdo It   Examples are great for interest, and often necessary for clarity, but sometimes less is more. One or two examples may enhance understanding, but six or seven will be confusing. An analogy will take you just so far, and pushing it until it breaks down doesn't help your audience. For example, yoga is a form of meditation, and meditation and prayer are similar. But the prayer traditions of some religions, such as the idea of "talking to God," are quite different from meditation and would lead your audience away from understanding yoga.

Turn the *Ear* into an *Eye*   The biggest problem with speech is that it's not visual: The audience can't *see* what you're talking about. You can help, however, with specific and visual examples, as well as concrete language that suggests an image, as we discussed earlier under "Mental Pictures." Do yoga practitioners put themselves in positions that look like pretzels? Not exactly, but the image of a pretzel gives a good visual hint about how difficult some yoga poses are.

Own It   Information won't be compelling to an audience if it's only about imaginary or hypothetical people. To help your audience relate to your speech, *personalize* it. Talk about *your* relationship to the information ("When I first heard people talking about yoga, I had no idea what they were talking about . . ."), why it interested you ("I was fascinated by the difficulty of yoga"), and the audience's potential relationship to it ("We all deal with the stresses of school, work, and family life, and wonder what would relieve some of it").

Choose Effective Organizational Patterns

We discussed organizational patterns thoroughly in Chapter 7, explaining the different patterns you can choose: the *topical pattern*, which takes listeners from one subtopic to another; the *chronological pattern*, which moves from the past through the present to the future; the *spatial pattern*, which moves from near to far or far to near; the *cause-and-effect pattern*; and the *problem-solution pattern*.

Once you choose an organizational scheme, stick with it. You'll confuse your audience if you begin with an introduction about yoga and *physical* health and then segue to subpoints about meditation's *mental* benefits. And, as we've said before, don't start with the most difficult concepts but, rather, with concepts that are simpler and closer to the audience's understanding and experience.

Choose Effective Language

Clear language is essential to informative speeches. Your audience needs you to translate or define unfamiliar and technical terms. See Chapter 8 for a discussion of these and other important points about language and style.

Translate the Technical Talk It's too easy to fall into the habit of talking like an expert when you've done good, extensive research on a topic, but that also means leaving your audience behind. To avoid doing so, explain all technical terms and spell out all abbreviations the first time you use them. If you end up with a long list of technical terms to define, you may want to think twice about whether they're all necessary for your audience. For example, in a discussion of yoga, you may decide it's important to include *chakras* but, depending on the length and focus of the speech, choosing to call them "energy centers" rather than defining *chakras* might be a better decision. The translation does a pretty good job of communicating what they are without requiring the audience to learn new vocabulary.

Define Your Terms Sometimes a term is important enough to define because a simpler one will create a misunderstanding. For example, if you're talking about the flexibility benefits of yoga, most people think in terms of "stretching their muscles," which is true, but it's also necessary to know that sustained yoga practice may stretch tendons and ligaments as well as muscles. To differentiate these tissues from muscle tissue, you should define tendons as "connective tissues that link muscle and bone" and ligaments as "connective tissues that link bones to bones." That will help you clarify the flexibility benefits (and disadvantages) of stretching tendons and ligaments.

Some choices work for every speech, and some are specific to a purpose. By keeping things simple, connecting to your audience, and using appropriate support and organization and clear language choices, you can ensure that you'll be delivering a well-understood and well-received speech.

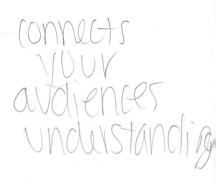

connects your audiences understanding

ALTERNATIVE SPEECH FORMATS

Two new speaking formats have become popular recently: TED talks and Pecha Kucha. Each has its fans and detractors, but many people find them to be useful and entertaining alternatives. Let's look at the structure, advantages, and disadvantages of each.

TED Talks

TED stands for the *Technology, Entertainment and Design* conferences sponsored by the Sapling Foundation, which originated in 1990 and became a yearly conference. These conferences were tied closely to the emerging Silicon Valley community, well as famous politicians and visionary thinkers. The goal of the talks at the TED conferences were for experts in their fields to talk to experts in other fields, as well as the public, sharing the best and most sophisticated current ideas in their areas of specialty. That's a tall order, because the format of TED talks is that speakers have only 18 minutes to explain their ideas in ways that anybody can understand, to use narrative as their basic structure, and if they use slides, to have few or no words and no bullet points. The rules given to speakers look like this, meant to mimic the Biblical Ten Commandments, complete with fake King James-style English:[5]

1. **Thou Shalt Not Simply Trot Out thy Usual Shtick.**
2. **Thou Shalt Dream a Great Dream, or Show Forth a Wondrous New Thing, Or Share Something Thou Hast Never Shared Before.**
3. **Thou Shalt Reveal thy Curiosity and Thy Passion.**
4. **Thou Shalt Tell a Story**
5. **Thou Shalt Freely Comment on the Utterances of Other Speakers for the Sake of Blessed Connection and Exquisite Controversy.**

6. Thou Shalt Not Flaunt thine Ego. Be Thou Vulnerable. Speak of thy Failure as well as thy Success.
7. Thou Shalt Not Sell from the Stage: Neither thy Company, thy Goods, thy Writings, nor thy Desperate need for Funding; Lest Thou be Cast Aside into Outer Darkness.
8. Thou Shalt Remember all the while: Laughter is Good.
9. Thou Shalt Not Read thy Speech.
10. Thou Shalt Not Steal the Time of Them that Follow Thee.

So the focus is on ideas, not the speaker and not selling. Telling stories and making the audience laugh is the aim. Keeping it short, focused and visual are highly prized; slides should have compelling images rather than lists of words. In *Talk like TED*, Carmine Gallo summarizes the "3 Laws of Communication."[6] Good communication is:

1. **Emotional: touches the audiences' hearts**
2. **Novel: teaches the audience something new**
3. **Memorable: presents content in ways the audience won't forget.**

Many of these things are truisms, which we have looked at in this book. What's interesting about the TED format is what it avoids— being boring. Choose one basic point or lesson that you want the audience to walk away with, keep it in sharp focus, and blend humor and passion into your presentation. Many speeches want more from the audience in persuasion than they are likely to get, or pack in so much information that they become more like a bad day in the classroom than an enjoyable chance to learn.

How do you create a TED style talk? First, obviously you have to stay within the constraints just listed. In addition, the TEDx site gives a process for preparing a TED talk (TEDx are TED-style events which can be held by any group anywhere).[7]

Step 1: *Get familiar with the form*
    18 minutes or less
Step 2: *Develop an idea*
    It should be new, interesting and factual/realistic
Step 3: *Make an outline and script*
    Here they have some advice on structure similar to what we discussed in Chapter 7, with these additional principles:

    1. The primary goal of your talk is to communicate an idea effectively, not to tell a story or to evoke emotions. These are tools, not an end in themselves.
    2. Your structure should be invisible to the audience. In other words, don't talk about how you're going to talk about your topic— just talk about it!

Step 4: *Create slides*
    Use slides only if they help. They should be mainly images or graphics, and no bullet points. They recommend a 42-point font.
Step 5: *Rehearse*
    Focus on staying in time and posture
Step 6: *Give your talk*
    "Inhale. Exhale. Do it like you practiced."
Step 7: *Savor the glory*

The TED format shares much in common with what we've provided in this book, and you can practice this format be setting up opportunities to practice. You can work with campus groups to organize a mini-TEDx conference. You also can use this format for class presentations in your courses throughout your education.

PechaKucha

The PechaKucha (pe-tcha koo-tcha) format was developed in 2003 by architects Astrid Klein and Mark Dytham.[8] Their concern was that presentations by architects and others are terrible because they just go on too long. (Notice a theme shared with the TED talks? Similar formats are called Ignites and Lightening Talks.) A PechaKucha consists of 20 slides shown for 20 seconds each; 400 seconds = 6 minutes and 40 seconds for a speech. The slides should be designed to advance automatically, so the speaker has no choice but to be concise and keep up with them. PechaKucha is Japanese for "chit-chat," and the intention was that these be quick, relaxed talks rather than formal speeches.

PechaKuchas typically are done at a "PechaKucha night," which includes a series of talks by creative professionals or academics, and may also include music. According to their website (www.pechakucha.org/faq):

> **Good PechaKucha presentations are the ones that uncover the unexpected— unexpected talent, unexpected ideas. Some PechaKuchas tell great stories about a project or a trip. Some are incredibly personal, some are incredibly funny, but all are very different, and they turn each PechaKucha Night into "a box of chocolates."**

PechaKuchas differ from TED talks mainly because the structure of the way they are organized. The TED conference is organized centrally, and the presenters are invited strategically. When a bar, restaurant, or other business decides to host a regular PechaKucha night, the people who present are the ones who show up that night.

To create a PechaKucha presentation, you will have to think about, just as in the TED talk, what main point you want to make. This is like the thesis of a regular speech, but maybe a little more limited and smaller. Then you have to think about the *story* of your point or lesson. This not just the "this happened, then this happened, then this happened" version of a story, but more like a story-type, or plot. Stories generally have a certain structure. If you think

What features of this photo, of a PechaKucha in Los Angeles, do proponents claim will make it a better experience for the audience?

Michael Buckner/Getty Images Entertainment/Getty Images

about movie genres, you get an idea of what these structures are like. An action movie starts with a conflict between two people or groups, moves through several iterations of them clashing, often exchanging who gets the upper hand, moving toward a climatic conflict or confrontation leading to a resolution. The hero's journey is somewhat different. The hero receives a quest, or goal, and goes through adventures and setbacks until he or she achieves the quest. Usually the conflicts in these stories are also internal to the hero, who learns memorable lessons in the course of achieving the goal.

So, as you think about the shape of the 20 steps of your PechaKucha, you might want to plot them out, or storyboard them, according to an intelligible structure. If you were talking about a new piece of technology, why not make it an action movie?

2 slides to set the context
3 slides for the Problem (what these people needed some technology for)
2 slides for The First Solution that didn't work
2 Slides for The Second Solution that didn't work
3 Slides for the developers go back to square one and start over creatively
3 Slides for the Creative Solution that Actually Works
2 Slides for How Things are So Much Better
1 Slide to Wrap Up

This storyline could be adapted to public policies or social programs—or just about anything ("How one high school solved its cheating problem"). It sustains the interest of audience members because it is focused and they want to see how the story turns out.

The downside of both of these formats lies in their limitations. They are great examples of an "infotainment" speech, an informative speech that is entertaining and easy to digest. When that's your goal, these formats work well. But often you have to be accomplishing other things with constraints, and these may not be flexible enough.

Summary

A skilled informative speaker presents information to an audience in a way that is easy to digest and remember. The information may even make a difference in how audience members think about the world. Informative speeches introduce new information, perspectives, and emotional connections to the audience, so informative speakers have to take responsibility for the choices they make. They are not just conduits for information but actively shape it for the audience. The topics for informative speeches include objects, events, people, processes, and ideas. Definition, description, and explanation are basic techniques for informative speeches. Skilled speakers also know the importance of simplicity, connecting to the audience, and wisely choosing supporting materials, organizational pattern, and language.

MindTap®

Reflect, personalize, and apply what you've learned.

Questions for Review

1. What is the difference between a persuasive speech and an informative speech?
2. What are the responsibilities of informative speakers? To the audience? To themselves?
3. What is the role of *defining* in an informative speech?
4. Why is it essential to use vivid descriptions and careful language choices in an informative speech? What kinds of techniques can you use to make your descriptions more vivid?

Questions for Discussion

1. Can any speech ever be simply "informative?" Is an informative speech in part persuasive? Is there a sense in which *all* communication is persuasive? Explain your answer.

2. If you're presenting new information, you'll present your topic differently than if you were encouraging a new perspective or creating a positive or negative feeling. How exactly do the different goals of informative speaking change the choices you will make in a speech? Give some examples.

3. Suppose you have a big topic and could talk about it for 30 or 40 minutes but you have only 7 minutes available to you. How do you choose what to include in your informative speech and what to leave out? Identify a couple of principles, and then, using a topic that interests you, illustrate how they would help you make choices.

Key Concepts   MindTap®

Practice defining the chapter's terms by using online flashcards.

analogy	description	informative speech
definition	explanation	supporting material

MAURICIO LIMA/Getty Images

LEARNING OBJECTIVES

- Clarify the difference between information and proofs

- Identify the dimensions of ethos, and why they matter for a speaker

- Assess the role of emotion, or pathos, in persuasion and the role of frames in producing emotion

- Compare and contrast the purposes of reasoning, or logos, in persuasive speeches

- Differentiate among fallacies and explain why they represent poor reasoning

- Choose different types of arguments, according to when they are most effective

- Explain the benefits of addressing counterarguments, and demonstrate how to deal with them

CHAPTER OUTLINE

- **Introduction: Giving the Audience Proofs**
- **Ethos: Why Audiences Should Believe You**
- **Pathos: The Framework of Feelings**
- **Logos: Who Needs an Argument?**
- **Making Connections: The Process of Reasoning**
- **Types of Arguments**
- **When Reasons Go Bad**
- **What About the Other Side? Dealing with Counterarguments**

Carol knows what topic she wants to talk about for her problem/solution speech, because it's a highly personal one for her. She believes in her position strongly already. The challenge is to bring the audience along. The topic is touchy, and one in which listeners are likely to say they agree just because they're uncomfortable, not because they've thought about it. How does she convince them? How does she supplement her personal belief with reasons that will convince skeptical people?

Overview

In this chapter, we'll analyze the choices you can make in designing a persuasive speech—a speech that moves the audience members to change their actions or the way they think about your topic. In the previous chapters, you've already learned how to choose a topic and present compelling information. Now you'll see the kinds of arguments that are used to shape information to create a persuasive speech.

MindTap®

Start with a warm-up activity about Carol's speech and review the chapter Learning Objectives.

INTRODUCTION: GIVING THE AUDIENCE PROOFS

Persuasion is an everyday tool. We regularly attempt to persuade others to do what we would like them to do. Asking for a raise, arguing for a rule change, and trying to convince a customer to buy a certain item all are forms of persuasion. And all can be successful or unsuccessful depending on how well we present our arguments to our audience.

In **persuasion**, speech is used to influence others' actions through reason, credibility, and identification. When we persuade someone, we do it largely by presenting better or more believable arguments or by getting the person to identify with or see an argument from our perspective.

The dark side of persuasion is manipulation. *Manipulation* means using deception in your speech, making unsound arguments appear to be strong, or attempting to appear to be someone you are not.

The light side of persuasion attempts to influence an audience in the context of an ethical speaking relationship, and the speaker undertakes this task with the good of the audience in mind. Instead of trying to pull the wool over someone's eyes, as in manipulation, persuasion gives people reasons to believe or act differently than they currently do.

Explaining persuasive communication has a long history, dating back to Aristotle's *Rhetoric* (written about 2,400 years ago). Some ancient Greeks were skeptical about rhetoric, or principles of speaking and writing persuasively, believing it was used too often for manipulation. But others, including Aristotle, believed rhetoric was the substance of high-quality public dialogue.

MindTap®

Read, highlight, and take notes online.

persuasion The use of speech to influence others through reason, credibility, and identification.

Imagine that you're the speaker and the topic is crime on campus.
Write two short paragraphs, one in which you describe or outline an informative approach, and one in which you describe a persuasive approach. How do the approaches differ? Why?

FAQ *Who was Aristotle?*

Aristotle was a Greek philosopher (384–322 BCE) who systematized many academic disciplines from biology to astronomy, ethics, and rhetoric by creating definitions for them and outlining how they work. He also was the *pedagogue* (personal childhood teacher) of Alexander the Great.

Persuasion is just as common in written communication as in verbal communication. When you hand in a paper, you are attempting to persuade your teacher of your argument and your mastery of the subject matter. The op-ed (opposite the editorial) pages of the newspaper are examples of written persuasion, or journalism that goes beyond reporting and explaining facts to take a position on the issues of the day. If you like to read blogs, you'll know that (depending on the author), they often are a mix of personal experience and arguments intended to sway the reader.

In the public speaking realm, citizens use persuasive techniques when speaking at local school board or city council meetings for or against a proposed policy. Another familiar example of persuasive speaking is the opening and closing arguments presented by the prosecution and the defense in a courtroom. Each side attempts to persuade the jury that its view of the case should prevail.

Sometimes we think that if others could only understand the situation, or "see things the way I do," they would quickly agree with us. If that were the case, just being informative

Gregory Peck starred as iconic attorney Atticus Finch in *To Kill a Mockingbird* (1962), in which he tried to prove that a man didn't commit a rape. How similar are legal arguments to the three proofs presented in this chapter?

Silver Screen Collection/Getty Images

would be enough to be persuasive. But most of the time, disagreement stems from more than a lack of understanding; it goes deep enough that new facts aren't enough to change people's beliefs or actions. What's needed is to turn facts into reasons to change, which takes us out of the informative speech and into persuasion.

Persuasion doesn't seek change only by establishing the "truth"; persuasion appeals to the relationship between arguers, to the listeners' emotions, and to the listeners' reason. These three appeals together are the tools of persuasion, or **proofs**. They are called ethos, pathos, and logos.

Ethos is the attempt to establish a relationship of trust *authority figure* with your audience and convince the members that you are someone they should listen to. The audience has to see the persuader as ethical, practical, and knowledgeable about the subject. A speaker who belittles others is not likely to be regarded as an ethical or responsible arguer. A speaker who argues that colonizing the moon is the only way to save the planet will not appear practical. And a plumber trying to persuade the audience to endorse nuclear energy will probably have little credibility.

Pathos is the speaker's attempt to put the audience *emotion* in a frame of mind to accept his or her point of view. Pathos is used to show the audience both how it is reasonable to feel a certain way about a topic and how those feelings can translate into actions and beliefs. A speaker who shows an audience pictures of the victims of a war, in an effort to get listeners to support humanitarian aid, is likely to get an emotional response from the audience. If listeners think, "What terrible pain those people have suffered; I feel I should send money to help," the speaker will have evoked the audience's emotions successfully and appropriately.

Logos is the use of reasoning to persuade an audience. *Logic* Statistics, surveys, polls, authorities on a certain subject, and the use of historical evidence are examples of logos. But these are only some of the types of reasoning that can be used in an argument. Presenting well-organized materials and drawing conclusions through an orderly sequence of claims and reasons also contributes to a logical case. Later in this chapter, we will discuss different types of arguments. (Chapter 7 discusses the details of organizing and concluding your speech.)

To be successful, a persuasive argument can't use just one or two of these appeals or proofs. For example, if an argument were eminently rational (logos) and even evoked an

proofs The three kinds of persuasive appeals: ethos, pathos, and logos.

ethos An appeal based on the speaker's trustworthiness and expertise.

pathos An appeal to emotions of the audience.

logos An appeal based on reasoning.

Queen Latifah (Dana Owens), speaking at the Boys and Girls Club of Newark Annual Evening of The Stars, derives part of her ethos from her accomplishments as a singer and actress.

Bryan Bedder/Getty Images

emotional response (pathos) in the audience, the listeners still wouldn't be likely to change if they thought the speaker had no credibility, or ethos. Similarly, if a speaker seems trustworthy and also plays on our emotions, we are still likely to resist if we feel like the speech is based on nonsense.

A persuasive argument should demonstrate balanced and integrated use of all the proofs, weaving them together throughout the speech. Ultimately, their coherence helps to persuade audience members. Consider an appeal for humanitarian aid. If the speaker mentions that she is a United Nations relief worker who spent time in the region in need, she demonstrates her credibility on the subject. If she also presents casualty statistics and identifies the sources of her information, she is being logical, too, supplying the audience with reasons to give money. If her case relies on how serious the problems are in the postwar country, she can gain the sympathy and pity of the audience through photos and stories that demonstrate the conditions of ordinary people there.

ETHOS: WHY AUDIENCES SHOULD BELIEVE YOU

The word *ethos* means "the character or knowledge of the speaker." A speaker has ethos if there is reason for audiences to think he or she is believable, reliable, or trustworthy. For the ancient Greeks, the word *ethos* meant "character," because speakers are judged partly on whether they characteristically tell the truth, judging wisely, and making good arguments.

When you seek to persuade, you are asking the audience members to trust you, and you have to provide reasons for them to do so. Some of these reasons are related to expertise: Have you done your homework? Do you know your subject? Do you have the sources and research to back up what you say? Organize your information clearly, and cite sources in your speech. Much of your ethos is built into the speech from the ground up in this way. (Chapter 6 covered how to locate credible sources and cite them in your speeches).

There are other dimensions of ethos for speakers, too. Ethos also means that *you*, a real live person, are standing in front of others, speaking words in your own voice and name. Naturally, audience members will ask themselves *why* you have chosen to speak to them about this topic and *who* you are that qualifies you to speak about it. If you can't show why playground accidents concern *you*, you probably won't be able to convince the audience members that such accidents concern *them*, because, as you know from Chapter 3, on audiences, good speakers try to construct an inclusive "us" to address as their rhetorical audience.

Demonstrating to the audience *why* you're speaking can be a challenge for students. There's always a temptation to say, "Whatever. It's just an assignment. I had to come up with something." Don't be surprised if you can't construct a good speech with that attitude. The audience can tell if you don't care. Get in the habit of investing yourself in your speech and your topic. Audiences value commitment in their speakers.

To integrate yourself into your speeches, look at your materials and ask yourself what you would be thinking, doubting, or wondering about if you were in the audience. You'd be asking yourself why this speaker cares about clean water, acquaintance rape, student government, rising tuition costs—the choice is yours. You can leave your audience wondering about your personal connection to the topic, or you can build ethos into the speech by explaining your reasons and credentials to the audience.

Stephen Spielberg is a speaker who has ethos, or believability and trust, in the field of filmmaking.

ZUMA Press, Inc/Alamy

LOOK FOR ETHOS TRY IT!

One of the most significant elements of ethos is projecting a sense of trustworthiness. You form your opinion of the speaker based on the qualities he or she conveys in the speech.

- On the Internet, find and watch two public speeches.
- Do the speakers seem like people you would trust? Why or why not?
- List at least three things speakers do that influence your perception of their character.
- Which ones are most important? Why?

Classical Dimensions of Ethos

Aristotle, in the second part of his book *The Rhetoric*, discussed the dimensions of ethos, emphasizing that it is not just a quality that a speaker possesses but also a quality that audience members attribute to the speaker. This means it's your responsibility to *prove* to the audience members that you're worthy of their trust. Aristotle's three dimensions of ethos—good judgment, excellence, and goodwill—illustrate how to show that you are trustworthy.

Good Judgment   Good judgment also could be called "common sense," but as is often pointed out, common sense isn't all that common. If you expect people to believe that you have good judgment, make sure to display its hallmarks:

- a balanced and fair treatment of opposing points of view,
- thoughtful adaptation to your listeners so you can take account of what they believe without talking down to them, and
- a judicious use of evidence.

Excellence To believe you, listeners also have to believe that you're a virtuous person. What Aristotle meant by this is that you strive to be excellent. Excellence doesn't mean that you're never wrong but, rather, that you're oriented toward your better self. Excellence also means a high level of competence ("virtuosity"): Are you good at communicating? Connecting to the audience? Do you have other skills or knowledge that you're sharing with the audience? You probably can think of public speakers or people you've known who communicate a sense of mastery that creates respect for them.

Goodwill Have you shown your listeners that you have *their* best interests in mind? Part of the reason salespeople sometimes are mocked in popular media is that people assume they're always looking to make an unfair profit at the buyer's expense. When your listeners decide, perhaps because of a one-sided presentation or poor adaptation, that you're in it for yourself rather than advising them in a fair way, they will believe that you lack goodwill toward them.

Why Are You Speaking on This Topic?

Even though you could reasonably see your classroom speeches as just assignments, other speaking contexts are different. You are speaking for a reason, and the audience wants to know what that reason is. Think about Aristotle's definition of goodwill: Does your reason for speaking converge with the audience's interests?

People listening to you *assume* that you have a connection to or interest in the topic. If you don't say what it is, they will speculate about it. Suppose you're giving a speech on rising tuition costs. Your listeners may be wondering, among other things:

- Does this speaker have trouble paying tuition?
- Do his parents pay his tuition?
- Does he have loans?
- Does he have a car (because cars are expensive)?
- Would he have gone to a more expensive school if he could have afforded it?

By addressing thoughts like these and relating your personal story to the subject of the speech, you will bring immediacy to your speech. Of course, we're not saying that you should build ethos by talking about yourself for 10 minutes. Instead, we're warning that speakers who remain aloof from their speeches, who just provide disembodied information, will likely have low ethos compared to those who show the audience their investment in the topic. Speakers have higher ethos when they share their firsthand experiences and concerns with the audience—when they make their speech appropriately *personal*. Of course, balance and appropriateness are the keys. Your persuasive speech isn't just a "research report"; it's your chance to speak on something you care about. Make sure the audience knows that.

PATHOS: THE FRAMEWORK OF FEELINGS

Pathos is the proof that appeals to emotion. But simply generating a lot of raw emotion by being outrageous or provocative won't be successful, and neither will be generating too little emotion, which will result in being boring. Rather, your goal should be to put your audience in a frame of mind consistent with your persuasive purpose. You're trying to evoke *appropriate* emotion.

Your audience's emotional reaction will be guided by what you're saying about your topic and how you're saying it. If you'd like to have a state legislator removed from office, you don't want the audience thinking, "Hey, but he's such a nice guy!" Rather, you want to portray his actions in a way that will rouse appropriate and justified indignation in the audience—indignation consistent with approving his removal from office. If you have *only* indignation (or some other emotion) but no arguments to back it up, you're not likely to change anybody's mind. And if you overdo the appeals to emotion, your audience may doubt your objectivity and judgment, which can harm your ethos, the trust in you as a speaker.

Emotion can provide consistency to your whole presentation. To incorporate pathos (or, more technically, "pathetic proofs") into your speech, begin by asking yourself: "How do I *expect* the audience to feel about my arguments? What do I feel? What emotions are appropriate?" Then make choices about language, examples, and arguments that support that frame.

There are as many ways of appealing to pathos as there are human emotions. But one useful appeal to pathos that can go wrong if misused is to create fear. Before we examine why, let's look at a few possibilities for eliciting positive emotions that you might include in your pathos toolbox.

Appeals to Positive Emotions

By appeals to positive *emotions*, we mean appeals that connect your topic or thesis to emotions that people typically want to feel, such as sympathy, nobility, and empowerment. Appeals to positive emotions work because people are predisposed to feeling these emotions, and they give an audience a sense of participation in an issue.

Sympathy   Audiences may identify with a claim based on *sympathy*, for example, in a speech about a social problem. One of the best ways to evoke sympathy is to argue by example,

Effective speakers use words to shape audience emotions such as fear, pity, hope, anger, disgust, fascination, or curiosity. Does generating really strong emotions help to advance the speaker's goals?

John Lund/Paula Zacharias

Salma Hayek, here speaking in London, England, promotes many charitable causes. She shows authority because she speaks out for her causes, in addition to her many contributions of time and money.

picking a specific person or group of people affected by a problem and telling their story in a vivid way. In evoking sympathy, you're inviting audiences to identify with the people who are affected by helping them to imagine themselves in the same position. For example, television commercials for organizations that promote animal welfare will earn your sympathy by showing images of animals that look sad or lonely.

Nobility   Sometimes you can convince listeners to do something by claiming that by taking up your cause, they are following their own best instincts. A speech that appeals to *nobility* usually frames the values that you assume that the audience already holds and then implores the members to live up to the best version of these values. For example, you might frame a controversial freedom of speech issue, such as the right to silently protest against war at a soldier's funeral, by pointing out how important freedom of speech is to our democracy, and by extension to the audience. This strategy works because it compliments the audience members by crediting them with good intentions or beliefs while simultaneously challenging them to live up to these values.

Empowerment   One of the most common audience responses to a speech goes something like this: "I agree with what you're saying, but what can I do about it?" Audience members may be fully on board with your claim but frustrated because they can do little to change the state of affairs. To use this situation to your advantage as a pathos-oriented appeal, focus on what the audience *can* do, such as making individual lifestyle changes or getting involved in the political process. Empowering the audience in this way is effective because it reaffirms that audience members aren't actually powerless and can be effective in making big and small changes toward solving a problem.

Activating Feelings and Senses

Pathos is one of your most important assets in making a persuasive speech. The point of pathos, on the most basic level, is to get your audience members to feel something, and then to use that feeling to move them to believe something. A number of theories throughout history have proposed to explain how this might happen: Aristotle, as we mentioned, believed that you got people to feel something because you could spur movement in their imaginations, or "bringing it before their (mental) eyes," as he would say. Others have suggested that pathos works because it draws on our past experiences or feelings, and uses these to help us process and understand our dispositions towards a claim.

Modern neuroscience has something to say about this. Researchers in Spain, Julio González and his colleagues, did a brain-imaging study on people reading words that had a strong smell association, words such as "garlic" and "cinnamon." What they found was interesting: When people read these words, not only did their centers for language processing light up, but their brain centers for processing smells and tastes also lit up. We all have practical experience of this when we're hungry and someone mentions food: If they mention a food that we really like, not only will we feel hungrier, but we may even salivate!

What this research shows is that language is powerful because it is associated with all kinds of smells, experiences, memories, and so on. When we evoke powerful sensory and emotional memories, people respond not only by processing the words that we're saying, but also by recalling specific sensory memories. It turns out that Aristotle was right (in part) on this account: Even though these memories aren't necessarily just about recalling visual images, well selected words can evoke powerful sense memories. These memories may be tied to the senses, but they also can be tied to emotional states such as nostalgia, fear, or pleasure. The best resource for you in this regard is your own stockpile of memories and experiences. If you can describe and evoke memories and experiences that you share with your audience, you will have gone a long way toward adding powerful pathos-based claims to your speech.

For information, see:

Julio González, Alfonso Barros-Loscertales, Friedemann Pulvermüller, Vanessa Meseguer, Ana Sanjuán, Vicente Belloch, and César Ávila, "Reading Cinnamon Activates Olfactory Brain Regions," *Neuroimage*, Aug 2006, 15;32(2):906–912; and Annie Murphy Paul, "Your Brain on Fiction" *New York Times*, 3/17/2012: http://www.nytimes.com/2012/03/18/opinion /sunday/the-neuroscience-of-your-brain-on-fiction.html?adxnnl=1&pagewanted=all&adxnnlx =1354716276-vBCJNxgtluIFGnU+PmkBpA&_r=1&

LOOK FOR PATHOS   TRY IT!

Think of a speech that moved you. Why was this speech effective for you?

- List three qualities of the speech that you connected with on the level of pathos.

Then think about one or two great speeches that you've seen in a movie or TV show. What specific elements of these speeches still stick with you?

- Try to re-watch or find the speech online and take notes about some of the compelling phrases, imagery, and ideas in the speech.
- What emotions did the speech evoke for you? Why do you think it evoked these emotions?
- What lessons can you take for your own speaking practice from these examples? Note three lessons.

Fear and Other Negative Appeals

In persuasive speeches, you often want people to change their behavior, to do something. One of the standard, and often appropriate, ways to do this is to use *fear appeals*.[2] Fear appeals identify a threat and then let audience members know what actions will prevent them—or someone important to them—from being harmed. If obesity, political advertising, global warming, or rising tuition costs can hurt us (physically, politically, financially), we naturally want to take steps to avoid the harm.

A related negative emotion is outrage, an emotional reaction to something we deeply feel is morally wrong. Sometimes we can be outraged by unfairness and injustice, sometimes by hearing about violence or aggression.

If you give just a clinical recitation of statistics, audience members may have no feeling of fear and, therefore, not do anything differently. You will have to make the problem seem threatening or scary—but fear appeals have to be gauged carefully because they're specific to each audience and can backfire. If you crank the fear level too high, the audience might be turned off to the topic, and maybe to you. Your audience could feel manipulated and just tune you out.

If you make people fearful of something they think they can't change, they'll ignore you to reduce their discomfort. Or if your fear appeals are over the top ("We're destroying the Earth!"), yet you offer only a limited course of action, your speech may not make sense to the audience. For example, many students end their speeches by advising their audience members to contact their senators and representatives and request that they vote a certain way. Is that response proportional to the problem? You should present solutions and actions steps that are in reasonable proportion to the size of the problem you've described. That might mean getting students organized, donating money, attending a demonstration, or something else.

Your speech has to arouse enough fear to make it reasonable for people to act, but not so much fear that they just ignore you. How do you find the balance? You'll want to create a level of fear or tension in proportion to your audience's ability to actively change the situation. So you can either tone down the fear (from "Coal-based pollution will destroy our world by the end of the century" to "Greenhouse gases will change our climate unless we act soon"), or you can increase the perception that audience members' individual actions do make a difference ("Every plastic bottle you recycle cuts down on our use of crude oil for manufacturing").

Framing *organization*

Emotional reactions can help to guide our interpretation of speakers (and situations), so they become a frame for a speech (as we discussed in Chapter 1). Imagine you're walking down the sidewalk and see two people rolling around on the ground together. Quick—How do you feel? What do you do? At this point, nothing—because you don't know what's going on. You don't have a *frame* for interpreting what you see. There are several possibilities:

- They're fighting.
- One person has picked the other's pocket and been caught.
- It's a practical joke.
- It's a practical joke gone wrong.
- They found a really inappropriate place for making out.
- These are students acting out a piece of street theater for an assignment.
- One person is having a seizure, and the other is helping him.

The challenge here is interpretation. If you know what's happening, you know whether to be angry or amused, and whether to clap or to call 911. In the same way, when you decide to persuade, you can't just present bare facts; you also have to provide a frame for your audience to interpret and understand those facts.

As we discussed in Chapter 7, much of the work of framing happens in the introduction to your speech. The way you set up your topic will determine, in part, how your audience hears it. Framing gives perspective to your audience members, a place from which to evaluate the information and what it means to them. And framing usually implies values, or

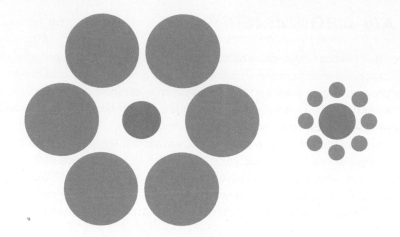

This optical illusion illustrates the principle of framing. The two center circles are the same size, but they appear to be different sizes because of the size of the circles that frame them.

judgments, about what's important and what actions follow from those values. To build on our example of two people on the ground, if one of them really is being mugged or having a seizure, most onlookers will call 911 because they value health and safety, and those values imply that they should help others.[3]

Often you can communicate a frame by using a mental image, as in the example above. Not only does "painting a picture" make your frame easy for the audience to understand and remember, but your picture also can make an emotional appeal. President Ronald Reagan was the first to create an analogy between the federal deficit (which is hard to picture) and your "checkbook," which stands for your personal bank account. Of course, the federal budget is nothing like your personal finances, but if you think about your checkbook and a billion-dollar deficit, you will find it alarming and scary.[4]

USING ETHOS, PATHOS, AND LOGOS **TRY IT!**

Find the outline and notes for a speech you have given already. What was your primary strategy for projecting a sense of credibility? What primary emotional appeals were you employing? Can you define your primary argument strategy? How would you compose and deliver the speech differently with these three modes of proof in mind?

Not every audience or public will find the same frames meaningful and emotive. Remember, in Chapter 3, when you identified a rhetorical audience for your speech (asking the audience to listen with a certain set of interests, as a consumer, as a citizen, or as some other role), you were picking out a set of interests that a frame might address.

Suppose you're speaking about a new medical procedure. If the rhetorical audience consists of consumers, a frame focusing on cost or savings or money will be effective in sparking appropriate emotion. If the rhetorical audience consists of people who care about being healthy, a frame focusing on health and avoiding sickness will be most effective. The contrast between "look how much you'll save" and "look how much sickness you'll avoid" is a contrast between two frames for the same material.

The frame should be visible "all the way down"—throughout your entire speech. For example, if you choose a health frame, while not completely ignoring cost, you'll probably want to organize your points around health and sickness, find more evidence to support those points, and draw a conclusion about health. Chapter 6 shows you how to find evidence to fit your topic and your frame, and Chapter 7 shows you different ways of organizing your points.

MindTap®

Watch a video, and do an interactive activity.

LOGOS: WHO NEEDS AN ARGUMENT?

argument A claim backed by reasons—logic and evidence—in support of a specific conclusion.

Usually we think of an argument as something we'd like to avoid. Few people enjoy "having an argument," especially when it means shouting and getting red in the face. However, the arguments in a persuasive speech are not the type that leaves you frustrated and hoarse. By **argument**, we mean the stuff of logos: statements or claims that are backed up with reasons. These reasons may be based on evidence, statistics, other forms of data, logical necessity, the opinion of experts, or any other kind of rigorous proof. Thus, this kind of argument is quite different from a shouting match. Making a good argument is an essential steps in giving a persuasive speech.

FAQ Is logos just logic?

The English word *logic* does indeed come from the Greek word *logos*. But the word *logos* in classical Greek had a much broader meaning. It meant "reasoned speech" (a logographer was a speechwriter) and "theory or rationale" (as in the many English words that end in *–ology*, such as *psychology* and *sociology*), and it also could mean "argument" (reasons given in speech), which is the sense we'll use here.

What makes a good argument? Well, you may not be surprised to hear that making good arguments is a matter of choices. This means you choose not just what you want to say but also how to defend your points. Making a good argument means giving a clear statement of a position and backing up this position with reasons. An argument addresses questions such as "Why is that statement true?" "Why should we believe you?" "How do you know that?" or even "So what?"

Here's an example of what we mean by making good argument choices. Imagine the sleepy guy in the back row—we'll call him Fred—gets up to give his speech in class one day. Fred has been paying some attention in class, but perhaps not enough. He at least knows that a speech must have an introduction, a body, and a conclusion, so he stands up and delivers the following speech:

> **Today we get much of our entertainment from free file-sharing services. I'd like to address the issue of downloading music and movies. We shouldn't download music and movies off the Internet that we haven't paid for. In conclusion, I think that everyone who's using free file-sharing services should stop.**

Obviously, that speech is on the short side. Are you persuaded? Probably not. Why not? Fred's speech has no significant details, and it contains no attempt to engage audience members or grab their attention. There's not even a hint of support for his main point that we "shouldn't download music and movies off the Internet that we haven't paid for." In the absence of supporting evidence, how do we know that we should agree with Fred?

With just a little more work, Fred could make a much more compelling case for his central point. To do this, he has to introduce some supporting evidence. He might state his central point, then add to it:

> **We shouldn't download music and movies off the Internet that we haven't paid for. *Free music and movies from the Internet are destroying the entertainment industry.***

Now Fred is approaching an argument—but he's not quite there yet. He has provided a reason to support his statement "We shouldn't download. . ." with "Free music and movies from the Internet are destroying the entertainment industry."

We still might not be convinced. How do we know that file-sharing is destroying the music industry? Fred's next step is to get more specific and cite some sources:

> **We shouldn't download music and movies off the Internet that we haven't paid for. Free music and movies from the Internet are destroying the entertainment industry. *Recent reports from the RIAA—the Recording Industry Association of America—and the MPAA—the Motion Picture Association of America—indicate that the practice of file-sharing has significantly reduced the profits of musicians and filmmakers.***

Christine Chew/UPI/Landov

In an interview with *USA Today* against file-sharing websites, musician Bono argued forcefully by calling the current system "madness."

Finally, Fred is on the right track, and the third version of his speech is shaping up as a decent argument. We now can see the line of reasoning that supports Fred's point about file-sharing. But we still might object that Fred hasn't really made a compelling case for his point, and we might ask, "So what?"

Fred makes one final attempt:

> **We shouldn't download music and movies off the Internet that we haven't paid for. Free music and movies from the Internet are destroying the entertainment industry. Recent reports from the RIAA (the Recording Industry Association of America) and the MPAA (the Motion Picture Association of America) indicate that the practice of file-sharing has significantly reduced the profits of musicians and filmmakers.** *Good profits for creative production in entertainment are important because they create a significant incentive for musicians to make the best music they can and for filmmakers to make great films. If you enjoy the things you are downloading from file services, you shouldn't jeopardize the future of the entertainment industry by undermining the profit motive that drives good-quality work. You get what you pay for, after all.*

Regardless of your opinion about file-sharing services, or even about Fred's line of reasoning, the final version of his speech is clearly much better than the original. In the final version, Fred has made a complete argument. He has

- made a statement,
- supported it with evidence, and
- related the argument to the concerns of his audience.

Let's explore the techniques that distinguish Fred's first try from his developed speech by addressing the relationships among arguing, persuading, and informing.

TRY IT! **LOOK FOR LOGOS**

Go to the White House Briefing website for speeches and pick one of the president's speeches that advances an argument for change in policy or belief. Identify the primary claim made in the speech. Then identify the supporting claims. Do the supporting claims adequately justify the main claim? Why or why not?

MAKING CONNECTIONS: THE PROCESS OF REASONING

You've been making arguments and giving reasons your whole life. For instance: "Why are you going to college?" "Because _____." Whatever you say to fill in the blank are your reasons for going. Reasoning is basically about *linking* things: a claim ("I should be going to college") and some kind of support or justification for it.

In preparing a speech, it's helpful to think of argument as a *movement* from reasons to claims, or conclusions. You start with what the audience members already know, believe, or value (the reasons) and move to what they should believe or value (the claim or conclusion).

Every speech also requires a *pattern of argument*: How are you going to support the claim that you'd like the audience to believe with reasons and evidence? There's much more to argument than citing a lot of statistics. Facts and statistics aren't useful unless they fit into a pattern of argument. All too often, speakers fire a barrage of numbers that amount to nothing to the audience, because these speakers haven't made clear the argument that the numbers fit into, and how. There's nothing wrong with having the numbers to prove your point, as long as you start with an argument.

Finally, keep in mind the saying that "the best persuasion is self-persuasion." Rather than imagining that your arguments will magically win over the audience, think about giving your audiences real reasons to believe and act differently than they do now. Think of empowering rather than conquering them.

Now, we'll consider six common types of reasoning that you can use to structure the arguments in your speeches. You can mix these types of argument; the typical speech contains several of them:

1. arguments from examples (inductive argument),
2. formal (or deductive) arguments,
3. causal arguments,
4. arguments from analogy,
5. arguments from signs, and
6. arguments from authority.

We'll conclude the chapter with a look at counterarguments, the ways you can respond to arguments against your position—either other speakers' arguments or arguments circulating elsewhere—so you can make your case effectively. There's always another side to an issue, and by acknowledging it, you not only assert your own side but also weaken the other side in the audience's mind.

TYPES OF ARGUMENTS

For each of the six common types of argument, we'll first define it, and then explain how it works and when it will be useful to you as a speaker.

Arguments from Examples (Inductive Reasoning)

In **inductive reasoning**, you draw a conclusion based on examples or instances. You make a general claim based on a number of examples. The examples serve as evidence for the claim.

inductive reasoning
Argument from form; a claim based on specific examples.

How It Works   If you want to argue that Milwaukee has good restaurants, you could base that claim on the restaurants you know: Kopps, Maders, Pizza Shuttle, Oakland Gyros, and so on. If each of them is good, it increases the strength of your general claim about Milwaukee's restaurants. If you gather even more information—making sure it's about different kinds of restaurants—you increase the strength of your support even more.

If you have only one or two examples, your argument can (fairly) be dismissed as anecdotal. If you have many examples, and they're varied in terms of time, populations, and circumstances, you can support your claim inductively.

You often can use statistics to good effect here: You might discover, for instance, that 80% of Milwaukee restaurants get a two-star or higher rating. Be sure, however, that the statistics are clearly connected to your claim and that the audience knows exactly what your argument is.

You also should be careful to tailor the strength of your claim to the strength of your evidence. The claim shouldn't be any stronger than the evidence for it. Depending on how good your evidence is, you can state the claim in a number of ways (in order of decreasing strength):

- Milwaukee *certainly has many* good restaurants.
- Milwaukee *undoubtedly has many* good restaurants.
- Milwaukee *has many* good restaurants.
- Milwaukee *probably has many* good restaurants.
- Milwaukee *might have many* good restaurants.
- Milwaukee *has some* good restaurants.

Especially if your evidence is statistical, your claim must match it. If only 15% of Milwaukee's restaurants have achieved a four-star rating, a claim that the city "certainly has many good restaurants" wouldn't hold up.

When It's Effective   Inductive reasoning is most useful when you're trying to support a general claim, often as a part of a larger argument. For example, if you were speaking about the problem of student cheating, you'd have to establish some facts, addressing the following questions:

- How many students cheat?
- What types of students cheat?
- How often do they cheat?
- In what ways do they cheat?

Each of these questions is answered by an inductive generalization about students, such as "80% of U.S. college students reported that they cheated last year." Notice the generalization here: The "80%" is an extrapolation from the number of students who completed a survey. If the sample was good one, this is a valid generalization. Notice also that the statement of the fact is qualified by the method ("they reported") and time ("last year"). A different method might produce a different number, and the number of cheaters might change over time.

To recognize the power of inductive reasoning, contrast the statistic with your personal experience. You might know a couple of students who cheat, but your description of your experience with them wouldn't help you prove there's a *widespread* problem with cheating. With inductive reasoning, you rely on a large number of examples taken from a reliable source.

Formal Arguments (Deductive Reasoning)

Sometimes the *form* of an argument persuades us. Any argument, no matter what content, with an *if–then* format is likely to be convincing. An **argument from form** is also called a

argument from form
Deductive, or if–then, reasoning.

deductive argument. Deductive reasoning, which is the subject of the field of logic, is a huge topic, and we can only touch on it here. Although setting up a deductive argument correctly in a speech can be challenging, it's convincing when it works.

How It Works Deductive reasoning typically takes an if–then form: If X is true, then so is Y. To create a deductive inference using this form, you establish the relationship between the "if" and "then" statements and the conclusion you want to draw.

1. If a town has 5 four-star restaurants in a town, then it is a good restaurant town.
2. Milwaukee has 6 four-star restaurants.
3. Therefore, Milwaukee is a good restaurant town.

Statements 1 and 2 are called the *premises*, and number 3 is the *conclusion*. The word *"therefore"* in Statement 3 asserts that there is an *inferential relationship*: You can logically infer the conclusion from the premises. The relationship between the conclusion and the premises is *extremely* tight. If the premises are true, the conclusion *must* be true also.

The if–then form or pattern is straightforward. You state the relationship between two actions, situations, or characteristics (*if* one is true, *then* the other is true). Then you show that the first one is true—so the second one must be true also.

1. *If* you're an adult, *then* you need health insurance.
2. We're *all* adults.
3. *Therefore*, everyone here today needs health insurance.

If the first two statements are true, the conclusion must be true also, creating a powerful argument.

When It's Effective The challenge in formal reasoning is to justify your premises. In the health-insurance example, you can do this through logic (everyone gets sick) and the nature of the occasion (we're all adults). Other ways to establish premises are to reason from authority (discussed later) and to reason from examples (discussed above).

Although deductive reasoning can be powerful, it can be difficult for an audience to follow. So be sure to make it clear, and avoid overwhelming the audience with a long chain of involved reasoning.

Causal Arguments

causal argument A claim that one event, situation, or attribute causes another.

We often have to be able to show *why* something happened—not its purpose, but what caused it. A **causal argument** tries to demonstrate that an event or a situation has a cause and that changing the cause or causes would change the situation.

How It Works Especially when you're talking about problems and solutions in your speeches, you'll want to establish the *causes* of situations or actions. Knowing the real causes allows you to propose effective solutions. What you're trying to do in causal reasoning is to show that two events, situations, or attributes

- occur together,
- vary together, and
- are connected by a describable mechanism.

For example, if you want to claim that studying hard causes better grades, you'll have to show that studying and grades are associated *and* that they vary together (more study produces higher grades; less study produces lower grades) *and* that there is some reasonable explanation for this relationship (studying produces more understanding, which enhances performance on exams).

If you were talking about a disease, the mechanism would be the underlying physical process that explains how we get (or treat) the disease. For instance, smoking and lung cancer occur together, heavy smokers have a higher incidence of lung cancer than nonsmokers do, and over time the chemicals in cigarette smoke damage the DNA in lung cells, causing them to reproduce wildly, resulting in cancerous tumors.

When It's Effective   When you show that two things are associated, you have demonstrated a *correlation* between them. Sometimes you'll be able to find statistics that show correlations between events. There are two kinds of causal claims: weak and strong.

In a *weak causal claim*, you know only that two situations or actions are associated, which doesn't always mean there's a causal relationship. For example, your heart is beating every morning when you get up, and the sun comes up every morning—but that doesn't show a causal relationship. Your heart isn't beating just because the sun came up (or vice versa). When you have strong statistical data but no good account of how the causality happens, limit your claims.

A *strong causal claim*, in contrast, relies on a clearly proven mechanism, usually a scientific explanation of a physical or biological process: how solar power cells convert light into electricity, for example, or how your body converts food into the energy that moves your muscles.

Arguments from Analogy

As you saw in Chapter 8, *analogies* are comparisons that link unfamiliar things to familiar things by highlighting a similarity. When you say, "Doing my math homework is like throwing myself against a brick wall," you're using an analogy to convey the challenging quality of the experience. Sometimes *as* rather than *like* announces an analogy: "This homework is as hard as nails." If you were to omit the *like* or *as* and say, "I'm hitting a brick wall on the math homework," you would be using a *metaphor*, wherein the comparison is only implicit.

An **argument from analogy** compares two things and asks the audience to believe that one of them has the characteristics of the other. If your body is like a machine, and if a machine must have fuel, your body needs fuel as well.

argument from analogy
A claim that a similarity exists between two objects or actions.

Thinking Through Analogies

Analogy is one of the most essential modes of human thinking. After all, it's understandable: When we learn or experience something new, we often understand the new thing or experience by comparing it to what we know already. We use our preexisting knowledge to find similarities, and to mark out differences, and we use these new similarities and differences to understand other things. Analogy is a crucial tool not only for learning, but also for categorizing and classifying information.

You can use human dependency on analogy to good effect in making a persuasive speech. Hammad Siddiqi studied investment decisions, and he looked at the ways by which people used the information provided to them to make choices about what assets to invest in. One of the most significant of his findings was that, for investment decisions, the best predictor of what someone would pay for an asset was the similarity (or the analogy) between it and other investments, rather than a way of thinking about prices of an asset that were determined by a more empirical model. As it turns out, we use analogies not only to think, but the presence of an analogy (or a similarity) between one thing and another has significant persuasive effects, even in situations such as investing, which we usually think are controlled by cool-headed and rational calculations of dollars and cents.

What does this mean for you? Having a carefully selected analogy that demonstrates the similarity between past experience and the case you're making can pay huge dividends in terms of persuasive punch. If you can say that something you're calling on an audience members to do is like a decision they've made in the past, there's a high likelihood that the similarity you construct in your analogy will be persuasive to them. So, for example, if you were trying to make the case, say, that people should eat well or exercise, pointing out other behaviors they're engaged in for the sake of future benefits (such as going to college or taking a public speaking course) might help to convince them to go to the gym or to cut down on fast food. The crucial thing in using analogies persuasively is to establish a similarity, and then to use the similarity to argue for the change in beliefs, ideas, or actions that you'd like to see your audience make.

For more information, see:
Hammad Siddiqi, "The Relevance of Thinking-by-Analogy for Investors' Willingness-to-Pay: An Experimental Study," *Journal of Economic Psychology*, *33*(1), Feb. 2012, pp. 19–29.

How It Works   You can use analogies to argue. By claiming a similarity between two things, you can claim that something that is true of one must be true of the other. George Washington said, "Government is . . . like fire, it is a dangerous servant and a fearful master." Accepting this analogy would mean you could infer that although government is useful (fire/energy is, of course, useful), we should be careful because it can be dangerous, and it can overwhelm us if we don't keep it under control.

When It's Effective.   For an analogy to work, it has to be appropriate ("The body is like a bowl of ice cream" is inaccurate, so probably wouldn't be useful in arguing anything). An analogy also has to start with something your specific audience will find familiar (like a machine as an analog for the human body).

The two types of analogies are:

- *literal:* The comparison has a factual basis.
- *figurative:* The analogy is suggestive and useful but not based in fact.

For an argument, a literal analogy is more useful than a figurative analogy. Your body *is* like a machine in many ways. But if you were to argue that the negotiations between the United States, the United Nations, and the European Union are like a ballroom dance, you could push the analogy only so far (for one thing, ballroom dance has only two partners!).

Analogies have their limits. Don't push them past what's plausible or helpful to your argument.

Arguments from Signs

Sometimes in a speech, we're trying to predict the future. How can we know what might happen? An **argument from signs** tries to show that an event, condition, or characteristic is a sign of some future event.

argument from signs   A claim that one event, situation, or attribute precedes another.

How It Works   Arguments from signs work when we're discussing relationships that are highly correlated but not causal. If you look for one thing, will you almost always find another? If so, the first is a *sign* of the second. Dark clouds are a sign of rain, because although they don't cause the rain, they are a reliable signal that it is approaching.

Signs can be conventional or realistic. A *conventional sign* is a human-created symbol, such as the white flag as a sign of surrender, or SOS as a distress signal. Conventional signs usually aren't useful for persuasive speeches. A *realistic sign* reflects a relationship in the actual world. For example, dark clouds mean rain, and if the leading economic indicators are down three quarters in a row, that's a sign that a recession is likely in the next year.

When It's Effective Signs require some support, because it's always possible that the relationship we've inferred is false or inappropriate. For instance, dark clouds could be smoke from a forest fire and not a sign of rain. Racial and gender stereotypes are signs that we sometimes use to predict what other people will do—but we shouldn't use them, because they're inaccurate and unethical. For example, if women truly were worse drivers than men (the stereotype), women's auto insurance rates would be higher than men's (though in fact they're lower).

One subject that does use argument from signs extensively is economics. Certain kinds of economic arguments rely on signs that, for instance, prices are going to rise, the Federal Reserve may change interest rates, and so on. These arguments often are based on a good deal of support in the form of research and understanding of the history of the economy.

Arguments from Authority

When you're speaking from expertise on a subject based on research or experience, you may make an **argument from authority**. The crucial thing is to figure out how to make your expertise clear to your audience.

argument from authority
A claim that a statement is true because of the expertise of its source.

How It Works When you do library research, you're finding out what other people, who presumably know more than you do, have said about a given claim. You can bring their authority to bear on factual claims in your speech, and sometimes on value claims, too—claims that something is "better" or "worse, "right" or "wrong."

If you want to argue that you know that the mostly likely reason for students' dropping out during their first year of college, you'll have to cite an authority in the field of higher education research. If you want to know how many students drop out of your own school, these figures should be available from the university administration.

Because your knowledge of any interesting topic probably is limited, you'll rely on authorities quite a bit. Make sure you're using them appropriately. For the most part, stick to factual claims; claims about values or policy are harder to support with an appeal to authority. For example, researchers can tell you how many people are killed each year in handgun accidents, but they can't tell you, in an authoritative way, how many accidents are morally acceptable to society (you'll have to make your own decision and claims about that). Make sure, too, that your authority is a specialist in the topic of the claim. You wouldn't cite a theologian about gun statistics, or a chemist about a point of Christian theology.

When It's Effective It's essential to ensure that your authorities aren't biased and don't have self-serving motives. Organizations now routinely create websites, hire impressive-seeming "experts," and post lots of information. Even if a site comes to the top in a Google search, though, it may be biased, so you shouldn't use it. Of course, such a site may refer you to legitimate sources of research. (See Chapter 6 for more about how to evaluate online sources.)

WHEN REASONS GO BAD

Our discussion of argument would be incomplete if we were to talk only about the uses of argument and not the abuses of argument. You have to know that not all arguments are equal and, further, that by thinking about the forms that arguments take, you will be in a position

Fallacious arguments are often tempting, but they're a bad idea. Why?

to unpack and analyze them more effectively. You also will be in a better position to evaluate arguments and to guard against the misuses of argument in your own speech if you are able to identify fallacies, the common errors in thinking that represent the dark side of argument.

Fallacies involve an error in the process by which someone comes to an argumentative conclusion. We have to be careful here to distinguish between the truth of a claim and the process by which someone arrives at it. Just because a person reaches a conclusion by using a bad process doesn't mean that the conclusion is wrong; it simply means that it can't be justified on the grounds the person provides. For example, if Frank says, in his defense of not down-loading illegal music, "Recording industry profits have declined significantly, and as proof, I'll punch you in the face if you don't agree with me," he isn't necessarily wrong about the claim about recording industry profits; he has just not provided you with evidence or arguments that show you how he came to this conclusion.

To help you sniff out some common bad forms of reasoning, we'll address four basic kinds of fallacies (though there are many others): fallacies of appeal, causal fallacies, inductive fallacies, and deductive fallacies.

Fallacies of Appeal

A fallacy of appeal occurs when an argument appeals to something that is inappropriate to proving the specific claim. Using a fallacy of appeal is a fairly common strategy for glossing over the weaknesses of a claim by playing on a set of our preconceived notions that, though not directly about an argument, influence the way we think about it. An appeal is always an appeal *to* something that is just outside of what is relevant in proving a claim. The Latin term for "to" is *ad*. Now, we're not simply including the term "ad" to be fancy but, rather, we include it here because fallacies of appeal are commonly known as "ad" fallacies. The most famous example, of course, is the ad hominem—a term you may have heard before that's just a technical way of naming an appeal to the person. We'll start our list with ad hominem because it's the most famous fallacy.

***Ad Hominen:* Appeal to the Person**   The classical appeal to the person is an indict-ment of a person's intelligence or character: "John believes that carbon emissions cause global

Ad hominem arguments sometimes are used against celebrity doctors who give advice on television. Are these fair?

warming, but he's a total idiot." Usually, the implication of such a statement is that because John is an idiot, he must not be correct about the claim that carbon emissions cause global warming. But note that the claim "he's a total idiot" doesn't really disprove the idea that carbon emissions lead to global warming. In appealing to the person, and specifically to the person's intelligence, the speaker has asked us to agree with an implication of the argument that is unsupported. Think about it this way: Even total idiots believe things that happen to be correct. The fact that a person making a claim is generally unintelligent does not excuse us from evaluating the merits of the claim. This also would hold in cases in which the person making the argument has lied in the past, has a criminal record, or holds controversial political views. In each case, you have to see how good the argument is, not just think about how much you dislike the speaker.

A more subtle version of the appeal to the person is the circumstantial ad hominem. The circumstantial ad hominem claims that because the circumstances that motivate people to make an argument cause them to be biased in some way, the conclusion that the person draws must be suspect. For example, someone might claim, "Well, of course, Susan B. Anthony argued for a woman's right to vote—she was a woman after all." The implication of this claim is that Susan B. Anthony's advocacy for a woman's right to vote is suspect because she had a personal stake in the argument. Two things are wrong with this implication. One, Susan B. Anthony's interests do not negate the logic of the argument she's making; we have to confront the merits of her claim before we dismiss it on the basis of her self-interest. Two, sometimes a person's interest in an argument puts him or her in a good position to judge the merits of the claim.

Inappropriate Appeals to Authority   Even though you rely on authorities in your speeches, you have to do it in the proper way. First of all, some appeals to authority may be appeals to an inappropriate authority. For example, someone might have said in the 1950s, "The government's official position is that smoking is good for your health." In this instance, the person is evoking the general authority of the government and not the specific, and perhaps more authoritative, proclamation of doctors or epidemiologists. Because we don't know *who* in the government, there's no real authority, so it carries no weight.

early childhood tests. When early childhood education specialists did a study, they found that kids who have a lot of books in their homes tended to do better on tests. Some politicians took up this connection and decided to sponsor legislation giving more books to children, with the assumption that if the state were to provide kids with more books, kids across the state would do better in school. But here's the difficulty: The correlation between doing well in school and being surrounded by books doesn't prove that having books in the home *causes* children to do well in school; it just shows that these two things (doing well and having books) happen together.

Concluding that having books at home causes children to do well in school commits the fallacy of inferring causation from correlation. There may be any number of other explanations for the correlation between books at home and performance on tests that don't rely on the direct causation of books. For example, having parents who are involved in their children's education, who make learning an important part of household life, and who have the means to buy books tends to cause children to do better in school and on tests. The correlation between books in the home and performance in school doesn't prove a causal link. It may be that books in the home and performance on tests are both evidence of an underlying commitment to education in a home, and it may be that this commitment is the cause of good school performance, instead of the simple presence of books in the home. This also may be an example of the fallacy of complex causation, which occurs when a person presumes that one cause among many is the *only* cause of an outcome. It may be that books in the home do cause higher test performance, but there are other important causes as well, and presuming that books are the sole cause is potentially misleading.

Inductive Fallacies

Amassing evidence in favor of a general conclusion can go wrong in many ways, and these are common problems with arguments. Let's look at some fallacious types of reasoning involving induction.

The Hasty Generalization   The goal of induction is to take as many specific examples of a phenomenon as possible, and to use these to make a generalization about a class of things. Sometimes people make generalizations of things without an appropriate sample size. A general statement on the basis of insufficient evidence is called a "hasty generalization." What if, for example, the first person to speak in your public speaking class gave a terrible speech and your instructor then stormed out of the room declaring, "No one in this class can give a decent public speech. You all fail!" This is, of course, a hasty generalization; your instructor would be engaging in fallacious thinking if he were to presume that one speech was indicative of the entire class.

If you think about it, hasty generalizations can have some nasty effects. For example, many forms of discrimination are supported by hasty generalization. People often have a tendency to take bad behavior by, or a bad experience with, a person from a specific group and transfer that bad experience in their mind to the whole group. Just because someone might have had a bad experience with one angry professor doesn't mean that professors are angry—any more than one bad speech in a public speaking class doesn't mean that the entire class is bad at public speaking.

The Slothful Induction   The opposite of a hasty generalization is a slothful induction. "Slothful" is another way of saying "lazy." You've committed a slothful induction if you refuse to make a generalization about something supported by most of the specific facts. For example, imagine that speech after speech in your public speaking class is phenomenal. The instructor is handing out high grades and compliments to everyone. Now imagine that the instructor says, "Well, we've had a bunch of phenomenal speeches, but I'm still not convinced that this is a very good public speaking class." When the facts are in and a reasonable person can't help but draw a conclusion, if you refuse to make a generalization that's supported by the facts, you're guilty of slothful induction.

Slothful induction has just as many dangers as hasty generalization. If every time you take a shortcut through a dark alley on the way back from a party you get mugged, you might consider walking back on an alternate route or hitching a ride. If you say, "Well that happened only the last ten times, and this time I feel lucky," you'll most likely experience the effects, yet again, of a slothful induction. In popular culture, this fallacy circulates as the saying, "The definition of insanity is doing the same thing over and over and expecting a different result."

Inappropriate Sample   You also can get into trouble in inductive reasoning by using the wrong evidence. For example, let's imagine that your public speaking instructor is a little spacey, and that the students watch speeches from another public speaking class. On the basis of those speeches, your instructor comes to your class and says, "This class is terrible; no one can give a decent public speech," and assigns everyone extra homework. Of course, the conclusion that your instructor has drawn ("this class is terrible") is based on an inappropriate sample. What happens in another public speaking class has little to do with what happens in your public speaking class. The point is that inductive reasoning doesn't go wrong only when people make conclusions based on too little evidence, or when they don't make a generalization that the evidence supports. Often, the biggest problems in inductive reasoning occurs when people pick bad samples on which to base their generalizations.

An interesting example of this phenomenon comes from political polling data. Most political polls are done by phone, typically by picking numbers for people's landlines from a phonebook. Political consultants may conclude that a policy is popular or unpopular based on these responses, but they can't do so with the same certainty that they used to. After all, people are increasingly getting rid of their landlines in favor of cell phones. If pollsters conclude that a policy is generally popular on the basis of phone polling, they may be implicitly guilty of the fallacy of inappropriate sampling because they excluded significant segments of the population by choosing to gather data only from people with landlines. This is not to say that pollsters can't draw some conclusions from these data ("people who had landlines generally liked this policy"), but they're falling into fallacious thinking if they presume that data gathered by landlines is representative of the entire population.

Begging the Question: The Fallacy of Circular Reasoning

Begging the question, or circular reasoning, occurs when people take for granted the things they're trying to prove. In deductive form, this means that one of the premises of the argument is essentially the same as one of the conclusions. For example, imagine an argument from a strange religion dedicated to Zorg:

> **Because Zorg exists as a supernatural being, his writings, such as the Book of Groz, are never wrong.**
> **The Book of Groz says that Zorg exists.**
> **Therefore, Zorg exists.**

Of course, the problem here is that the conclusion is fully present in the premises. The premises don't just support the conclusion; they assert it. This is like saying, "Zorg exists; therefore, Zorg exists"—which gets you nowhere if you're in doubt about the existence of Zorg in the first place.

This fallacy isn't limited to followers of Zorg. A common occurrence in public dialogue is for arguers to presume the very thing that they're trying to establish. For example, in debates about economic issues, defenders of the free market and defenders of a regulated economy both often argue that a policy is bad because it deviates from the vision of the economy that

Greg Mankiw of Harvard (left) and Paul Krugman of Princeton University (right) are experts on economics who frequently speak with authority on issues of the day. How can you decide which of these authorities to believe?

they are arguing for. The same tendency to presume the very thing they're trying to prove happens almost every time that people argue for something based on an ideological commitment as opposed to the facts of everyday life.

WHAT ABOUT THE OTHER SIDE? DEALING WITH COUNTERARGUMENTS

counterargument An argument in opposition to your or someone else's argument.

The way you think about **counterarguments** makes a difference in the way you approach public speaking. Normally, when we think about presenting our position on something, we tend to de-emphasize counterarguments. Objections to our positions often make us uncomfortable, so we may try to avoid them. And some speakers are more concerned with getting their way or pulling the wool over the audience's eyes than with providing all the facts to help the audience make a wise decision. But if you've internalized the idea that an argumentative speech is always in dialogue with its audience, you might want to approach counterarguments differently.

If your speech is in a process of dialogue and discovery with an audience (and we hope you think of it that way), it's often better to deal directly with counterarguments to your position. If the goal of your speech is to help the audience make a more informed choice about your topic, laying out the possible objections to your position gives the audience a sense of the full range of issues at stake. More important, if you address the counterarguments to your position, you give the audience the essential tools to work with you in a dialogue.

Why Addressing Counterarguments Is Persuasive

Dealing directly with counterarguments also can make your speech more persuasive. By laying out the objections to your position and countering them, you can achieve three goals that will help you persuade your audience:

1. *You recognize that your audience is smart.* The members probably are already thinking of a number of important counterarguments to your position. By naming and

addressing the counterarguments, you open up an opportunity to persuade them on these points that you wouldn't otherwise have had.

2. ***Addressing counterarguments adds to your credibility.*** Your audience will be listening for evidence that you've researched your position thoroughly and thought through the main objections to your points. Addressing counterarguments explicitly demonstrates that you've done the groundwork to support your position. It also shows the audience members that you're in control of the issues surrounding your speech and that, despite the objections, there are still good reasons for them to believe your position is defensible.

3. ***You can control and frame the terms of the discussion.*** The way you choose to introduce the counterarguments helps to define them in the mind of your audience. If you frame the counterarguments a way that benefits your claims, you will have gone a long way toward persuading your audience even before you've presented your primary conclusions.

Tips for Dealing with Counterarguments

Let's imagine we're coaching Nathan, who is arguing with Heather about the benefits of welfare. Nathan is to give a speech in class defending his position that expanding welfare is economically beneficial. Here are some tips we might offer him:

1. *Reference the counterargument specifically*, and define who's making it. Nathan might say,

   Conservative critics of welfare argue that welfare benefits decrease the incentives for people to work.

2. *Give a charitable version of the counterargument*, one that the other side might make, preferably by citing a specific source. This will add to your credibility by showing that you understand the counterargument, and it will help set up the reasons why you disagree. Nathan might say,

   For example, John Q. Taxpayer argued in last week's *City News* that people have no incentive to work when the government is willing to pay their living expenses.

3. *Point out that although the counterargument has merit, there is a reason why the audience should not accept it.* Some of the best techniques of rebuttal are to say that the counterargument ignores an important fact, oversimplifies the case, or runs contrary to empirical evidence. For instance, Nathan might say,

   There's a certain logic to what Mr. Taxpayer is saying. After all, who would work if the resources to achieve their loftiest aspirations were provided free of charge? But what criticisms like this ignore is that the purpose of these programs is not to provide a luxurious lifestyle but instead to provide their basic needs so they can get a job. For instance, the program that Mr. Taxpayer is criticizing provides housing assistance so people will have an address to put on a job application, job training so they will have a marketable skill, and basic subsistence needs so they can focus on a job search.

4. *Finally, remember the benefits of framing.* The way you choose to represent the counterargument helps to define its power for your audience. Nathan could frame the counterargument that welfare hurts economic productivity in a number of ways. Which of the following is the best frame?

The vast majority of qualified economists who have studied welfare demonstrate that it does depress economic productivity.

Economists argue that welfare reduces the incentives for work.

Some economists claim that providing the basic subsistence necessary for a job search might also risk reducing the incentives for people to work.

Counterarguments are necessary to maintain the dialogic framework that we discussed in Chapters 1, 2, and 3. They anticipate your audience's interaction with what you say. If you're going to engage the audience, you have to engage their arguments—especially the ones that attack your claims and your reasons.

As you design your counterarguments, ask yourself the following questions:

- What are the main objections to my argument or position? (You probably know this from your research.)
- How can I integrate my response into my speech? (At what point in the speech will audience members be likely to think about objections?)
- Can I frame my position as a way to answer the counterarguments that might come up?

For example, a counterargument to the claim "Our town should lift the ban on smoking in public places" is that smoking bans protect public health (one of the primary reasons for the ban in the first place). You could narrow the claim to deal with this counterargument by arguing that "Our town should lift the smoking ban only in bars." Smoking would still be prohibited in public places such as schools and restaurants, but bar owners would be able to regain valuable smoking customers. Thus, narrowing the topic from lifting the smoking ban in *all* public places to lifting it *only* in bars better positions the speaker to answer the counterargument of public health.

You also can answer counterarguments by saying that your position is better than the other side's position (technically, this is called a "comparative advantage" case). Using the smoking example, you could argue that bars are essential local businesses that supply jobs and pay taxes, and in tough economic times their need to grow and profit should be valued more than public health.

Summary

Giving a persuasive speech requires attention to ethos, pathos, and logos—three factors that classical rhetoricians labeled "proofs" because they contribute to the persuasive force of your speech. A persuasive speech requires attention to presenting yourself as credible, well researched, and well intentioned—all the reasons why an audience should not only listen to you but also believe what you're saying. Rhetoricians call this quality of a speaker *ethos*. To be persuasive, you also have to use *pathos*, to connect with your audience emotionally by moving them to connect positive or negative emotions with your topic, your description of the world, your thesis, and the action you're calling for.

Finally, it is to your benefit to make arguments that rely on solid logical connections between your claims, evidence for the claims, and the ways you use them to paint a picture of the world or call on audience members to change their beliefs or actions. Rhetoricians call this proof *logos*. Six types of reasoning that you can employ are inductive arguments, formal (deductive) arguments, causal arguments, arguments from analogy, arguments from signs, and arguments from authority.

Finally, speakers must be prepared to address, in their own speeches, what others will say about a topic. An issue always has more than one side, and even though you have the floor during your speech, it should address, accurately and cogently, some of the arguments against your side.

MindTap®

Reflect, personalize, and apply what you've learned.

Questions for Review

1. What are pathos, ethos, and logos? Why are they called "proofs?"
2. What characteristics give a speaker credibility?
3. What kinds of emotional appeals might a speaker employ in a speech?
4. What are the six types of argument? How does each one work?
5. How do speakers benefit from addressing counterarguments?

Questions for Discussion

1. Sometimes, speakers seem like they're working too hard to make an emotional connection with an audience, and audiences are put off by it or feel manipulated. What, in your opinion, makes the difference between a successful and an unsuccessful emotional connection?
2. There's a fine line between a well-supported argument and one that loses the audience in details. What makes a speech seem well argued to you? Can you identify some consistent strategies that make arguments seem engaging?
3. Speakers appear credible to audiences for a number of reasons. What qualities make speakers seem believable to you? What qualities make speakers less credible to you?

Key Concepts

MindTap®

Practice defining the chapter's terms by using online flashcards.

argument	argument from signs	logos
argument from analogy	counterargument	pathos
argument from authority	ethos	persuasion
argument from form	inductive reasoning	proofs

David T. Foster III/Charlotte Observer/MCT/Tribune News Service/Getty Images

LEARNING OBJECTIVES

- Identify the differences between special speaking situations and informative and persuasive speeches

- Characterize speaking techniques and strategies for special situations such as weddings, graduations, and memorials

- Choose appropriate communication techniques associated with ceremonial speaking situations

CHAPTER OUTLINE

- **Introduction: Adapting Your Skills to New Challenges**
- **Speeches at Life Transitions**
- **Speeches at Ceremonies**

Stacey was asked to speak in commemoration of a person or a group of people. She knew that she wanted to honor soldiers of past conflicts but wasn't sure what to do with that. Talking about death is difficult, and it's hard to sound sincere. What is this kind of speech supposed to be like anyway?

Overview

This book has focused on the most basic types of public speeches: informative and persuasive speeches. The skills you've learned in constructing these speeches can be transferred to other speaking situations. In this chapter we'll be examining what those situations require and how you can boost your skills to be successful in special types of presentations.

MindTap®

Start with a warm-up activity about Stacey's speech and review the chapter Learning Objectives.

INTRODUCTION: ADAPTING YOUR SKILLS TO NEW CHALLENGES

In an informative speech, you want to create understanding, whereas in a persuasive speech, you want to inspire a change in belief or action. Yet, on many occasions, you don't really want either of these, and your goal is to honor a person, a community, or some common values. Although you still may create feelings or beliefs in your listeners, you'll do it in a different way than we've discussed so far. You will still have choices to make, but they will have to be appropriate to the goals of special occasions such as wedding toasts, eulogies, graduation ceremonies, and others.

How do you have to refine your skills to succeed at the speech types discussed in this chapter? Basically, you need to increase your ability to adapt to the constraints of these situations. Ceremonial speeches are often called **occasional speeches**, not just because they happen only once in a while, but because so much about them depends on the nature of the occasion on which they are given—a wedding, funeral, graduation, awards presentation, and so on.

In occasional speeches, special constraints emerge from the expectations about the life transition involved. A graduation celebrates an accomplishment. A wedding celebrates a life to come. A funeral usually celebrates a life well-lived. In each of these cases, you can imagine rhetorical constraints on what can be said (obviously, these are not times to deliver criticism or to say anything negative). In many cases, these constraints are embodied in traditions about what to say, which offer guides to appropriateness for specific contexts. Still, traditions, over time, can curdle into a set of meaningless clichés. The speaker is responsible for identifying the constraints on appropriate speech, and then finding a way to say something fresh and new within them.

You should regard the audiences of occasional speeches—even if they are mainly friends and family—as publics. Why? Because at each of these special occasions, you're celebrating

MindTap®

Read, highlight, and take notes online.

occasional speeches
Speeches given "on the occasion" of ceremonies, such as weddings, funerals, graduation, and birthdays.

values that are shared by communities (which, understood rhetorically, are publics), and you can address the people present as members of the relevant public. For example, if you were giving a eulogy for a person deeply devoted to environmental activism, you don't have to assume that all the friends and family attending the occasion feel the same. Instead, you could address them as part of a public that benefited, and continues to benefit, from this person's good works.

SPEECHES AT LIFE TRANSITIONS

Every culture has customs in which family, friends, and others come together to mark significant life transitions. Some of these transitions create anxiety or sadness; some create joy or reason for celebration; still others arouse in us a mix of emotions. Your job as a speaker is to find fitting words to address the occasion, and perhaps even to help yourself and the members of the audience to experience the occasion in a meaningful way.

We'll first look at the main goals of occasional speeches—celebrating, praising, and inspiring. Then we'll look in detail at some specific kinds of occasional speeches. The basic principles that make you an effective speaker in informative and persuasive speaking all apply here: You still have to think carefully about the choices you make, and you want these choices to produce good results for your public even if the only effect is to enrich a celebration or to honor someone.

The most important factor guiding your choices in an occasional speech is the character of the occasion. Each occasion provides a *reason* for people to get together, and your remarks must address that reason, amplifying it, extending it, making it specific to the time and place, making it personal for you and your audience. For example, every wedding toast has the same audience: two people who've made a commitment and a group of people who would like to honor and celebrate that commitment. So in a way, every wedding toast is the same, yet because every wedding is unique, every wedding toast will be different.

The goals of praising, celebrating, and inspiring require identifying a value and connecting it to the person or thing at the center of the occasion. For instance, a graduate may be praised for achieving an outstanding academic record, and a graduation is inspiring because it represents overcoming hardships and difficulties and the possibility of change and improvement. What values might we invoke in this setting?

If you think carefully about the person you'd like to praise or celebrate, you usually can find that one or more of the values in the listing below describe what you think is unique about the person. Because many people share these values, they create an automatic connection for you between the person, the occasion, and the audience.

bravery, courage, daring, heroism	finishing a difficult task
caring for others, putting others first, selflessness	flexibility
charity, benevolence, kindness	frankness
commitment	growth, maturity
compassion, warmth	hard work
creativity	having an impact
dependability	humility
determination	humor
diligence	making a contribution
effectiveness	mastery
energy, vivacity	open-mindedness
enthusiasm	passion
excellence	perseverance, persistence
fairness	playfulness
faith	poise

receiving an honor or award	teamwork
resilience	wittiness
spunk	wonder

FINDING THE RIGHT VALUES TRY IT!

Think about yourself and your best friend.

- If you were going to choose some values to celebrate each of your lives so far, what would they be?
- Would they be the same for both of you, or different? Why?

Toasts

Traditionally, when a meal is held to celebrate a major life transition, a short speech, accompanied by the raising of a glass (the literal "toast") is given: Drinking the beverage at the end of the toast completes it in much the way that a handshake completes an agreement. Toasts typically are a way to mark the significance of the event and communicate affection and respect for the people present. Toasts are offered at many occasions, including birthdays, retirements, and births, but the situation for which people are most likely to prepare a toast is a wedding.

The wedding toast is a way for friends and relatives to honor the newly married couple. A toast typically is 2 to 3 minutes long and traditionally is given by the groom, the best man, the maid or matron of honor, or one of the parents. Nowadays, though, many people choose more informal arrangements, in which toasts are given by best friends and relatives who have been notified in advance. The key things to remember if you expect to be speaking in this setting are these:

Prepare   Think about what you want to say in advance. If you think you'll be nervous, jot down two or three words on a slip of paper; glance at it before your turn comes, then put it away.

Stand Up to Speak   It's traditional, though not obligatory, to stand when giving a toast. Standing makes it easier for people to hear you and gives your words importance and dignity.

Introduce Yourself   Begin by briefly giving your name and stating your relationship to the couple—for instance, "My name is Mike Rogers, and I went to college with Jim."

Keep It Short   Shorter celebratory speeches and toasts are more memorable and enjoyable than long, rambling ones.

Keep It Personal   Abstract definitions or explanations of big ideas, such as "love" or "commitment," aren't effective in this moment. Instead, because this is *your* toast, make it about *your* relationship with the bride and groom. You might want to think about what makes them special, such as one or more of the values listed earlier. Looking to their future, does a certain value come to mind? Resilience? Compassion? Wonder?

> **David and Beth, we all started out on this journey together six years ago. From the bowling league where you were the best team and beat me easily, to graduation where you had the highest grades and outshone everyone, I've taken enormous pleasure in your successes. And now I'm proud to take pleasure in your latest achievement—becoming the most beautiful and happy bride and groom in the world at this moment.**

Marvin Joseph/The Washington Post/Getty Images

Is it OK to use humor in a wedding toast?

Stay Original   Keep any quotations brief and relevant. Please leave song lyrics to the wedding singer.

Use Only Appropriate Humor   Witty and clever remarks can be great, but crude ones never are. Sometimes, guests who are overwhelmed with the intensity of the moment try to lighten it, but embarrassing the bride or groom doesn't do much to honor them. Jokes about lazy husbands or nagging wives, for example, are best left at home.

Speak Directly to the Couple   Ignore the photographer or videographer (if there is one), and speak directly to the couple. Hold a glass in your right hand, raise it as you finish speaking, and then take a sip. The toast is basically a wish that their lives will contain this value, or that virtue. For this reason, the conclusion of a toast usually starts with, "May you. . ." or "May your. . . ."

Be Pithy When Possible   Often, a toast is expressed as an antithesis or a repetition (see Chapter 8). No limericks, please. Here's a traditional toast as an example:

> **May you be poor in misfortune,**
> **Rich in blessings,**
> **Slow to make enemies,**
> **And quick to make friends.**
> **May you never forget what is worth remembering.**
> **Or remember what is best forgotten.**
> **May you live each day like your last, and live each night like your first.**

Here's another sample wedding toast. The speaker begins by introducing himself, then explains his relationship to the couple, keeping his remarks short and appropriately positive.

> **I'm Mike Rogers. I went to college with Jim, and I'd like to wish Juanita and Jim much happiness in their new life together and remind them both that the same formula for success in college will bring them success in marriage: Put in the hard work, and enjoy everything.**

Toasts, and the wedding toast in particular, can seem like a heavy responsibility if you aren't sure what to do. But when you use your knowledge about audience, adaptation, and style and keep your message personal and appropriate, you can create a meaningful and memorable toast.

Eulogy

When someone has passed away, those who cared about the person gather to honor the significance of his or her life. Thus, every **eulogy** in some way is a reflection of what makes a life meaningful. With a little thought, you can find original and personal reflections for a eulogy that express how someone's life has been meaningful to you, to others who knew the person, or even to the larger community. Following are some ideas and suggestions to think about in preparing a eulogy:

MindTap®
Watch a video, and do an interactive activity.

eulogy A speech given to remember and honor someone who has died.

Make Sure You're Able to Speak If you're still so emotional that you feel like you'll break down, it's acceptable to pass on the opportunity to speak. It's not disrespectful; rather, it's an acknowledgement that the memorial service has come too soon in your personal grieving process.

Say Less Rather Than More Just as in any speech, if speakers haven't thought through what they want to say, they may ramble. At this time of intense emotion, hearing a speech that goes nowhere can be difficult for the attendees. Your eulogy doesn't have to be a polished gem, but it's best to decide ahead of time on at least a thematic value and one or two specific examples from the person's life. You can't—and shouldn't—say everything about that person's life. Other speakers will want to make their own contributions.

To organize your thoughts, think about what you found most impressive about this person and his or her life. See whether you can express it in terms of one of the values listed above. This gives you a theme to pull together what you want to say:

> **Joan was, more than anything, a compassionate person.**

Now you can fill it out with concrete examples, supplying details as appropriate and with an eye on how much time you want to speak.

> **We all know of Joan's extensive work with the food pantry for the poor. . .**
> **For those of you who don't live in our city, you may not know that Joan trained assistance dogs for the visually disabled. . . .**
> **I remember the time I went to Joan with a problem that was crushing me, and I've been endlessly grateful for what she told me. . . .**

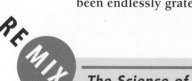

The Science of Eulogies

A eulogy is the kind of speech that you never want to give but may have to do at some point. As we have said, it's an opportunity for celebrating the person and reaffirming shared values. As with anything that we're studying in the course of learning public speaking, some valuable scholarly resources can help to guide you. Adrianne Kunkel and Robert Dennis have developed an integrated framework for thinking about eulogies, and it includes not only insight from the rhetorical traditions but also from social psychology and grief counseling. Their suggestions might help you do the difficult work of composing a eulogy if the sad occasion arises. In addition to the goals we've suggested, they suggest a number of things that you might think about including in a eulogy:

- *Self-disclosure*: One of the functions of a eulogy can be to talk about your own process of grief. Including some examples of how you're working through or coping with a passing can be constructive for an audience that undoubtedly is working through the same issues.
- *Problem-focused coping*: Being specific about the difficulties that you or other friends of the deceased are dealing with, and talking in some detail about how you're approaching them may help others do the same.
- *Positive reappraisal*: Often, people have mixed emotions when a person passes, and one of the significant things that you can do in a eulogy is to be honest but also to try to reappraise elements of your experience with the person who has passed to put him or her in a charitable light.
- *Affirmation and continuation of relationships with the deceased*: Reaffirming that even though the person is gone, his or her memory or deeds will live on in meaningful ways in the life of the attendees can help people to process their grief.

For more information, see:

Adrianne Dennis Kunkel & Michael Robert Dennis, "Grief Consolation in Eulogy Rhetoric: An Integrative Approach" *Death Studies* 27(1), 2003.

Share a Memory   The departed person lives on in memory, so we should share our memories with each other. The best memories to share in your speech will be connected to a theme you've chosen from the values listed earlier. Say what, in your experience, was exceptional or praiseworthy about this person, then give examples that vividly display that virtue.

Saying "Sarah was sweet, kind, and loving to everyone" is fine, but it's abstract, and repeating it with variations doesn't bring *you* into the eulogy or help listeners take away a specific picture of Sarah with them. Many people may have noticed how kind Sarah was, but they haven't experienced *your* memories of her kindness. Choosing to share your memories makes it easy for you to prepare, because all you have to remember are the thematic virtue you've chosen and a story to go along with it.

Whitney Houston's coffin is carried to a hearse in Newark, New Jersey. At the funeral service, filmmaker Tyler Perry drew upon a memory of a conversation with her to frame a message about grace and forgiveness in his eulogy.

Acknowledge the Community of Mourners   Memorial services are community events. They allow a group of people to recognize and honor the memory of the deceased. So it's helpful to keep in mind that the value you've chosen is not their value but also *our* value, something of significance to everyone's life. Knowing that the community shares your value allows you to bring your audience into the eulogy: "We all admired Jorge's determination in the face of life's difficulties" or "All of us struggle sometimes to keep the passion in our work, but Tonya never gave up when a client needed something."

Eulogies work as a kind of rhetoric. We want to make sense of this person's passing—and life. We do this as a group. Individuals' lives make sense in the context of their communities, of the *publics* they belong to. So eulogies not only invoke values but they also do so with respect to a public, which is an audience that shares those values. In the same way that in an informative speech you invoke an audience that cares about health so you can talk about yoga, in a eulogy you can invoke an audience that allows you to make public sense of this person's life and accomplishments.

Graduation

Graduations take place from kindergarten and elementary school through middle and high school to college and training programs. These academic accomplishments often are celebrated with a ceremony, and you may find yourself called upon to "say a few words," or even to give a full commencement speech, at one of them. Here's how to make your words count.

Recognize Everybody   Even if you're there for just one friend or relative, be sure to congratulate the entire group. Often, special honors will be handed out to a few celebrants, but try to make clear that everyone who graduates is a success.

> **I'd like to thank everyone for coming today: Graduates, this is your day. Friends and family, you are so important to success. And, of course, our teachers and faculty, without whom we wouldn't be here.**

Oprah Winfrey, speaking during Harvard University's commencement ceremonies in May 2013 tries to inspire graduates to excellent and public service.

Use Only Appropriate Humor Appropriate humor adds zest, but inappropriate humor is weird and unhelpful, and it often makes the audience uncomfortable. Humor typically has a target and is, to some extent, negative, so when you're speaking in praise of others, use humor directed at yourself if you want to be funny:

> **I'm truly honored to be speaking today. And surprised. I know it's probably a big surprise to my parents and many of friends—and to me as well. There are so many talented and impressive people in our graduating class.**

Focus on Values Again, to focus your remarks, decide on the one or two values that will be at the core of your speech. A speech in this setting honors all of the students who are graduating, so choose a value that, to you, is the essence of what all these people have accomplished by graduating. For example, if you choose "courage" as the central value to speak about, you could develop this theme in several ways:

- The courage to work hard. . .
- The courage not to give up. . .
- The courage to take chances. . .
- The courage to believe in ourselves. . .
- The courage that comes from friendships we'll never forget. . . .

Each of these (or just two or three, depending on your time constraints) can be filled out with specific anecdotes about you and people you know, making the abstract value of "courage" concrete and memorable.

Keep Clichés Under Control In hearing graduation speeches, we know the familiar clichés:

- You are the future. . .
- This is the first day of the rest of your life. . .

- Follow your dreams. . .
- You'll always remember these days. . .
- As we look back, we should also look forward. . .
- This isn't just an end, but a beginning. . .

These phrases and themes became trite because they're actually so appropriate. A graduation is a certainly a time to reflect on times past and those to come, to relish what has been accomplished and what can be achieved in the future, and so on. Your challenge is to find a way to express these ideas without using the same stock phrases.

How do you do this? One way is to draw on personal experience. Look back on your own educational experiences and think about specific incidents or stories that can illustrate the clichés concretely and vividly so you can invoke the truth in them without merely restating them. You might choose a story from current events as well, as long as it is sufficiently well known. But whether you're talking about the latest news or pop culture or music, you have to be sure you know your audience or you'll be leaving some people in the dark.

Consider Metaphors Another rich source for ceremonial speaking is metaphor (see Chapter 8). Perhaps you have some area of expertise that could provide you with a rich set of metaphors for talking about the passage of time, accomplishments, lessons learned, goals for the future, and so forth.

Metaphors or similes from sports can be trite unless they're enlivened by personal experience. "College (or high school) is a team sport" becomes an effective metaphor when it's filled out with your experience or the experiences and accomplishments of people in the audience.

Graduation remarks and commencement speeches allow you to recognize an accomplishment of a group of people with reference to the values of that group. A graduation is a public ceremony, and the speech that accompanies it should invoke the relevant publics as the audience for it. Excellent graduation speakers reframe the significance of the experience for the people graduating, allowing them to see the value of their achievement in the context of the larger world outside of school.

FAQ *What should I keep in mind for any speech at a significant life event?*

- *Prepare.* You get only one shot at the toast, eulogy, or other speech, so you should have an idea in advance of what you want to say.
- *Words are a gift.* Your main goal should be to give the couple, the mourners, or the audience the gift of a good or comforting memory, and if you do it right, your speech will become a memorable part of how they remember the occasion.
- *It's not about you.* Your primary concern should be the person or persons you are honoring, so you should speak in a way that honors and draws attention to them, as opposed to showcasing yourself.

SPEECHES AT CEREMONIES

As you become more involved in your workplace and community, you will have even more opportunities to use your communication skills. Ceremonial events may take place in a professional context (an awards ceremony at your workplace, for example) or be occasioned by another group that you belong to (an annual banquet with a civic group, such as the Independent Order of Odd Fellows, the Masons, the Junior League, or the Rotary). Any of these events may have speakers whom you are asked to introduce, speeches of entertainment to give, and awards given and received.

Introducing a Speaker

Although in informal settings, speakers can introduce themselves, in more formal situations someone else will introduce them, and that someone might be you. In introducing a speaker, your task is to arouse the audience's interest in the person and to honor him or her in the process. If you do this well, you can help to generate excitement and interest in the speaker's talk and make the occasion more enjoyable for the audience. You're trying to connect the speaker to the audience, and the audience to the speaker. In effect, you're serving both as an ambassador to the speaker on behalf of the audience and as an ambassador for the speaker to the group.

In all professional settings, if you're introducing or talking about someone, be sure to pronounce the person's name correctly. If you're not sure, ask in advance, write it out phonetically, and practice it. Nothing creates ill will or damages your credibility faster than a mispronounced name. In professional settings, you'll usually be able to contact either the speaker or an organizer, and you can do research not only about correct pronunciation but also about additional information to create a great introduction.

The two most important goals for your introduction are to boost the speaker's ethos (see Chapter 12) by indicating why the audience should be interested in him or her and demonstrate why the speaker either has an interesting perspective on the topic of the speech or is uniquely qualified to address it.

Make It a Complete Speech   Even though it may take only one or two minutes, an introduction for a speaker has the structure of a complete speech—a beginning, a middle, and an end—but all in miniature. Just as in any other speech, the body is the important part, in which you have to clarify your topic and purpose and explain why it's important to the audience—why the speaker is especially qualified to be holding forth on this topic.

Start It Right   The opening of your introduction speech should be light and brief, and it should have a strong topical connection to either the speaker or the content of his or her speech. For example:

> **We have the privilege tonight of being able to hear a stranger who is actually a friend and who can tell us a lot about improving our service work to the community.**

Give It Substance   You can cover some basic information in the body of the introduction. Here's a basic list for you to adapt to the specific situation:

At an April 2012 speech, University of Colorado student Daniel Paiz worked his personal experience and concerns into his introduction of guest speaker President Barack Obama. How much information did he need to give about President Obama?

R. Marsh Starks/UNLV Photo Services

- Basic biographical information about the speaker
- The speaker's qualifications or special accomplishments, or both
- Information that helps the audience understand why the speaker was invited to speak
- The title or topic of the speaker's talk
- A reflection of excitement about the speaker's talk.

When you talk about the speaker's accomplishments, focus especially on those that are relevant to this audience. Rather than read a laundry list of awards and milestones, it's often better to pick a couple of them and give a brief explanation of why each is noteworthy.

Clinch It   End your speech of introduction by stating briefly why you're looking forward to the speaker's talk or thanking the speaker in advance. Acknowledging the speaker's generosity in coming to address your group creates an inviting climate that will help to put him or her at ease. A good introduction helps the audience understand the speech and puts the speaker in the best position to be compelling and memorable.

CREATING AN INTRODUCTION   TRY IT!

Think of two people, one a friend and one a relative. Suppose they're both winning an award for "Best Person of the Year." Write a brief introduction for each.

- How were your introductions similar and different?
- How much information did you feel you needed about each person to create an appropriate speech of introduction?

After-Dinner Speaking

An **after-dinner speech** is just what you would guess: a talk given at a dinner event or meeting, after everyone has eaten. Typically, if the purpose of meeting is serious and focused on a topic relevant to the group, such as sales reports, new products, or scholarly research, after-dinner speaking is meant to be more like entertainment. But it shouldn't be just comedy or a series of jokes. It should strike a balance between fun and information, and the humor must be gentle.

after-dinner speech A humorous talk given after a meal with a serious point, but not the reason the group has gathered.

The best way to understand the after-dinner speech is as a humorous speech with a serious point. Why humorous? Because after dinner it's hard for the attendees to listen. They're full of dinner (and maybe working on dessert), and it's been a long day, so you'll need some humor to wake them up and get their attention. After-dinner speaking actually may be one of the most challenging speaking situations. With a hostile audience, in contrast, at least you can be assured that the attendees are listening—if only so they can refute you!

An after-dinner speech must have a topic or theme. It can be related to the purpose of the group or occasion, or you may have the freedom to choose what you want to talk about. In that case, you can find a topic using the techniques we discussed in Chapter 5, by taking inventory of what you know or what you're interested in. For example, you could start with a big-picture issue such as climate change and do a humorous take on it:

> Have you ever thought about all the different places that oil—in the form of energy or plastic—comes up in our daily lives? It heats our homes, fuels our cars. We're even wearing oil, though most of us don't know it.

You could say several funny things about petroleum-based fabrics and products and then move on to the larger point about our dependence on oil. Or you start with something seemingly ordinary and gradually work toward your real topic:

Neil deGrasse Tyson, Director of the Hayden Planetarium at the American Museum of Natural History, is famous for his ability to communicate passion and relevance along with substantial scientific knowledge. Does being a distinguished physicist make it easier or harder for him to be a good speaker?

AP Images/Invision for FOX/Frank Micelotta

Have you ever noticed how many times a day you check your phone? For email, for texts, for phone messages, tweets, Facebook, and more? It's almost like my phone controls me, and it's saying "Hey. Hey! HEY!" and I just can't ignore it. Wait—maybe our phones do run our lives, and we don't even realize it.

You could give many different humorous examples, illustrating ways in which technology can turn from a tool into a lifestyle.

After-dinner speeches typically fall flat when they go to one of two extremes: stand-up comedy or an attempt to be completely serious, such as a persuasive speech. Instead, use all the skills of audience adaptation you honed for informative and persuasive speeches to find a topic that will be intrinsically interesting, then give it a light and enjoyable treatment.

What's funny? You have to start, of course, with your own sense of humor and what you find amusing. But then you'll have to ask hard questions about your ideas, because humor can go wrong quite easily. First, avoid political or religious controversy; there's almost no way you can find humor in these topics that won't offend someone in the audience. Second, don't use humor that relies too much on stereotypes: Men are like this; women are like that. Instead, try to stick with common human situations, the grist of what's known as "observational comedy"—the challenge of relationships, dealing with difficult people, struggling with technology, finding motivation when things get difficult, learning from travel or a hobby.

Even when you're talking about something that is, in the big picture, a problem, try to keep things relatively positive. Don't try to hammer home a point; just keep the relevance obvious. If you can work-in some lightly self-deprecating humor, it will endear you to audiences. Clearly, you'll want to avoid sarcasm and irony, because not only are these often perceived negatively, but you also run the risk of letting the audience members feel left out of the joke if you use irony, or worry that it's aimed at them if you use sarcasm. And, of course, nothing X-rated or even off-color is acceptable.

Presenting an Award

Sometimes you'll find yourself being an award presenter, which is a bit different from being an introducer. Here you will both introduce the person and make clear what the award is and why the person deserves to receive it. To prepare well for a speech in which you will present an award, you have to understand the *meaning* of the award and master the *mechanics* of this special type of speech.

Meaning of the Award You should begin by saying something about what this award means. Why is it given? What history or traditions are associated with it? Are there any outstanding previous recipients who should be mentioned? Are any of them present? You should acknowledge them and do so by name if not too many. You also should explain why this recipient is being given the award. What were his or her accomplishments? Who made the decision to give the award? Although you'll want to research the answers to these questions—typically by reading the information provided by the organization giving out the honor—you should try to explain in your own words and make them sincere. For example:

> It's truly my pleasure to be presenting the 25-Year Length of Service award to Emily Vanderpool. This award, which comes from the president of our company, acknowledges the important service provided by long-time employees. In a world where people change jobs and careers on a regular basis, it's no small achievement to work 25 years in one company. I know myself—and anyone here who has received a 10- or 20-year award will back me up—that it takes determination and dedication not only to remain on the job for 25 years, but to do it in an outstanding way. Let me tell you a little bit about Emily's accomplishments. . . .

The Mechanics of Presenting It You can use a few specific strategies to heighten the sense of drama that accompanies the presentation of an award. First, don't call the person to come up while you're making the introduction; that just forces him or her to stand there awkwardly. If there's a plaque or a trophy, hold it where people can see it while you speak, and hold it as if it were something truly precious. Sometimes the name of the winner is known to the audience (and it may be in the program), but in other cases you may be building drama by *not* saying the name until later in your speech. Describing the person and his or her accomplishments before saying the name can be exciting, though you shouldn't let it go on so long that it becomes annoying.

Celebrity chef Jamie Oliver, recipient of an award from the Harvard School of Public Health, speaks widely to promote healthier diets for school children

At the conclusion of your speech, invite the winner to come up; with a gesture, look him or her in the eye and smile while shaking hands, then hand over the award and invite the audience members to applaud, if they haven't started already. Be sure not to turn your back on the audience, or to stand between the audience and the recipient. To continue the previous example:

> **And so, in light of these accomplishments, I'd like everyone to congratulate Emily on her award. Not only is it well deserved, but it makes us appreciate her all the more.**

People long remember the moment they received an award, and you can use your speaking skills to make it special and memorable.

Situations in your personal and professional life may require you to "get up and say a few words." With the skills you've gained from this book, you have the tools to master these occasions. Everything you've learned about audiences, adaptation, organization, language, and delivery will enable you be to be outstanding.

Summary

Even though occasional speeches impose a number of unique demands on a speaker, the basic rules for composing a good speech still apply. You can use what you've learned already about audiences, publics, and adaptation by thinking about the constraints of the occasion. This will allow you to make appropriate choices in deciding what to say at these ceremonial events.

MindTap®

Reflect, personalize, and apply what you've learned.

Questions for Review

1. How do occasional speeches differ from the typical persuasive or informative speeches? What advice would you give someone about composing a speech for an occasion such as a wedding or a funeral? An after-dinner speech?
2. What are the some of the qualities or characteristics of the speeches that you might give at any of the following life occasions: weddings, funerals, graduations?
3. How should you give an introduction for a speaker? What factors about the occasion should you consider?

Questions for Discussion

1. Which ceremonial occasions are most difficult to speak at? For you? In general?
2. Think of a time when you spoke about someone's life transition—whether to a group or to that individual person. How did you decide what to say? Did you use a formula or cliché, or try to be original? How would you do it differently if you could?

Key Concepts   MindTap®

Practice defining the chapter's terms by using online flashcards.

after-dinner speech	eulogy	occasional speeches

Appendix 1: Sample Speeches

Informative Speech
Persuasive Speech
Special Occasion Speech

INFORMATIVE SPEECH

Why Laughter is the Best Medicine

By Michael Fisher

Everybody always says that an apple a day keeps the doctor away. And of course that may be true, but why have we never heard anybody say that a laugh a day keeps the doctor away? Today I am going to tell you why laughter is the best medicine since it leads to a healthier physical, mental, and social lifestyle.

First, I want to stress that although many feel that if there is no pain, there is no gain in relation to physical health, I feel that if there is no grin, there is no win. It has been scientifically proven that laughter can improve your physical health. According to Lee Berk, who is an associate professor for the Allied Health Studies and Physical Therapy Departments at Loma Linda University in California, the benefits of laughter that he found through an experiment that he conducted where people watch 20-minute video clippings of comedic television programs were equivalent to those of a moderate 20-minute workout. Exercising comes a long way in that it makes you feel stronger and more energized. However, trying one of Lee Berk's "laughersizes" can yield similar benefits. Laughing also helps to prevent disease and infection, since laughing aids in protecting the heart and circulatory system, as well as boosts our immune systems.

One interesting example that I found from Berk's research was actually that if an expectant mother laughs an ample amount during her pregnancy, her breast milk will be of better quality and therefore helping her newborn infant's immune system through breastfeeding. This is because, according to helpguide.org, which is a well-trusted, nonprofit resource for help in resolving health challenges, laughing helps in decreasing stress hormones while increasing immunity cells and infection-fighting antibodies. Laughing also causes a release of endorphins from your body. Endorphins, in short, are a chemical that your body contains and emits when it needs to physically feel good, and this can even alleviate pain for brief periods of time. Now that we have covered how grinning is winning for physical health, let's take a look at how turning that frown upside down can improve your mental well-being.

Laughter has been proven to reduce stress and alleviate anxiety. By doing so, you'll be able to stay focused on a task for a longer period of time, and this will prevent the feeling of becoming overwhelmed and needing to multitask by finishing five things all at once. For example, this will help you to finish your homework on time or get that job promotion you've been waiting for, or even just maintain personal as well as professional relationships. It is also naturally impossible to harbor negative emotions while you are laughing. One way to laugh easily and get that peace of mind that you have long awaited for is through *laughter yoga*. Laughter yoga is a method of mental cleansing where you pair breathing exercises with self-initiated laughter.

According to Angela Haupt from the *US News World Report*, who has also been a laughter yoga instructor since 2007, activities at laughter yoga include things such as childlike playfulness and *Visa laughter*. Visa laughter, for example, is where you open up ridiculously high credit card bills that are fake and just laugh at them because in reality you don't actually need to pay them. By doing exercises like those that I mentioned, you have the opportunity to look on the brighter side of negative situations, and this will help you in the long run when you are faced with a difficult dilemma that might require you to make an even more difficult decision.

Deborah Williams, who has been a laughter yoga instructor for many years for many different types of people, states that "At first I thought it was a goofy idea, but since I started doing it, I react to things in a more lighthearted way. It helps to brush away some of the gray clouds, and it's a fun thing to do."

Lastly, I want to emphasize how laughter helps you to become a more positive, openly sociable person. Social health is something that not many people take into consideration throughout their life, but it is actually one of the most important aspects of your life and according to helpguide.org can easily be improved by laughter. Laughter helps to neutralize communication during conflict. You will have the ability to forget the notions that caused the conflict to arise, such as judgments or opinions while you are trying to solve the conflict instead of just making harsh or cruel remarks in return. Therefore, while communication is more open and direct, it will be more calm and collected. Laughter is also contagious, so it will attract others to you. Humans, and even animals, are more naturally tempted to gravitate towards you while you are laughing, since it is releasing positive energy from your body rather than to run away from you if you were to emit negative energy from your body by not laughing. Speaking of this—there is a countless amount of ways to conjure up laughter, such as having a game night with your friend, going to see a funny movie, going to comedy clubs, playing with your pet, partaking in simple fun activities like crafts and adventures, or going to a laughter yoga session like I previously mentioned.

Lastly, laughter helps to promote teamwork and bonding skills. One story that I read from helpguide.org is the perfect indicator that when you can laugh together, you can bond and work together more effectively. This story was about a man named Roy, who really enjoyed the sport of golf. However, he started to overanalyze all of his mistakes because the players that he was playing with were affecting his attitude since they were all very serious about the game. However, when he started to play with people who were more lighthearted about it, he was able to score better without trying harder and he stopped being so critical of himself. He was able to have more fun and bond with those people better.

As you can see, there is ample evidence as to why laughter is the best medicine, so let me review the highlights. Laughter contributes to an overall healthy lifestyle physically, mentally, and socially. A 20-minute laughter size will provide you with benefits equivalent to a moderate 20-minute workout. Laughter yoga will help you to mentally erase any stressors or anxieties that you may be facing. And it has been proven that when you can laugh together you can work together. Laughter is more than a simple smile from ear to ear and a few chuckle noises. It's a means of achieving that picture perfect life that everyone hopes for: healthy, happy, and wholesome. Thank you.

PERSUASIVE SPEECH

Statement to the Iowa House Judiciary Committee

By Zach Wahls
January 31, 2011

Good evening Mr. Chairman. My name is Zach Wahls. I'm a sixth-generation Iowan and an engineering student at the University of Iowa, and I was raised by two women.

My biological mom, Terry, told her grandparents that she was pregnant, that the artificial insemination had worked, and they wouldn't even acknowledge it.

It wasn't until I was born and they succumbed to my infantile cuteness that they broke down and told her that they were thrilled to have another grandson. Unfortunately, neither of them lived to see her marry her partner Jackie of fifteen years when they wed in 2009.

My younger sister and only sibling was born in 1994. We actually have the same anonymous donor, so we're full siblings, which is really cool for me.

Um … I guess the point is our family really isn't so different from any other Iowa family. You know, when I'm home we go to church together, we eat dinner, we go on vacations. Ah, but, you know, we have our hard times too, we get in fights … you know.

Actually my mom, Terry, was diagnosed with multiple sclerosis in 2000. It is a devastating disease that put her in a wheelchair. So we've had our struggles. But, you know, we're Iowans. We don't expect anyone to solve our problems for us. We'll fight our own battles. We just hope for equal and fair treatment from our government.

Being a student at the University of Iowa, the topic of same-sex marriage comes up quite frequently in classroom discussions … you know the question always comes down to, well, "Can gays even raise kids? In question, you know, the conversation gets quiet for a moment because most people don't really have any answer.

And then I raise my hand and say, "Actually, I was raised by a gay couple, and I'm doing pretty well. I scored in the 99th percentile on the A.C.T. I'm actually an Eagle Scout. I own and operate my own small business. If I was your son, Mr. Chairman, I believe I'd make you very proud. I'm not really so different from any of your children. My family really isn't so different from yours. After all, your family doesn't derive its sense of worth from being told by the state: 'You're married. Congratulations'."

No. The sense of family comes from the commitment we make to each other—to work through the hard times so we can enjoy the good ones. It comes from the love that binds us. That's what makes a family.

So what you're voting here isn't to change us. It's not to change our families. It's to change how the law views us, how the law treats us. You are voting for the first time in the history of our state to codify discrimination into our constitution, a constitution that but for the proposed amendment is the least amended constitution in the United States of America. You are telling Iowans that some among you are second-class citizens who do not have the right to marry the person you love.

So will this vote affect my family? Will it affect yours?

In the next two hours I'm sure we're going to hear plenty of testimony about how damaging having gay parents is on kids. But in my 19 years, not once have I ever been confronted by an individual who realized independently that I was raised by a gay couple.

And you know why? Because the sexual orientation of my parents has had zero effect on the content of my character.

Thank you very much.

SPECIAL OCCASION SPEECH

"I am an African." (Statement on Behalf of the African National Congress, on the Occasion of the Adoption by the Constitutional Assembly of the Republic of South Africa Constitution Bill)

By Thabo Mbeki
May 8, 1996, Cape Town

Chairperson, Esteemed President of the Democratic Republic, Honourable Members of the Constitutional Assembly, Our distinguished domestic and foreign guests, Friends:

On an occasion such as this, we should, perhaps, start from the beginning.

So, let me begin.

I am an African.

I owe my being to the hills and the valleys, the mountains and the glades, the rivers, the deserts, the trees, the flowers, the seas and the ever-changing seasons that define the face of our native land.

My body has frozen in our frosts and in our latter day snows. It has thawed in the warmth of our sunshine and melted in the heat of the midday sun.

The crack and the rumble of the summer thunders, lashed by startling lightning, have been a cause both of trembling and of hope.

The fragrances of nature have been as pleasant to us as the sight of the wild blooms of the citizens of the veld.

The dramatic shapes of the Drakensberg, the soil-coloured waters of the Lekoa, iGqili noThukela, and the sands of the Kgalagadi, have all been panels of the set on the natural stage on which we act out the foolish deeds of the theatre of our day.

At times, and in fear, I have wondered whether I should concede equal citizenship of our country to the leopard and the lion, the elephant and the springbok, the hyena, the black mamba, and the pestilential mosquito.

A human presence among all these, a feature on the face of our native land thus defined, I know that none dare challenge me when I say: I am an African!

I owe my being to the Khoi and the San, whose desolate souls haunt the great expanses of the beautiful Cape—they who fell victim to the most merciless genocide our native land has ever seen, they who were the first to lose their lives in the struggle to defend our freedom and independence and they who, as a people, perished as a result.

Today, as a country, we keep an audible silence about these ancestors of the generations that live, fearful to admit the horror of a former deed, seeking to obliterate from our memories a cruel occurrence which, in its remembering, should teach us not and never to be inhuman again.

I am formed of the migrants who left Europe to find a new home on our native land. Whatever their own actions, they remain still part of me.

In my veins courses the blood of the Malay slaves who came from the East. Their proud dignity informs my bearing, their culture a part of my essence. The stripes they bore on their bodies from the lash of the slave-master are a reminder embossed on my consciousness of what should not be done.

I am the grandchild of the warrior men and women that Hintsa and Sekhukhune led, the patriots that Cetshwayo and Mphephu took to battle, the soldiers Moshoeshoe and Ngungu-nyane taught never to dishonour the cause of freedom.

My mind and my knowledge of myself is formed by the victories that are the jewels in our African crown, the victories we earned from Isandhlwana to Khartoum, as Ethiopians and as the Ashanti of Ghana, as the Berbers of the desert.

I am the grandchild who lays fresh flowers on the Boer graves at St Helena and the Bahamas, who sees in the mind's eye and suffers the suffering of a simple peasant folk: death, concen-tration camps, destroyed homesteads, a dream in ruins.

I am the child of Nongqause. I am he who made it possible to trade in the world markets in diamonds, in gold, in the same food for which my stomach yearns.

I come of those who were transported from India and China, whose being resided in the fact, solely, that they were able to provide physical labour, who taught me that we could both be at home and be foreign, who taught me that human existence itself demanded that freedom was a necessary condition for that human existence.

Being part of all these people, and in the knowledge that none dare contest that assertion, I shall claim that I am an African!

I have seen our country torn asunder as these, all of whom are my people, engaged one another in a titanic battle, the one to redress a wrong that had been caused by one to another, and the other to defend the indefensible.

I have seen what happens when one person has superiority of force over another, when the stronger appropriate to themselves the prerogative even to annul the injunction that God created all men and women in His image.

I know what it signifies when race and colour are used to determine who is human and who subhuman.

I have seen the destruction of all sense of self-esteem, the consequent striving to be what one is not, simply to acquire some of the benefits which those who had imposed themselves as masters had ensured that they enjoy.

I have experience of the situation in which race and colour is used to enrich some and impoverish the rest.

I have seen the corruption of minds and souls as a result of the pursuit of an ignoble effort to perpetrate a veritable crime against humanity.

I have seen concrete expression of the denial of the dignity of a human being emanating from the conscious, systemic, and systematic oppressive and repressive activities of other human beings.

There the victims parade with no mask to hide the brutish reality—the beggars, the prosti-tutes, the street children, those who seek solace in substance abuse, those who have to steal to assuage hunger, those who have to lose their sanity because to be sane is to invite pain.

Perhaps the worst among these who are my people are those who have learnt to kill for a wage. To these the extent of death is directly proportional to their personal welfare.

And so, like pawns in the service of demented souls, they kill in furtherance of the political violence in KwaZulu-Natal. They murder the innocent in the taxi wars. They kill slowly or quickly in order to make profits from the illegal trade in narcotics. They are available for hire when husband wants to murder wife and wife, husband.

Among us prowl the products of our immoral and amoral past—killers who have no sense of the worth of human life; rapists who have absolute disdain for the women of our country;

animals who would seek to benefit from the vulnerability of the children, the disabled and the old; the rapacious who brook no obstacle in their quest for self-enrichment.

All this I know and know to be true because I am an African!

Because of that, I am also able to state this fundamental truth: that I am born of a people who are heroes and heroines.

I am born of a people who would not tolerate oppression.

I am of a nation that would not allow that the fear of death, torture, imprisonment, exile, or persecution should result in the perpetuation of injustice.

The great masses who are our mother and father will not permit that the behaviour of the few results in the description of our country and people as barbaric. Patient because history is on their side, these masses do not despair because today the weather is bad. Nor do they turn triumphalist when, tomorrow, the sun shines. Whatever the circumstances they have lived through—and because of that experience—they are determined to define for themselves who they are and who they should be.

We are assembled here today to mark their victory in acquiring and exercising their right to formulate their own definition of what it means to be African.

The Constitution whose adoption we celebrate constitutes an unequivocal statement that we refuse to accept that our Africanness shall be defined by our race, colour, gender, or historical origins.

It is a firm assertion made by ourselves that South Africa belongs to all who live in it, black and white.

It gives concrete expression to the sentiment we share as Africans, and will defend to the death, that the people shall govern.

It recognises the fact that the dignity of the individual is both an objective which society must pursue, and is a goal which cannot be separated from the material well-being of that individual.

It seeks to create the situation in which all our people shall be free from fear, including the fear of the oppression of one national group by another, the fear of the disempowerment of one social echelon by another, the fear of the use of state power to deny anybody their fundamental human rights, and the fear of tyranny.

It aims to open the doors so that those who were disadvantaged can assume their place in society as equals with their fellow human beings without regard to colour, race, gender, age, or geographic dispersal.

It provides the opportunity to enable each one and all to state their views, promote them, strive for their implementation in the process of governance without fear that a contrary view will be met with repression.

It creates a law-governed society which shall be inimical to arbitrary rule.

It enables the resolution of conflicts by peaceful means rather than resort to force.

It rejoices in the diversity of our people and creates the space for all of us voluntarily to define ourselves as one people.

As an African, this is an achievement of which I am proud, proud without reservation and proud without any feeling of conceit.

Our sense of elevation at this moment also derives from the fact that this magnificent product is the unique creation of African hands and African minds. But it also constitutes a tribute to our loss of vanity that we could, despite the temptation to treat ourselves as an exceptional fragment of humanity, draw on the accumulated experience and wisdom of all humankind, to define for ourselves what we want to be.

Together with the best in the world, we, too, are prone to pettiness, petulance, selfishness, and short-sightedness. But it seems to have happened that we looked at ourselves and said that the time had come that we make a super-human effort to be other than human, to respond to the call to create for ourselves a glorious future, to remind ourselves of the Latin saying: "Gloria est consequenda"—Glory must be sought after!

Today it feels good to be an African.

It feels good that I can stand here as a South African and as a foot soldier of a titanic African army, the African National Congress, to say to all the parties represented here, to the millions who made an input into the processes we are concluding, to our outstanding compatriots who have presided over the birth of our founding document, to the negotiators who pitted their wits one against the other, to the unseen stars who shone unseen as the management and administration of the Constitutional Assembly, the advisers, experts, and publicists, to the mass communication media, to our friends across the globe: Congratulations and well done!

I am an African.

I am born of the peoples of the continent of Africa.

The pain of the violent conflict that the peoples of Liberia, Somalia, the Sudan, Burundi, and Algeria suffer, is a pain I also bear.

The dismal shame of poverty, suffering, and human degradation of my continent is a blight that we share.

The blight on our happiness that derives from this and from our drift to the periphery of the ordering of human affairs leaves us in a persistent shadow of despair.

This is a savage road to which nobody should be condemned.

This thing that we have done today, in this small corner of a great continent that has contributed so decisively to the evolution of humanity, says that Africa reaffirms that she is continuing her rise from the ashes.

Whatever the setbacks of the moment, nothing can stop us now! Whatever the difficulties, Africa shall be at peace!

However improbable it may sound to the sceptics, Africa will prosper!

Whoever we may be, whatever our immediate interest, however much baggage we carry from our past, however much we have been caught by the fashion of cynicism and loss of faith in the capacity of the people, let us say today: Nothing can stop us now!

Thank you.

Appendix 2: Sample Outlines

INFORMATIVE SPEECH OUTLINE

Why Laughter is the Best Medicine

By Michael Fisher

I. Laughter improves physical health.

   A. Many feel that if there is no pain, there is no gain to physical health.
   B. I feel that if there is no grin, there is no win.
   C. It has been scientifically proven that laughter can improve your physical health.

      1. According to Lee Berk (associate professor, Allied Health Studies and Physical Therapy Departments, Loma Linda University, California), the benefits of laughter in an experiment that he conducted, in which people watch 20-minute video clips of comedic television programs, were equal to those of a moderate 20-minute workout.

         a. Exercising comes a long way to make you feel stronger and more energized.
         b. Trying one of Berk's "laughersizes" can yield similar benefits.

      2. Laughing also helps to prevent disease and infection.

         a. Laughing aids in protecting the heart and circulatory system and boosts our immune systems.
         b. One interesting example is in Berk's research:

            i. If an expectant mother laughs an ample amount during pregnancy, breast milk will be of better quality.
            ii. Her newborn infant's immune system is helped through breastfeeding.
            iii. This is because, according to helpguide.org (a well-trusted nonprofit resource for help in resolving health challenges), laughing helps decrease stress hormones while increasing immunity cells and infection-fighting antibodies.

      3. Laughing also causes a release of endorphins from your body.

         a. Endorphins are a chemical that your body contains and emits when it needs to physically feel good.
         b. This can even alleviate pain for brief periods of time.

Transition: Now that we have covered how grinning is winning for physical health, let's take a look at how turning that frown upside down can improve your mental well-being.

II. Laughter improves mental well-being.

   A. Laughter has been proven to reduce stress and alleviate anxiety.

      1. By doing so, you'll be able to stay focused on a task for a longer period of time.
      2. This will prevent the feeling of becoming overwhelmed and needing to multitask by finishing five things all at once.

3. For example, this will help you to finish your homework on time, get that job promotion you've been waiting for, or just maintain personal and professional relationships.

4. It is also naturally impossible to harbor negative emotions while you are laughing.

B. One way to laugh easily and get that peace of mind that you have long awaited is through laughter yoga.

1. Laughter yoga is a method of mental cleansing where you pair breathing exercises with self-initiated laughter.

2. According to Angela Haupt, *US News & World Report,* who has also been a laughter yoga instructor since 2007, activities at laughter yoga include childlike playfulness and Visa laughter.

3. In Visa laughter, you open up ridiculously high credit card bills that are fake and just laugh at them because you don't actually need to pay them.

C. By doing exercises like those, you have the opportunity to look on the brighter side of negative situations.

1. This will help you in the long run when you are faced with a difficult dilemma that might require you to make an even more difficult decision.

2. Deborah Williams, who has been a laughter yoga instructor for many years for many different types of people, states, "At first I thought it was a goofy idea, but since I started doing it, I react to things in a more lighthearted way. It helps to brush away some of the gray clouds, and it's a fun thing to do."

Transition: Last, I want to emphasize how laughter helps you become a more positive, openly sociable person.

III. Laughter improves social lifestyle.

A. Social health is something that not many people take into consideration throughout life.

1. It is actually one of the most important aspects of life.

2. According to helpguide.org, life can easily be improved by laughter.

B. Laughter helps to neutralize communication during conflict.

1. You will have the ability to forget what caused the conflict to arise, such as judgments or opinions, while you are trying to solve the conflict, instead of just making harsh or cruel remarks in return.

2. When communication is more open and direct, it will be more calm and collected.

C. Laughter is also contagious, so it will attract others to you.

1. Humans and even animals are more naturally tempted to gravitate toward you while you are laughing because it is releasing positive energy from your body.

2. They might run away from you if you emitted negative energy from your body by not laughing.

D. There are a countless number of ways to conjure up laughter.

1. You can have a game night with your friend.

2. You can go see a funny movie.

3. You can go to comedy clubs.

4. You can play with your pet.

5. You can partake in simple fun activities such as crafts and adventures.

6. You can go to a laughter yoga session as previously mentioned.

IV. Laughter helps to promote teamwork and bonding skills.

    A. One story that I read from helpguide.org is the perfect indicator that when you can laugh together, you can bond and work together more effectively.

    B. This story was about a man named Roy, who really enjoyed playing golf.

        1. He started to overanalyze all of his mistakes because the players that he was playing with were affecting his attitude since they were all very serious about the game.

        2. When he started to play with people who were more lighthearted about it, he was able to score better without trying harder, and he stopped being so critical of himself.

        3. He was able to have more fun and bond with those people better.

Transition: There is ample evidence on why laughter is the best medicine, so let me review the highlights.

Conclusion

I. Laughter contributes to an overall healthy lifestyle physically, mentally, and socially.

    A. A 20-minute laughersize will provide you with benefits equivalent to a moderate 20-minute workout.

    B. Laughter yoga will help you to mentally erase any stressors or anxieties that you may be facing.

    C. It has been proven that when you can laugh together, you can work together.

II. Laughter is more than a simple smile from ear to ear and a few chuckling noises.

    A. It's a means of achieving that picture-perfect life that everyone hopes to have.

    B. It is a means of being healthy, happy, and wholesome.

PERSUASIVE SPEECH OUTLINE

Statement to the Iowa House Judiciary Committee

By Zach Wahls

Introduction

I. *Narration:* I'm a sixth-generation Iowan and an engineering student at the University of Iowa, and I was raised by two women.

    A. My biological mom, Terry, told her grandparents that she was pregnant, that the artificial insemination had worked, and they wouldn't even acknowledge it.

        1. It wasn't until I was born that my grandparents told Terry that they were thrilled to have another grandson.

        2. Unfortunately, neither of them lived to see her marry her partner Jackie of fifteen years when they wed in 2009.

    B. My younger sister and only sibling was born in 1994.

        1. We actually have the same anonymous donor.

        2. We're full siblings, which is really cool for me.

Transition: Our family really isn't so different from any other Iowa family.

Body

I. When I'm home, we go to church together.

    A. We eat dinner.
    B. We go on vacations.

II. We have our hard times, too.

    A. We get in fights.
    B. My mom was diagnosed with multiple sclerosis in 2000. It put her in a wheelchair.

Transition: We've had our struggles.

III. But we're Iowans.

    A. We don't expect anyone to solve our problems for us.
    B. We'll fight our own battles.
    C. We just hope for equal and fair treatment from our government.

IV. At the University of Iowa, the topic of same-sex marriage comes up quite frequently in classroom discussions.

    A. The question always comes down to, well, "Can gays even raise kids?" Most people don't really have any answer.
    B. I was raised by a gay couple, and I'm doing pretty well.

        1. I scored in the 99th percentile on the A.C.T.
        2. I'm an Eagle Scout.
        3. I own and operate my own small business.
        4. If I was your son I'd make you very proud.

Transition: I'm not really so different from other children.

V. My family really isn't so different from yours.

    A. Your family doesn't derive its sense of worth from being told by the state they are married
    B. The sense of family comes from the commitments we make to each other.

        1. We work through the hard times so we can enjoy the good ones.
        2. It comes from the love that binds us.

VI. The vote here isn't to change us.

    A. It's not to change our families.
    B. It's to change how the law views us and how the law treats us.

        1. You are voting for the first time in the history of our state to codify discrimination into our constitution,
        2. The Iowa constitution, except for the proposed amendment, would be the least amended constitution in the United States of America.
        3. You are telling Iowans that some among you are second-class citizens who do not have the right to marry the person you love.

Conclusion

So will this vote affect my family? Will it affect yours?

Peroration

In the next 2 hours, I'm sure we're going to hear plenty of testimony about how damaging having gay parents is on kids. But in my 19 years, not once have I ever been confronted by an individual who realized independently that I was raised by a gay couple. And you know why? Because the sexual orientation of my parents has had zero effect on the content of my character.

SPECIAL OCCASION SPEECH OUTLINE

Statement on Behalf of the African National Congress, on the Occasion of the Adoption by the Constitutional Assembly of the Republic of South Africa Constitution Bill 1996

By Deputy President Thabo Mbeki

Introduction

I. Narration: I am an African—what does it mean to be an African?

    A. I owe my being to the land and the seasons

        1. Snow and heat.
        2. Thunder and lightning.

    B. To nature (fragrances, blooms, the veld)

    C. And to the specific places that make up Africa (Drakensberg, the Lekoa, iGqili noThukela, the sands of the Kgalagadi)

II. A challenge: Africa is the backdrop for the political dramas of our time; the "natural stage on which we act out the foolish deeds of the theatre of our day."

    A. The guiding question: "At times, and in fear, I have wondered whether I should concede equal citizenship of our country to the leopard and the lion, the elephant and the springbok, the hyena, the black mamba, and the pestilential mosquito."

    B. The answer: a declaration of hope in African citizenship: "A human presence among all these, a feature on the face of our native land thus defined, I know that none dare challenge me when I say: I am an African!"

Body

I. Africa has been defined by a series of historical conflicts, each of which is woven into Mbeki's being.

    A. The Khoi and the San.
        1. Genocide
        2. They perished in the fight for freedom.

    B. The history of conflict and migration, which I am a part of, should teach us lessons:
        1. European migrants.
        2. Malay slaves.
        3. Warrior men and women.
            a. With military victories
            b. And as victims of conflict: "I am the grandchild who lays fresh flowers on the Boer graves … who sees … the suffering of a simple peasant folk."

4. My family has benefitted from and suffered because of global trade.
   a. I am the child of a man who benefitted from global trade.
   b. And a man descended from people (Chinese and Indian) who were forced into labor by global trade.

Transition: "Being part of all these people, and in the knowledge that none dare contest that assertion, I shall claim that I am an African!"

II. One version of the story of Africa: Africa is defined by conflicts, and these conflicts continue to the current day.

A. Disparities in power deny equality
B. Racism denies equality

1. It denies equality by destroying self-esteem.
2. Racism creates material inequality.

C. Racism corrupts the soul.
D. Racism destroys human dignity.
E. Racism creates a number of social ills.
F. Racism motivates violence.

1. "To these the extent of death is directly proportional to their personal welfare."

   a. Political violence in KwaZulu-Natal.
   b. The taxi wars.
   c. The drug trade.
   d. Murder for hire.

G. Among us prowl the products of our immoral and amoral past.

1. Killers.
2. Rapists.
3. "Animals" who benefit vulnerable children, the disabled, and the old.

Transition: All this I know and know to be true because I am an African!

III. Another version of Africa's story: the fundamental truth of Africa is a history of heroic struggle

A. People who would not tolerate oppression.
B. South Africa would not allow that the fear of death, torture, imprisonment, exile, or persecution should result in the perpetuation of injustice.
C. Our forefathers and foremothers would not tolerate behavior that frames African history as barbaric.

1. They were patient.
2. They were not triumphalist.
3. They were determined to define themselves.

Transition: We are assembled here today to mark their victory in acquiring and exercising their right to formulate their own definition of what it means to be African.

IV. The Constitution is the culmination of this historic struggle.

A. It declares that South Africa belongs to all who live in it, black and white.
B. It gives concrete expression to the sentiment that the people should govern.
C. It recognizes dignity of the individual and the right to material well-being.
D. It rejects oppression.

E. It creates equal opportunities under the law.
F. It promotes free speech.
G. It enforces the rule of law.
H. It enables the resolution of conflicts by peaceful means rather than resort to force.
I. It rejoices in diversity in the context of unity.

Transition: As an African, this is an achievement of which I am proud, proud without reservation and proud without any feeling of conceit.

V. The Constitution is an incredible victory because it defines what it means to be an African.

A. It draws on the best insights of all humanity.
B. It recognizes that we can also be prone to pettiness and short-sightedness.
C. It represents a super-human effort to go beyond the worst human tendencies: " 'Gloria est consequenda'—Glory must be sought after!"
D. It represents the culmination of efforts by stakeholders across South Africa.

Transition: I am an African.

VI. There is still more work to do in the rest of Africa.

A. Liberia, Somalia, the Sudan, Burundi and Algeria.
B. Poverty
C. Lack of influence in global affairs

Conclusion

I. South Africa and the South African Constitution provide hope for the rest of Africa

A. It demonstrates that Africa is continuing her rise from the ashes.
1. Nothing can stop us now!
2. Peace is on the way
3. Africa will prosper!

B. Our success is the antidote to cynicism: nothing can stop us now!

Endnotes

Chapter 1

1. For more on rhetorical situations, see Bitzer, L. F. (1968). The rhetorical situation. *Philosophy and Rhetoric, 1*, 1–14; and Vatz, R. E. (1973). The myth of the rhetorical situation. *Philosophy and Rhetoric, 6*, 154–161.

Chapter 2

1. Perkins, H. W. (2002). Social norms and the prevention of alcohol misuse in collegiate contexts. *Journal of Studies on Alcohol, 14*, 164–172. Retrieved from http://www.collegedrinkingprevention .gov/supportingresearch/journal/perkins2.aspx

2. Jonsen, A., & Toulmin, S. (1990). *The abuse of casuistry*. Berkeley, CA: University of California Press, especially Chapter 10.

3. Davidson, D. (1984). *Inquiries into truth and interpretation*. Oxford, England: Clarendon Press, especially Chapter 13: On the Very Idea of a Conceptual Scheme.

4. Johnstone, H. W., Jr. (1965). Some reflections on argumentation. In M. Natanson & H. W. Johnstone, Jr. (Eds.), *Philosophy: Rhetoric and argumentation* (pp. 1–9). University Park: Pennsylvania State University Press.

5. Keith, William M. (2007). *Democracy as Discussion*. Lanham, MD: Lexington Books. Arnett, R. C., & Arneson. P. (1999). *Dialogic civility in a cynical age*. Albany, NY: SUNY Press.

6. Brockriede, W. (1972). Arguers as lovers. *Philosophy and Rhetoric, 5*, 1–11; Natanson, M. (1965). The claims of immediacy. In M. Natanson & H. W. Johnstone, Jr. (Eds.), *Philosophy: Rhetoric and argumentation* (pp. 10–19). University Park: Pennsylvania State University Press.

Chapter 3

1. Booth, W. C. (1963). The rhetorical stance. *Composition and Communication, 14*, 139–145; Brockriede, W. (1972). Arguers as lovers. *Philosophy and Rhetoric, 5*, 1–11.

2. Lake, R. A. (1990). The implied auditor. In D. C. Williams & M. D. Hazen (Eds.), *Argumentation theory and the rhetoric of assent* (pp. 69–90). Tuscaloosa: University of Alabama Press.

3. McGee, M. C. (1975). In search of "the people": A rhetorical alternative. *Quarterly Journal of Speech, 61*(3), 235–249.

4. Johnstone, H. W., Jr. (1981). Toward an ethics of rhetoric. *Communication, 6*, 305–314.

5. Dewey, J. (1927). *The public and its problems*. New York, NY: Holt.

Chapter 4

1. Booth, W. C. (1963). The rhetorical stance. *Composition and Communication, 14*, pp. 139–145.

Chapter 6

1. Deer, B. (2009, February 8). Hidden records show MMR truth. *Sunday Times*. Retrieved from http://www.timesonline.co.uk/tol/life_and_style/health/article5683643.ece

2. Dales, L., Hammer, S., & Smith, N., (2001). Time trends in autism and in MMR immunization coverage in California. *Journal of the American Medical Association, 285*(9), 1183–1185; Kaye, J., Melero-Montes, M., & Jick, H. (2001), Mumps, measles, and rubella vaccine and the incidence of autism recorded by general practitioners: a time trend analysis. *British Medical Journal, 322*(7284):460–3.

Chapter 7

1. This set of expectations is often called the *genre* of the speech. For some classic work on genre, see Campbell, K. K., & Jamieson, K. H. (Eds.) (1978). *Form and genre: Shaping rhetorical action*, Falls Church, VA: Speech Communication Association; Jamieson, K. H. (1973). Generic constraints and the rhetorical situation. *Philosophy and Rhetoric, 6*, 162–170; Miller, C. (1984). Genre as social action. *Quarterly Journal of Speech, 70*, 151–167.

2. U.S. Department of Labor, Bureau of Labor Statistics. (2008). *American time use survey*. Retrieved from http://www. bls. gov/tus/datafiles2008. htm

Chapter 8

1. For examples of scholars who analyze style, see Fulkerson, R. P. (1979). The public letter as a rhetorical form: Structure, logic, and style in King's "Letter from Birmingham Jail." *Quarterly Journal of Speech, 65*(2), 121–136; Carpenter, R. H. (1998). *Choosing powerful words: Eloquence that works*. Boston, MA: Allyn and Bacon.

2. [Cicero]. (1954). *Rhetorica ad Herrenium*. Trans. H. Caplan. Cambridge, MA: Harvard University Press.

3. Representative Cleo Fields may have introduced a longer version in February 2008, which then was shortened by the rapper Jay-Z. Fields, C. (2008, February 23). State of the Black Union 2008, morning session [Video clip]. *C-SPAN Video Library*. Retrieved from http://www.c-spanvideo.org /clip/2156642; Hershkovits, D. (2009, January 23). Sourcing the quote: "Rosa Parks sat so Martin Luther King could walk. Martin Luther King walked so Obama could run. Obama ran so we can all fly" [Web log]. *Papermag*. Retrieved from http://www.papermag.com/2009/01/sourcing_the _quote_rosa_parks.php; yaddab. (2008, October 29). "Rosa sat so Martin could walk, so Obama could run, so our children can fly" [Web log]. *Daily Kos*. Retrieved from http://www.dailykos .com /story/2008/10/29/645922/--Rosa-sat-so-Martin-could-walk-so-Obama-could-run-so-our -children-can-fly

Chapter 9

1. Song, S. (2004, July 19). Health: The price of pressure. *Time*. Retrieved from http://www.time .com/time/magazine/article/0,9171,994670-1,00.html

2. Rarig, F. (1955, Nov. 1). Audio interview. Audio-Visual Register of the WSCA Oral History Project, A0327. University of Utah Archives. Frank Rarig, a professor of speech at the University of Minnesota beginning in 1911, recalls talking to someone who was present at the Gettysburg address.

Chapter 10

1. Katt, J., Murdock, M., Butler, J., & Pryor, B. (2008). Establishing best practices for the use of PowerPoint as a presentation aid. *Human Communication, 11*(2), 189–196.

2. Schrodt, P., & Witt, P. L. (2006). Students' attributions of instructor credibility as a function of students' expectations of instructional technology use and nonverbal immediacy. *Communication Education, 55*, 1–20.

3. Norris, J. (2011, April 28). Five myths about foreign aid. *The Washington Post*. Retrieved from http:// www.washingtonpost.com/opinions/five-myths-about-foreign-aid/2011/04/25 /AF00z05E_story.html

4. These criticisms are taken from Tufte, E. (2006). *The cognitive style of PowerPoint: Pitching out corrupts within*. Cheshire, CT: Graphics Press.

Chapter 11

1. University of Texas Health Science Center. (2011, June 27). Waistlines in people, glucose levels in mice hint at sweetener's effects [News release]. Retrieved from http://www.uthscsa.edu/hscnews /singleformat2.asp?newID=3861

2. Centers for Disease Control and Prevention/National Center for Health Statistics. (2011, November 17). Obesity and overweight. *FastStats*. Retrieved from http://www.cdc.gov/nchs /fastats/overwt.htm (2011, November 17)

3. Health Discovery. (n.d.). Tips for keeping your New Year's. Retrieved from http://www .healthdiscovery.net/articles/Tips_New_Year.htm (2011, November 17).

4. Surgeon General Regina Benjamin, The Prevention Imperative: Protecting the Health and Well-Being of America's Families, in *America's Health Rankings: A Call to Action for Individuals and Their Communities*, 2011 edition (United Health Foundation: 2011), p. 4. http://www .americashealthrankings.org/SiteFiles/Reports/AHR%202011edition.pdf

5. http://www.timlonghurst.com/blog/2008/05/16/the-ted-commandments-rules-every-speaker -needs-to-know.

6. Gallo, C. (2014). *Talk like TED: The 9 public speaking secrets of the world's top minds*. NY: St. Martin's Press.

7. http://storage.ted.com/tedx/manuals/tedx_speaker_guide.pdf

8. http://www.pechakucha.org

Chapter 12

1. Kenton, S. B. (1989). Speaker credibility in persuasive business communication: A model which explains gender differences. *Journal of Business Communication*, 26(2), 143–157. A good source for research on source credibility updated to the information age is Andrew Flanagin's and Miriam Metzger's website Credibility and Digital Media @ UCSB: http://www.credibility.ucsb.edu

2. Ruiter, R. A. C., Abraham, C., & Kok, G. (2001). Scary warnings and rational precautions: A review of the psychology of fear appeals. *Psychology and Health*, *16*, 613–630.

3. Significant work on framing has been done by the linguist George Lakoff: Lakoff, G. (2002). *Moral politics: How liberals and conservatives think* (2nd ed.) (Chicago: University of Chicago Press); Lakoff, G. (2004). *Don't think of an elephant: Know your values and frame the debate* (White River Junction, VT: Chelsea Green Publishing).

4. For a different example of a mental image, think about the cliché you may have heard before. The speaker is talking about a danger growing so slowly that people may not take action until it's too late, and he compares the public to a frog being boiled to death in a pan of water: Supposedly, if the water is heated slowly enough, the temperature will never change quickly enough to cause the frog to jump out and avoid being boiled. The analogy ("in this situation, we are like a frog in a pan of water…") serves to frame the problem you're talking about, implying that it's a more serious problem than it seems at any one moment. If you're trying to make a case about cumulative physical, social, or moral damage, this visual analogy would help your audience frame any given instance as part of a larger problem. Of course, frogs do try to escape from boiling water if they can http://www.snopes.com/critters/wild/frogboil.asp so it wouldn't be responsible to use this analogy, even though it's a common one.

Index

A

abstract, 118
academic journals, 112, 113
Academic OneFile, 113
Academic Search Premier, 113
active listening, 70–71, 72
ad consequentiam, 272
ad hominem argument, 270–271
ad populum, 272–273
adaptation, 10
Address to the March on Washington (King), 58, 163
advertising, 7
advocacy, 31
advocacy organizations, 116
after-dinner speech, 291–292
Allen, Will, 90
alliteration, 162
alternative viewpoints, 42–43
America: History and Life, 113
American Sign Language (ASL), 10
analogy, 267–268
ancient rhetorical practice, 12
and, 137
animation, video, and other moving images, 215
answering questions, 193–195
antithesis, 164–166
anxiety, 22
APA citation style, 125
apathetic audience, 56
appeal, 44
appeal to consequences, 272
appeal to popularity, 272–273
appeal to tradition, 273
appropriate clothes, 191
appropriating ideas, 39
argument, 19, 32, 262, 264
argument from analogy, 267–268
argument from authority, 269
argument from form, 265–266
argument from signs, 268–269
Aristotle, 251, 252, 255, 259
Armstrong, Karen, 72
Armstrong, Neil, 164
articulation, 186–187
"as" test, 54
attention, 135, 147
audience, 10, 17–18, 48–67
    apathetic, 56
    "as" test, 54
    be directive, 58
    common interests, 57
    common premises, 58
    demographics, 51–53
    engagement, 36–38, 60–61
    ethics, 39–40, 63–64
    hostile, 56
    interests, 55–57
    literal, 51–53
    marketing, 60
    from "me" to "us," 55
    occasional, 56–57
    public, and, 11, 61–63
    respect for, 24, 39–40
    rhetorical, 53–55
    shared experience, 57
    sympathetic, 56
audience analysis, 50
audio clips, 215
authority, 238, 269
award presentation, 292–294

B

balance, 35, 43
bandwagoning, 45
bar graph, 211, 212
because, 137
begging the question, 275–276
bias, 31, 120
biased speech, 31–32
bibliography, 125–126
Black, Ed, 46
blog, 120
body, 135–139
    attention, 135
    functions, 136
    internal preview, 138, 139
    points, 136–137
    transitions, 137–138, 139
    understandability, 135–136
Bono, 263
books, 113, 118
Bowser, Muriel, 103
Brady, James, 144
brainstorming, 93–95, 100
breathe, breathe, breathe, 193
business settings, 100
Business Source Premier, 113
but, 137

C

Caesar, Julius, 162
Canada, Geoffrey, 108

card-stacking, 45
Carlson, Kurt, 131
Carter, Majora, 121
Catt, Carrie Chapman, 165
causal argument, 266–267
cause-and-effect pattern, 143
ceremonial speaking, 289. *See also* special-occasion speech
Chan, Jackie, 171
charisma, 166–167
chart, 210–213
choices, 12, 24
chronological pattern, 141–142
Churchill, Winston, 4, 166
Cicero, 98
circular reasoning, 275–276
circulation, 64
circumstantial ad hominem, 271
citing sources, 125–126
civic engagement, 37
claim, 32
clarity, 234
classroom situation, 98–99
clavicular breathing, 184
Clinton, Bill, 133
Clinton, Chelsea, 194
common sense, 255–256
communication, 246
Communication & Mass Media Complete, 113
communication process, 9–10
comparison, 168–170
concept map, 79
conclusion, 139–140
concrete and lively language, 159
Congressional Record, 10
constructive feedback, 80
contrast
    figures of, 164–166
    verbal emphasis on a word, 187
conventional sign, 269
conversational framework, 7–9
conversational rate (speed of talking), 185
Cooper, Anderson, 150
coordinate points, 152
Cornell style notes, 79
corporate web pages, 122
correlation, 267, 274
counterargument, 276–278
CQ Researcher, 113
credibility, 256
credible sources, 20
critical feedback, 80–83
critical listening, 71–72
cropping, 208, 209
CUTS, 204–205, 215, 219

D

Dalai Lama, 29
databases, 112, 113
Davidson, Donald, 35
deaf people, 10
deceptive speech, 29–30

deductive reasoning, 265–266
definition, 238–239
DeGeneres, Ellen, 37
delivery, 12, 22, 174–200
    answering questions, 193–195
    anxiety, 177–179
    articulation, 186–187
    attire/appearance, 191–192
    breathe, breathe, breathe, 193
    extemporaneous speaking, 180–181
    eye contact, 190–191
    gesturing, 190
    group presentation, 196–199
    impromptu speaking, 181
    inflection, 187–188
    manuscript speech, 180
    obstacles, 176
    posture, 188
    rehearsal, 192–193
    speaking aids, 182–183
    speech from memory, 179–180
    speed of talking, 185–186
    time limit, 181–182
    vocal fry, 195–196
    volume, 183–185
    walking, 189
democracy, 6, 7
democratic conversation, 7
demographics, 51–53
demonstration speech, 218
Dennis, Robert, 285
description, 239–240
Dewey, John, 62
diagram, 214
dialogue, 7
Dickens, Charles, 165
digital media, 223
direct democracy, 6
distractions, 75–76
divergent viewpoints, 42–43
dollar bill, 6
donation, contribution, gift, 21
double-reverse antithesis, 166
Duggan, William, 93–94
Dytham, Mark, 247

E

EBSCO, 113
EconLit, 113
editorials, 120–121
emotion, 257
empowerment, 258
engagement, 36–38, 60–61, 98
ethics, 17, 26–47
    balance, 35
    biased speech, 31–32
    deceptive speech, 29–30
    defined, 27
    engaging the audience, 36–38, 63–64
    fallacies/prejudicial appeals, 44–45
    generosity, 34

ethics (*Continued*)
  honesty, 33
  listening, 72–74
  openness, 34
  plagiarism, 38–39
  poorly reasoned speech, 32–33
  present alternative viewpoints fairly, 42–43
  respect the audience, 39–40
  respect your topic, 40–42
  responsible use of sources, 36
  taking appropriate risks, 36
ethos, 253, 254–256
eulogy, 285–287
evaluating sources, 120–122
Evernote, 120
exaggeration, 171
examples, 238, 239, 241–242
explanation, 239, 240–241
expressive communication, 50
extemporaneous speaking, 180–181
extemporaneous speech, 152, 153
eye contact, 190–191, 223

F

fallacies
  fallacious arguments, 269–276
  prejudicial appeals, 44–45
fallacy of causation, 273–274
fame, notoriety, 234
familiar locations organization, 142
fear appeals, 259–260
feedback, 80–83
figurative analogy, 268
figure, 161–167
figure of contrast, 164–166
figure of repetition, 162–163
figure of speech, 22
flip charts, 217
focus, 187
foul language, 160
frame, 21
framing, 260–261
framing an image, 208, 209
Franco, James, 88
Freakonomics (Dubner/Levitt), 273
from "me" to "us," 55
funny stories, 133

G

Gale Reference Library, 113
Galileo, 272
Gallo, Carmine, 246
Gates, Bill, 231
general purpose, 98
generosity, 34
geography (spatial organization), 142
gesturing, 190
Gettysburg Address (Lincoln), 162, 187
Giunta, Salvatore, 99
glittering generalities, 44
goals, 18–19

Golden Rule, 40, 41
Goldwater, Barry, 166
González, Julio, 259
Goodall, Jane, 164
Google News, 112
Google Scholar, 112, 121
Google search, 112
Gorgias of Leontini, 4
graduation speech, 287–289
grammatical repetition, 162
graph, 210–213
grounds, 32
group presentation, 196–199

H

handouts, 216, 217
hasty generalization, 274
Hayek, Salma, 258
head-to-toe organization, 142
Hippocratic Oath, 65
historical pattern, 141
honesty, 33
hostile audience, 56
Houston, Whitney, 286
hyperbole, 171
hypercorrectness, 186

I

"I Have a Dream" (King), 162, 163, 176
I statements, 83
idea appropriation, 39
impromptu speaking, 181
inappropriate appeal to authority, 271–272
inappropriate sample, 275
inappropriate support, 33
inappropriate testimonials, 44
inductive fallacies, 274–275
inductive reasoning, 265
inflection, 187–188
informative speaking, 12, 226–249
  connect topic to your audience, 243–244
  defining, 238–239
  describing, 239–241
  explaining, 241–242
  goals, 228–233
  language choices, 244–245
  new information, 229–230
  new perspectives, 230–231
  organizational pattern, 244
  PechaKucha, 247–248
  positive/negative feelings, 231–232
  sample outline, 302–304
  sample speech, 295–296
  simplicity, 243
  speaker's responsibilities, 233–235
  supporting material, 244
  TED talks, 245–246
  thesis statement, 102
  topics, 235–238
informative thesis statement, 102

informing, 14, 98
InfoTrac, 113
interested, disinterested, 120
interests, 55–57
  audience, 89–90, 97
  speaker, 89, 92–93
internal preview, 138, 139
interviews and conversations, 113–114
introduction, 131–135
  functions, 132
  narration, 133–134
  preview, 135
  thesis, 134–135
introduction speech, 289–291
inverted pyramid, 133
invited speaking situations, 99. *See also* special-occasion speech
"I've Been to the Mountaintop" (King), 22

J

jokes, 133
Jolie, Angelina, 93
journal articles, 112, 113, 118
JSTOR, 112, 113

K

Kennedy, John F., 166
Kennedy, Joseph P., 166
Kenton, Sherron, 256
Keynote, 219
King, Martin Luther, 4
  Address to the March on Washington, 58
  "I Have a Dream," 162, 163, 176
  "I've Been to the Mountaintop," 22
  repetition, 162–163
Klein, Astrid, 247
Krugman, Paul, 276
Kunkel, Adrianne, 285

L

language choices, 22. *See also* verbal style
lapel mic, 184
laptop notes, 80
lecture, 37
LegalTrac, 113
legendary speeches, 5
LexisNexis Academic, 113
librarian, 126
Lihua, Tai, 10
Lincoln, Abraham, 162, 187
line graph, 211, 212
listening, 68–84
  active, 70–71, 72
  critical, 71–72
  distractions, 75–76
  ethics, 72–74
  feedback, 80–83
  hearing, contrasted, 70
  mental zone, 76–77
  note taking, 77–80
  passive, 70, 71

literal analogy, 268
literal audience, 50, 51–53
litotes, 171
logical definition, 238
logos, 253, 262–263

M

manipulation, 251
Mankiw, Greg, 276
manuscript speech, 180
maps, 213
marketing, 60
master of ceremonies (MC), 198
Mbeki, Thabo, 298, 306
McMillan, Corey, 186
memorized speech, 179–180
mental picture, 240
metaphor, 22, 168–169, 289
metonymy, 170
Milk, Harvey, 162
Ming, Yao, 189
Monroe's Motivated Sequence, 146–148
Moon, Ban Ki, 65
Mueller, Pam, 80
multi-modal engagement, 158

N

name calling, 44
narration, 133–134
negation, 239
negatively/positively charged terms, 232
news articles, 118, 120
Nixon, Richard, 164
nobility, 258
noise, 75
note taking, 77–79
  concept map, 79
  Cornell style notes, 79
  distractions, 75
  handwritten notes *vs.* laptop notes, 80
  outline, 78
  practical concerns, 80
  research, 119–120
notoriety, fame, 234

O

Obama, Barack, 166, 290
objects, as presentation aid, 217–218
occasional audience, 56–57
occasional speech, 281. *See also* special-occasion speech
Occupy Wall Street rallies, 81
off-color language, 160
Oliver, Jamie, 293
online search, 114–116
Online Writing Lab (OWL), 126
openness, 34
operational definition, 238
opinion or advocacy pieces, 120–121
Oppenheimer, Daniel, 80
opposing viewpoints, 42–43

organization, 20–21, 128–154
  basic three-part structure, 130–140
  cause-and-effect pattern, 143
  chronological pattern, 141–142
  combination of formats, 148–149
  defined, 129
  Monroe's Motivated Sequence, 146–148
  outlining, 151–153
  primacy/recency, 150
  problem-solution pattern, 144
  spatial pattern, 142–143
  supporting materials, 150–151
  topical pattern, 144–146
outline, 151–153
  coordinate/subordinate points, 152
  informative speech, 302–204
  persuasive speech, 304–306
  samples, 138, 302–308
  special-occasion speech, 306–308
  taglines, 123
  working (research), 153
outline style notes, 78
outrage, 260
overenunciating, 186
overstatement, 171

P

Paiz, Daniel, 290
paraphrasing, 38–39
part-to-whole organization, 145
passive listening, 70, 71
past-present-future organization, 141
pathos, 253, 257–261
patterns of organization, 140–146. *See also* organization
PechaKucha, 247–248
Peelle, Jonathan, 186
peer review, 112
peer-reviewed articles, 121
performing, 17
peroration, 140
personification, 171–172
persuading, 15, 98
persuasion, 251
persuasive speaking, 12, 250–279
  argument from analogy, 267–268
  argument from authority, 269
  argument from signs, 268–269
  causal argument, 266–267
  counterargument, 276–278
  deductive reasoning, 265–266
  ethos, 254–256
  fallacies/fallacious arguments, 269–276
  inductive reasoning, 265
  logos, 262–263
  pathos, 257–261
  sample outline, 304–306
  sample speech, 296–297
  thesis statement, 102
persuasive thesis statement, 102
physical parts (spatial organization), 142
pictures and photos, 207–209

pie chart, 212–213
pitch, 100
plagiarism, 38–39, 125
plain double antithesis, 166
plain-folks appeal, 45
pluralism, 6, 7
points, 136–137
Pollan, Michael, 230
Poo, Ai-jen, 117
poorly reasoned speech, 32–33
Porter, Zeam, 9
position papers, 120–121
positively/negatively charged terms, 232
post hoc fallacy, 273
posters, 217
posture, 188
PowerPoint slides, 221–222
praiseworthy characteristics, 282–283
preconceptions, 76
preparation choices checklist, 13
preparing, 13, 16
presentation, 100
presentation aids, 22–23, 201–224
  audio clips, 215
  charts and graphs, 210–213
  CUTS, 204–205, 215, 219
  defined, 203
  demonstration speech, 218
  digital media, 223
  guiding principles, 204–207
  handouts, 216, 217
  maps and diagrams, 213–214
  objects, 217–218
  pictures and photos, 207–209
  posters and flip charts, 217
  PowerPoint slides, 221–222
  presentation software, 219–222
  text, 214–215
  uses, 203–204
  video, animation, and other moving images, 215
  visual composition, 205
presentation of an award, 292–294
presentation software, 219–222
preview, 135
Prezi, 219, 220
primacy, 150
principle of charity, 35
private *vs.* public issue, 61
problem-solution pattern, 144
progression, 163–164
Project Muse, 112, 113
proofs, 253
Pryor, Burt, 216
public, 11
public forums, 74
public issue, 61
public situations, 99–100
Purdue University's Online Writing Lab (OWL), 126
purpose
  choice of topic, 91, 92, 98
  general, 98
  specific, 91, 98

Q

Queen Latifah, 253

R

racist language, 160–161
reading strategies, 118
Reagan, Ronald, 180
realistic sign, 269
reasoning, 32, 264
reasons (topical organization), 146
recency, 150
reciprocity, 40, 41
reference librarian, 126
rehearsal, 192–193, 222
relay presentation, 198
relevance, 234
remix, 4
    activating feelings and senses, 258–259
    Address to the March on Washington (King), 58
    analogy, 267–268
    bias, 31
    brainstorming, 93–94
    charisma, 166–167
    definitions, explanations, 239
    ethics and effectiveness, 28
    ethics and the audience, 45–46
    eulogy, 285–286
    Golden Rule, 41
    Google search, 115
    graphs and charts, 210
    handouts, 216
    helping audience to do something, 146–147
    public or publics?, 63–64
    public speaking and democracy, 8
    speaking in images, 158–159
    speed of public speaking, 185–186
    structure and persuasion, 130–131
    taking notes, 80
    vocal fry, 195–196
repetition, 162–163
representative democracy, 6
research, 20, 105–127
    choosing appropriate research materials, 124
    citing sources, 125–126
    designing a research strategy, 111
    evaluating sources, 120–122
    gathering the materials, 117–118
    getting help, 126
    note taking, 119–120
    online search, 114–116
    organizing the information, 123
    reading strategies, 118
    refining the argument/modifying your claims, 122–123
    resources, 111–113
    steps in research process, 109
    what do you already know?, 109–111
research outline, 153
respect the audience, 24, 39–40
respectful language, 160–161
responsible choices, 23–24
responsible use of sources, 36

responsive communication, 50
restatement of the thesis, 140
review, 140
rhetoric, 4
Rhetoric (Aristotle), 251, 255
Rhetorica ad Herennium, 162
rhetorical audience, 50, 53–55
rhyme, 162
risk taking, 36
Rock, Chris, 161
Rogers, Fred ("Mr. Rogers"), 73
Roosevelt, Franklin, 4
Rosling, Hans, 78
Ruffalo, Mark, 191

S

sample outlines, 302–308
sample speeches, 295–301
scholarly articles, 112, 113, 118, 121
ScienceDirect, 113
search engines, 111–112
Seinfeld, Jerry, 176
self-efficacy, 146
self-risk test, 36, 61
sexist and racist language, 160–161
Shu, Suzanne, 131
Siddiqi, Hammad, 267
signposting, 135
signs, 268–269
simile, 169–170
slide-based presentation software, 219
slothful induction, 274–275
spatial mapping software, 219
spatial pattern, 142–143
speaking aids, 182–183
speaking situations
    business settings, 100
    classroom situation, 98–99
    invited, 99
    public situations, 99–100
special-occasion speech, 12, 280–294
    after-dinner speech, 291–292
    eulogy, 285–287
    goals, 282
    graduation speech, 287–289
    introducing a speaker, 289–291
    praiseworthy characteristics, 282–283
    presentation of an award, 292–294
    sample outline, 306–308
    sample speech, 298–301
    toasts, 283–284
specific purpose, 91, 98
speech from memory, 179–180
speech of introduction, 289–291
speeches
    basic three-part structure, 130–140
    changing course of history, 5
    changing course of your life, 6
    delivery. *See* delivery
    general purposes, 98
    legendary, 5

speeches (*Continued*)
  research. *See* research
  samples, 295–301
  speaking situations, 98–100
  time constraints, 100–101
Spielberg, Stephen, 255
SpringerLink, 113
stage fright, 177–179
stakeholders, 6
Stanton, Elizabeth Cady, 4
staying "in the moment," 76
step-by-step organization, 141
stereotype, 60, 75–76
student government, 7
style, 157. *See also* verbal style
subordinate points, 152
substitution, 170
Sunday feature, 133, 134
supplemental media, 203. *See also* presentation aids
supporting material, 150–151, 244
sympathetic audience, 56
sympathy, 257–258

T

tablet notes, 80
tagline method of taking notes, 119
taking notes. *See* note taking
Tal, Aner, 210
Tale of Two Cites, A (Dickens), 165
Talk like TED (Gallo), 246
technical terms, 245
TED talks, 245–246
TEDx site, 246
testimonials, 44
text, as presentation aid, 214–215
thesis, 134–135
thesis statement, 90–91, 101–103, 134, 135
think tanks, 116
3 laws of communication, 246
time constraints, 100–101
To Kill a Mockingbird (film), 252
toasts, 283–284
topic, 86–104
  audience interests, 89–90, 97
  brainstorming, 93–95
  defined, 88
  focusing (narrowing) your topic, 96–97
  informative speaking, 235–238
  process of choosing a topic, 92
  purpose, 91, 92, 98
  respect for, 40–42
  speaking situations, 98–100
  thesis, 91–92
  time constraints, 100–101
  topic choice dos and don'ts, 96
  what do you care about?, 92–93
  what do you want to know more about?, 93

  what is the occasion?, 90–91
  your interests, 89, 92–93
topical pattern, 144–146
transitions, 137–138, 139
trope, 161, 167–172
trope of comparison, 168–170
trope of exaggeration, 171
trope of substitution, 170
trope of voice, 171–172
Trout, J. D., 239
Tufte, Edward, 130
types (topical organization), 145
Tyson, Neil deGrasse, 292

U

uncredited "borrowing" of ideas, 38
understandability, 135–136
understatement, 171
unity, 6, 7
unrealistic assumptions, 80–81
U.S. dollar bill, 6

V

values (praiseworthy characteristics), 282–283
verbal style, 156–173
  concrete and lively language, 159
  figures, 161–167
  matching style to topic and occasion, 172
  respectful language, 160–161
  tropes, 167–172
video, animation, and other moving images, 215
visual aids, 23. *See also* presentation aids
vivid language, 241
vocal fry, 195–196
voice, effective use of, 183–188

W

Wahls, Zachary, 296, 304
Wansink, Brian, 210
Warner, Michael, 64
Warren, Elizabeth, 242
weak support, 33
web-based search engines, 111–112
websites/web pages, 122
wedding toast, 283–284
wiki, 121
Wikipedia, 121–122
Winfrey, Oprah, 288
word choice, 21–22. *See also* verbal style
working document, 119
working (research) outline, 153

Y

"yabbut" problem, 77
Yousafzai, Malala, 55